The Censorship of British Drama 1900–1968

Volume One: 1900–1932

This book is based on a systematic exploration of the Lord Chamberlain's Correspondence archives, which contain files for every play submitted for a public performance licence in Great Britain.

Volume One covers the period before 1932, when theatre was widely seen to possess an almost unique power to shape the future of society, determining what people believed and how they behaved. It is not just about the relatively small number of plays which were banned outright (though these are important): it is more about how and why themes, characters, speeches and lines had to be removed or rewritten, and how action, gesture, costume and even advertising were restricted.

Censorship is also examined in relation to contemporary debates and arguments about freedom and the role of the artist within the historical, social and political contexts of the plays. The emphasis is not exclusively on the professional theatre, for it is often in relation to apparently obscure or unimportant plays that policies and practices were most clearly defined.

The book uncovers the disputes which occurred among and between the Lord Chamberlain and his Readers and Advisers, and discusses the extensive pressures exerted on him by bodies such as the Public Morality Council, the Church, the monarch, government departments, foreign embassies, newspapers, powerful individuals and those claiming to represent national or international opinion. For all of these sought—often successfully—to control what could be said and done on stages throughout Britain.

Exeter Performance Studies

Exeter Performance Studies aims to publish the best new scholarship from a variety of sources, presenting established authors alongside innovative work from new scholars. The list explores critically the relationship between theatre and history, relating performance studies to broader political, social and cultural contexts. It also includes titles which offer access to previously unavailable material.

Series editors: Peter Thomson, Professor of Drama at the University of Exeter; Graham Ley, Reader in Drama and Theory at the University of Exeter; Steve Nicholson, Head of Theatre Studies and Principal Lecturer at the University of Huddersfield.

The Censorship of British Drama 1900–1968

Volume One: 1900–1932

Steve Nicholson

UNIVERSITY
of
EXETER
PRESS

In 1990, John Johnston, a former member of the Lord Chamberlain's Office,
dedicated his apologia for theatre censorship to

'the Lord Chamberlains who wielded their blue pencil
and
to their Examiners of Plays'.

I would like to dedicate my study to those who corresponded,
and especially argued, with the Lords Chamberlain.

First published in 2003 by
University of Exeter Press
Reed Hall, Streatham Drive
Exeter EX4 4QR
UK
www.ex.ac.uk/uep/

British Library Cataloguing in Publication Data
A catalogue record for this book is available
from the British Library.

ISBN 0 85989 638 2

Typeset in 10pt Plantin Light
by XL Publishing Services, Tiverton

Printed in Great Britain by Antony Rowe Ltd, Chippenham

Contents

Preface

This is the first of two volumes which, together, will chart and analyse censorship in Britain between 1900 and 1968, when the unique system of control and licensing exercised through the Lord Chamberlain was finally abolished. This present volume covers the period up until 1932, and Volume Two will continue from 1933. The basic structure within each volume will be chronological, although specific themes and issues will also be followed.

Although the books will be contextualised in relation to social, political, cultural and theatrical history, and although other sources relevant to censorship will be referred to, the central story and analysis is based very largely on the extensive theatre and correspondence archives of the Lord Chamberlain's Office. These archives have never previously been subjected to a comparably systematic or thorough analysis, and it is this focus which will make these books unique, and which will provide a distinct perspective on British theatre history and activity in the first two-thirds of the twentieth century. Remarkably, with the exception of a relatively small amount of material which has gone missing, these archives contain files in relation to every single script which was submitted to the Lord Chamberlain as required by the Acts of 1737 and 1843, as a prerequisite for obtaining a licence to allow public performance; in most cases, the scripts themselves are also preserved in a separate archive. Crucially for any attempt to understand the full range of theatrical activity and its control, the archives cover scripts which were accepted but amended as well as those which were refused, those which were published and unpublished, and those which were intended not only for professional but also for amateur public performance anywhere in Britain. The most notable exception is music-hall material, which remained more or less unofficially exempt from the same process of licensing and censorship.

It is perhaps worth saying that when I began working on this project, my original intention was to produce one book which would cover the whole period, and which would have been rather shorter than this first volume on its own has turned out to be. Since that proposal was accepted by the publisher, and since I began more detailed research, it has more than doubled in length. Previous work had already given me some familiarity with the archive, and I knew it was a rich resource which deserved a much fuller exploration than it had previously received. Yet I had no real idea of the extent or the range of the material which was preserved, or that there would be so many stories to be uncovered. Funding from the University of Huddersfield, the Society for Theatre Research and, especially, the Arts and Humanities Research Board (AHRB) enabled me to spend time reading not just a broad sample or cross-section of the material in the archive (as I had previously intended) but every single file. It is only this extensive research that allows me to claim that these books are, at least in relation to that archive, authoritative—though by no means, of course, definitive. And it is also this which has yielded many of the insights which these two books aim to present. Primarily, of course, those insights are into the history of theatre censorship itself; but they also extend more broadly into other aspects of theatre history in the twentieth century, and into social and political attitudes and practices beyond the theatre.

Though originally I admitted it with some reluctance, it gradually became apparent as I undertook the research for this study that the material I was uncovering demanded to be dealt with at greater length and in more detail, and that I should considerably expand the scope of what I was writing. I am particularly grateful for the enthusiasm with which the University of Exeter Press accepted and embraced this revision of my original intentions. I should add that even when the two volumes are completed, there will be much that remains untold and which deserves to be brought into the light of day. I have never previously told my publisher that there was a point when I seriously considered proposing that I should write not two volumes, but six.

Future scholarly explorations of this archive may well take narrower and more focused perspectives on the material than I have done, in order to pursue and reveal a specific aspect in greater depth than will be possible in this present study; they may well choose to structure their discussion in ways other than the chronological. In some ways, then, I see my two volumes as groundwork, which may help to encourage other kinds of investigation and other ways of approaching the archive. For that reason, the broadly chronological approach —while the most obvious and perhaps unimaginative—has seemed to me to be the most useful. Yet to have followed this pattern slavishly would, I think, have concealed more than it would have revealed. I have therefore tried to construct a balance between the sequential and the thematic. I have also chosen to quote directly and sometimes at length from the contents of corre-spondence files. Inevitably, such quotations are highly selective and are both dependent on and mediated by my arguments; nevertheless, I would hope that the extent of the quotations has the added advantage of allowing the reader as much direct contact with the archive as would be appropriate in a study of this kind, and perhaps the opportunity to reach different conclusions from my own. A strong case could be made for publishing an annotated selec-tion of material from the correspondence archives in its own right.

I refer elsewhere—especially in the introduction to this first volume—to the nature and content of the Lord Chamberlain's Correspondence archive, and also to the fact that a considerable quantity of files has only recently been released into the public domain, actually after I thought I had completed my research and was engaged in writing my analysis. Frustrating though it may have briefly been to have been first forced to abandon writing in order to confront new material, and second to adjust significantly some of what I had written, I am fortunate indeed that it was released in time for me to access it. However, this should perhaps also serve as a reminder that, however extensive the archive seems, there is much that is absent from it and which might be significant in shaping and re-shaping our understanding. It is possible that there may still be papers which have not yet been released and which have been withheld, but doubtless there are also some missing papers which will never be recovered, let alone identified. Perhaps most frustrating of all for the researcher is the moment where a correspondence about the censorship of a particular play ends with a note indicating that the issue will be taken up in a personal or telephone discussion between the Lord Chamberlain's Office and someone else. On the other hand, one of the most valuable discoveries has been the extent to which not only official letters but internal notes, memoranda, annotation, jokes and scribbled remarks—some of them surprisingly unguarded—have been preserved for us in the files. In analysing the practice of theatre censorship between 1900 and 1968, it is obviously important to remember that we do not have all the evidence; but if, at least, we take the time to explore thoroughly the evidence we do have available, then there is much to be learned. I hope and believe that each volume of this present study will tell us important things we didn't know.

Acknowledgements

I would like to thank the following for their support, assistance and contributions to the process of research which lies behind this book: the Arts and Humanities Research Board, whose financial support was crucial in allowing me the time to work on the archive material; the Society for Theatre Research and the University of Huddersfield, both of whom also made generous grants to assist the process of research; Kathryn Johnson, archivist in charge of the Lord Chamberlain's material (and much, much more) at the British Library, for her expertise, her unfailing responses to bizarre queries, and for conversations and fantasies about the Lord Chamberlain's staff shared over doughnuts; staff in the Manuscript Room of the British Library and the Study Room of the Theatre Museum; Peter Ettridge, Carol Quinney and Clare Walters for transcribing and checking; Alasdair Burman for cover photography; staff at the University of Exeter Press, especially Simon Baker, Peter Thomson, Graham Ley, Genevieve Davey and Anna Henderson, for their perceptions and their encouragement; Martin Banham and Dominic Shellard for advice and comments; colleagues at the University of Huddersfield; Miss Webster and the other silent staff in the Lord Chamberlain's Office who, over many years, organised and maintained this archive, and without whom there would have been little here to research; and finally Heather, for support, ideas and questions, and my daughter, Katya, for making the writing process more challenging by her deft (and permanent) removal of the letter 'b' from my keyboard.

Because Lions Ain't Rabbits

> No petty tyranny which has gone to such lengths of absurd abuse as the
> present administration of the Lord Chamberlain's department has any
> parallel in history. To future ages it will appear as darkened and ridicu-
> lous as the Inquisition, but for us, alive, working, giving our time on earth
> and our worldly goods in the cause of dramatic art it is a jest only in the
> abstract.[1]

At a recent conference on theatre censorship, I told a contemporary British
playwright that I was writing this book. He was old enough to have had his
own brushes with the Lord Chamberlain in the early part of his career, but
for him censorship had only been a minor and a rather silly irritant; as a result,
he was sceptical about the significance of censorship to twentieth-century
British theatre, or the need for a book on the subject: 'Were there any really
good plays to censor?', he asked, sipping his wine. Strangely, I had never actually asked myself that question. 'Does it matter if they were good?', I asked,
hesitantly. 'Of course it does', he insisted; 'if they weren't any good then it
doesn't matter if they were censored'.

I thought about this encounter a lot. I could have replied that there were
indeed some fine and famous plays—*Miss Julie*, *Ghosts*, and *Six Characters in
Search of an Author*, for example—which had been withheld from public
performance for many years, and that I also knew of a handful of effective
and powerful scripts consigned to oblivion largely as a result of the refusal to
license them. 'WE ARE EFFECTIVELY PROHIBITED FROM
PRESENTING THE MASTERPIECES OF TODAY', complained the
director Terence Gray in the early 1930s.[2] But somehow the question missed
the real point of what I was writing about, and I want to challenge the premise
that it is only the censorship of great plays that matters. On one level, of course,
it is true that the silencing of a good play matters more than the silencing of
a poor or an average one—though this obviously begs the question of how we
all agree on which is which. Yet censorship, I suggest, is at its most effective
when it is invisible. So often when exploring its practice in relation to British
theatre one has the sense of touching the tip of an iceberg; the rest of that

iceberg can never be seen, for it consists of plays that were never submitted for licence, and probably never written. One of the fundamental strategies deliberately and consciously employed by the Lord Chamberlain's Office was to refuse one play, perhaps innocuous itself, *pour décourager les autres*. In a sense this was a perfectly reasonable strategy, since it becomes much harder to defend the refusal to license a particular word or theme if the author or manager can complain that something the same or very similar has already been licensed elsewhere. 'Unborn' plays, as one playwright and critic called them, can never be looked at or properly taken into account. But somehow we need to be aware of their non-existence—of the silenced voices.

Banning a play was a last resort, avoided by the Lord Chamberlain whenever possible. Before that came the process of removing certain elements and of persuading the manager—since it was managers rather than playwrights who submitted texts for licensing—to alter the script. Next time round, perhaps the manager would anticipate the difficulties and either refuse to touch the script or save time by insisting it must be altered before submitting it for licence; the time after that, perhaps, the playwright would censor the play before sending it to the manager, or censor his or her own thoughts while writing. Preventing the unacceptable from being written or even imagined is probably the ultimate goal of censorship. Some artists may persist in their work and their principles even though they anticipate that what they produce will be disallowed; but others, with livings to make, surely will not. There were plenty of novelists and poets in the early part of the twentieth century who claimed that the censorship was one of the main reasons why they refrained from writing plays. It is perhaps no coincidence that one of the strategies used by the English Stage Company in the 1950s as part of its attempt to revitalise theatre with new plays was to contact novelists and encourage them to write for the stage.

So my first response to the suggestion that only the censorship of good plays matters, is that the censorship of poor plays may lead directly to the prevention of much better ones being written. Furthermore, I would argue that we should take into account the place and function of theatre within society. During the period covered by this present volume, theatre was obviously far more important and influential as a medium for communicating, discussing and responding to what was going on in the world than it is in the twenty-first century. That is precisely why it was seen as so necessary to control it. The playwright Laurence Housman, who suffered more than most from the activities of the Lord Chamberlain's Office, was certainly convinced of this, as the report in *The Times* of his address at a public meeting on theatre censorship in October 1910 makes evident:

> To-day, when men had to a large extent left off going to church and to a large extent left off reading anything except the newspapers, the stage was

probably the most valuable platform left for the development of new thoughts; yet here it was that they had the fiat of an essentially average man imposing itself, and imposing itself so vaguely that they did not know where the prohibition began or ended.[3]

Moreover, and crucially, in the 1920s the activity of creating and watching theatre was not only—or perhaps primarily—to do with professional artists seeking to produce great work; a 240-page government report on the state of drama across the country gave equal weight to detailing how villages, factories, churches, political parties, schools, prisons and others were using drama as 'a powerful instrument for the conveyance of ideas'. The report argued that it was above all through active participation that theatre had the potential to heal the 'warring elements in our national life'.[4] The system of licensing for public performance extended to all plays—professional and amateur, 'highbrow', twice-nightly melodramas, local pantomimes, propaganda plays, and so on. While they may often have based themselves in clichés and stereotypes, a surprising number of those plays reflected in one way or another on contemporary political and social issues. The plays themselves now have little to recommend them for study or performance; but whether they were good plays or dreadful plays, an analysis of how they were controlled through censorship may tell us much about the relationship between power and freedom at this time, and flag up for us the potential fault lines in the prevailing ideology where the British establishment felt itself vulnerable and in need of defence. For this reason too, then, the censorship of all plays matters.

The practice of theatre censorship often involved complicated negotiations and compromises, and was not necessarily consistent. Partly because of the sheer volume of material being submitted—and the ambiguities of language and intent which so easily make censorship look ridiculous—contradictions are not hard to find. Opinions and policies were generally fluid rather than stagnant, and the precise meaning and implications of the laws governing theatre censorship proved to be incapable of precise definition. No doubt, too, there were hypocrisies, self-deceits and attempts to mislead or conceal in the way the Lord Chamberlain's Office worked. But the censors rarely saw either the overall 'quality' of a play as having much relevance to their decisions—though they did sometimes take into account the reputation of the playwright—or even the 'truth' of a play, 'Historical accuracy being no part of censorship', as the Lord Chamberlain noted in 1930.[5] Certainly the fact that a play was not 'truthful' could sometimes be held against it, but the fact that it *was* 'true' counted for little or nothing in terms of securing a licence. That is why it is appropriate that this book should focus, not on the censorship of great art, but on how and why the medium of theatre was controlled in day-to-day practice. It is not an exact analogy, but control and censorship of tabloid newspapers is as, or more, important as control and censorship of classic novels, and I do not think that we need any longer justify the refusal to privilege 'great art' when selecting our texts for analysis.

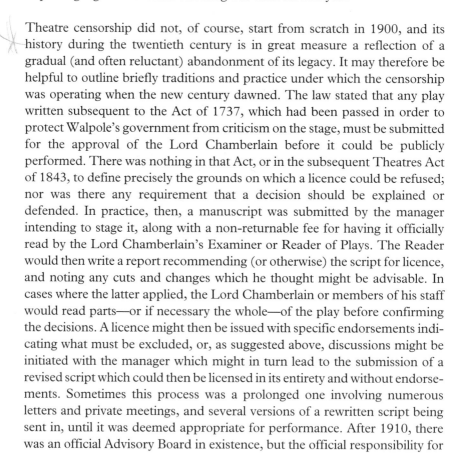

Theatre censorship did not, of course, start from scratch in 1900, and its history during the twentieth century is in great measure a reflection of a gradual (and often reluctant) abandonment of its legacy. It may therefore be helpful to outline briefly traditions and practice under which the censorship was operating when the new century dawned. The law stated that any play written subsequent to the Act of 1737, which had been passed in order to protect Walpole's government from criticism on the stage, must be submitted for the approval of the Lord Chamberlain before it could be publicly performed. There was nothing in that Act, or in the subsequent Theatres Act of 1843, to define precisely the grounds on which a licence could be refused; nor was there any requirement that a decision should be explained or defended. In practice, then, a manuscript was submitted by the manager intending to stage it, along with a non-returnable fee for having it officially read by the Lord Chamberlain's Examiner or Reader of Plays. The Reader would then write a report recommending (or otherwise) the script for licence, and noting any cuts and changes which he thought might be advisable. In cases where the latter applied, the Lord Chamberlain or members of his staff would read parts—or if necessary the whole—of the play before confirming the decisions. A licence might then be issued with specific endorsements indicating what must be excluded, or, as suggested above, discussions might be initiated with the manager which might in turn lead to the submission of a revised script which could then be licensed in its entirety and without endorsements. Sometimes this process was a prolonged one involving numerous letters and private meetings, and several versions of a rewritten script being sent in, until it was deemed appropriate for performance. After 1910, there was an official Advisory Board in existence, but the official responsibility for decisions lay always with the Lord Chamberlain, a member of the royal household. Moreover, much to the disappointment and disapproval of many of those who opposed the lodging of authority with one individual, the members of this Board were themselves appointed by the Lord Chamberlain, who anyway consulted them only when he wished to do so.

Licences for plays were issued only when a specific venue had been stipulated, but, once licensed, it was normally assumed that the same script could be performed in other public theatres without further consideration, provided no changes were made to it. Nevertheless, even laws are open to different interpretations, and there were several occasions when the practices above were varied, or when Lords Chamberlain sought advice from the government and the law lords about the exact extent of their powers and duties. When this occurred, the answer given was almost invariably ambiguous rather than clear-cut. To mention just one example, the precise definition of what did and

did not count as a stage play was never properly specified and became the subject of disputes to which we shall return on more than one occasion.

It has often been argued that theatre suffered from a unique form of censorship, in that the act of silencing took place before a work had been presented to a public. As James Barrie complained to the Joint Select Committee appointed by the government in 1909 to report on stage censorship, 'in no other art is a man treated as the dramatic author is treated under the Censorship, namely, as a criminal without being heard'.[6] Why, we must ask, was theatre censored with such care and relative assiduity by comparison with other forms of expression? One simple answer is 'because it mattered'—or, at least, because the authorities and the political establishment believed it mattered, which is much the same thing. Wherein lay its danger? In his recent book about theatre in the 1950s, admittedly focusing on a later period than that covered in the present volume, Dan Rebellato discusses the criticisms and recommendations of an official sent by the Lord Chamberlain to report on the public performance of a drag revue which he had cautiously licensed. The official's report was dominated by concerns about how the audience was responding, and Rebellato suggests that this was an illegitimate focus for attention since the Lord Chamberlain's jurisdiction did not extend to the ways in which audiences behaved.[7] But in fact fear about the behaviour of those who witnessed performances—both while they were actually watching and especially subsequent to the performance—was one of the crucial factors which drove theatre censorship. This preoccupation was not without some basis in the 1843 Act or the spirit of the recommendations of the government's Joint Select Committee on theatre censorship in 1909, which confirmed that it was incumbent on the Lord Chamberlain to disallow any performance which was 'calculated to cause a breach of the peace'.[8] There can be little doubt that the authorities would have considered it a breach of the peace if audiences leaving a drag revue had in any way imitated what they had witnessed on stage. The authoritative advice given with the backing of the King by Spencer Brabazon Ponsonby—who had served as Comptroller to the Lord Chamberlain's Office from 1857 until 1901—to the Lord Chamberlain at the time of that enquiry was that 'his first duty is in regard to probable results consequent on the production of the play'.[9] Similarly, the definition of the role of stage censor offered by a Reader of Plays in the 1890s (and still being held up to the 1909 Committee) declared:

> It is only at the point where public manners affect public morals that his responsibility begins. The guardianship of abstract morality must always belong to the pulpit . . . No legislation can make a moral theatre or a moral audience; it can only prevent a deliberate corruption of public manners, and a systematic debasement of the moral currency by theatrical entertainments which pander to the lowest tastes and passions, and count upon scandal

for success. With the widest freedom of abstract political opinion and sentiment in stage Plays I have never deemed it my right or duty to interfere.[10]

In other words, it was the actual rather than the abstract—what happened
outside theatres as 'a result' of what happened inside and on-stage—which it
was crucial to control.

The concern about audiences was not, in fact, limited to theatres. In 1903
the Lord Chamberlain and his officers met a representative of the Home
Office, Henry Cunynghame, to discuss whether theatre clubs should be
permitted to give 'private' performances to select audiences of material which
would not be permitted on the public stage. The Home Office advised the
Lord Chamberlain that, so far as it was concerned, unlicensed plays could be
performed provided they 'would not create a public scandal'; it was 'the policy
of the Home Office to leave things alone, unless there was danger to the Public
Morality', and it would 'probably not take action in cases of hole and corner
performances'. In principle, then, it was who saw a play and what the effect
might be which concerned the government; a fascinating internal memorandum in the Lord Chamberlain's files shows that an explicit link was drawn
on this occasion between the control of theatre and of literature:

> Mr Cunynghame cited cases within his Home Office experience where
> the publication of questionable literature, which would not be likely to
> come before the Great Masses in a cheap form had not been suppressed,
> notably Burton's *Arabian Nights*, which was expensively published at 5
> pounds, and would not be within the reach of schoolboys and schoolgirls,
> and the other classes, on account of its price. In this case the Home
> Secretary would certainly not have sanctioned the publication of the work,
> which was intended for a select few, if it was thrown open to the Public
> eyes, and thus it is with stage plays.[11]

It is beyond the scope of this study to compare the practice of censorship in
theatre with that in other art forms, but perhaps the uniqueness of the system
of theatre censorship has sometimes been exaggerated.

Another assumption frequently made is that the Lord Chamberlain's jurisdiction encompassed only those plays written after 1737 when the Censorship
Act was passed. It is true that only plays written after that date were to be
formally submitted for licence—though we should note first that this was
taken to include subsequent translations of much older plays (notably *Oedipus*
and *Lysistrata*) since these were made after 1737; such plays would not have
required licensing to be performed in the original Greek, yet they were subject
to considerable constraints in English versions. However, another section of
the Act also gave the Lord Chamberlain the right to intervene and prevent a
performance in any case where he considered a breach of the public peace to

be likely; so although Jacobean and Restoration plays, for example, did not have to be submitted for licence, the possibility and threat of intervention were not wholly absent. This was doubtless one reason why classical texts were habitually and automatically censored by managers without the necessity of direct intervention from the Lord Chamberlain. Whatever the reason—and whoever the censor—it seems that older texts were habitually presented only in bowdlerised versions. When *The Country Wife* was performed in 1926, the Public Morality Council bitterly denounced the production and demanded that the law should be changed to bring such plays within the direct control of the censors, even while acknowledging that the management had already cut one-third of the text as too indecent to be performed.[12] From an opposite stance, when during a parliamentary debate of 1913 the MP Francis Neilson attacked the restrictions imposed on theatre, he chose as a key example, not a contemporary playwright, but Shakespeare:

> I wish to point the difference between the way Shakespeare is played in Germany, where they are unfettered, and the way it is done in this country. I have never seen in *Romeo and Juliet* the scene between Lady Capulet, Juliet, and the nurse. If I want to see that scene I have to go to Germany to see it . . . The same is true with regard to many other scenes from Shakespeare.

The repertoire itself, Neilson claimed, was being significantly limited:

> They boast in Vienna that they have performed every one of Shakespeare's plays, including *Troilus and Cressida* and *Measure for Measure*. Why are we in London not to see these plays?

Although such censorship had nothing directly to do with the Lord Chamberlain, the MP attributed considerable responsibility to his control:

> Not because the Censor would censor a Shakespearean play, nor would he I think debar any particular scene in Shakespeare from being acted. But because of the whole sense of restriction that the Censor has brought about, managers themselves when they are considering the production of a Shakespeare play have to emasculate the whole force of the drama itself time and time again, and cut out essential scenes.[13]

In trying to understand the extent of theatre censorship, then, it is necessary to be aware of more than the explicit interventions by the Lord Chamberlain.

One of the implications of the system of censorship—often attacked as a weakness by those who wanted tougher restrictions—was that the licence was essentially granted or refused on the basis of the written text rather than how

it was performed. The Chief Constable of Newcastle once suggested to the Lord Chamberlain that, when granting licences, 'regard should be paid to enquiring as to the gestures and settings that will be used in connection with certain phrasing'.[14] It was even proposed on one occasion that no action or gestures at all should be allowed on stage which had not been detailed in the script! Of course, even had it been possible to meet such obviously impracticable demands, this still would not have allowed for the way in which lines would be spoken or mediated by facial expressions. Only the censors of cinema would enjoy the luxury of knowing the performance they had licensed could not be varied. But certainly, to censor only the spoken word would have been an ineffective method of control. As the playwright Henry Arthur Jones evocatively put it in 1909 in his attack on the bias of censorship:

> One reason that makes the Censorship impossible today lies in the fact that modern plays are no longer chiefly pieces of declamation and lengths of dialogue . . . The Censor sits in his office vetoing Sophocles and Shelley and Ibsen, and their kin ancient and modern, with the full text of their plays before him. Meanwhile Mr. Slangwheezy and Mr. Bawlrot are almost out of his reach, and Mr. Bluewink and Mr. Leerit slip away from him altogether.[15]

In fact, costumes, settings and actions were frequently included by the Lord Chamberlain in his list of required emendations—though there remained some uncertainty about how far the law actually gave him jurisdiction over these—and, on occasions, staff would inspect rehearsals and require changes to be made before agreeing to issue a licence. Equally, performances might be inspected after a licence had been granted, though for practical reasons of resources such inspections happened relatively rarely, invariably where a potential problem had been identified, and never outside London. However, after 1922, chief constables were routinely asked by the Lord Chamberlain to inspect and report on performances taking place elsewhere. It is important to realise that the Office charged with controlling the censorship of the stage throughout the country was hardly a well-organised, dedicated, efficient or well-resourced outfit befitting the authority it seemed to wield. Most of the duties and energies of the Lord Chamberlain himself were devoted to other fields. To stray for a moment into the territory of the second volume, it is strangely comic and yet poignant that the Office's notes on a bitter anti-war and anti-establishment play of the 1960s, submitted by Tynan and Olivier under the title *What Were We Fighting For* (and featuring burning soldiers screaming in a tank), should be written partly on the back of the agenda for a meeting of the Queen's Gallery Executive Committee in the Tapestry Room to discuss a proposal from the Lord Chamberlain's Comptroller that 'the "ascending" staircase be covered with carpet to match the "descending" stair-

case', and partly on the back of the instructions for the State Funeral of Sir Winston Churchill.[16] To imagine a Lord Chamberlain and his Comptroller constantly switching between organising trivial and momentous affairs of state and considering, for example, how much whip they could allow to be used in the latest touring version of *Enslaved by the Mormons* is perhaps to gain an insight into how the Office may really have operated throughout the century.[17]

In 1899 Bernard Shaw had described the Lord Chamberlain as 'the Malvolio of St James's Palace', probably quite accurately suggesting that most of his time was taken up supervising Court pageantry.[18] Of course, Shaw was setting out to be provocative and antagonistic, but the evidence certainly indicates that the importance of stage censorship was not always fully recognised throughout the monarchical household. At the end of the 1920s, the Lord Chamberlain consulted the Keeper of the Privy Purse and the Treasurers to the King about the possibility of paying a retaining salary to his Examiner (in addition to the reading fees) so that he could afford to take an occasional holiday; the response was outrage at the suggestion that the censorship should not be self-financing from the fees charged for reading: 'the King should not be asked to pay anything', insisted his financial advisers. They proposed, instead, that the Reader (who was then producing reports on 700 plays or more per year) should take on additional employment to support himself, and indicated that the only grounds on which they could pay him a salary would be if they docked half of the reading fees, and if the Reader himself paid for the secretary who typed out his reports. The only other possibility was to increase the reading fees charged to managers, but since these were enshrined in the Act as one guinea for a one act play and two for anything longer, the amounts could not be altered without passing amendments to the law.[19] Successive Lords Chamberlain and governments always feared that to attempt to make even minor changes in that law would inevitably stir up a hornet's nest in which every aspect of theatre censorship would be questioned and debated, so even the fees had to remain unchanged. Those who complained that the Lord Chamberlain's Office failed to inspect enough performances or to read every play carefully enough did not realise the extent to which stage censorship was being done on the cheap.

Why is this book necessary? At the start of his immensely valuable and scholarly study entitled *The Censorship of English Drama 1824–1901*, John Russell Stephens defines his aim as being

> to trace the changing faces of censorship and—just as important—of the censors . . . in the belief that, within a properly illuminated theatrical context, it will serve as a contribution to the history of nineteenth-century drama and to an understanding of the manners, attitudes, and preoccupations of its time.[20]

It is now over twenty years since that book was published, but strangely, there has been no attempt to follow Stephens's excellent example in relation to twentieth-century theatre. Several books have taken aspects of theatre censorship between 1900 and 1968 as their topic, but none can lay claim to emulating the thorough research and the properly academic approach of Stephens which together allow his work to cast light so widely. My two volumes represent an attempt to do just that. This is not to denigrate the important and interesting work which has been done by others. There are, for example, two valuable and unpublished Ph.D. theses on which I have drawn; one, by John Florance, under the title 'Theatrical Censorship in Britain: 1901–1968', was written with the handicap of having no proper access to the Lord Chamberlain's Correspondence, which, since it became available in the early 1990s, has been the crucial starting point for all such work. On the other hand, Florance's use of other relevant material is important and informing.[21] More recently, Anne Etienne's thesis, written in French under the title 'Les Coulisses du Lord Chamberlain: La Censure Théâtrale de 1900 à 1968', is based on a very thorough exploration of examples from the Lord Chamberlain's papers, properly set within social and historical contexts.[22] However, Dr Etienne's research and thesis, while full of valuable discoveries, focuses almost exclusively on those plays which were actually banned and refused licences; while such an approach provides a perfectly reasonable focus, the range of these two volumes goes beyond that and reflects my contention that there is as much or more significance in the detail of how plays were altered and then licensed as in the reasons why others were never licensed.

As regards published work, Richard Findlater's *Banned*—which was actually written before the abolition of censorship and necessarily excluded the 'end' of the story—was for a long time the only available work; however, for all its ground-breaking importance and the fascinating examples which he presented, Findlater had only limited access to the Lord Chamberlain's papers, and was perhaps ultimately inclined to seek out good stories rather than attempt anything more thorough.[23] Writing as an insider and former Comptroller of the Lord Chamberlain's Office (and presumably with potential access to all the relevant papers) John Johnston published *The Lord Chamberlain's Blue Pencil* in 1990, immediately before St James's Palace released the material for public access.[24] It is probably inevitable that much of Johnston's book should read like an apologia for the censors, and while again there is much intriguing material, he barely begins to consider the real significance of what he himself was part of. Indeed, some of the selectiveness reflected in the examples he cites perhaps speaks of a continuing instinct for suppression, or at least sensitivity about what should become public knowledge. More recently, the journalist and author Nicholas de Jongh has published valuable and focused work drawing on some of the Lord Chamberlain's papers, first in a study of homosexuality on the stage entitled

Not in Front of the Audience and more recently in *Politics, Prudery and Perversions*, a highly readable volume which also utilises interviews with some who had direct contact or involvement with the censorship in its final death throes.[25] De Jongh's work is important but limited, since he appears to have chosen specific plays and issues and then sought out relevant material. Of course, given how much material is available, any treatment is bound to be highly selective and based on exemplars, and will to some extent reflect the interests of the researcher; there are many different perspectives which could be taken and books which could be written drawing on that material. Nevertheless, I would contend that a scholarly approach should at least select its examples after making a reasonable attempt to explore the whole range of what is available; even with regard to the issues on which de Jongh focuses, my rather more extensive research sometimes allows me to support and amplify what he says, but at other times to challenge or to contradict it.

In addition to these full-length studies, a number of writers have drawn on the Lord Chamberlain's files for shorter pieces of research, exploring specific plays or writers or themes in relation to stage censorship. But for understandable reasons, most previous research has tended to focus on relatively well-known plays, by relatively well-known writers, usually performed professionally and more often than not in London. If we wish to get a fuller picture of the censorship and how it operated, there can be no such bias. With the exception of the early part of the century (when a less effective system of maintaining records in the Lord Chamberlain's Office was in existence) and occasional missing files (mainly as a result of bombing during the Second World War) there exists a folder for every single script that was submitted for licence in the twentieth century—this includes every play that was legally performed in public, and those which were refused licences or put in Waiting Boxes pending decisions which were never made. Together that constitutes some 300 boxes with an average of perhaps 150 files in each, available since 1991 for consultation in the Manuscripts Room at the British Library (not, as de Jongh mistakenly suggests, in the Public Record Office at Kew), covering all amateur and professional performances throughout Britain. Many of those files contain little other than a synopsis of the play, written by the Lord Chamberlain's Examiner or Reader, and an indication of the date and theatre for which the first performance was licensed. But often—whenever doubts were raised about issuing a licence or when there were subsequent complaints—the files contain much more: letters, comments, minutes of discussions, scribbled notes, official policy documents, private memoranda, suggested revisions to scripts, complaints, newspaper articles, programmes, photographs and drawings, and evidence of detailed negotiations about whether and on what conditions a script could be licensed. The material typically incorporates correspondence between a theatre manager and a senior member of the Lord Chamberlain's Office (probably the Comptroller) but

may also include letters or occasionally telegrams involving the playwright, the Lord Chamberlain and his staff, government departments, MPs, foreign embassies, organised campaigning bodies, the monarch, the Archbishop of Canterbury, other religious leaders, members of the Lord Chamberlain's Advisory Board, famous public figures, the Church, the military establishment, justices of the peace, local authorities, chief constables, and members of the public. In the case of some plays there is too much material to fit into one or even two folders, and reading it all (especially when many items are handwritten or scrawled) takes a considerable time. However, one of the discoveries which comes from reading the material more exhaustively is that some of the most potent discussions of principle or important formulations of policy may be found in files related to obscure plays, which no amount of pre-selection or guessing on the part of a researcher would allow him or her to anticipate.

As if this material were not enough, even while I was in the throes of writing this first volume I was alerted to the fact that St James's Palace had decided to disgorge a further 150 boxes containing material from the Lord Chamberlain's Office which was not filed under the titles of individual plays. Thanks to the co-operation of the British Library (and most especially the generous assistance of Kathryn Johnson, the archivist and researcher with detailed knowledge of these papers), I was able to explore the most relevant files within days of their arrival and before they had even been catalogued. They yielded some important new information which previous researchers have not had access to, and which I have been able to refer to and to integrate in my work. Even now, it is unclear whether more material still remains at St James's Palace, and, indeed, whether someone had been carefully through the recently released files in order to extract—to censor—anything still deemed too sensitive for public knowledge. Although I draw on other important sources in my research—including published and unpublished scripts, parliamentary debates and reports, books, articles and letters by playwrights and critics, and the annual reports of the Public Morality Council—the systematic analysis of the Lord Chamberlain's Correspondence files is central to this study, and, I am certain, a prerequisite for an equivalent scholarly book to Stephens's *The Censorship of English Drama 1824–1901* or to L.W. Conolly's *The Censorship of English Drama 1737–1824*.[26] While I make no claim to closure or to having achieved the impossible concept of exhaustiveness—there are other stories which could be told—I would wish that my contribution will be seen to follow those books and to constitute the final part of a trilogy covering the period from 1737, when the Act of Licensing was passed, until its abolition in 1968.

This volume is divided into ten chapters within two sections. Although neither the chronological nor the thematic divisions are inevitable or absolute, they are not arbitrary. The first section is broadly chronological and deals with

the period from 1900 until 1918. Chapters One and Two focus on the first decade, which concluded with the publication of a report by the government's Joint Select Committee of Enquiry into stage censorship. Chapters Three to Five focus on the period between 1910 and the end of the First World War, with Chapter Three concentrating primarily on the arguments and debates between the Lord Chamberlain, his readers and advisers, playwrights and MPs in the early part of that period, Chapter Five on the use of the theatre as an instrument of anti-German and pro-war propaganda, and Chapter Four on the censorship of other areas. The second section explores the period between 1919 and 1932 through focusing on some of the most important themes and issues. Chapter Six discusses some of the theoretical debates, practices and general principles, Chapter Seven discusses plays about religion and horror, good and evil, Chapter Eight covers morality, and Chapters Nine and Ten discuss issues of national and international politics.

The year 1932 marks a point roughly (though not precisely) halfway through the period covered in these two volumes, and there are several reasons why I have used it as the dividing line. One is related to the censorship of politics in the theatre, which will be a key and recurring theme in both volumes; from 1933 onwards, scripts making reference to Hitler or the Nazis or Fascism began to be submitted, and since such plays became a major source of conflict it seems essential to discuss them together. And 1932 was also the year in which Terence Gray, one of the most innovative and challenging theatre directors who had fought constant battles with the Lord Chamberlain over the previous five years, not only resigned from the Festival Theatre in Cambridge, but abandoned all theatre and emigrated to France to cultivate grapes and racehorses. It was in 1932, too, that the playwright Laurence Housman complained poignantly to the Lord Chamberlain after yet another play of his had been refused a licence that 'to feel indignant is one of the few compensations left to a defrauded author'; Housman also expressed the hope that the censorship would pass away before he did. Lord Cromer replied: 'While I understand your prayer as an author for the death of the Censorship, whether or not this may be answered lies on the lap of the Gods'.[27]

Ironically, perhaps, one of the principal findings to emerge from a thorough exploration of the Lord Chamberlain's Correspondence files is that he and his Office were not supreme in their authority but only one element controlling and censoring theatre—and by no means always the most extreme one. Those who suffered under his restrictions sometimes described the Lord Chamberlain as a god, wielding absolute power and influence. On one occasion when the use of the word 'God' was banned from a play he was producing, Terence Gray even sought (and obtained) permission to substitute the phrase 'Lord Chamberlain' into the performance at the relevant

moments. But at most he was a god rather than the God, and the complexity of the forces contributing to the process of censorship has not generally been recognised. We know now that the Lord Chamberlain's position and legal duty lasted until 1968, and certainly he remained an important figure; but no one—least of all the successive holders of the position—knew for sure that it would last so long. The responsibility of controlling plays could have been shifted elsewhere—to the Home Office, for example—or the whole system of centralised licensing could have been abolished, leaving local authorities and other laws to decide and limit what could be performed. One of the imperatives influencing the policies of the Lord Chamberlain in the 1920s was actually the wish to hang on to power; in seeking to avoid confrontation and bad publicity, many decisions were motivated less by absolute principle or even personal whim, than by a consideration of what would give him the best chance of retaining his position and resisting the challenges to his authority from all sides. In fact, it turns out that, far from being the strongest advocate of suppression, the Lord Chamberlain's Office during this period was constantly resisting powerful campaigners and representatives of the political and moral establishment who were demanding that the Office should be much, much tougher and more draconian in its decisions. The efficiently organised and well-connected Public Morality Council is the most obvious such example, but other nations' governments and foreign embassies were sometimes also dissatisfied with the Lord Chamberlain's leniency and strove—often successfully—to put pressures on the Office to be more restrictive. The Comptroller of the Lord Chamberlain's Office between 1907 and 1920, Sir Douglas Dawson, may have held the sort of narrow and self-righteous views which match the clichéd view of a censor as someone constantly disgusted and appalled by the world around him—though even he had a secret penchant for risky French plays which he nevertheless thought unsuitable for the lower classes—but other advisers to the Lord Chamberlain had much more liberal instincts. In the 1920s, the Earl of Cromer (the Lord Chamberlain) declared:

> In censorship I hold it is not a question of liking or disliking a play, its theme or the form in which it is to be presented. The question for discussion is whether it is right or wrong for a play to be licensed for public performance. If it is wrong, there must be some valid ground for considering it so.[28]

Such a statement invites many questions—it is certainly not against censorship, and nor can it be taken as a guarantee of how censorship would act in practice—but it is not quite the voice of someone seeking to measure everything by his own tastes.

Stephens concludes in the Epilogue to his study:

The question of whether dramatic censorship had any profoundly serious effect upon the drama of the nineteenth century is not easy to answer. It may hardly be doubted that the drama was seriously restricted in many areas, sometimes in the subject-matter itself, sometimes in its treatment; but the degree of responsibility to be laid at the door of the censor is less clear . . . It was the authorities' habitual defence to claim that censorship was merely reflecting the wishes of the public, whose voice the Lord Chamberlain's Office listened to attentively throughout the century. In religion, political allusion, and morality the Victorians could always easily find to hand enough evidence to support and sustain the idea of an institution of censorship that could control the frightening power of the theatre to influence opinions, encourage imitation, or mould attitudes.[29]

Much of this remains true at least up until 1932.

In November 1913 the Haymarket theatre in London staged what the Lord Chamberlain's official Reader called 'a pointed burlesque' under the title *The Censor*; this 'bitter caricature of censorship standards' by Wilfred Coleby centred on a playwright whose Piccadilly agents are adamant that it would be a waste of time to submit his script to the Lord Chamberlain:

> POCHIN: We've both read your Sketch—very clever—brilliant—but— you tell him Cobb.
> COBB: The Censor wouldn't pass it, Mr Gosset to begin with.
> GOSSET: Oh!
> POCHIN: You see, it isn't a question of altering some of the lines. It's the whole subject—or rather the way it's treated.
> COBB: Realism—they won't have it, you know . . . you make your characters say just what they would say.

The 'realism' to which they insist the Lord Chamberlain would object is not only in the form and the language, but also, we are given to understand, in the content; the play is about 'something that happened' and the writer has 'treated it sincerely'. The target of Coleby's satire, then, is not the strictness of the theatre censorship *per se*, but the perceived discrepancy between the severity with which the serious play is treated and the relative leniency afforded towards the frivolous—in spite of its evident immorality. This, as we shall see, was a frequently and passionately voiced complaint by many of those most opposed to the existing system of stage censorship. To the disgust of the moralistic playwright in Coleby's script, he is forced to work in a business in which cynical theatre managers have mastered the art of tantalising audiences' imaginations with provocative sexual displays, ridiculously disguised in order to lend them the most spurious respectability:

> GOSSET: I saw a girl last night . . . she couldn't dance—She didn't try to dance. Her whole entertainment consisted in presenting this conundrum to the audience. Had her bare flesh got any covering upon it, and if so, where did that covering begin?
>
> POCHIN: (*eagerly, with great animation*) Ah, but that's done by the lighting you know . . .
>
> COBB: (*eagerly*) You couldn't see the join? Where were you sitting? Close up? . . .
>
> POCHIN: . . . She didn't do a dance, you say. What was it exactly?
>
> GOSSET: It was just waggling about.
>
> POCHIN: Yes, yes, I know, I know. All of them are that. What did they call it, I mean?
>
> GOSSET: The most revolting thing she did of all was called The Temptation of St Agatha, a tale of the Early Christian Church . . . The applause was terrific they wouldn't let her go. So at last for an encore turn to St Agatha, she came on and took off her halo . . .
>
> POCHIN: Martin Crane's running that show . . . Symbolism. It's an extraordinary thing but Crane always does know just what the audience want—symbolism—he knows—they're taking that this year.
>
> GOSSET: (*savagely*) Taking it—yes, that's exactly what they were doing—taking it—just like trout—gulping it down and your Mayfly—what a maggot.

Coleby implies that the Lord Chamberlain's focus on the spoken word was simply having the effect of driving unscrupulous managements further into increasingly immoral visual displays. But he also described his play as 'an attempt to illustrate the attitude of the British mind towards Art in general', and he dramatises the perennial debate over whether managers are simply giving the public what they want, or whether they and the agents—the 'muck-rakes' as his frustrated playwright calls them—are manipulating and creating the situation. The agent insists that no one can change the way things are:

> POCHIN: You complain, you complain, instead of accepting it Mr Gossett. You're like a lion tamer who grumbles when he goes into the cage because the lions ain't rabbits. The British public—is—the British public.[30]

Coleby's satire was by no means misplaced; between 1900 and 1932 it was above all those playwrights, directors, managers and enthusiasts for whom theatre was something other than an entertainment and a business who most consistently objected to the restrictions of the censorship, and who were most reluctant to make amendments. This reluctance to compromise infuriated the Lord Chamberlain's Office, which rarely showed much respect for writers.

When the exasperated playwright in *The Censor* eventually storms out of the agents' office, he passes an exotically clad dancer on her way in. 'Who was that who went out then?', the dancer asks one of the agents. 'Oh nobody', the agent replies, 'an author'. That seems as good a place as any to start a study of theatre censorship in the twentieth century.

SECTION ONE
1900–1918

.

CHAPTER ONE

From Ibsenity to Obscenity
Principles and Practice 1900–1909

> If you really want to lead the London stage out of Gomorrah
> you must abolish the Lord Chamberlain.[1]

In May 1900, Samuel Smith, the MP for Flint, introduced a motion to Parliament stating that the House of Commons 'regrets the growing tendency to put upon the stage plays of a demoralising character, and considers that a stricter supervision of theatrical performances is needed alike in the interests of the public and the theatrical profession'. His supporting speech attributed a remarkable power to the stage to influence the future health of the nation:

> Multitudes of young men and young women form their ideas of what is right and wrong in no small degree from what they witness on the stage . . . Is it not certain . . . that a decadent drama, and, what always accompanies it, a decadent literature, will produce a decadent nation?

And he even extended this to the British Empire:

> Would it not be the highest patriotism to keep the heart of this great Empire sound? Is it not lamentable to find that our Colonial and Indian fellow-subjects, when they visit the Metropolis of the Empire, are often staggered at the orgies of vice they witness? If we wish to maintain the loyalty of this great Empire we must keep a standard at home which will command its respect.[2]

Some MPs suggested Smith was exaggerating the importance of theatre, but there was plenty of support for his views, both inside and outside the House. One member lamented the fact that 'there was something about the tradition of the theatre that prevented people exercising that control over themselves there which they exercised in church and in other places'. Eventually, the first of many parliamentary debates on theatre censorship during the twentieth

century ended with Smith's motion being 'talked out'; no vote was taken, and the House generally acknowledged that it was not qualified to make judgements on theatre and would harm its own reputation if it tried to do so:

> Nothing that the House could do would prevent people laughing at a questionable joke . . . public taste had, to some extent, advanced in this matter; but it had not advanced through resolutions of that House, and, whatever estimation of that House might be formed in the country, nobody attached any importance to it when expressing its opinion on literature or art . . . he begged them for Heaven's sake not to make that House ridiculous by pretending that it was an authority on a subject on which it knew next to nothing (*Cheers from both sides of the House.*)[3]

The first decade of the twentieth century witnessed growing demands for the abolition or radical reform of theatre censorship; led by writers such as Granville Barker, Shaw and Pinero, and in parliament by the MP Robert Harcourt, the campaign brought sufficient weight on the government to force it to establish a Joint Select Committee in 1909 to consider the principles and the practices of controlling theatres. Yet simultaneous to this pressure for greater freedom, were campaigns which insisted that the Lord Chamberlain had become too lax and the theatre too decadent. Supporters of these campaigns insisted that much more rigorous policing should be introduced, in order to prevent the performance of what Samuel Smith had called 'foul and corrupting plays that no good actor or actress should touch with a pitchfork, and which no youth can witness without taint'. Several newspapers regularly used editorials or headline stories to lambast the Lord Chamberlain and demand that he should 'Keep Our Theatres Clean',[4] and Smith himself had drawn from the complaints of a leading theatre critic, Clement Scott, about an upsurge in the presentation of 'heathen plays' which were 'destitute of any moral sense'. Scott, no less than Smith, feared the persuasive capacity of theatre to seduce audiences into abandoning virtue and embracing immorality by means of 'plays artfully contrived to attract sympathy for vice . . . with a glamour of romance and sickly sentiment; plays that bring the power and allurement of good acting, or show, or spectacle, or personal charm, to deaden our moral force and moral fibre'. Above all, Scott blamed the playwrights, mourning the fact that 'dramatists of the first-class have one after the other broken away from the beautiful, the helpful, and the ideal, and coquetted with the distorted, the tainted and the poisonous in life'.[5] Theatre was also one of the key targets in need of reform identified by the Public Morality Council, which had been formed in 1899 under the chairmanship of the Bishop of London.

Thus it was not only the opponents of stage censorship who favoured the removal of the Lord Chamberlain and his Examiner of Plays; those

demanding more restrictions and tighter control frequently argued that the power to license or refuse plays for public performance should be handed over to magistrates or local authorities, who would be tougher in their decisions, and who would also be in a better position to inspect the actual performances which took place. The Home Secretary admitted to the 1909 Joint Select Committee that a censorship which based its decisions almost entirely on a script seen in advance of a performance could not be fully effective. Further confusion was caused by the fact that some of the performances which provoked the most hostility from the Public Morality Council and other vigilante groups were staged in music-halls; although the law did not exempt these venues from the same process of censorship imposed on theatres, in practice they were not required to submit their material to the Lord Chamberlain to be licensed, and were only liable for prosecution for indecency or for other reasons after a performance had occurred.

Technically, the granting of a licence for a play did not preclude a prosecution being instituted against those involved in its production, and the Lord Chamberlain's Office covered its back by requiring that the theatre manager should take full responsibility for the nature of a production; licences contained an endorsement that 'no indecency of dress, dance, or gesture' was to be permitted, and official letters to managers frequently pointed out that 'the fact of the piece having been licensed for representation does not relieve you from the responsibility of the *representation*'. This statement was also intended to devolve to the manager the duty of ensuring that actors did not add lines or deviate from the licensed script. Yet to take legal action against a play which had been licensed by the Lord Chamberlain would be to challenge the authority of a member of the royal household; in practice, therefore, once a script had received its licence it was extremely unlikely that it would be challenged in a court of law. This was the reason that most theatre managers continued to oppose any significant change in a system which effectively offered them an immunity against prosecution.

Legally, as we have seen, censorship was still based on the 1843 Theatres Act, which instructed the Lord Chamberlain to refuse a licence whenever 'he shall be of opinion that it is fitting for the preservation of good manners, decorum, or of the public peace so to do'. However, the actual wording on the licences being issued by 1900 also promised that the play 'does not in its general tendency contain anything immoral or otherwise improper for the stage'. More specifically, it required 'strict observance' by the management of four regulations; the first simply indicated that the Examiner of Plays must be informed of any change in the play's title, but the other three were more significant:

> No profanity or impropriety of language to be permitted on the Stage.
> No indecency of dress, dance, or gesture to be permitted on the Stage.

> No offensive personalities or representations of living persons to be permitted on the Stage, nor anything calculated to produce riot or breach of the peace.

As the Joint Select Committee of 1909 pointed out, these regulations had no legal status, because the wording was not part of any Act; however, most of the members of that Committee accepted the assurances of the Comptroller of the Lord Chamberlain's Office that 'the words on the licence may be considered as the Lord Chamberlain's interpretation' of the 1843 Statute.[6]

The written evidence of Viscount Althorp (the incumbent Lord Chamberlain) to that Committee—which went unchallenged—explicitly revealed that his rulings were primarily based, not on the content of a play *per se*, or even necessarily on the way in which it was interpreted in performance, but rather on its predicted effect upon an audience. Whether or not this was a legitimate interpretation of the 1843 Act may be open to question, but it was a shrewd position to adopt since it allowed for an effective response to the accusations of inconsistency and variation which were frequently levelled at the Lord Chamberlain's Office; such accusations invariably depended on a comparison of content rather than on the more nebulous and hypothetical effect of a performance. Althorp's argument, derived from the advice of a previous and experienced official, also offered a plausible justification of why a play which had already been licensed could subsequently have that licence revoked (as famously happened with *The Mikado* in 1907) on the basis of the changed historical or political context of a particular production, of the venue and likely composition of an audience, of how the play was being interpreted, or even of the particular performers involved. Similarly, it provided a legitimate pretext which would sanction the Lord Chamberlain's undeclared habit of consulting government departments, foreign embassies and others as sources of advice.

But how did the censorship operate in practice and—equally important—how did its functionaries, its supporters and its critics perceive it to be operating? In 1899 Bernard Shaw, one of its most committed and eloquent opponents, had summed it up in an essay for the benefit of American readers. In a typically witty and mocking onslaught he described the Lord Chamberlain as 'the Tzar of the drama', pointing out that the office was not democratic and that its holder was responsible only to the monarch. Because the Lord Chamberlain was so taken up with other duties, power effectively devolved onto one of his 'breath-bereaving retainers', his Examiner of Plays, who thus became 'the most powerful man in England or America'; the Examiner had an authority which, according to Shaw, was greater and more significant than that of the monarch or a Cabinet minister: 'Other people may make England's laws; he makes and unmakes its drama'. Yet in attacking the censorship, Shaw was keen not to lay the blame on the Lord Chamberlain as

an individual, explaining rather that the rules by which he was bound to operate 'simply codify the present and most of the past prejudices of the class he represents'. The fault, Shaw argued, was located primarily in the English character, which seemed strangely willing to grant the right to make judgements on behalf of the individual to a spurious authority. Most people, he said, seemed to be

> absolutely convinced that only by a strenuous maintenance of restrictive laws and customs . . . can society be withheld from casting all moral considerations to the winds and committing suicide in a general Saturnalia of reckless debauchery . . . the normal assumption in England is that without a Censor the stage would instantly plunge to the lowest practicable extreme of degradation.

In this sense, the actual censor is as much a victim as an autocrat; but his effect, says Shaw, is devastating, since 'he is doomed . . . to shut the stage door against the great dramatic poets'.

As regards the actual subjects which a playwright must avoid, Shaw claimed that

> You mustn't dramatize any of the stories in the Bible. You mustn't make fun of ambassadors, cabinet ministers, or any living persons who have influence in fashionable society, though no notice will be taken of a gag at the expense of . . . a Socialist Labor member of the County Council, or people of that sort . . . If you introduce a male libertine in a serious play, you had better 'redeem' him in the end by marrying him to an innocent young lady. If a female libertine, it will not matter if she dies at the end, and takes some opportunity to burst into tears on touching the hand of a respectable girl.

The ultimate and governing principle, he maintained, was embodied in an unwritten rule which never changed: 'that a play must not be made the vehicle of new opinions on important subjects, because new opinions are always questionable opinions'.[7] While Shaw's rhetoric may sometimes have exaggerated the situation, that last comment was not very far from the truth.

Although there were examples of religious and political themes being censored, most contemporary observers of theatre during the first decade of the century saw personal and sexual morality as the main target. In a series of articles in 1907 explaining the history of stage censorship, *The Times* correctly informed its readers that

> The censorship is, therefore, political in its origin. But curiously enough,

> it is not on the political side that its exercise is much criticised today . . .
> It is with questions of morality and decency on the stage that the censor-
> ship now mainly occupies itself.[8]

In its annual report on the same year of 1907, the Public Morality Council
was proudly identifying its greatest achievement as the partial success of its
attempt to drive living statuary out of the music-halls of London by
persuading the London County Council to discourage such performances.
The campaign had been based on the arguments that 'exhibitions of apparently nude men and women were demoralising to both spectators and
performers', that 'the efforts being made to raise the spirit of purity and self-
control amongst boys and girls are being seriously impeded by such
exhibitions', and that it was 'the duty of the inhabitants of London to set an
example, as what is allowed in London will be introduced elsewhere'.[9] Yet if
this was a success then it was a partial one. Writing about the state of drama
at the end of the decade, one theatre critic still found it

> impossible to deny that the sexual instincts of young men are often
> provoked to an extreme degree by the sight upon the stage of beautiful,
> half-nude young women . . . The degree of nudity, of display of the human
> form in our theatres, and, of course, music-halls as well, to those unac-
> customed to such matters is certainly quite startling, and by many people
> such displays are regarded as being entirely demoralizing to hot-blooded
> young men . . . Lately the degree of nudity considered permissible has
> been largely increased . . . it is difficult for stern moralists to stomach the
> danse du ventre.[10]

As with the living statuary, the writer was referring directly to presentations
of the unclothed (or underclothed) body on stage. Surprisingly little distinction was made between the explicit and the implicit. One of the plays which
provoked the most hostile attacks on the Lord Chamberlain for having
licensed it was the fairly well known example of Pinero's A Wife Without a
Smile in 1904.[11] The visual image which provoked the outrage was a doll
attached to a string suspended from a couch in an unseen room above, which
becomes agitated when characters off-stage are supposed to be on the couch
together. Under a headline 'The Dirty Drama', one newspaper, which
described this image as 'grossly indecent', accused the Lord Chamberlain of
having 'gone straight from Ibsenity to unashamed obscenity'. While contemptuous of Pinero for having written a play 'which no self-respecting writer
should ever have begun, much less completed', it was George Redford (the
Reader of Plays) and Lord Clarendon (the then Lord Chamberlain) who were
singled out for blame for not having 'saved the British stage a greater degradation than it ever suffered at the hands of the Restoration dramatists'.[12] A

typically private and discreet meeting between Redford and the manager of Wyndham's Theatre in the light of such criticisms resulted in alterations to the action: 'I need hardly say that we are very anxious to do all in our power to meet your wishes', wrote the latter; 'we have moderated the transports of the doll considerably'.[13] But Clarendon still blamed his Examiner for the bad publicity caused; Redford—an enthusiastic admirer of Pinero's work—had failed to anticipate any problems and had therefore not referred the play for another opinion before recommending it for licence. The subsequent furore caused him to seek to protect himself by obtaining and sending to the Lord Chamberlain a letter from a barrister which 'expressly absolves me from any blame'.[14]

Perhaps an even clearer example of the importance attributed to censoring the unseen occurred over *Monna Vanna*, which was refused a licence in 1902 and again in 1908. Maeterlinck's play had been staged in much of Europe, but Redford had reservations about the general theme, in which a woman agrees to sacrifice herself sexually to her husband's military enemy in return for the sparing of her city; since this supposed enemy, having secretly loved her since childhood, does not take advantage of her offer, many people argued that the play was in fact a highly moral and romantic one. However, the particular cause of anxiety was that when the wife goes for her secret tryst with the enemy, she is, according to his request, 'clad only in her mantle'. There is no reason to suppose that the actress playing Monna Vanna would actually have needed to be naked beneath her cloak; even if she had been this would not have been visible to an audience, since the character neither removes nor is asked to remove her garment. But the mere suggestion of semi-nudity was considered too provocative, not least by the King, who subsequently told the Lord Chamberlain that he 'would have wished *Monna Vanna* to be licensed with alterations as to clothing'.[15] Even when the play was eventually allowed in 1914, the then Reader of Plays found the idea 'prurient in its suggestion for the spectator' and cut all references to it.[16] Was such censorship absurd—or a recognition that, in performance, the suggested and the unseen may be more charged than what is visible?

Supporting the banning of *Monna Vanna*, the theatrical newspaper *The Era* described the play as 'more insidiously corrupting than the most cynical French comedy or the most impudent frivolity from the Palais-Royal'.[17] But one of the complaints increasingly made against the censorship by advocates of what was often known as the 'advanced' drama was that plays which dealt seriously with complex moral questions were frequently refused licences, while plays which touched on the same subjects in lighter or comic ways were allowed. Curiously, therefore, the opponents of censorship frequently presented themselves as moralists—even puritans—and the Lord Chamberlain and his Examiner as more or less dissolute rakes. As Shaw provocatively wrote in 1905:

> There is in London an enormous trade in illicit sexual intercourse. Certain
> forms of art unquestionably stimulate that trade; and certain others
> depress it. The Censorship of Plays is tolerated and supported because,
> whilst it pretends to suppress the first and encourage the second, it really
> does exactly the reverse.[18]

Another critic who supported the demands of serious playwrights for greater
freedom argued that 'the real sin of the Censor's office lies as much in what
it permits as in what it forbids'.[19] Many of the aggrieved victims of censorship not only insisted that their own dramas were absolutely moral, but also
called for more severe censorship of what they considered to be immoral.
They were particularly galled by the string of 'cynical' and 'impudent' French
farces imported from the Palais-Royal in the early 1900s and licensed for
commercial theatres in London, which depended for their humour on promiscuity and unfaithfulness.

What the censors seemed to resent was dramatists who wanted to make
people think and perhaps to change: 'the theatre insists strongly upon being
regarded simply as a place of entertainment, and objects almost savagely to
dramas which really show sin as ugly and vice as harmful', wrote one theatre
critic.[20] Sir Herbert Tree, a leading theatre manager, informed the 1909 enquiry
about his meeting with the censor after a serious play about adultery had been
refused a licence: 'I was told', he said, 'it would be acceptable if it could be
made more comic'.[21] In fact, although the Lord Chamberlain did refuse
licences or impose restrictions in relation to some French comedies, these were
habitually dealt with on a different basis from British plays, and the Office
acknowledged—at least internally—that 'many plays have been licensed in
French which in English would not pass muster'. In 1909, when concerns were
raised over a series of Sacha Guitry plays being staged in London, Redford
recommended licensing *L'Assommoir* and informed the Lord Chamberlain:

> there are no doubt some passages more outspoken than we are accustomed
> to hear on the English stage, but I fear this latitude is inevitable with French
> plays, and has always been recognised. There would be no French season
> if it were not so.

Redford said he observed the principle of his predecessor 'that the audiences
in London Theatres when they go to see French Plays should imagine themselves in Paris', and even proposed that the theatres should be treated 'as you
would treat the French Embassy, as part of France'.[22] Yet according to
Dawson, the Reader had a very specific reason to be more cautious about
another play in the same season:

> Mr Redford stated that he had heard by a 'side wind' that the King had
> indicated to M. Guitry through Lord Knollys that he would prefer that

L'Assommoir should be given on the first night (when he would be present) rather than *La Griffe*. I imagine therefore that the King has seen *La Griffe* in Paris . . . One might draw an inference from this that H.M. objected to the Play.[23]

In 1905 Shaw cited examples of serious modern plays by Ibsen, Brieux and himself, all of which dealt with 'sex problems', and all of which censorship had kept off the public stage.[24] *Mrs Warren's Profession* was submitted for licence in 1898 and not passed until 1926, *Ghosts* had been rejected in 1891 and remained unlicensed until 1914, and *Damaged Goods* (*Les Avaries*) was eventually licensed in 1917 in very particular circumstances. Each of these plays might have been described as having a lesson to teach, and it would be hard to argue that any of them revelled in the exploitation of irresponsible sexuality and immorality which featured in many of the plays licensed for performance. A newspaper column in May 1909 claimed that the effect of the censor's practice was to 'warn off the artist and the preacher, and to clear the path for the scoffer and the clown'; drama which was 'audacious in its glorification of lying, adultery, mockery, and light-mindedness' was routinely licensed:

> The drama that they pass on and therefore commend to the people is a drama that is always earthly, often sensual, and occasionally devilish; the drama which they refuse to the people is a drama that seeks to be truthful . . . and that might, if it were encouraged, powerfully touch the neglected spheres of morals and religion.[25]

In the couple of years before the playwrights' deputation to Downing Street, the presentation of Robert Harcourt's Bill in Parliament, and the establishing of the Joint Select Committee, a series of confrontations occurred between the censor and the 'advanced' dramatists. For all its limitations, Edward Garnett's *The Breaking Point*, in which a young woman drowns herself after becoming pregnant by a married man, was undoubtedly intended as a serious and tragic play, and the refusal of a licence for it in 1907 provoked the playwright's wrath. Garnett published not only the play, but, along with it, a letter written by George Redford, in which the Examiner explained that he had suggested to the manager 'the desirability of withdrawing this piece' before it was refused a licence, in order 'to avoid any possible appearance of censure on anyone'. This was one of the traditional practices by which the censor discreetly operated, and the best that could be said of it was that it represented an attempt to save a playwright from the supposed stigma of having a play banned. Conveniently for the Office, it also allowed the Lord Chamberlain to keep down the number of plays which had formally been refused licences and thus to play down the extent of censorship. The

letter infuriated Garnett: 'Is it possible', he asked Redford rhetorically, 'you really imagine that any intelligent person feels the slightest stigma in your disapproval?'. He insisted that the opposite was the case, and that there was no respect among serious theatregoers for the judgement of Redford or his master: 'Your disapproval carries with it no more dishonour than your approval carries honour'. In his introduction to the published text, Garnett calls for the creation of 'A Society For The Defence Of Intellectual Drama' and complains about the huge power being exerted by Redford:

> the deeply harmful effect of the Censor's influence is his power of hindering the development of intellectual drama. He terrorises would-be dramatists. Serious dramatists . . . are deterred from making a deep analysis of actual life . . . You are suppressed by fear of the Philistine before you begin, or you are suppressed by the Censor after you have finished.

Garnett goes on to define what he believes the role and the duty of the Lord Chamberlain's Office should be:

> It is not the Censor's function to suppress works of art . . . It is the Censor's business to prevent gross or prurient indecency on the public stage. Nothing else . . . It is not the Censor's business to suppress intellectual plays that criticise contemporary life or plays . . . that introduce new moral teaching. Half the best works of art in literature, the drama, and the arts are revolutionary to the taste of their times; they do not flatter the tastes, feelings, or prejudices of the great public; they would not be works of art if they did.[26]

The refusal of a licence for Granville Barker's *Waste* in 1907 was another catalyst which contributed to the demands by supporters of the 'intellectual' drama for a change in the law. *Waste* famously depicts an independent politician who is about to join the Tory Cabinet and steer a Bill through Parliament to dis-establish the Church of England. After making a married woman pregnant in a brief affair, he refuses to help her procure an abortion, and she dies in a back-street operation. The politician then commits suicide when the Prime Minister decides it is now too risky to include him in his Cabinet. When the Lord Chamberlain refused a licence, suspicions abounded that it was the political dimension to the narrative which was to blame. Barker himself stated that 'whether it is that important sexual questions are treated in it seriously instead of flippantly, or whether it is the political background that there is to the play to which he objects, I cannot tell'.[27] In order to improve the chance of obtaining a licence, Barker was specifically instructed to 'moderate and

modify the extremely outspoken references to sexual relations', and to remove 'all reference to a criminal operation', but, as he pointed out, he had recently received a licence to stage another play which contained references to abortion.[28] If—as some commentators asserted—audiences would have recognised and identified actual politicians in the characterisations, that alone would have made the play hard to approve. Yet it is equally certain that the censors and critics were genuinely disturbed by the sexual references, and especially by the suggestion that respectable members of the medical profession could be found who were willing to carry out abortions. What is also clear is that Barker's struggle with the censor had extremely negative effects on his management of the Court Theatre, where he had been attempting through the introduction of a 'theatre of ideas' to offer a model for what a National Theatre might be. In November 1907 he claimed that '*Waste* has wasted me', and much of his time and energy over the next few years were spent fighting to escape what he called the 'Dry Nurse', whom he held responsible for having 'retarded the advancement and especially the development of English drama', and for helping to ensure its 'extreme narrowness', by excluding 'any original or unusual point of view'. [29]

One avenue which had been at least half opened for serious playwrights or managers who could not get permission for their work to be publicly staged was to pursue a private performance. The movement had effectively begun in 1886 when the Shelley Society had been created in order to mount a production of *The Cenci*, to be viewed only by those who joined the society. It blossomed with the Independent Theatre Society and the Stage Society in the 1890s, and the strategy of creating clubs at which fee-paying members would be entitled to watch plays which had not been passed for public performance did offer a way of partially circumventing the censorship. This was far from satisfactory; performances were usually restricted to Sundays, and were not necessarily as fully realised or resourced as public performances. Moreover, their status was still questionable. In 1902 a licence was refused for Laurence Housman's play *Bethlehem* on the grounds that plays based on the scriptures were not permitted. At the playwright's instigation, a private performance was then given at the University of London. This was seen by the Lord Chamberlain's Office as a direct challenge to its authority, and on the advice of the King the Comptroller wrote to the Law Officers of the Crown to try and obtain a ruling on the legality or otherwise of private performances of unlicensed plays, so that the Lord Chamberlain would 'know what his powers are in the future with regard to these cases where the law is being so continually evaded'. In March 1903 they received a lengthy and typically convoluted reply; the Comptroller, Sir Arthur Ellis, was driven to seek further advice from Cunynghame at the Home Office: 'My dear Henry, Neither the Lord Chamberlain, nor I, nor anybody here can quite grasp the meaning of

the legal opinion in the enclosed reply from the Law Officers'. At a subsequent meeting with the Comptroller, the Assistant Comptroller, and the Examiner of Plays, Cunynghame suggested that the crucial issue was whether or not tickets had been sold. There was, he said, 'a wide distinction between a bona fide club who could perform what they liked with or without license [*sic*] for the recreation of their members, and a society got up for the express purposes of giving performance of unlicensed plays, and advertising the sale of tickets, which could be bought by anyone to witness such performances'.[30] On the other hand, he intimated that whether or not a prosecution would be pursued depended less on an absolute principle and more on the notoriety and possible significance of the performance. The written statement presented in 1909 on behalf of the Lord Chamberlain to the Joint Select Committee echoed this vagueness:

> During the last 3 or 4 years owing to non-interference on the part of the Lord Chamberlain the matter of Sunday performances gradually took root and has broken out galore with the result that most of the outlying Theatre Managers let their Houses on Sundays to various Societies which have sprung up some of which are *bona fide* . . . and others which are only bogus . . . The Lord Chamberlain has therefore felt during the past two years that these performances must come under his aegis . . . and thus he has felt it his duty to give sanction to the Theatres being open on Sundays providing that the proceeds of the Entertainment are given for some recognised Charity.[31]

In effect, the issue of club and private performances, and their legality or otherwise, remained unresolved. They continued to offer a loophole for what the Office dismissively called the 'insignificant clique of Dramatic Authors who prefer to advertise themselves, rather than yield to any kind of restraint', but they were not, on their own, a solution.[32]

It was by no means only plays dealing with sexuality that provoked censorship during the first decade of the century. Shaw claimed to the 1909 enquiry that 'I have to ascertain, before I know what sort of play will pass, what the politics of the Censor are'.[33] There was probably very little doubt in anybody's mind what the broad politics of the censor were likely to be, and inevitably they dictated policy and practice. As Redford told the Joint Select Committee: 'The stage is not a political arena, and it is not considered desirable that important political questions, involving, perhaps, diplomatic relations with foreign Powers should be dealt with there'.[34] The censors were also extremely touchy about how the military was depicted; in 1907 they insisted on cutting a reference to 'khaki cut-throats' from Synge's *Playboy of the Western World*, along with 'any allusions derogatory to the Army', and the issue of the use of

uniforms on stage recurred regularly.[35] In 1903 Cecil Raleigh wrote a play called *Flood Tide*, set partially within the British army.[36] Coming so soon after the wars in Southern Africa and at a time when the assumed invincibility of the forces of the Empire was beginning to be questioned, the criticisms of the British army—and especially of the institutional class prejudices which drove its practices—touched on a sensitive area. The play gained a licence and was performed at Drury Lane, but only after interference with the script by the Lord Chamberlain's Office and, less publicly, the King. Raleigh probably had no idea that the objections came from so high, but he complained bitterly about the singling out of theatre for such strict repression:

> The journalist, the public speaker, the cartoonist, or the man in the street can say whatever he likes about current affairs; the only person who can be gagged according to law is the unfortunate dramatist, and the Lord Chamberlain is seeking to gag him without mercy . . . I wonder what would happen if a Censorship of the Press existed as well as a Censorship for the Drama.[37]

Written in a popular form and with the most conventional of love plots, *Flood Tide* was hardly part of a 'theatre of ideas', but within a popular and traditional form it carried a strong political message. The narrative of what its author described as a 'Spectacular Melo-Farce' focuses largely on Jack, the son of a publican who has won the Victoria Cross during the recent war and been promoted to the rank of officer. But because of his social background, Jack is contemptuously dismissed by his fellow officers as a 'ranker'. He then speaks out against the whole basis of power in the army:

> JACK: I say we should take our officers only from the ranks! Let a man learn to obey before he is put in command. Let him learn in the Ranks, how the Ranks live . . . let him learn to be a man before he leads men in battle, then you'd have an Army![38]

Such general criticism of the army—made by a sympathetic character—was not welcomed by the political establishment or by staff in the Lord Chamberlain's Office, military aficionados to a man. But what really provoked their ire was a scene at the end of the second act in which Jack's fellow-officers display their contempt for him by invading his room, indicting him in a mock court-martial, demanding that he leave the regiment, and beginning to smash up his possessions. Resentment focused particularly on the climax of this 'ragging' scene, when Jack actually draws his sword on his fellow-officers. According to Raleigh, a member of the Lord Chamberlain's staff attended a rehearsal and 'took exception to the incident', declaring that 'under no circumstances . . . would an officer who was being ragged use a

weapon'. In fact, recounts Raleigh, a similar real-life incident was reported in newspapers even while his arguments with the Lord Chamberlain were going on.[39]

In a private letter from Windsor Castle, Sir Arthur Ellis, the Comptroller, informed the Lord Chamberlain of the King's views:

> From what the King said to me . . . about 'military ragging' I do not hesitate to say that this play should be declined at once . . . and no play with any allusion to such practices should receive a licence—I am sure I am speaking according to H.M.'s wishes . . .
>
> The author seems to have 'ragging' in the brain—and to be a very persistent tiresome man.[40]

This was not the end of the story, and the following day Ellis wrote again to the Lord Chamberlain:

> Dear Clarendon,
>
> Mr Redford to my amazement sends me another manuscript of the 'Ragging Case' Play with some alterations and changes and says he now sees 'no harm in it'. I have looked thro' it and I find the mock court martial in full. It is written by the same ass at Blackpool who was so persistent about it some time since. When last I spoke to the King about it he was superlatively strong on the subject and said that no play with an allusion to such a thing should ever be licensed—and I am sure if he thought that Redford recommended it HM would make short work of Mr Redford!!
>
> I really am astonished that Redford should not see the impropriety of airing the subject on the stage at all.

The play was finally licensed on the understanding that there must be neither representation of, nor references to, any such incident. Redford even attended the first public performance to ensure these requirements were observed, while the King sent a message to the Lord Chamberlain after reading the reviews, in which he expressed 'much satisfaction', but indicated he was still concerned about the costumes: 'he hopes you will go even further, and will not allow, either, actors to be dressed exactly like officers on the stage'. This broadest of hints was evidently followed by a discreet attempt to interfere with the production after it had opened, for a few days later Raleigh published an article in the *Daily Mail* under the headline 'Banishing The Army From The Stage' in which he accused the Lord Chamberlain of 'doing his best to prevent the appearance of soldiers on the stage at all'. Presumably he still had no idea of the real source of the demands, but he identified it as an issue of class:

> The Lord Chamberlain is an ex-Guardsman. There has been ragging in

the Guards; the Lord Chamberlain desires to stop any allusion to ragging on the stage . . . Not only any representation, but any comment upon it . . . Here we have a man representing a class who wants to send the Army out as above criticism . . . even the clothes of the soldier must be preserved from the contamination of the stage . . . all stage uniforms are purposely made inaccurate. Ours . . . looked too like the sacred vestments worn by the Lord Chamberlain's young friends who uphold the dignity of the British Army by spanking each other with hair brushes . . .[41]

Raleigh's article provoked, in turn, several angry letters of reply, including one from a major-general at the Army and Navy Club which possibly confirmed the playwright's claims:

Mr Cecil Raleigh has written a play in which officers of the Army are depicted as the most outrageous cads, who refuse to associate with a brother officer promoted from the ranks, on the ground that his father is a publican . . . Anything more untrue to life has seldom been seen on the stage . . .

Mr Raleigh does not appear to realise that in insulting his Majesty's Army he is insulting the King, who is the head of the Army.[42]

Flood Tide was not the only play Raleigh wrote which brought him into confrontation with the censorship.[43]

Diplomatic pressure from international allies was a not infrequent cause of censorship. In 1908 the Russian Ambassador in London expressed concern about *The Woman of Kronstadt*, a spy play; at a private meeting, the Lord Chamberlain 'explained to the Ambassador the difficulties that would occur were he to take official cognizance of His Excellency's objections', and they therefore agreed, according to the minute, 'to let the matter rest on condition that the Russian uniforms were as unlike the real ones as possible, and that the Russian Imperial eagle should be not too much shown, and that the Ikon should be treated with proper respect'.[44] Such pressures often came via the Foreign Office, as with *The Secrets of the Harem*, a play about which Sir Douglas Dawson, who became the Comptroller of the Lord Chamberlain's Office in 1907 in succession to Sir Arthur Ellis, was asked at the 1909 enquiry. This play had actually been licensed in 1896 and had toured extensively, but in April 1900 the Lord Chamberlain received a letter from the Turkish Ambassador (forwarded from the Foreign Office) which claimed it 'tended to excite political and religious passions against Turkey in favour of the Armenians'. The response of the Lord Chamberlain to continuing Turkish protests is instructive:

Later in the year the Ambassador approached the Lord Chamberlain

direct, when Lord Hopetoun informed his Excellency that the play was not likely to be performed again in the neighbourhood of London, that it was played only in Theatres of the lower class and that more importance would be given to the subject if the very unusual course of withdrawing the license [*sic*] was pursued.

However, when the play was revived the following year at the Shakespeare Theatre in Clapham Junction, the Ambassador complained again; as a result, the licence for performance was actually withdrawn by the Lord Chamberlain—an unusual occurrence—because, according to an answer to a parliamentary question, it was deemed 'offensive to the Sovereign of a friendly State'. On the Lord Chamberlain's suggestion the play was then rewritten and re-licensed 'with the objectionable matter removed'.[45]

As international tensions between Britain and Germany increased and were publicly recognised, the Lord Chamberlain's department had to deal with a number of not very good plays making reference to this. In December 1907 the Office licensed *Send Him Victorious* with the provisos: 'No character in the piece to represent the German Emperor' and 'No references to a political conspiracy to promote a war between England and Germany'. Then, at the end of 1908, a play called *An Englishman's Home* was submitted. Written by 'A Patriot' (actually Guy du Maurier), the play depicted an invasion of Britain by a foreign army and was presumably intended as a warning which would encourage more people to volunteer for military service and prepare to defend the nation. The narrative centres on the Browns, a middle-class family naively complacent in their confidence that Britain will never be attacked, and that if it is they will be able to rely on others to defend it. Even after the invading army (abetted by Fritz, the local hairdresser) has commandeered their property, the Browns fail to take the invasion seriously. In exasperation at their blindness, the one character who is facing up to what is going on spells out the nature of the threat in a speech directed primarily at the audience:

> Are you all mad? Don't any of you understand? How can you stand here, and laugh and joke in the same rotten old way . . . Don't you realise it yet—that the whole damned country is coming down like a house of cards, and that you, and thousands like you, are saying it's not your business, as long as it doesn't interfere with you let it go on. And others are just the same, shouting and singing music-hall songs, and thinking they are going to see some fun. Fun—oh my God![46]

It so happened that Sir Douglas Dawson was himself an active member of the National Defence Association and in favour of universal voluntary service; he was undoubtedly very sympathetic to the propagandist message of the play,

and described it as 'a grim serious useful lesson which it is to be hoped will be taken to heart'. Nevertheless, he was worried about potential controversy in the press coinciding with the King's forthcoming visit to Berlin, and the play was licensed 'subject to the understanding that the scenes, situations, etc. in the play are kept to a <u>supposed invasion</u> of England by an imaginary enemy of <u>no recognised nationality</u>'. All the German costumes and references of the original script were duly altered, but Dawson knew that people would still identify Germany as the invading force, and some of the press did exactly that. In a confidential memorandum, the Comptroller commented that until recently the play 'would not have borne any particular significance, but everybody knows that, just now, the only Continental Power which the cap fitted would be Germany'.[47] This private admission did not prevent Dawson from proposing a series of misleading and disingenuous replies for the Lord Chamberlain to send in response to a 'bothering letter' criticising the Office for having passed the play: 'You have been misinformed . . . I need hardly say that had Germany or any other friendly Power been alluded to, the Play would not have received his Lordship's Licence'. The 'bothering letter' in fact came from a prospective liberal MP, G.C. Ashton-Jonson, who was closely associated with the International Peace Society and concerned that the play might damage relations between England and Germany and make war more likely. Ashton-Jonson began a campaign to contact every MP to seek support for the withdrawal of the licence which had already been granted. Dawson, meanwhile, who had been advised by the Foreign Office that there was insufficient reason to ban the play, continued to negotiate with the manager about how to tone down the allusions to Germany.

> Sir Douglas asked Mr Vaughan if it would be possible to make the incidents of the Play occur as it were, a few years later than the present time, say 1915, that sort of thing . . .
>
> Mr Vaughan said there could not be the slightest objection to this proposal.
>
> Sir Douglas Dawson then . . . requested Mr Vaughan to undertake that the head-dress should not be a helmet with a spike or a spike at all, and that the dress should be non-distinctive of any particular country, as the desire was to get as far away as possible from Germany . . . Mr Vaughan undertook . . . that the names of the various Officers of the opposing force should not bear any affinity to those of Germany, and that there should be no suggestion in the make-up or no moustache brushed up, as is the custom now so much in Germany.

Despite this, when the play opened at Wyndham's Theatre, the press immediately identified the play as dealing with a German invasion. Ashton-Jonson wrote again to Dawson:

I was present at the first night. The names and make up of the invaders were unmistakeably German, and the fact that the Play dealt with a raid made during fog on our Eastern Coast still further dotted the i's and crossed the t's . . .

However useful the play may be as providing propaganda for those who are in favour of universal military service I am still of opinion that the play cannot but still further embitter the relations between this Country and Germany. I do not think we shall have to wait very long before we see proof of this. Whatever mischief there may be is now irreparable . . .

Dawson's reply was deliberately misleading:

You will perhaps allow me to say that I never saw anything less German in my life than the dress, manners and general appearance of the Invaders . . . With all my experience of Continental armies, their uniforms, habits and customs I was totally unable to fit the Cap to any foreign Power, European or otherwise.

Even more revealing of the willingness to use censorship for political ends is the refusal of a licence a few weeks later for a burlesque version of *An Englishman's Home*, *Chips*. Dawson later denied the Joint Select Committee's suggestion that the decision was made explicitly because performance of the script might have had a detrimental effect on recruitment to the territorial army; when queried, he spuriously claimed that—unlike du Maurier's play— the burlesque specified the identity of the invading force, and that if *An Englishman's Home* had done likewise, it too would have been refused a licence. Considering what he had acknowledged privately about that play and the modifications he had negotiated, his answers were more than misleading. In March 1909, however, another play about an invasion of Britain—again aimed at British complacency—*was* licensed by Redford. The original script of *Mr Turnbull's Nightmare*, written by the MP Mark Sykes, suggested that the invading army was from Scandinavia, though most of the enemy were actually aliens already working in Britain as waiters. This play focused as much on domestic as on international politics, and actually came close to proposing that Britain was in need of an invasion to flush out those who were destroying it from within and to restore its—presumably Victorian—great- ness. As he explains in one of his speeches to the British, the altruistic aim of the leader of the invading forces seems to be rather to redeem the true Britain than to conquer it, and to save it from itself by subsuming it within a great Empire:

The acquisition of such a hopeless ganglion of inefficiency would be no material gain to the Empire. It was decided therefore to take you in hand

at once and reform you as one would reform a drunkard. At present your education system is deplorable, your poorer children are degenerate, your working classes more and more debauched by doles and bribes, your industries are declining . . . and your sources of morals, manhood and material are either degenerating, spent or neglected. We shall, therefore, disenfranchise you for ten years, impose a sound system of education both moral and physical on all classes, introduce compulsory military service . . . and in fact firmly but kindly put you on your legs. Those who do not choose to live under our rule may depart with what they have, in that way we expect to rid ourselves of the worser elements of your somewhat congested population.[48]

Finally coming to his senses, Mr Turnbull declares that Britain has become decadent; he turns on his son, who had been planning to stand for Parliament to help the working classes, and tells him that it is

because we're over fat, having had no war—not a real one, the last was an episode—no plague, no famine, no pestilence to purge us, that, as a people, we're apt to catch a disease like you when it comes along . . . you are a national danger, because there's just an off chance of your being successful . . . everything that makes this country rotten you encourage and play down to; you preach down Patriotism, you encourage thriftlessness, idle-ness and waste, you stir up every ill feeling, you jeer at responsibility . . . you run about making mischief every hour of the day, you teach women not to bear children, and men to cadge and beg.

Redford said the play 'could not possibly be considered harmful or objec-tionable'. Not all politics, then, was considered inappropriate for the stage.[49]

As has already become clear, the relationship between Redford, as Reader or Examiner of Plays, and his superiors was not always an easy one. Frequently attacked for his leniency by sections of the press, and reviled by playwrights whose work he refused, Redford was also accused of making too many deci-sions himself instead of consulting with those above him. The formal letter of instruction, with which he had apparently been issued when he took up the post (though Redford denied that he had ever received it), informed him:

The Manuscripts pass through the Examiner's hands alone, excepting in cases of doubt, when he is bound to consult the Lord Chamberlain who in all other cases has been in the habit of accepting without question the recommendations of the Examiner.[50]

While Redford may have had a streak of arrogance which made him disin-

clined to consult as often as he might have done, it is worth noting that he had received no training for the post, which he had obtained in 1895 through his personal friendship with his predecessor, Edward Frederick Smyth Pigott. Prior to that, he had sometimes unofficially substituted for Pigott, and had thus become familiar with the system and requirements of the post. Yet he had no particular connection with the theatre or qualifications for his work, and claimed, rather naïvely, to be simply continuing the policies and practices of his predecessor.

Under Dawson and Althorp (who had succeeded the Earl of Clarendon as Lord Chamberlain in 1905), and as the arguments over censorship raged more strongly than before, Redford's attitudes and practices became increasingly embarrassing for the Office. In 1909, immediately before and during the Joint Select Committee enquiry, two further plays caused problems and discomfiture for the censorship. In the spring, Redford licensed a sub-Faustian play, *The Devil,* for the Adelphi Theatre, without referring it upwards for consideration. However, Franz Molnár's play, which showed the Devil luring people from the path of virtue, was immediately condemned in a number of newspapers. Redford described it as 'comparatively harmless', though he acknowledged that some might find it 'unpleasant and shocking'.[51] Indeed, merely showing the Devil—albeit in a modern costume and setting—successfully encouraging people to behave against conventional morality would probably have been troubling enough. The psychological thesis of this play—that the Devil is simply 'a looking glass . . . A candid friend who shows you what you are'—carried some very disturbing implications. Moreover, the play seems to end in the Devil's triumph and his victory over God, as he suddenly changes, according to the stage directions, 'from cynical jeering to terrible defiance' before 'shaking his clenched fist toward Heaven' and challenging it with the provocative question: 'What says The Other Side?'[52]

To give such an opportunity for criticism of the censorship less than three months before the Joint Select Committee was due to begin its deliberations was unfortunate. Redford and his wife were recuperating from illness at Weston-Super-Mare when the Lord Chamberlain, having read the attacks in newspapers on the *The Devil* and on those who had licensed it, wrote to him requiring that he should explain his decision to pass the play. Redford replied that he, also, had 'found much to condemn' in what he called 'a vulgar, and somewhat unpleasant, highly coloured rendering of the Faust motive'; but with a touch of possibly unintended condescension he went on to inform the Lord Chamberlain that it was 'inevitable that a play on this theme should be "unpleasant"'. He went on, reasonably enough, to argue that 'the fact is these are a good deal matters of opinion, and even the critics, who never lose a chance of having a dig at the poor "Examiner", are not agreed'. Althorp was not satisfied, and replied to Redford the following day:

I am afraid that some considerable comment is being made at my having it licensed at all. The Play seems to be not only coarse, but distinctly improper, and nearly indecent. I have been written to privately imploring me to stop the Play, owing to its 'unmitigated wickedness', and I very much fear that an agitation may arise out of it . . . It is unfortunate, to say the least of it, that nothing was known by me or Sir Douglas about this Play, as now it may be extremely hard to deal with it.

Incidental strayings from virtue in a Play can generally be dealt with, but in this case the whole Play seems to be founded on absolute impropriety . . . Of course, I hold myself responsible, though I could not easily say that I knew anything about the Play.

At the same time the Lord Chamberlain wrote to Dawson, trusting the views of the critics and putting the blame heavily onto his Reader's shoulders: 'Evidently the play at the Adelphi is disgusting . . . How on earth Redford could have passed such a play passes my comprehension.'

Redford's next letter to Althorp was apologetic:

I beg to thank you for your most kind and considerate letter . . . It did not strike me, considering the theme, as any more risky than dozens of others . . . And I am equally confident that any one of experience reading the play would be of the same opinion . . . I have always shown myself ready, nay anxious to refer any difficulties or doubtful cases, and to keep your Lordship informed as far as possible on everything . . . This play appeared to me quite an ordinary commonplace and tawdry affair such as I have dealt with many times before in the course of my 14 years experience and I did not deem it necessary to call special attention to its production.

It was at this point that Althorp asked Dawson how his plans were progressing for setting up an Advisory Board to assist in and to help legitimise the process of censorship. 'We might be again in this dilemma if Redford considers this a play that . . . should be licensed', he wrote.[53] To the considerable discomfiture of the Lord Chamberlain's Office, the publicity surrounding *The Devil* was still going on during the Joint Select Committee's enquiry, with performances receiving complaints and hostility from local authorities as it toured the country.

In September, in the middle of the enquiry, those seeking to maximise the problems of the Lord Chamberlain by exposing his supposed laxness focused next on *The Proud Prince*, a play based on a legend (also used by Longfellow) in which the King of Sicily behaves with such arrogance and immorality that an Archangel turns him into the likeness of his own jester and himself takes the place of the King until the latter has learned humility. One of King Robert's chief crimes is to persecute a young woman who has rejected

his lewd advances, forcibly handing her over to his harem of prostitutes for them to ruin and humiliate. Although the play has a conventional moral and a happy ending—everyone is redeemed (with the exception of the prostitutes who are banished to Naples)—the erotic dances in the harem and the threatened cruelty provided an opportunity for some to condemn once again the decadence of the British stage. The Lord Chamberlain was upset, not least at the timing of this controversy:

> I cannot help feeling that Mr Redford has not read the play, or if he has that he chose to ignore its evident coarseness. It does seem rather hard just now when the whole question of the censor is so much before the public, that this very unfortunate handle should be given to the anti-censor people with which they can legitimately belabour me.

In the event, it transpired that the play had actually been licensed some years previously, before either Lord Althorp or Sir Douglas Dawson had been in office. This left Redford exposed, as Dawson's emphasis probably implies:

> This play having been passed in 1903, we do not seem to be culpable even if it is objectionable. I should say the best line is to take no notice of objections, but if acknowledging to state that the play was licensed six years ago.[54]

Two new plays by Bernard Shaw were also timed to cause maximum embarrassment for the Lord Chamberlain's Office. Without suggesting that Shaw was deliberately trying to provoke or even humiliate the censorship in the light of the forthcoming enquiry, there can be little doubt that he would have anticipated and relished the problems he would be causing. *The Shewing Up of Blanco Posnet* was rejected for licence because, even though it depicts the conversion of an atheist, Shaw refused to remove lines in which one of the characters refers apparently to God in derogatory terms:

> He hasn't finished with you yet, He always has a trick up His sleeve . . . He's a sly one. He's a mean one. He lies low for you. He plays cat and mouse with you. He lets you run loose until you think you're shut of Him . . . He cometh like a thief in the night . . . a horse-thief . . . He caught me and put my neck in the halter. To spite me because I had no use for Him . . . He caught me out at last . . .[55]

The manager for whom Shaw wrote the play, Sir Herbert Tree, was apparently quite prepared to compromise over these lines, and even suggested to the enquiry that this was a case where the censor might have served as a convenient and useful buffer to help prevent a confrontation between manager and playwright:

one always desires to have friendly relations with one's authors, and there were certain passages in that play which I personally should not have regarded as quite suitable for the stage . . . I accepted the play knowing that the passages to which I objected would be cut out.[56]

Shaw, however, refused to cut the references to God, later claiming that to do so would have made it a 'senseless, rowdy, blasphemous, coarse play'.[57] He complained in a letter to *The Times*:

Except when the name of God is taken altogether in vain, by way of swearing, the Divine Antagonist must be spoken of, even by the most hardened and savage outlaws, with the decorum and devotional respect observed by our Bishops.[58]

Press Cuttings was another short play written by Shaw for the Women's Suffrage Society, which included jokes aimed at the military and at senior government ministers; two of the central characters were the Prime Minister, Balsquith, and the War Minister, Mitchener, whose names were based on the conglomeration of those of real public figures, Balfour, Asquith, Milner and Kitchener. One of the most regularly invoked grounds for censorship was against the offensive depiction of living personalities, although in practice this depended on who was being depicted; Shaw himself had complained about being portrayed on stage in a bathing costume, and even claimed that 'on another occasion my appearance was so exactly imitated that a near relative of my own was deceived by the resemblance'.[59] As the Lord Chamberlain's Office sought a way to prevent *Press Cuttings* from being performed without actually being seen to impose a ban on it, Redford injudiciously, but not unusually, wrote a private letter to the manager of the theatre where it was intended for performance, pointing out the rules about offensive depictions. Unfortunately for the Lord Chamberlain's Office, the letter was leaked to the press and used by Shaw to attack the inconsistency and hypocrisy of the censorship; Redford again found himself apologising to the Lord Chamberlain for the bad publicity he had attracted:

I regret to learn that considerable annoyance has been caused to your Lordship by the unwarrantable and quite unforeseen use that has been made in the Press, of a very simple and ordinary official communication addressed by me on Friday last to the Manager of the Court Theatre . . . This was simply a preliminary and tentative step designed to bring the play within the terms of the Licence . . . I followed the usual and ordinary routine which I have practised for the last fourteen years, solely with a view to assist the Lord Chamberlain and facilitate his decision. This has always been my endeavour, and has hitherto proved perfectly successful.[60]

Two months later, *Press Cuttings* was licensed, though in a revised form and with some continuing reluctance: 'It is almost inevitable that the caps will be fitted etc., but in my judgement after careful re-reading, I see no reason for witholding the Licence', wrote Redford. In this instance Shaw did agree to make changes, but—with a playful joke on the gap which exists between script and performance—he deliberately mocked the censorship by changing not the names of the characters as they appeared on the page, but the way they would be heard on the stage: 'Throughout the representation the name printed "Mitchener" is to be spoken as "Bones" and the name printed "Balsquith" is to be spoken as "Johnson".'[61]

If the leaking of Redford's 'private' letter to the press was not the first occasion on which his misjudgements had caused discomfort for the Lord Chamberlain, then Althorp and Dawson certainly found it convenient to blame Redford when he failed to protect the censorship from criticism. It was in part their dissatisfaction with what they perceived as his incompetence and inefficiency that encouraged them in developing an Advisory Board as an extra layer of protection and insurance for the Lord Chamberlain. To his subsequent humiliation, this plan was kept secret from Redford; in June 1909 Dawson wrote to the Lord Chamberlain following a meeting with Redford: 'I said nothing whatever to him about the Advisory Committee: it was better that he should hear of it from you rather than from me'.[62] Redford seems to have heard nothing of it from anyone until the middle of the enquiry, when his public denial of the existence of any plans to create such a Board was contradicted by his own superiors.

In October 1907 seventy-one writers signed a letter to *The Times* calling for an end to the control of the Lord Chamberlain and of a censorship

> which was instituted for political, and not for the so-called moral ends to which it is perverted—an office autocratic in procedure, opposed to the spirit of the Constitution, contrary to common justice and to common sense.
>
> They assert that the Censorship has not been exercised in the interests of morality but has tended to lower the dramatic tone by appearing to relieve the public of the duty of moral judgement.
>
> They ask to be freed from the menace hanging over every dramatist of having his work and the proceeds of his work destroyed at a pen's stroke by the arbitrary action of a single official neither responsible to Parliament nor amenable to law.
>
> They ask that their art be placed on the same footing as every other art.
>
> They ask that they themselves be placed in the position enjoyed under the law by every other citizen.
>
> To these ends they claim that the licensing of plays shall be abolished.[63]

The impressive list of signatories to the letter included Henry James, Joseph Conrad, W.B. Yeats, John Masefield, Somerset Maugham, J.M. Barrie, John Galsworthy, W.S. Gilbert, Laurence Housman, H.G. Wells, Thomas Hardy, J.M. Synge, George Meredith, Henry Arthur Jones, Arthur Wing Pinero, Elizabeth Robins, Israel Zangwill, Edward Thomas, Alfred Sutro, and of course Shaw and Granville-Barker. It is notable that the signatories included not only writers who wrote primarily for the stage but also writers who did so rarely or not at all; one of the central arguments put forward by proponents of the 'advanced' theatre was that the censorship was actually preventing some of the best writers of the age from working in the theatre.

In February 1908 Barrie and Pinero led a deputation to the Home Office, where a petition against the censorship was handed to the Home Secretary, and a letter was published in *The Times* in their support. This was signed by, amongst many others, Max Beerbohm, Hilaire Belloc, Sidney and Beatrice Webb, Rider Haggard and Winston Churchill. In December the Liberal MP and dramatist Robert Vernon Harcourt introduced a Private Members Bill on the subject of stage censorship, seeking to 'abolish the powers of the Lord Chamberlain in respect of stage plays', but it progressed no further than a first reading. The following year, however, with the agitation against the censorship growing, the Prime Minister, Asquith, set up a Joint Select Committee; it met for the first time on 29 July 1909.

People Who Eat Peas With Their Knife

The Government Enquiry of 1909

Ten gentlemen in frock-coats, five lords and five commoners at a long green table—not by them ever are dawns of new eras ushered in. Their business is to find with dignity a common denominator in the opinions severally held by them . . . an humble offering upon the altar of the god Compromise.[1]

Between July and November 1909, the Joint Select Committee, made up of five members of the House of Lords and five of the House of Commons, listened to the evidence of forty-nine witnesses over twelve sittings. Their duty, as required by the government, was to discover how theatres and places of public entertainment were regulated and controlled through the current provisions of censorship, and 'to report any alterations of the law or practice which may appear desirable'.[2] Surprisingly, the Committee ultimately produced a series of recommendations which might have gone a considerable way towards ushering in a new era. Though it is true that those recommendations were often contradictory, reflecting the antagonistic views of different members of the Committee, it was rather the fact that no legislation was subsequently enacted to turn those recommendations into practice which meant that the system remained essentially the same. This lack of legal alteration might seem to reduce the significance of the enquiry, but the arguments and deliberations which occurred within committee sessions, the assumptions, the exposures and the justifications of conflicting positions and actions, make the record of the twelve sittings a key document in understanding the debates about theatre censorship in the twentieth century. Nor does the lack of change in the law necessarily indicate that the recommendations were without influence on subsequent practices. Moreover, it is important to recognise why the recommendations were never translated into law and, given that some of the proposals were perhaps surprisingly radical, to identify not only how the Lord Chamberlain and his officials constructed their defence during the enquiry, but how they helped ensure that the recommendations made would not be enforced.

The enquiry was certainly not one which had been sought or welcomed by the Lord Chamberlain's Office. Sir Douglas Dawson, who had been Comptroller of that Office for only two years when the enquiry took place, believed it had been forced upon them unnecessarily; he blamed 'one very noisy section' of the theatrical community for 'the ridiculous waste of time and the prominence which has been, quite needlessly, given to the subject'. While it was still taking place he rather patronisingly wrote: 'I believe that important members of the Committee have long ago realised the nonsense of the whole thing, and are fretting over the ridiculous waste of time'.[3] Dawson was for ever distinguishing between 'important' people, whose opinions mattered, and people whose views were not worthy of attention, and he repeated the *Daily Telegraph*'s claim that the entire crusade had 'arisen out of the *saeva indignatio* of four gentlemen'—Shaw, Granville Barker, William Archer and Edward Garnett. While these four were indeed significant leaders and perhaps even orchestrators of the campaign, they had extensive support; indeed, when the enquiry began, the Lord Chamberlain himself, Lord Althorp, was noting with some despair that not only the whole of the press but 'the Theatrical profession generally' appeared to be demanding an end to the current system.[4] That was not, in fact, the case, and the Committee's final report summed up fairly effectively the balance of the arguments they had heard:

> With rare exceptions all the dramatists of the day ask either for the aboli-
> tion of the Censorship or for an appeal from its decisions to some other
> authority . . . On the other hand, with exceptions equally rare, the
> managers of Theatres ask for the retention of a control over plays prior to
> their production . . . It is clear that the retention of the Censorship is
> desired also by a large body of public opinion, of which the Speaker of the
> House of Commons . . . may be regarded as representative.[5]

It is perhaps hard to know what grounds other than sycophancy the Committee had for regarding the Right Honourable J.W. Lowther, the Speaker of the House of Commons, as especially representative, though a decade or so later, as Lord Ullswater, Lowther would actually become one of the important members of the Advisory Board for the Lord Chamberlain to call on. A couple of playwrights did actually speak in favour of the censorship, but one, Comyns Carr, admitted under questioning that he was actually there at the behest of the Society of West End Managers; what he did not reveal was that he had also already agreed in principle to be a member of the Lord Chamberlain's Advisory Board. The other was W.S. Gilbert, who made one of the most directly explicit statements of the whole enquiry:

> Committee: Why do you think a Censorship of some kind is desirable?

Gilbert: Because I think that the stage of a theatre is not a proper pulpit from which to disseminate doctrines possibly of Anarchism, Socialism, and Agnosticism. It is not the proper platform upon which to discuss questions of adultery and free love before a mixed audience composed of persons of all ages, of both sexes, of all ways of thinking, of all conditions of life, and of various degrees of education.[6]

It was to be expected that most managers would support the current system of censorship, because it gave them an effective guarantee that a play they had financed was not going to be closed down or to face prosecution once it had opened; they were assuring their security before committing their money. Managers who took shows to different towns and cities were in particular need of such security, for if the power of veto had devolved to local authorities, the variations would have been such as to make touring almost impossible. A play in performance, as one witness insisted to the Committee, was not to be seen as a work of art belonging to its writer, but as 'a commercial commodity' with which a manager dealt 'for the purpose of profits'.[7] Indeed, in his evidence supporting the abolition of stage censorship, the writer and philosopher Israel Zangwill commented that 'in England you do not need any Censor, because you already have the censor of the box office'.[8] *Plus ça change.* Given their vested interest, it is probably surprising to note that rather than flocking to give evidence to the Committee, as playwrights had done, most managers had to be more or less coerced into appearing. In July, Dawson wrote to William Fladgate, the solicitor representing the managers of West End theatres, pointedly informing him that 'the Lord Chamberlain supposes that, in addition to your appearance as the representative of West End Managers Association, some of the Managers will appear in person to give evidence before the Censorship Committee'. Fladgate replied: 'I have asked five of the principal Managers to give evidence, but whether I shall get them to do so I am not clear'.[9] He did.

One of the first tasks of the Committee was to clarify the legal position under which censorship was currently operating, and how this related to prevailing practice. A number of anomalies were quickly exposed, chief among them being the fact that music-halls were treated, for no good reason, as though they were outside the authority of the censor. Witnesses agreed that there was no logical justification for songs or sketches to be immune from censorship, but it became clear that it would simply be impractical for the Lord Chamberlain's Office to deal with the quantity of new material being continuously generated by the halls. The Committee also elicited some fairly remarkable responses when trying to define the difference between plays and songs. The Assistant Under-Secretary of State for the Home Department, for instance, when asked for his view as to whether a licence should be required for 'a song interspersed with dialogue', pronounced that in his view 'any song

calculated to move the emotion is a stage play'.[10] Similarly, a manager with responsibility for both music-halls and theatres suggested that 'a song with a plot is a stage play'.[11] Wisely, perhaps, the Committee chose not to pursue this line of questioning too far. More significant in terms of the irregularity was the revelation that dramatic sketches were being regularly produced in the music-halls, and it was even harder to see any possible grounds on which these could be exempt from the censorship applied to theatres. It had been the 1892 Select Committee on theatre censorship which had recommended that music-halls should be allowed to produce small stage plays, and while this had initially angered many theatre managers—who had taken to informing on their new rivals for staging unlicensed material—what the Lord Chamberlain termed a 'modus vivendi' had been established in 1907. By this code, theatre managers had agreed to cease reporting their music-hall counterparts for prosecution provided their dramas were limited to two unconnected sketches in one evening, of no more than thirty minutes each, and employed no more than six actors. From one point of view, this left writers with considerable freedom to produce what were in effect plays without requiring a licence for them, and Shaw was among those who took occasional advantage of this way of bypassing the censorship by writing for the halls. Furthermore, it was not uncommon for music-halls to exceed the unofficial time limit, or for them to present edited highlights from full-length plays—either what the Lord Chamberlain called 'the cream', or perhaps just a series of the more provocative scenes and moments—which might or might not have already been licensed.

These somewhat unscrupulous practices of the music-halls were acknowledged by the Lord Chamberlain's Office in an internal memorandum as acts of 'trespass' and 'piracy'; in a statement summarising his attitude to 'the vexed question of Dramatic Sketches in Music-Halls' which he prepared for the Chair of the Committee, the Lord Chamberlain accepted that the law was being broken on a regular basis. He also conceded that it was to the financial and artistic detriment of 'the theatre proper' that the law should be so flouted:

> These dramatic sketches are in themselves objectionable, as being presentations either of unlicensed stage plays or of condensed and mutilated versions . . . They withdraw from the theatres many who are tempted by the freedom, the smoking, the promenades and the drinks in the auditorium . . . Some of these people will not go to the theatre if they can see Actors and Actresses in the Halls in 'Sketches', and they tend to produce a degraded taste for hurried, frivolous and brainless Drama.

Yet despite the admitted illogicality of exempting the music-halls from the censorship imposed on theatres, Lord Althorp was adamant that he would

have nothing to do with them: 'the Lord Chamberlain does not . . . want, and does not intend, to be drawn into a policy of prosecuting them'.[12] This was a risky line to pursue because it was hard to defend; if the music-halls were not to be brought into line with the theatres and lose their privilege, then the logical step—advocated by at least one member of the Committee—was that censorship in theatres should be brought into line with that of the halls. Indeed, the Committee's final report recommended the removal of any legal differentiation and proposed that 'the same provisions for licensing . . . should apply also to all words sung or spoken in any unlicensed place of entertainment'.[13] Of course, the barely hidden justification for the discrepancy was the differing social backgrounds of the audiences. As Dawson told the Committee, it would be 'most undesirable' for the two to move closer together; when asked whether the division between music-halls and theatres should be removed he replied that

> The public interest is to divide the theatre from the music-hall . . . people
> who go to a theatre are largely composed of a different class to those who
> go to a music-hall . . . and I think it is well to retain that distinction.[14]

Since those who attended music-halls were not 'important' people, it presumably mattered less what they saw or how it influenced them.

The pressure for the enquiry to take place had come primarily from those seeking to abolish the current system of censorship; the grievances of censored artists, and their arguments against both the principle and the practice of censorship, were therefore strongly to the fore throughout. Playwrights wanted at least the right to know the grounds on which their work had been censored. Redford had specifically warned the Lord Chamberlain against conceding to this demand, arguing that to publish such a code would 'play into the hands of *the enemy* [my emphasis], by affording opportunities for circumventing it'; he insisted that managers, anyway, possessed 'a very shrewd idea of the proscribed limits, and are only too glad to avail themselves of an independent and recognised authority as a buffer between themselves, and the advanced school of irreconcilable Dramatists who would, if unrestrained, drive out of the theatre a very large proportion of their paying public'.[15] Playwrights wanted the right to be able to deal directly with the censor themselves; they also wanted to be able to appeal against decisions, and for their appeals to be heard by a committee in which they felt confidence and on which they were represented. In terms of content, authors specifically demanded the right to deal with serious moral, political and contemporary affairs, and to treat historical and religious subjects; some claimed the right to include elements of immorality and vice only within an ultimately moral work, others the right to challenge conventional morality itself. There were

also specific complaints that Redford was too rigid and limited in what he was prepared to allow:

> The average play that is always passed by the Censor is one that corresponds to the average instincts of the ordinary man. He likes a certain level of moral maxim to which he is accustomed. He does not, as a rule, like any serious study or anything like a serious examination of moral or social points with which he is unfamiliar . . . he will always fall back on the conventional, and refuse the original work.[16]

Some witnesses emphasised the effects of censorship in relation not only to an existing and identifiable body of work but also to unwritten plays and to writers who chose not to work in the theatre. The critic William Archer told the Committee that the effect of the censorship was

> to depress and mutilate, and not only to destroy, but to keep out of existence, serious plays, for many authors will not write serious plays under the threat of having them destroyed by a single veto . . . About 1885 the present British drama came into existence, and since that time the Censorship has had a very distinct and growingly repressive influence upon the development of English drama.[17]

Galsworthy alleged that the system of censorship 'deters men of letters from writing for the stage' and that 'its continuance will have a disastrous effect on the development of the drama at what I consider a most critical and important moment of its life in this country'. He also cited a comment made by Arnold Bennett:

> Immediately you begin to get near the things that really matter in a play, you begin to think about the Censor, and it is all over with your play . . . that is why I would not attempt to write a play . . . at full emotional power. The Censor's special timidity about sexual matters is an illusion. He is equally timid about all matters.[18]

Several opponents of the censorship claimed that a new cultural era had arrived, and that a system which might have been appropriate in the past was becoming a serious handicap to artists of the future; as Pinero explained,

> I do not think it has very seriously retarded the growth of the drama up to the present moment, but what I do say is that we are entering upon a period of new fertility and dignity and power, and that this development must be seriously impeded by the continuance of an irresponsible Censorship.[19]

To what extent the claims about writers having been driven away from theatre by censorship were true it is impossible to judge. Comyns Carr, who was presented as a playwright though he was better known as a manager (and who spoke generally in favour of the censorship) took a sceptical and disparaging line; he suggested that the real reason why a writer did not write for the stage was simply because 'the intending author cannot do it'. Yet even Carr argued strongly for the system to be reformed so that control would no longer reside 'in the hands of a servant of the court', and decisions would be subject to appeal. Anyway, his position was at least partially undermined when it emerged during questioning that Carr (the author of just two plays) appeared at the behest of William Fladgate, solicitor to the Society of West End Managers, 'because he thought from my evidence in 1892 that I upheld the position of Censor'.[20]

Other witnesses felt the whole conflict had been over-inflated, and questioned whether theatre and the censorship of it actually mattered very much at all; this, to the understandable disgust of several playwrights, was the position adopted by A.B. Walkley, theatre critic of *The Times* and President of the Society of Dramatic Critics. He argued that playwrights who complained were exaggerating their grievances and that it was always possible for them to get their work performed privately; they should learn, he declared, to 'take the rough with the smooth'. Walkley publicly mocked the self-deluding arrogance of 'advanced' authors for 'believing that art is very important' and for taking the theatre too seriously:

> Personally, I venture to think the importance of all art, and more especially the importance of drama, is apt to be over-rated nowadays, and that we take these things a little too solemnly . . . it probably matters very little either to the art of drama or to public welfare whether the Censor exists or not . . . if . . . I had to decide . . . probably it would end in my tossing up a coin.[21]

The underlying subject informing many of the debates was the proper function of theatre in contemporary society. One manager insisted that censorship had been instrumental in helping to give Britain 'the cleanest stage in the world', and was quite explicit in informing the Committee that 'the main object of the theatre is to provide harmless entertainment, brightness, gaiety, and amusement for the public'.[22] By contrast, those opposed to censorship on principle always argued that theatre had a higher function than to entertain, and that it therefore needed freedom rather than the petty and blinkered restrictions imposed by small-minded administrators and politicians. James Barrie, for instance, insisted that censorship 'makes our drama a more puerile thing in the life of the nation than it ought to be' and maintained that it was founded on practicalities rather than anything more high-minded:

The important objections to abolition are not founded on what is best for the drama, but on the practical difficulties, real or imaginary, of running theatres without such an official to simplify matters for the managers . . . the drama must make most progress when it is untrammelled, and the work of authors anxious to say, whether sportively or seriously, what is in them to say, and allowed to do it . . . Their minds, not necessarily more original, are more unconventional; they think many of the accepted views are wrong, and they work out their ideas on the subject in plays. But to the official mind, whatever is not the accepted conventional view is a thing suspect—officialdom is created to carry out the accepted view.[23]

Like Gilbert, Comyns Carr was critical of those authors whom he accused of 'using the stage as a pulpit'. Revealingly, he suggested that the plays which ran into problems with censorship were almost invariably those which contained 'some strong feeling or desire not to paint life, but to change it'. It was the authors of such plays whom he believed to be in error.

When Harcourt subsequently led another attempt in Parliament in 1913 to abolish censorship, Dawson insisted that 'the most important duty of the censor is in connection with plays dealing with Foreign Powers'; the Comptroller informed the Home Office that about once a week he amended plays which had been written 'tactlessly' and from which 'international complications might ensue' if they were performed as written. 'We have dozens of such plays submitted here: they leave us so altered as to obviate trouble', he proudly informed Sir William Byrne.[24] However, a strong argument presented by the abolitionists to the 1909 enquiry—and never effectively countered—was that such strict control of political drama was only really necessary because the fact that censorship operated through a member of the royal household seemed to signal that any play which had been permitted spoke with the consent and even the *approval* of the monarch. As Shaw put it:

The Lord Chamberlain's Censorship is open to the special objection that its application to political plays is taken to indicate the attitude of the Crown on questions of domestic and foreign policy, and that it imposes the limits of etiquette on the historical drama.[25]

In the case of moral issues, those seeking to reform or abolish the present system of censorship maintained that it was ineffective because it was aimed at the wrong targets, and that theatres were in fact full of depravity. Shaw protested, almost as the Public Morality Council might have done, that 'a very large percentage of the performances on the English stage at present under the censorship have for their object the stimulation of sexual desire';[26] the Lord Chamberlain, complained Shaw, habitually allowed plays which were

'exceedingly revolting and disgusting'. The critic William Archer similarly argued the censorship was 'indulgent to all the lighter forms of frivolity', and had been 'ineffective in keeping off the stage plays which are offensive to the feelings of people who have at all a keen sense of decency, whereas it has been entirely effective in keeping off several plays of very considerable intellectual power and of very stern morality'.[27] Frederick Whelen, the founder and chairman of the Incorporated Stage Society also insisted:

> It does not protect the public from vulgar or indecent plays. Its working
> mainly is to prevent the writing of a certain number of moral plays, and it
> prevents the English public from seeing some of the finest foreign plays.[28]

Even the manager Sir Herbert Tree regretted that 'the tragedy of the great human passions should be barred while the belittlement of those passions as exemplified in a French farce should be favourably regarded'.[29] Several playwrights also sought to assuage any fears about the unbridled liberties which might result from the abolition of censorship by suggesting, perhaps not with absolute candour, that without the Lord Chamberlain the restrictions would actually become tougher. The argument that because managers would be unable to shelter behind the Lord Chamberlain they would become less inclined to take risks would doubtless have proved true in the majority of cases, but Shaw, for example, would surely have intended to take advantage of the greater freedom.

The wish to control the theatre was based on a perceived need to protect audiences from any possibility of offence or disturbance, and the belief that all plays must be suitable for family viewing. It was as though audiences must have the right to choose their evening's entertainment at random and without checking on its nature first. As the *Daily Express* put it:

> In Paris a British visitor knows that there are certain theatres to which he
> cannot take his wife or daughter . . . But in London we have come to
> consider that practically all our theatres are suitable for the attendance of
> our girls and boys. It will be an evil day for the drama if it ever becomes
> necessary to placard certain plays upon a moral blacklist for the sake of
> fathers of families.[30]

Some of the abolitionists questioned this: 'Why should not a part of the community be offended?' asked Israel Zangwill,[31] and Gilbert Murray, Regius Professor of Greek at Oxford and a member of the Council of the Stage Society, argued against the assumption that 'we should take such very great care to avoid hurting people's feelings. I do not want to hurt people's feelings, but literature has only done its work at the expense of shocking people's feelings.'[32] Even the Bishop of Southwark, speaking with the support of the

Archbishop of Canterbury, agreed that it would not be 'at all desirable to limit stage plays to plays which a man would naturally take his daughter to see. There are books . . . of very great value—which one would not give to a girl but it would be the greatest mistake to prohibit them.'[33]

But for many witnesses, the need to protect others from being exposed to the dangers of taboo subjects and unconventional views was the most important imperative. 'I have seen plays that I should be very sorry to take my daughter to', W.S. Gilbert told the enquiry. It was not sufficient even to know that the conclusion would be exemplary, for Gilbert complained that in his experience 'the audience may be required to wade through a great deal of moral mud before they appreciate the excellence of the author's intentions'.[34] The Speaker of the House of Commons less charitably referred to plays 'that I should be horrified to think that my daughter had been to see'; indeed, he added, he would 'not be best pleased if I thought my son had been to them'. Others expressed concern for the man who unwittingly escorted female members of his family to a play, confident that anything passed by the censor must be suitable for all eyes and ears, only to discover that it contained unsuitable material:

> Committee: Do you see any reason why these authors of what are called 'advanced ideas' should use the stage as a means of ventilating their doctrines?
>
> Speaker: I do not at all. There is a French saying, 'Toute vérite n'est pas bonne à dire'—you are not obliged to say everything. There are certain facts in human nature with which we are all acquainted, but we do not drag them out constantly in private conversation. Why, then, should we produce them on the stage, and so cause offence to a certain number of people who are anxious to go to the theatre and enjoy it?[35]

Oswald Stoll, who was managing-director of no less than thirty-three music-halls and six theatres, acknowledged that *Monna Vanna* was 'a great play by a great writer', but he considered that because its message was 'inconclusive' it was therefore 'dangerous in its teaching'. He rejected on principle the notion of a theatre that asked difficult questions, insisting that criticism of the government should never be allowed and that 'great moral issues should not be raised merely because a great poet has a powerful imagination'.[36] The critic of *The Times* told the Committee he had found *Waste* 'a play of remarkable power' but that he had 'had no hesitation in approving the Censor's prohibition' because it was 'wholly unfit for performance before a miscellaneous public'.[37] Even J.T. Grein, a pioneer of intelligent theatre and the man who had first brought Ibsen's *Ghosts* to the London stage, was on record as supporting the Lord Chamberlain's public ban on the performance of such plays 'in the ordinary theatre, accessible to the unthinking and still imperfectly

educated crowd of woman, man and child'.[38] Fundamental to the argument was a paternalistic or patronising wish to protect those seen as being easily susceptible to influence, including women, the young, and the uneducated. Assumptions about class were also significant, and the need so clearly articulated by Dawson to keep theatres unattractive to those who relished the vulgarity of music-hall language and morality. Sir Herbert Tree, for example, declared that a censor was necessary in order to protect the public 'from the people who eat peas with their knife'.[39] In effect, through controlling what was staged in theatres, one section of the public was to be protected from another part.

There were some influential witnesses to the Enquiry who demanded that the censorship should be much more restrictive than at present. One such was the Speaker of the House of Commons, who was utterly antagonistic not only towards the arguments of the playwrights but to the whole notion of a theatre of ideas. He complained that the Lord Chamberlain was 'too lax' and that his control needed 'tightening up'. Invited to comment on whether the development of drama had been held back by the censorship, he put the blame on the writers, replying confidently:

> I should think no healthy minded author with a wholesome plot would
> have any difficulty in writing a good drama . . . He is not obliged to go to
> these very unhealthy and disgusting subjects as so many authors do. They
> seem to revel in them.[40]

The playwrights' argument that theatres were unfairly singled out for a degree and system of censorship which was not applied elsewhere was countered by those who insisted that the theatre's potential dangers were indeed uniquely harmful. W.S. Gilbert cited a woman taking off her clothes and getting into a bath as something which was permissible in a novel but not on the stage.[41] Lowther also claimed that 'a play with an immoral tendency' was calculated to do 'much more harm than a book' because its depravity was expressed 'in public and laughed at by a great number of people night after night', while Herbert Tree averred that 'passages that may read quite commonplace in a book come out in letters of fire on the stage'.[42] The critic of *The Times* was even more portentous in his predictions of the particular dangers accompanying performance:

> To read something obscene in private may do the individual a certain
> amount of harm. It will do much more harm, I submit, if the individual
> listens to the same words uttered in the company of some hundreds of
> other human beings . . . Take the case of a political play produced in the
> time of political stress; if it is read by a man in his study the effect on him,
> whatever his political opinions may be, will not be dangerous, but the effect

on a crowd in a theatre might incite them to pillage, to go out and burn the city.[43]

Some witnesses challenged these claims, suggesting that the private experience of reading was actually *more* dangerous in its potential to pervert:

> the corrupt book is likely to be far more pernicious and operative than the corrupt play. We are all virtuous in public . . . and if anyone is shocked he instantly declares it . . . But a book works more slowly and subtly.[44]

However, such arguments failed to convince the Committee, whose report concluded that

> Ideas or situations which, when described on a printed page may work little mischief, when represented through the human personality of actors may have a more powerful and more deleterious effect. The existence of an audience, moved by the same emotions, its members conscious of one another's presence, intensifies the influence of what is done and spoken on the stage.[45]

Another area of anomaly in the censorship to which attention was drawn was the fact that it apparently only applied to plays written since the 1737 Act came into being. Redford hardly helped his situation or prospects by the evident uncertainty and confusion he expressed when he was asked about plays from the Restoration period, which were frequently held up as the epitome of a decadence and immorality to which even contemporary playwrights had not yet sunk:

> The Restoration dramas are probably the most indecent plays that have ever been written. Several of Wycherley's comedies could not be produced in a theatre today without producing a riot. Have you no control over such plays?[46]

George Redford, presumably confused, at first indicated that such a play would have to be submitted for licence, then conceded that this was not the case and that he had previously informed a would-be producer of a Restoration play that no licence would be required. He then claimed that 'if it was a really bad case' it could be stopped by the Lord Chamberlain as the licenser of theatres rather than of plays. *The Stage* pointed out with incredulity the Examiner's confusion and continuing errors. It also publicised how much more extensive were the powers of the Lord Chamberlain than was generally recognised:

> The Lord Chamberlain only licenses a comparatively small number of theatres; hence 'the bad case' could not come before him in the capacity of licenser of theatres, except through one of those theatres. Mr Redford is looking at the wrong section of the Act of 1843. Under section 14 the Lord Chamberlain would in his discretion forbid 'the bad case', acting as censor of plays. No play, old or new, is free of the Lord Chamberlain's right to prohibit its performance.[47]

Interestingly, when Dawson took the precaution of seeking confirmation from the Home Office in August 1909 regarding the legal position of older plays, he was advised that 'if a new play by Shakespeare or by Congreve were discovered, which had never been acted, it would be necessary to obtain the licence from the Lord Chamberlain before it could be presented'.[48] He wisely chose not to share that detail with the enquiry. Several of the abolitionists argued that had Shakespeare been writing under present conditions, his plays would have been refused licences—either because they dealt with dubious sexual morality or because their settings would have been considered too recent history for the stage. 'Was Shakespeare a healthy-minded author?', asked Granville Barker on another occasion, responding to the attack on contemporary playwrights by the Speaker of the House of Commons; 'Is the plot of *King Lear* a wholesome plot?'.[49] William Archer publicly doubted whether *Hamlet* or *Othello* could be licensed today.[50] Another playwright took up the same theme, suggesting that

> The Censorship of today would put an end to the public representation of nearly every play of Shakespeare. It would banish from the stage nearly every work of the Elizabethan dramatists. There is scarcely an English drama more than 100 years old that could stand up for five minutes against the theory of the Censorship properly administered.[51]

As a theatre manager, Sir Herbert Tree was almost bound to speak broadly in favour of the principle of censorship, though he dared to suggest that more freedom should be permitted to playwrights; but he understood that perhaps the real danger of censorship was the self-censorship to which it led: 'I don't think', he told the committee, 'if Shakespeare were alive now he would write such plays'.[52]

Religion was another area where the exemption of older plays from the censorship rigidly applied to their modern equivalents seemed to lack a certain logic. In 1902, for example, Laurence Housman's entirely orthodox nativity play, *Bethlehem*, had been refused a licence for public performance, and Redford had informed the playwright that any plays based on the scriptures were ineligible for licence. Indeed, Redford confirmed to the enquiry that when plays based on the scriptures were submitted, 'I do not even read them'.

There was, as the Committee realised, nothing in the existing law specifically to justify this, but Redford explained it as 'the custom' which was 'generally understood in the theatrical business'.[53] Yet the year before Housman had submitted *Bethlehem*, God had famously been portrayed on stage in William Poel's production of the medieval morality play *Everyman*. Redford protested to the Committee that this should not be regarded as a scriptural play, and that if it had been a modern play he would have licensed it; but this muddied rather than clarified matters. Various ways had been found around the supposed absolute ban on scriptural plays, and this too made a certain mockery of the censor's actions; a 'Bethlehem Society' had been founded to stage Housman's play privately and under club conditions, though, according to Housman, at the first night the management had turned away 'an agent provocateur sent presumably by the Censor to offer gate-money and so bring us within the reach of the law'.[54] Other religious plays had circumvented the censorship by altering the setting or the names of the characters, as in 1904 when Stephen Phillips had transferred his play about David and Bathsheba to the English Civil War. Even more bizarrely, Redford admitted to the Committee that the Office had 'recently stretched the rules in the cases of *Samson and Delilah*'—a decision he appeared to justify on the grounds that it had proved 'the most popular production of the season'—and of *Eagerheart*, because it had been 'a slight thing, done at Christmas time, in imitation of a miracle play'.[55]

The recommendations in the Committee's final report were bound to be a compromise, given the conflicting views of its members about whether theatre censorship should be abolished entirely or made tougher. 'Into this controversy we need not enter', said the report in an unconvincing but inevitable evasion of responsibility. It acknowledged that a system of pre-censorship was 'open to grave objection', and even that 'its effect can hardly fail to be to coerce into conformity with the conventional standards of the day dramatists who may be seeking to amend them'; whether such coercion was positive or negative remained open to different opinions. Significantly, the report also noted that although the figures returned by the Lord Chamberlain's Office suggested that only a small number of plays were refused a licence outright, 'this is not the measure of the activities of the Censorship or of its effects'. Apart from the fact that many plays were licensed only after negotiations and sometimes extensive alterations, witnesses had pointed out that it was

> a frequent practice of the Censor to write letters to managers, and mark them private, ostensibly to give the opportunity of avoiding the stigma of having a play rejected . . . a considerable number of plays were thus withdrawn, and the return does not therefore give a faithful repetition of the facts.

Yet the Committee declared that the system operating was a necessary one and confirmed that 'special laws' to regulate theatre were required in 'the public interest'—thus dismissing the argument that the ordinary laws of the land were sufficient. They also rejected as 'contrary to sound principles of government' the principle of allowing a playwright or any other individual to appeal to arbitration against the decision of a Minister of State, conceding that the author 'should have a right . . . to receive a copy of the Lord Chamberlain's decision', though not the reasons for that decision.[56]

Various possible alternatives to the present system had been mooted before and during the enquiry. One was to hand over the power of censorship to the Home Office, which would have made it answerable to Parliament and open to criticism in a way which the Lord Chamberlain and his examiners were not. Another possibility was to remove the single authority and give power to magistrates, local authorities and the police; in all probability this would have resulted in less emphasis on pre-licensing and would have meant censorship operating primarily through post-performance prosecutions. The Committee rejected all such proposals. Though it approved the continuation of a limited role for an Examiner of Plays, it was insistent that authority and absolute responsibility should remain with the Lord Chamberlain. However, it did recommend that 'distinct Parliamentary responsibility should attach to the Lord Chamberlain who should be held accountable primarily to the House of Lords, and secondarily to the Lower Chamber, for his decisions'. Had this become law it might have had very significant implications, since it would for the first time have made the censor definitely answerable for his actions to an elected Parliament.

The Report attempted to make some firmer proposals with regard to content, though again the need to encompass contrasting views led to compromise and a lack of specificity. Cautiously, the Committee recommended that the Lord Chamberlain should not in future 'act with greater stringency than hitherto in dealing with serious plays touching on moral problems', and slightly more daringly proposed that there should be no automatic ban on 'the presentation upon the stage of painful or disturbing ideas or situations'. On the other hand, it insisted that a play was 'not necessarily moral because its ultimate tendency claims to be moral', and that no licence should be granted to a play 'which presents vice in an alluring guise' even if that vice was ultimately condemned. More specifically, it proposed that the ban on scriptural plays, 'now only partially observed', should be lifted, though it left considerable leeway for the censor by insisting that such plays 'must not do violence to the sentiment of reverence', and that 'persons held to be divine' should not be represented 'in ordinary theatres, or places of public entertainment'. The Committee also attempted to produce detailed guidelines which would indicate the grounds on which the Lord Chamberlain should refuse a play:

It should be his duty to license any play submitted to him unless he considers that it may reasonably be held—

(a) To be indecent;

(b) To contain offensive personalities;

(c) To represent on the stage in an invidious manner a living person, or any person recently dead;

(d) To do violence to the sentiment of religious reverence;

(e) To be calculated to conduce to crime or vice;

(f) To be calculated to impair friendly relations with any foreign Power; or

(g) To be calculated to cause a breach of the peace.

Inevitably, these terms would still have left very considerable powers of interpretation in the hands of the censors; however, since they never became law, the Lord Chamberlain remained free to make use of or ignore them as he chose.

By far the most fundamental and far-reaching suggestion of all those put forward by the Committee was the proposal that the licensing of a play should be optional, and that managers should be entitled to present plays without licences and take the risk of prosecution if they wished to do so. The report recognised the importance and legitimacy of serious drama being free to take on difficult issues, and recommended that the censorship should not be able to prevent this:

> if it were right that the law should prevent the presentation upon the stage of painful or disturbing ideas or situations, it would be necessary to veto tragedy and melodrama, and to license comedy alone . . . In view of the danger that official control over plays before their production may hinder the growth of a great and serious national drama . . . we conclude that the licensing authority, which we desire to see maintained, should not have power to impose a veto on the production of plays.[57]

Given that the support of the managers for the existing system was rooted in the security from prosecution it afforded them, the recommendation that they should be free to apply or not apply for a licence as they chose did carry a logic with it; it would have left those managers—the majority—who sought the guaranteed protection to continue to enjoy it, while allowing those such as Granville Barker at the Court who wished to go ahead regardless to do so, leaving it up to the law to initiate a prosecution *after* a performance had taken place. The Lord Chamberlain's office, however, judged that the proposal to make applying for a licence optional for theatres (as it was for music-halls) would, if enacted, 'destroy the position of the Censor and turn it into ridicule', taking away his authority and turning him into 'the target, the buffer for abuse,

without the power to remedy abuses of which he himself is cognisant'.[58] Of the recommendations made by the Committee it was this one which most worried Althorp and Dawson, and which they were most determined to scupper.

Even before the enquiry by the Joint Select Committee had been announced, the Lord Chamberlain's Office had been on the defensive as a result of Harcourt's Bill with its explicitly stated aim 'to abolish the censorship of plays exercised in Great Britain under the authority of the Lord Chamberlain'. Harcourt was a key member of the Committee, so the Office knew its position would be under strong attack. One of the central planks of the defence it constructed was the plan to introduce an Advisory Board, which would allow it to refute accusations that theatre censorship depended on the whim of a single individual. Dawson claimed that the Board had been planned for a long time and was not simply a response to recent criticisms; only legal difficulties had held it up, he said, and though it had still not formally met, this was because it was necessarily in abeyance until the conclusion of the enquiry. In fact, right up until the first sitting of the Joint Select Committee, Dawson was still trying to secure promises from potential members of such a Board, as his private letter to the Lord Chamberlain on 14 June shows. The tone of his letter also demonstrates the extent to which he believed that such a Board would be a trump card in the coming battle:

> My dear Bobby,
> We have done a big thing this morning. If only Rufus Isaacs sticks to his word, we shall have an unanswerable argument in our favour. Comyns Carr has accepted with pleasure, and he says this idea of an Advisory Board will sweep away all the difficulties and objections, except perhaps in isolated instances like B.S. who wishes to rule alone . . . I think this stroke is a fine weapon when the 'committee' discuss the question.[59]

The Lord Chamberlain, probably trying to head off the enquiry, promptly wrote to the Prime Minister to inform him that, with the promise of an Advisory Board, 'the difficulties will be almost, if not entirely, at an end'.[60]

The Board did indeed become the subject of widespread discussion and general approval during the enquiry, though its terms of reference and especially its power and its relationship to the Lord Chamberlain were more contentious. A possibility favoured by several witnesses was a committee of three people, one appointed by the Society for Dramatic Authors, one by the Lord Chamberlain and the other by those two jointly or by the Prime Minister. Some argued strongly that the role of this committee should not be limited to advising, and that in cases of dispute it should have the final and absolute power to arbitrate. Comyns Carr even made his membership of the Board dependent on just such a ruling; when Dawson wrote in July 1909 to the four

prospective members—Rufus Isaacs, Squire Bancroft, John Hare and Carr—
to say it would 'strengthen my hand considerably' if he could give their names
confidentially to the Chair of the enquiry, Carr alone withheld permission
until the issue had been resolved: 'the action of such an Advisory Committee
as you propose must be wholly unfettered and its decisions absolutely final.
The position of such a committee would I think be wholly intolerable on any
other terms', he wrote.[61] Dawson promised him that the Lord Chamberlain
would consider the matter, and instead of Carr's name the phrase 'a distinguished playwright' was included on the list of proposed Board members
handed to the Chair; even without a name being specified, it certainly seemed
like a significant concession that the playwrights and their views could hope
to be represented. But this was not at all the sort of Board the Comptroller
and the Lord Chamberlain had in mind, and they had no intention either of
allowing the membership of the Board to be chosen by anyone other than
themselves, or of allowing the Board the final say in matters of censorship.
The Speaker of the House of Commons was emphatic that if he were the Lord
Chamberlain he would 'not submit to that for a moment' but would insist on
his right to make the final decision and to choose for himself whom he should
consult.[62] As we know, the Lord Chamberlain spoke, as a member of the royal
household, with the authority of the monarch, and the King was certainly not
prepared to see his power eroded in any way. In August 1909 Althorp received
a letter sent on his behalf:

> The King hopes you are keeping an eye on his interests in the matter, and
> that it is clearly understood that the ultimate decision rests entirely in his
> hands. While H.M. will be only too glad to consider any recommendation
> of the Commission, and to discuss with the Prime Minister the best solu-
> tion of the question he hopes that no attempt will be made to force his
> hand.[63]

The Lord Chamberlain was also categorically informed that the King 'will not
agree to the theatres being removed from the jurisdiction of the Lord
Chamberlain', and in January 1910, when Althorp wrote to him with official
plans for establishing an Advisory Board, the reply showed how seriously the
issue was taken:

> His Majesty entirely approves of the appointment of the Advisory
> Committee . . . but he regrets that he cannot agree to your proposal that
> 'you should be empowered to accept the advice of a majority of a Board',
> if by that you mean on no occasion will the Lord Chamberlain have the
> power of veto.
> Your recommendation is in the effect to abolish the Lord Chamberlain's
> right of censorship, as possessed by him at present.

> The King thinks that the veto of the Lord Chamberlain should be retained
> as a dormant factor, on the same principle as the Sovereign has the power
> of making use of his veto in cases of emergency or of an exceptional char-
> acter.[64]

It seems likely that this was exactly the reply the Lord Chamberlain expected, and that his proposal to which the King was unable to agree was probably a discreet manipulation which would allow Althorp to shelter behind his master. The Board was duly established with nothing other than the right to advise on those occasions when the Lord Chamberlain chose to consult it, and its members were selected and invited by the Lord Chamberlain and his Comptroller. Carr never sat on the Advisory Board, and no alternative 'distinguished playwright' was substituted.

Another part of Dawson's defensive strategy during the Enquiry was to allow the blame for poor and arbitrary decisions to fall solidly on the shoulders of George Redford, as Examiner of Plays. Redford was disliked intensely by what he himself called 'the advanced school of irreconcilable Dramatists', and it was not hard to demonstrate his incompetence.[65] Redford frequently proved himself inept both in his practice and in his responses to the Committee's questions, and was probably fairly accused of arrogance; the press expressed its astonishment at the gaps exposed by his evidence, and *The Stage* predicted that this alone would be sufficient to bring down the existing system:

> A remarkable exposition was given by Mr G.A. Redford . . . full of inex-
> actitude, showing how responsible officials do not understand the Acts
> governing amusements nor the way in which these Acts operate . . . The
> dramatic censorship, in its present form at any rate, will not survive the
> enquiry in Committee Room A.[66]

In the event, Redford was used more or less as a fall guy by Althorp and Dawson, someone who could be sacrificed in order to save the system. The Speaker of the House of Commons, for example, spoke denigratingly of Redford's relationship to the Lord Chamberlain, describing him as merely 'a clerk in his office, who does the drudgery for him', and Dawson's evidence on more than one occasion left Redford deliberately exposed and unsupported.[67] The Comptroller never informed him of the intention to introduce an Advisory Board, so Redford told the Committee that to have several people discussing whether or not a play should be licensed 'would be absolutely unworkable' and said that he knew of no plans to introduce such a Board; Dawson subsequently told the Committee that the Board had been planned for some time and was now in existence. Redford said he had never received anything in writing itemising his duties and responsibilities; Dawson insisted

that the Examiner's brief included inspecting theatres to check how plays were being performed, and that this had been stated in his letters of service; when it was pointed out that his answers were 'not in keeping' with Redford's claims, Dawson replied: 'I cannot say that they are; I can only tell you what Mr Redford's instructions were'. Redford spoke of his policy of communicating privately with theatre managers and insisted it was 'improper' for his letters marked as confidential to be made public; Dawson said that such communications should not be considered confidential and that there should be no secrecy. Redford told the Committee that his own judgement 'never has been reversed'. Dawson told them that 'such cases have occurred'. Redford had no effective answer when he was asked why he sometimes accepted a précis for a play in a foreign language; Dawson stated that it would have been better always to insist on a full translation.[68]

Redford's position had actually been undermined even before the enquiry began, when the Assistant Comptroller of the Lord Chamberlain's Office wrote to him, querying his competence and warning him that he must show his proposed statement and evidence to Althorp before speaking to the Committee. Redford was clearly taken aback, insisting he had simply carried on the policies of his predecessor, and expressing surprise at the demand: 'I cannot quite understand what is required of me in 'letting Lord Althorp know what evidence I am prepared to give'. I hold myself entirely at his disposal, and will of course carry out any instructions.' A further letter then reminded Redford of his lack of authority, and again accused him of having overstepped the mark in the past:

There is however one very strong point which you will never lose sight of and it is that the Lord Chamberlain is the (so called) Censor and the Examiner of Plays is not.

I really feel that, in the past, you have lost sight of this to some extent and taken more upon yourself than advisable—not, I am sure, for 'mean and contemptible reason', but I think you have slided into the practice by degrees somewhat unconsciously.[69]

In a preparatory interview with Althorp and Dawson before appearing at the enquiry, Redford was instructed to 'make his replies as brief as possible' and to 'take care not to be carried away'; he was to 'volunteer no information' nor 'anything personal to himself', and was to 'say yea and nay in reply to any questions'. It is perhaps hardly surprising that Redford should then have had a difficult time with some members of the Committee, coming across as naïve and cosily complacent; he admitted that he relied on his wife to enlighten him if the synopses of plays in German were offensive, and on theatre managers who 'generally do anything I ask them' and were 'most ready to do what I desired'. When the Committee asked what control over a performance the

censors had if a play which they had licensed should be altered or interpreted in ways they had not anticipated, he replied that he would act 'if it came to my knowledge', but conceded that whether it did so was dependent on his reading newspaper reports, and would be largely 'a matter of chance'. The Committee was understandably keen to try to pin down the precise grounds on which plays were censored, and since the Lord Chamberlain, who actually had full responsibility for every censorship decision, declined, on the advice of the King, to appear before the Committee, his Examiner of Plays had to try to explain his policy:

> Committee: On what principle to you proceed in licensing plays that come before you?
> Redford: . . . it is really impossible to say on what principle I proceed. There are no principles that can be defined.
> Committee: You base yourself mainly on custom and precedent?
> Redford: Yes. I follow the principle established in the office of the Lord Chamberlain for many years . . . There is no limit to the number of things which may justify a refusal.[70]

In one sense Redford's last remark here was admirably honest, but it gave the game away by admitting to an apparent vagueness which was exactly what so upset the abolitionists. As we know, such vagueness was, in fact, a deliberate strategy. However, by directly comparing material he had licensed and material he had refused, the Committee exposed a series of discrepancies and inconsistencies which Redford was unable to justify, and he was reduced to claiming that he was 'bound . . . by unwritten law'—without being able to explain what that law was.

On occasions during the enquiry, Redford was even expected to cover for his superiors. As mentioned previously, he was made to appear inconsistent in his attitude to religious plays when he admitted having granted a licence for the opera *Samson and Delilah* in 1908. What Redford—like all good servants—refrained from telling the Committee was that his master had given him no choice in that particular matter. In August 1908, Harry Higgins, the putative producer of the opera, had written privately to 'My dear Bobby', asking the Lord Chamberlain to tell his Examiner to license it; Althorp had replied: 'My dear Harry . . . if you would kindly forward a copy of the libretto to Mr Redford as usual, he knows my decision'.[71] In another instance, Redford declined to accept all the blame; discussing the refusal of a licence earlier that year for the burlesque on *An Englishman's Home*, the Committee asked Redford why he had informed the manager, not just that a licence was refused for this piece, but that 'No skit will be permitted' based on that particular play. Redford claimed that he had 'acted under orders' and was not responsible for it: 'I had better say at once I obeyed instructions in respect of that entirely.

Personally and individually I had nothing whatever to do with it.'[72] When Dawson was challenged about the issue, he directed the blame back onto Redford, accusing him of having expressed to the manager 'an opinion which he was not authorised to give';[73] but in fact the relevant file in the Lord Chamberlain's Correspondence contains a telegram from Althorp to Redford saying 'any skit on that subject is inadvisable and might cause complications'. Redford's error was in having passed on what was intended to be private.[74]

For all Redford's incompetence, it did strike some people as perverse that, even while it was being insisted that the Reader had no authority and that the only censor was the Lord Chamberlain, Althorp made no appearance in front of the Committee but left it to Redford (and Dawson) to answer questions. Once again, it was actually a royal wish that Althorp was observing; he had sought leave from the King to be allowed to give evidence, and had been advised against it unless he was specifically asked by the Chair to do so. Dawson was relieved by this recommendation, fearing the risk of exposing Althorp to questions: 'From our point of view I consider it most inadvisable', he wrote; 'I am so glad you talked it out with the King and that he was so nice about it'.[75] For his part, after his ordeal with the Committee was over, Redford wrote apologetically to the Lord Chamberlain: 'I need scarcely say how very much I regret the turn matters took at the Committee and I sincerely hope that you absolve me from any blame. Indeed, I wish I could have taken anything on my own shoulders.'[76]

One further part of the Comptroller's defensive strategy which requires mention was his attempt to make sure sympathetic witnesses were called. I have already referred to the pressure Dawson exerted to try to ensure that a series of West End managers spoke in favour of the censorship, and it was also revealed under questioning that Comyns Carr had been actively approached and asked to speak by the Society of West End Managers. At another point during the enquiry, Dawson set out to find an individual who would be 'prepared to give evidence from the point of view of the British public'; such a person would supposedly be independent and neutral, but in fact he would have been chosen for his sympathy with the censorship. William Fladgate, the solicitor to the Society of West End Managers, proposed George Russell, an MP, and in September 1909 Dawson wrote to Fladgate with some enthusiasm, displaying a level of calculating and manipulative hypocrisy: 'If you are sure of G.W.E. Russell's views on the Censor question, I think he would be a very good name to suggest, with the object of giving the Committee at least one independent representative of the general public'. Dawson told Althorp that 'Russell is sure to be alright or Fladgate would not suggest him', but he acknowledged that it would be inappropriate for the Office to propose him since 'it could only be taken as a request for the examination of a witness whose views we were already aware of'. He therefore proposed that Russell should suggest himself, confident that he was too well known for the

Committee to refuse. However, as someone who cheerfully admitted that he went 'much less to the play than most people', Russell fought shy of taking this initiative, fearful that he might be exposed as 'an incompetent witness' and would be too easily 'disposed of by the anti-licensing committee'. Dawson was forced to drop the idea of the 'independent' witness.[77]

In the autumn of 1909, the Lord Chamberlain's Office awaited the publication of the Committee's recommendations and report with some trepidation: 'I hear from Herbert Samuel that the Censorship Committee have agreed unanimously to the substance of their report . . . I am rather surprised and not altogether pleased to hear it', wrote W.P. Byrne, the Assistant Under-Secretary of State at the Home Office to the Comptroller. Dawson agreed that 'a <u>unanimous</u> report from the Committee looks ominous', though he could 'hardly believe seriously that the views of the extremists are shared by the rest of the Committee'.[78] He was duly appalled by the extent and the implications of the recommendations when they became known in November. But Byrne was able to advise him that, for all the disconcerting features of the report, no legislation was imminent; he informed Dawson that the press was not generally supportive of the proposals and suggested they should 'allow opinion gradually to form and express itself' and that 'it would be inexpedient for the Lord Chamberlain to express any <u>immediate</u> opinion or to tender any <u>immediate</u> advice to H.M. in the matter'.[79] The Lord Chamberlain's Office was determined there should be 'no drastic change' in the law, and in January 1910 Dawson set up a meeting with Sir Almeric Fitzroy of the Privy Council, Sir Charles Mathews, the Director of Public Prosecutions, and Byrne, representing the Home Office, to produce a case against the recommendations. Mathews sought to prove in particular that the principle of making a licence optional was 'unworkable', since a prosecution of an unlicensed play would be convoluted and by no means certain to succeed, and any failure would at once fatally undermine the system: 'one Juryman could entirely defeat the whole proceedings, and once the Director of Public Prosecutions failed to carry his case his prestige would be gone for ever'. He also claimed that coverage of the prosecution in the press 'would have a most pernicious effect, and that it would certainly tend to increase the harm done by the production of the play'. Having agreed unanimously that they did not wish the recommendations to be adopted as law, Dawson, Fitzroy, Mathews and Byrne next considered the simplest way of exerting influence on ministers. Not for the first time, the solution was to invoke the authority and preference of the monarch; as the minutes of the meeting delicately put it, 'both Sir Charles Mathews and Mr Byrne were of opinion that were The King to express it as his wish that things remained in <u>status quo</u> the Government would be bound to fall in with that view'.[80] A couple of weeks later, following discreet consultations, Dawson was able to write to Mathews: 'The King wished me to tell you specially that H.M. quite agreed with you that things should remain in

status quo'; Mathews duly confirmed that 'every effort will be made to fulfil His Majesty's wishes'.[81]

'I should have liked the artists to wrench a victory', wrote Max Beerbohm after the Committee's report had been published, but he confessed that a 'knowledge of the English character, and of the official mind, had sufficed to save me from hoping for anything better'.[82] Yet it was a mistake to lay the blame entirely at the door of the Committee, for had their recommendations become law then the change in how censorship was practised would have been profound. It is hard to imagine that many of the plays which were refused licences or significantly cut during the next sixty years would have had successful post-production prosecutions brought against them. Although one can only speculate, it is no exaggeration to say that if theatre managers and playwrights had been allowed to choose whether or not to submit their work for pre-censorship, the history of British theatre in the twentieth century might have been very significantly different. Probably the whole system of censorship would have been abolished much earlier than it was, and there would have been at least the opportunity for more innovative, more challenging and more serious work to be performed on the British stage.

In terms of day-to-day practice, the censorship had not, at least on the face of it, come off particularly well during the enquiry, having often being made to look at best well-meaning and at worst inept. Redford, who had been in post for much longer than either Dawson or Althorp, was a casualty of the enquiry—thrown to the playwrights and the press for them to devour. But for the Office, this was a sacrifice made all too willingly, for Redford was perceived to have caused many of the recent difficulties, and his departure would allow Dawson and Althorp to make their own appointment. Within a few years, Redford would be President of the Board of Film Censors, able to exercise power legitimately and on his own behalf, and it is striking that he quickly developed a much more specific code of what was and was not allowed than had ever been created for use in connection with theatre.

In effect, though, the existing system of theatre censorship was set to continue with little alteration other than the addition of an Advisory Board, which would be controlled by and entirely subject to the authority of the Lord Chamberlain. It remained to be seen whether and how the enquiry and its report would influence practice. Moreover, although we now know that there was to be no comparable investigation until the one which finally removed the Lord Chamberlain from his position nearly sixty years later, it would be wrong to assume that this was inevitable and that the abolitionists would retire, defeated, leaving the Lord Chamberlain's authority unchallenged and secure. Within four years, Harcourt would attempt to introduce another Bill to Parliament calling for the abolition of the system of pre-censorship, and for the removal of the 'antiquated legislation' which attempted to discriminate between performances in music-halls and in theatres. Though that and other

attempts to change the law failed, the policies and practices of the Lord Chamberlain would be constantly influenced by the need to be seen to court public opinion, for fear that his powers would be swept away if he appeared out of touch.

While urging the Lord Chamberlain at least not to become more restrictive of plays which attempted to use the theatre for something other than pure entertainment, the report of the Joint Select Committee had boldly suggested that 'a somewhat stricter guard than hitherto might be exercised against the indecencies that sometimes tend to appear in plays of a frivolous type'. One example of a deliberately frivolous play—cited on several occasions to the Committee—was *Dear Old Charlie* by Charles Brookfield. Little over a year after the Committee published its report, this same Charles Brookfield—in what the *Observer* called 'a stroke of grotesque and impudent cynicism'—had been appointed in place of Redford as Examiner of Plays.[83] As one critic put it, the Lord Chamberlain had 'publicly put out his tongue' at those who had challenged him.[84]

Cats, Canaries and Guinea Pigs

Principles and Practice, 1909–1913

> One reason against abolishing the Censorship of the Stage is that there
> would cease to be a Censorship question, which has for some time been a
> much surer source of amusement than the Stage itself.[1]

The Lord Chamberlain's position after the 1909 Joint Select Committee of
enquiry was not necessarily any more secure than it had been before. On the
one hand, continuing demands for the imposition of a stricter code of
morality, and for theatres—and especially music-halls—to be 'cleaned up',
were made in several newspapers which delighted in exposing the Lord
Chamberlain's inconsistencies or contentious decisions. On the other hand,
the campaign by those committed to using theatre as a forum for discussing
social issues was maintained on several fronts. Harcourt, who had undoubtedly been responsible for many of the liberalising recommendations included
in the final report (even though his anti-censorship views had been in a
minority on the Committee), was one of a group of MPs who tabled a series
of questions in Parliament about how the government intended to respond to
the conclusions of the Select Committee. This also allowed them the opportunity to highlight some of the difficult situations in which the Lord
Chamberlain's Office continued to become embroiled. No one was really able
to defend the logic of the discriminatory treatments of the theatres and the
music-halls; in a 1913 parliamentary debate, the Home Office representative,
speaking in support of the status quo, admitted that the present system was
'illogical and indefensible in theory', though he claimed it had proved 'work-
able' in practice. Even he accepted that legislation bringing theatres and
music-halls together under common procedures was bound to come:

> The Joint Committee in 1909 found, and rightly found, that there ought
> to be one licence for both these classes of entertainment. I think that is a
> position nobody can quarrel with, and when the proper time comes no
> doubt legislation will take that form.[2]

Long before then, leading managers were demanding the introduction of a 'dual licence' which would allow theatres the freedom to put on vaudeville and other entertainments; this would have created a more level playing field with music-halls, which they accused of stealing their plays, audiences and performers. But for the Lord Chamberlain's Office to take on the licensing of all music-hall material was impractical, and what went on in the halls continued to be seen as less important from a political point of view than what went on in theatres. In January 1910 Dawson advised the Home Office: 'I feel we have to hold the theatres at all costs, and with that as our goal must frame our action in the future'.[3]

By the autumn of 1910, a series of difficult confrontations had left the Lord Chamberlain's authority in crisis. Althorp was moved to confess to Dawson that he was 'beginning to feel what a relief it will be' to have an Advisory Board to share responsibility for what he called 'the awful nuisance of deciding about plays'.[4] Apart from the plays themselves, there was the problem of the Reader, George Redford, exposed by the Committee and increasingly drawn into conflict with superiors who were all but openly looking for a way to get rid of him. Following complaints in 1910 about *The Sins of London* at the Lyceum, the Lord Chamberlain's Chief Clerk watched a performance and reported that some of the scenes were 'in the worst possible taste'; Redford, asked why he had approved the play without consultation, was once again forced onto the defensive:

> These sensational plays . . . are all on much the same lines; it's only a ques-
> tion of degree . . . I have had rather a busy time of late, and had to get
> through things under some difficulty. It is not difficult to miss a line or
> two under these circumstances.

The Lord Chamberlain told Dawson that 'some notice must be taken of this' and expressed concern that so long as the Office was seen to approve such plays 'we never shall be safe'; he showed little sympathy towards Redford: 'Surely if he is so very busy he should say so and we could make other arrangements.—It would have been quite easy for him to have had these passages omitted before the play was produced.'[5]

One of the main charges levelled by the 1909 Committee had been that there was no adequate way of ensuring that changes required by the Lord Chamberlain were actually observed in performance. In November 1910 the editor of a London magazine complained to the Lord Chamberlain about lines in *How Girls Are Brought to Ruin*, in which a landlady encourages a young woman to solicit men for money to pay her rent. Althorp insisted that these lines had not been included in the text he had licensed, and the editor broadened his attack:

There are very many plays now being performed all over the country in which the version played contains such indecencies that these versions cannot be identical with the licensed versions. I should be glad to know whether your Lordship desires your attention specifically called to each of these seriatim, or whether the Censorship has any other means of seeing that its authority is not further mocked.[6]

Although Dawson had informed the Committee that one of the Examiner's duties was to inspect performances, there was no possible way of systematically checking what was really happening in most theatres—as Redford had, perhaps foolishly, conceded. In their book on censorship, published in 1913, Fowell and Palmer also suggested that abuse of the system was widespread and common knowledge:

> Corrections have been acquiesced in for the sake of securing a licence, and afterwards ignored . . . one actor . . . was such a favourite with the public that he had full liberty to do as he liked, and whatever the Lord Chamberlain struck out of the dialogue he took care to put in again with additions . . . it is largely a matter of chance whether any alterations come to the ear of the Censor or not, so that in actual practice he has largely to rely on the good faith and discretion of the managers and author.[7]

Not for the first or last time, Oscar Wilde's *Salomé* proved the starting point for yet another awkward confrontation in the autumn of 1910, and one on which the beleaguered Lord Chamberlain was outmanoeuvred. Although a dance version of the controversial scene involving Salome, Herod, and the head of John the Baptist had been performed to critical acclaim in February 1908, that had taken place in a venue outside the remit of the Lord Chamberlain; in October 1910, however, he refused to license the libretto of Richard Strauss's opera for Sir Thomas Beecham's Company at Covent Garden. Beecham immediately threatened never to conduct in London again, and insisted that his Company had invested heavily in its current season and that only this opera could save it from bankruptcy. Moreover, he insisted, it would be 'nothing short of a national calamity' if the result of the Lord Chamberlain's actions was that 'England alone in the world should be deprived of the opportunity of hearing the finest opera of modern days'.[8] Beecham's tactic—which proved extremely effective—was to appeal over the head of the Lord Chamberlain to the Prime Minister, Asquith, and the conductor was soon in conference with Althorp and Dawson to discuss how, in Beecham's words, *Salomé* would be trimmed so as to make it palatable to the taste of that large army of objectors who would never see it'. Beecham mocked these negotiations as 'a solemn sacrifice on the altar of an unknown but truly national god', describing the process as absurd and comic:

> The first thing we did was to eliminate the name of John, who was to be called simply The Prophet; and having invested him with this desirable anonymity, we went on to deprive every passage between him and Salomé of the slightest force or meaning. The mundane and commonplace passion of the precocious princess was refined into a desire on her part for spiritual guidance.[9]

Then, part-way through rehearsals, the Lord Chamberlain decided to object to the idea of Salomé singing to the prophet's decapitated head. A blood-stained sword was substituted for the head, but the singer asked to be allowed to substitute a tray covered with a cloth, to represent the head. Dawson attended a rehearsal, and he himself described what occurred at the climactic moment:

> As Salomé descended, carrying the charger, she suddenly stopped in her song, and burst out—'j'en ai assez. Je n'eu peux volus' [sic].
>
> I was hurriedly asked to go on the stage and calm the excited manager and lady, both loudly protesting the opera could not proceed without the head. I did what I could, but that night I received a note—'monsieur, je vous prie, donnez moi la tête'.[10]

It is hard to believe that the confrontation was as spontaneous as Dawson imagined it was, and it seems much more likely to have been a strategy to which Beecham was at least party. In any case, it was not unsuccessful. Althorp conceded that the performance could make use of a tray covered with a cloth, though he tried to maintain his position by insisting that 'care must be taken not to build up a great heap in it which would look suggestive'. But the final ridiculing of his authority occurred in the performance, when, according to Beecham, the singers 'forgot' the changes imposed on the libretto and sang the original, unlicensed version 'as if no such things existed as British respectability and its legal custodians'. Even in the Lord Chamberlain's presence this went either unnoticed or judiciously unremarked, and Beecham describes with relish Lord Althorp's fulsome post-performance congratulations 'for the complete way in which you have met and gratified all our wishes'.[11]

Beecham had managed to play the system, thanks mostly to the authority of his own position, and in particular his ability to gain the ear of the Prime Minister. He could therefore afford to speak of the censorship in a tone of gentle mockery. At exactly the same time, however, Laurence Housman was expressing bitter and angry frustration over the refusal of *Pains and Penalties*, a play about Queen Caroline, the wife of George IV, which was (somewhat ambitiously) submitted for licence just two months after George V had acceded to the throne. Dawson met the putative manager, Gertrude Kingston,

and warned the Lord Chamberlain that 'the lady appears to be very obstinate' and that the play was one which might 'cause us some trouble if prohibited'. Meanwhile, he suggested to Kingston that a licence might be more possible if the names of the characters and the country were changed. She, however, apparently failed in her attempts to persuade the playwright to make these changes, and tried a different approach to the Comptroller:

> May I remind you with no disrespect to your office, that when Shakespeare's play 'Richard II' was to be produced in the reign of Queen Elizabeth for purposes of political propaganda, Her Majesty summoned her advisers in order to stop it and the great Lord Burleigh counselled her to take no notice of it but to let it proceed. The play was produced and nothing ever came of it but good.

Though Kingston's argument did not convince Dawson, he was evidently impressed by her; when she complained subsequently of the refusal to license another play, and suggested that the Office unfairly favoured some managers over others, Dawson replied in an unusually flirtatious vein:

> If any bias were possible as far as I am concerned, I might plead guilty to have had a wish to do all I can to oblige you from the moment I first had the pleasure of making your acquaintance.
>
> But I fear I cannot persuade you that anything good can come out of this office. I don't despair; will you show you bear no ill feeling and come and let us discuss what you feel aggrieved about, and I can promise you a hearty welcome.[12]

Whether or not Kingston took up this dubious invitation is not recorded.

In the case of *Pains and Penalties*, the Office could find no ordinary reason to refuse the licence: 'The trouble is that we can't bring in The King', wrote the Comptroller to the Lord Chamberlain. However, they managed to make a private agreement with the Home Office that ministers would back the decision to ban the play if it were questioned in Parliament, and the licence was duly refused. Housman responded by provocatively organising a public reading of the play, and then challenged the Lord Chamberlain to license a full performance on the grounds that no breach of the peace had occurred. Althorp was not to be swayed:

> Housman's new move is rather adroit but I do not think that he can really imagine that I am going to reverse the decision about his play. A read play is very different from an acted one . . . Of course, Housman's object is to get me into a public correspondence and that I will not do.

Housman asserted that the Office could only have rejected his play because they thought it liable to undermine the 'Preservation of good Manners, Decorum, or of the Public Peace', since there were no other plausible grounds for turning it down. However, this view was based on the false supposition that the recommendations of the 1909 report were binding and had effectively defined the limits of the Lord Chamberlain's powers. Nevertheless, Althorp was unsure of his ground, and sought advice from the Attorney General; he confirmed that, in the case of new plays, there remained 'no limitation upon the exercise of the discretion by the Lord Chamberlain'. Dawson took delight in immediately writing to Housman to tell him that 'you appear to have been misinformed'. Despite doubts about the advisability of indicating the reason for a refusal, the Comptroller (evidently with the approval of the King) intended telling the playwright that it was because his play 'dealt with a sad episode of comparatively recent date in the life of a lady of Royal Rank'. On the advice of the Lord Chamberlain—who knew that Housman would be likely to publish the correspondence, and wished to avoid revealing such a narrow bias—the last phrase was amended to refer only to 'the life of an unhappy lady'. Though ignorant of this discreet alteration, Housman immediately publicised this justification in *The Times*, insisting that his play's primary aim had actually been to salvage Caroline's reputation:

> I am now officially informed that this rehabilitation of her character is not to be allowed; and it is for the prevention of such an attempt that the Censor's powers have been exercised. Truly the age of chivalry is not dead!

But for all his storming, and unlike Beecham, Housman was powerless to persuade the Lord Chamberlain to change his mind. He probably never realised that the King's own views were decisive in rejecting even a sympathetic portrait of a former monarch; it was another twelve years before *Pains and Penalties* was licensed, when Dawson would recall: 'There is nothing in writing on record to say that The King was consulted in 1910, but . . . I am sure H.M. <u>was</u> approached and objected to the Licence'.[13]

In many respects, Brigadier-General Sir Douglas Dawson was the power behind the thrones of successive Lords Chamberlain. The Advisory Board had been his idea, and it was he who orchestrated much of what went on in the Office. He was an old Etonian with an extensive background in the army during the late nineteenth century, who had then served as a military attaché in Vienna and Paris. The author of a published report on horse breeding in Hungary, Dawson had achieved a string of public honours before taking up the post of Comptroller of the Lord Chamberlain's Office in 1907. In the years after the 1909 enquiry, it was Dawson who stamped his authority on the Office, while rarely or never attracting publicity or taking the flak that was

thrown at the Lord Chamberlain or his Readers. He remained in that position until 1920, though Lords Chamberlain changed as governments
changed; his influence over Althorp was considerable, and his power
continued unabated when Lord Sandhurst replaced Althorp in 1912.
Sandhurst was a former Liberal Peer and a member of the Coldstream
Guards, and he had served in a number of public roles, including Governor
of Bombay, Under-Secretary in the War Office and Lord in Waiting to Queen
Victoria. However, even a eulogising obituary in *The Times* suggested that
Sandhurst 'laid no claim to conspicuous political talents', and was content to
conclude that since 'he was never seriously attacked' it might be presumed
that his term as Lord Chamberlain had been a success.[14] Dawson, meanwhile,
would remain extremely influential even after 1920, when he became State
Chamberlain. However, his reputation and health suffered to some extent
after a financial scandal erupted around a business company of which he was
a director, and which involved his cross-examination in a court of law and his
near breakdown. Moreover, the new Lord Chamberlain, Lord Cromer, who
took up his post in 1922, was altogether a shrewder and a more authoritative
figure in office, canvassing and balancing a much wider diversity of opinions
than his predecessors, with the result that Dawson had become almost isolated
by the time he resigned his commitment in January 1931 to be replaced by
Allardyce Nicoll.

For Lord Althorp, however, Dawson's strategy of appointing an Advisory
Board was an attempt to try to restore some of the credibility which had been
damaged by the government enquiry, and which had been further weakened
and undermined since. Many had begun to feel his authority over the theatre
was beyond saving; as *The Times* put it in 1910:

> He reminds us of the elderly Academician in M. Pailleron's famous play
> who was always being given out for dead in the evening papers and always
> being revived next morning . . . What with the combined attack of enraged
> dramatic authors and a Select Committee of both Houses, it was thought
> that the Lord Chamberlain—in his theatrical aspect—was bowled over.
> Yet here he is, as fresh as paint, reinforced by an Advisory Board.

The Times described the members of that Board as 'an incongruous medley',
and rather dismissively compared them to 'the "happy family" cages one used
to see at street corners, with cats, canaries, and guinea-pigs all dwelling together
in amity'. They were, of course, hand-picked by the Lord Chamberlain and
his Comptroller—something which had certainly not been envisaged by most
of those who had given evidence to the 1909 Committee in support of such
a Board—and *The Times* suggested that while 'this or that gentleman in the
list may be all right; it is their combination that is so odd'. Apart from the Lord
Chamberlain himself and Colonel Sir Douglas Dawson as *ex officio* members,

the Board consisted of five men; two (the Right Honourable Sir Edward Carson—who was also an MP—and Stanley Owen Buckmaster) were senior barristers and members of the King's Counsel, while two (Sir Squire Bancroft and Sir John Hare) were famous actor-managers, whose experiences were largely rooted in the nineteenth century and whose theatrical preferences were known to incline to the conservative and the old-fashioned. For all their achievements in another era, it was highly questionable whether these adequately prepared them for dealing with 'the constant pressure of new ideas, new moral forces on the art of drama'. *The Times* put it bluntly:

> No one would be surprised to see either of them there; but few could have expected to see them both there . . . the distinction between Sir Squire and Sir John, as theatrical experts, is, we confess, too fine for us to grasp. Sir Squire's celebrated eye-glass and Sir John's no less celebrated 'pair of spectacles' must show to both virtually the same theatrical world—which, in the nature of things, cannot be a brand-new theatrical world.

The final member of the Board, Professor Walter Raleigh from Oxford, was a surprise for different reasons:

> This sudden introduction of the Professor into the company of Court officials, distinguished K.C.'s, and honoured veterans of the theatrical 'boards' almost takes your breath away. You ask yourself, how on earth did they come to hear of him? He is a brilliant critic, an erudite man of letters, a University professor—what . . . is he doing in that set?

Yet the choice was somewhat cleverer and more strategic than this allowed, for the Lord Chamberlain could claim he had 'called in the New World to redress the balance of the Old'; indeed, *The Times* acknowledged that he had 'got hold of a trump-card', which would give him credibility and allow him to pre-empt objections from disappointed playwrights:

> With the old machinery the condemned author could always say, 'Oh, it's only Mr. Redford!' or 'only the Lord Chamberlain!' . . . But he will not be able to say, 'Oh, it's only Professor Raleigh!' In the world of letters the Professor's verdict will be final. [15]

However, though Raleigh did indeed prove generally more liberal in his recommendations than the other Board members, this argument conveniently neglects the near certainty that he would frequently find himself outvoted and in a minority of one. Indeed, this is exactly what happened almost immediately, when both *Waste* and *Mrs Warren's Profession* were resubmitted and he found himself alone in supporting their applications for licences. Moreover,

the Lord Chamberlain was not required to accept the Board's views, and Dawson sometimes made it clear when he sent plays out to its members what advice the Lord Chamberlain expected to receive back—as with Barker's play in 1911:

> I have no hesitation in saying that, however cleverly written the play is, I consider the procuring of abortion, by cabinet ministers or anyone else, to be a subject which is, to say the least, unnecessary and undesirable to produce on the public stage, even in these days.[16]

Later that year, Dawson sent out a religious play, again with the strongest possible hint that it must not be licensed. His intention to manipulate the Board could hardly be more obvious: 'It is no place of mine to give an opinion to the Advisory Board, but I thought you would not mind me sending you a line in strict confidence'.[17]

Raleigh came close to resigning from the Board at the end of 1912 over Strindberg's *Miss Julie*, which, once again, he alone supported. The Reader had described it as 'a revolting play' and accused its anti-heroine of having 'socialistic tendencies', while another member of the Board, Lord Buckmaster, disliked the play as being 'painful and false to life'; Buckmaster was prepared to admit that 'women do stoop to servants now and again', but claimed that 'rarely, if they be knowledgeable people like Miss Julie, do they begin in the kitchen'. The Lord Chamberlain was adamant that if the censorship passed such a play, 'there would be good reason for saying such an institution was useless'. Raleigh, however, took a different view, suggesting that to reject such a significant work would be in effect to 'hand over . . . some very heavy ammunition to the enemies of the Censorship'. He tried to establish a principle:

> I can quite understand the attitude of those who do not want to see the play. It is a grim ordeal. But surely it would be a disaster for the English public to be forbidden to see the best dramatic work of the best and most honoured names among foreign men of letters.

Here was a play, argued the professor, which 'really succeeds in doing what its English imitations try to do, and fail', and therefore it deserved to be seen. So adamant was Raleigh that Buckmaster was prepared to alter his own position and concede for purely pragmatic and longer-term reasons; he recognised that the Board needed the continued presence of Professor Raleigh, in order to retain its credibility:

> If refused I greatly fear he will resign his place on the Advisory Board and thereby cause a loss to the Lord Chamberlain . . . In the circumstances,

> being extremely anxious to retain Raleigh, whose name adds greatly to . . .
> our authority, I am quite ready to withdraw my advice against production.

It seems highly probable that pressure must then have been put on Raleigh to change his view, for he backed down and contradicted his previous position, though without denying his admiration for Strindberg's play:

> I would not have made a fuss, if the play had not hit me hard. But I don't
> want to see it myself, and I admit it might be terribly mishandled on the
> stage . . . I have bought it, and put it on my shelf; which closes this chapter.

Instead, he rather touchingly asked that, though it was condemned, at least respect must be shown for the play: 'the committee should stand with uncovered heads at its funeral, and should not call it names'.[18] In the event, Raleigh would remain on the Board for almost ten years before eventually resigning because of a continuous and growing disquiet about decisions; he increasingly realised that his views carried no real weight, and that he himself was little more than a convenient cloak for the Lord Chamberlain to wear in particular company.

The Advisory Board, then, can be seen partially as a cynical invention by Dawson, designed less to influence the decisions of the Lord Chamberlain than to prop him up. When Dawson retired twenty years later, he proudly claimed it as his 'child', the birth of which had 'completely pulverised Asquith's Committee' in 1909, and, by doing so, saved the censorship.[19] Not everyone was deceived by the Board; Housman, for example, quickly dismissed it as 'merely a device to take in weak minds and bolster up a bad system' and described it as 'the self-preserving device of an autocrat in difficulties'.[20] Yet in fairness, the Board's first effective decision was a positive one. Previous translations of Sophocles's *Oedipus Rex* had been refused because of the theme of incest, and when a new version was submitted in November 1910, Redford viewed it as a deliberate attempt to court controversy; he recommended an automatic ban without even considering the particular text. However, the Advisory Board took a different view. Despite concern that 'many writers will not I fear scruple to shelter themselves behind this licence', they were in favour of allowing it as a play which could 'neither create nor gratify unclean and morbid excitement'; crucially, they were also confident it would 'make no appeal to the general public'. In a decision which—perhaps not coincidentally—further undermined the Reader's judgement, Sandhurst accepted their views.[21] For Redford, worse was to follow.

The main reason for the dissatisfaction of Althorp and Dawson with their Reader was what they saw as his tendency to usurp power, making decisions himself instead of passing on contentious plays, and too often provoking bad

publicity as a result of his misjudgements. In August 1911, without reference to anyone else, he licensed a sketch called *Invasion* for Glasgow. Not least because of the direct family connection between the British throne and the German leadership, the Lord Chamberlain continued to feel duty-bound to refuse anything deemed likely to suggest a coming confrontation, and although in this case the manager promised to change any lines which made reference to Germany or other friendly powers, Dawson realised the performance was still liable to provoke embarrassing and unwanted attention. He wrote to Althorp:

> Here is Redford again. It appears he has, off his own bat, sent the usual 'permission to perform' this play *Invasion* . . .
>
> I have no doubt the uniforms are German, probably the accent and general appearance of the invaders ditto. It is too bad. Redford will wreck us if we don't put a stop to him at once.

Dawson suggested the time had come to get rid of him: 'Either we should at once change the Reader of Plays, or let Redford down easy by dividing the work and starting a sort of syndicate of play readers'.[22] On Althorp's advice, Dawson suddenly advised Redford that it had been decided that there was too much work for him to do alone, and that two further readers were to be appointed to assist him; the carefully placed bombshell was that there would be no extra money and that Redford's salary—consisting entirely of the fees paid by managers for having their plays read—would henceforth be divided equally between all the readers. They knew that such an insult would be too great to accept; Redford recognised by now that Dawson was his enemy, and he immediately appealed to Althorp:

> I should never have contemplated my present mode of living and expenditure if I had entertained the least idea that I was liable at any moment to be deprived of the income I had reason to expect, and depend upon.

He was swiftly rebuffed, with a rather patronising reminder that none of them could assume their positions would last for ever, and confirmation that Dawson had written to him with the Lord Chamberlain's authority and approval; 'the present system is not working to my satisfaction', wrote Althorp. [23] Meanwhile, in planning to replace Redford, Dawson also saw an opportunity to establish greater control and centralisation, and he spoke to the King about the need in future for staff to be based within St James's Palace; this, he insisted, would enable the Lord Chamberlain to keep more of an eye on them, 'controlling their work more than hitherto has been done', and ending a system which had been 'subversive of the Lord Chamberlain's authority'. The Comptroller declared his determination to establish a new

system which would support the Lord Chamberlain and the monarch by helping to 'accentuate his authority and preserve the prerogative of the Crown'.[24] Dawson's next move was to provoke Redford by sending him a message requiring that in future a full précis should be written of every play submitted. Redford replied that it would be 'physically impossible for any man to make a précis of every stage play submitted for licence', a reply described by the Comptroller as 'an impertinence, which is made worse by the proof it is that he does not read the plays as he should'.[25]

Redford's days as Examiner of Plays were numbered, and another, further embarrassment for which he was held responsible soon occurred. In November 1911 Redford had turned down a script submitted by Laurence Cowan—a writer whom he described as having an 'evil reputation', and one worthy of contempt since his 'acquaintance with police courts was more extensive than his knowledge of playwriting'. Unfortunately for Redford, Cowan claimed that the script which had just been rejected had been extracted by him, wholesale and unchanged, from within a longer play which had already been licensed two years earlier. Redford refused to take any blame, insisting he had 'forgotten all about the wretched tissue of prurient rubbish', and could hardly be expected to remember everything he read:

> It should be understood that plays of this nature make no lasting impression on my mind, and are dismissed ten minutes after reading. If it were not so I should be much nearer softening of the brain, than I trust I am at the present moment.

However, this hardly explained the inconsistency of judgement. Worse followed for Althorp, when Cowan's solicitor issued a summons against him personally, for refusing to return the copies of his scripts: 'There is nothing in the Act . . . which gives your Lordship any power to retain plays licences for which are refused'. Even more embarrassingly, the press then got hold of a story that Althorp had claimed that, as a member of the King's household, he was 'immune from the ordinary processes of the law', and was refusing to accept the summons. Such publicity was hardly calculated to help the cause or the public profile of the censorship:

> ABOVE THE LAW
> The latest action of the Lord Chamberlain obliges renewed attention to the Censorship question. This remarkable functionary now announces to a wondering world that he is above the law . . . on the ground of his being an officer of the King's household. The magistrate, helpless before a musty act of parliament which the Department had raked up in support of its outrageous claim, had to revoke the summons . . . we are grateful that the Lord Chamberlain has been driven to declare this the uttermost absurdity

of the office which he wields, and we hope one result will be that the people over whom its tyranny is exercised will bestir themselves to set right quickly an intolerable anomaly.[26]

Althorp was forced to deny the claim, pinning the blame on a clerk who, he said, had merely been intending to inform the magistrate that, for constitutional reasons, 'a summons on the Lord Chamberlain could not be effected in the Royal Palace of St James's'. He had little option other than to declare himself happy to receive the summons and to co-operate, but by the time the case came to court in March 1912 Althorp was no longer Lord Chamberlain. His successor, Lord Sandhurst, was quickly cleared of the charge.

Redford, too, had gone by then. His letter of complaint to Althorp—rejecting the new conditions of service being imposed on him—had been deliberately taken by the Lord Chamberlain as a letter of resignation, even though it had not been specified as such by its writer. Redford felt he had been trapped, and treated in an underhand way:

> You accept my resignation before it was even intended. I now understand for the first time, the real meaning, and intention of the correspondence . . . this discovery leaves me no alternative, but to comply with your Lordship's wishes.

But Althorp's letter had gone further in insulting the Reader:

> You must pardon my saying that after this most serious mistake about Mr Cowan's play . . . I should have been compelled, however reluctantly, to have asked you to have handed in your resignation.
>
> It is not kindness to disguise the fact that I have been uneasy at the way in which the reading of plays has been conducted on several occasions.

Anticipating Redford's response, Althorp also wrote to Dawson: 'I can't recollect at this moment the several occasions when we had to haul Redford over the coals, but please tell me, so that I can be ready with chapter and verse'. Redford was mortified, and wrote bitterly to the Lord Chamberlain. He knew it was primarily Dawson who had done for him:

> I am afraid you must have been very much misinformed as to my part in the Cowan business. I venture to think you never could have penned the paragraph which has pained me far more than giving up my appointments, or losing my means of living.
>
> It is so unjust, and completely out of harmony with the rest of your letter, that it is difficult to believe that you could have written it except under some malign influence.

Redford realised that the attempt to force him out of his post could be traced back to its origins nearly three years earlier:

> Of course I see now, only too clearly that I should have resigned immediately after my interview with Sir Douglas Dawson on the 26th of June 1909. Everyone advised me to do so, and it was only my consideration for others that outweighed my own feelings, and judgement. I have had to suffer ever since, and feel a positive relief at the prospect of freedom from a position that has been made unbearable.

Receiving no satisfactory reply from the Lord Chamberlain's Office, Redford wrote next to the King to complain about his treatment, detailing his 'long years of individual energy, and exceptional exertions' which, he claimed, had successfully transformed the censorship into the 'high state of efficiency' in which it now functioned:

> It was mainly by the exercise of personal knowledge, individual influence, and business capabilities that I was able to organise and work up the system which had been very much neglected, maintaining its prestige, and increasing the income from fees.

Implausibly, he also claimed credit for the fact that the system had survived the enquiry of the Joint Select Committee: 'I have the best reasons for knowing that the evidence I gave before the Commission of 1909 did more than anything else to maintain the censorship and retain the office of Examiner of Plays'. However, Redford's main purpose in writing to the King was apparently to try to secure a better pension for himself; he explained that the £300 per annum which he had so far been granted was 'insufficient to meet engagements entered into' and, given that at the age of sixty-six he was unlikely to secure another position, would consign him to 'penury'. To address the monarch on such a subject was a breach of royal etiquette, and for all his inadequacies, it is hard not to read into the treatment of Redford an element of snobbery directed against a retired bank manager whose background was in neither the military nor the court élite. The King's private secretary, Francis Knollys, forwarded Redford's letter to the Lord Chamberlain, and Dawson's reply to Knollys was openly contemptuous of the Reader; he even accused him of having made false declarations of his income for tax purposes, and he was dismissive of Redford's self-congratulations:

> It is as you say, most improper addressing the King on such a subject and it is just what I would expect of him. I have long wished to get rid of him and used to tell Bobbie that he would wreck us if we did not . . . .
>
> His service, of which he speaks so much, has been in my opinion of the

very worst description and we are very lucky to have got rid of him.

On one occasion when he had put the Lord Chamberlain in the cart Sir William Byrne told me that had he been a Civil Servant in the Home Office he would have been dismissed offhand.[27]

In the event, Redford became the first President of the British Board of Film Censors, holding that post from 1911 until his death in 1916.

Before his resignation from the post of Examiner of Plays took effect, Redford had briefly overlapped with a new Examiner, Charles Brookfield, who in 1911 had been handpicked and invited by Althorp and Dawson without having even applied for the post. While Redford's departure was widely celebrated—not least by the 'serious' playwrights who had suffered at his hands—the appointment of Brookfield was like a red rag to bulls. According to the *Saturday Review*, it was

> a deliberate insult and a deliberate threat to every author, manager, and actor who is in touch with the cleaner, young theatre of today, and a deliberate affront to the Royal Commission . . . by putting into a position of trust a man avowedly prejudiced against anything of the nature of severe criticism of life, and avowedly lenient towards the aphrodisiac plays with which he himself is so conspicuously associated.

Brookfield was known partly as the author of *Dear Old Charlie*, a comedy which, as the article pointed out, had been referred to on several occasions during the 1909 enquiry as 'exactly the kind of play which the Censor, if he were to be of any real use at all as a guardian of public morals, would refuse to pass'.[28] Critics had compared the play to a Restoration comedy in 'its glorification of lying, adultery, mockery, and light-mindedness' and suggested that 'the man who would pass *Dear Old Charlie* would pass anything'.[29] The Bishop of Winchester declared that the author of such a play was not fit to hold office, and though Dawson was at pains to point out that Brookfield had merely adapted the play from a French original, and should therefore not take all the blame for its vulgarity, the Bishop still questioned his judgement in choosing to adapt such a play. Such responses surely exaggerate the immorality of Brookfield's text, for while it contains dim echoes of Restoration wit, it has none of the darkness of that period and is rather innocuously sentimental. It is true that the central character's imminent marriage is threatened by secret affairs he has had in the past, and that he has cuckolded several friends; but the audience are left in no doubt that Charlie both intends and is capable of fidelity within the marriage to which he has now made a commitment. The slight plot is built on his having falsely told his wife that he has never loved anyone previously, and on his comic attempts to hide his past life; when these are revealed, his wife forgives him.

Nor was it true that Brookfield was likely to 'pass anything'. Far from it. As Dawson told the Bishop of Winchester:

> I cannot help thinking that were you to see as I do, daily, the reports sent in by Mr Brookfield on the various plays submitted, his opinions and remarks upon them, you would be convinced that in appointing him the Lord Chamberlain has not committed that outrage on the community which some people seem to imagine.[30]

Brookfield's views on theatre were unabashedly old-fashioned and conservative. Writing shortly before his appointment was made public, he hailed the period between the mid-1860s and the mid-1880s, before the advent of the modern 'problem play', as a 'Golden Age', and one from which 'lustre appears to me to shine forth all the more effulgently from the contrast in dullness of the last twenty years, during which time I cannot see that our stage has produced anything new of which we are entitled to be artistically proud'. It was this disdain for progressive, intelligent drama—not least his well-publicised contempt for the plays of Ibsen—which so angered some contemporary writers. Brookfield had declared that he especially disapproved of

> the earnest young writer who, far from underestimating the importance of the drama, pays it the highest compliment he can imagine by regarding it as the heaven-sent trumpet through which he is to bray his views on social problems of his own projection . . . His only equipment for his self-imposed task is a morbid imagination—an ingenuity for conceiving horrors in the way of unusual sins, abnormal unions, inherited taints. And this is the kind of young man who inveighs against the discretionary powers of the Lord Chamberlain.

Such writers, believed Brookfield, took not only themselves but also the theatre (and probably life) much too seriously:

> I think the influence of the theatre either for good or evil is much over-rated. But if a young person *could* be harmed by seeing a play, I think it would more probably be by a sombre dissertation on the right of a wife to desert a degenerate husband—or one of the many kindred topics so dear to the New Dramatist—than by the frivolous burlesque of ill-assorted marriages, such as one finds in the old French vaudevilles . . . I don't myself think it is the business of a dramatist to preach or try to teach a lesson . . . But, assuming for a moment that I am wrong and that he really *has* a mission to trying to salve the souls of his audience, I think he is far more likely to achieve such an end by making vice ridiculous than by making it interesting.[31]

While the appointment of Brookfield was condemned by moralists who thought he would be too frivolous and too liberal in his recommendations, it was therefore equally disturbing for the supporters of 'serious' drama who believed he would be too blinkered and too intolerant to recommend intelligent plays. A long petition sent to the Lord Chamberlain on behalf of the Manchester Playgoers Club, for example, inveighed passionately against 'the complete disregard of the Modern Drama' which was evident in the appointment of someone whose own writings showed him to be 'avowedly prejudiced against the work of some of the best dramatic authors of our time'.[32] In a speech at the Savoy Theatre, Granville Barker told the audience at a private performance of Housman's *Pains and Penalties* that 'this action of the Lord Chamberlain's is but further proof, if further proof were needed, that he is hopelessly out of touch with the theatre over which he exercises despotic control and that the continuance of his legalised tyranny is inimical to the Drama's welfare and its good name'.[33] There were even some who wondered whether the appointment of Brookfield was actually 'a jest', intended by the Lord Chamberlain 'to cover the Censorship with ridicule, and ultimately to laugh it out of existence', and in Parliament, Robert Harcourt asked the government to annul the appointment.[34] Somewhat disingenuously, though not without justification, Dawson insisted that the role of the Examiner was being exaggerated for ulterior motives:

> If the true nature of the post were understood, and its entire absence of responsibility as to rejection of plays, it would be seen that all this fuss about the appointment is a waste of time. It is of course inaugurated by the small but very noisy clique whose object it is to abolish the censor.[35]

In the event, Brookfield held the post for only two years before he died in 1913. For most of that time he had worked alongside Redford's replacement, Ernest Bendall, an experienced drama critic chosen because he enjoyed the explicit support and trust of most theatre managers. Indeed, according to the Office, Bendall was 'a favourite with all connected with the theatrical profession, the authors included, of course excepting the extremists with whom no appointment would be popular'.[36] After Brookfield's death, Bendall was joined by George Street, who remained Reader for over twenty years, effectively taking sole responsibility after the death of Bendall in 1920.

As already indicated, pressure for the abolition of censorship was maintained through a series of questions in Parliament designed to expose the shortcomings of the system. In November 1911 the Home Office was asked if it intended to respond to the recommendations of the 1909 enquiry. Another question in the same week focused on the role of the Lord Chamberlain; it pointedly and provocatively queried 'whether means exist within his power

of checking the alleged tendency to the encouragement of plays with a low intellectual and moral character at the expense of drama opening up new vistas of thought in social, political, and ethical matters'.[37] Dawson warned the Home Office that such questions were 'part of an organised plan, by a very small but noisy section of the community to hunt the censor and bring about his abolition'; in urging Sir Edward Carson, an MP who also served on the Lord Chamberlain's Advisory Board, to speak in the debate, Dawson advised him:

> There are four or five authors whose plays have been rejected in the last ten years, and four or five MPs who are I hear disappointed authors. These eight or ten people are on the warpath to abolish the censor. They are very violent, noisy, and have prolific pens, and the ear of the Press . . . The General Public who are all for the retention of the censor are misled by their statements, which are usually mis-statements of fact.[38]

Serious playwrights, goaded by Brookfield's presence, also maintained their attack. In 1912 the banning of *The Secret Woman* by the well-established writer Eden Philpotts caused a huge outcry. Philpotts, who had previously had no serious brushes with the censor, wrote a long letter to the Lord Chamberlain about the insult which he felt had now been dealt him, and the implied criticism of his character; he had refused to compromise on a line in which someone watching in a mist sees two characters 'thicken into one'. As a later Lord Chamberlain put it when he rescinded the ban in 1922:

> Any one who has been in the mist on a hill and has seen two objects making towards each other and meeting can easily understand this phrase, and I do not for one moment accept the interpretation which appears to be put on it.[39]

As far as Dawson was concerned, however, Philpotts was guilty of intransigence and had allowed himself to be used as part of a deliberate strategy to challenge the Lord Chamberlain: 'He is, alas, prompted I presume by Granville Barker, who with Shaw and Zangwill seem to have banded themselves together to break down the system of a Censor, by refusing point blank to cut out one word'.[40] There were questions in Parliament about the banning, and a forceful letter signed by twenty-four writers was sent to *The Times*:

> Mr Philpotts is the victim today, but of course it may be any of us tomorrow . . . There is not perhaps another field so fine in the England of today for a man or woman of letters, but all the other literary fields are free. This one alone has a blind bull in it.
>
> We who sign this letter may be otherwise engaged; some of us may be

old and done, and no longer matter. Our chance has gone by. But there are men and women who are coming—are they also to be warned off? Can we strike no blow for the young?[41]

Dawson insisted that in order to win the war, the Office must unite to resist this assault:

> May I urge that it is most important we should adhere to our decision, or we risk grave consequences as regards the principle for which we work . . . The refusal to cut out a few words which alter nothing is only the outcome of an organised plan on the part of two or three authors to upset the whole system of the Censorship.[42]

His strategy prevailed.

Dawson may well have been right in identifying such a deliberate policy of refusal to negotiate. For any writer with the pride to take writing seriously, the assumption that nothing significant would be lost as a result of someone else cutting and altering their text would obviously be anathema. By contrast, the Comptroller was easily able in January 1912 to persuade the manager, Arthur Bourchier, that he should substantially rewrite a play he had submitted. Dawson flattered Bourchier by telling him that it was future productions by less talented companies which would be the problem: 'What is humorous and harmless played by actors of your calibre is turned into a very different story in the Provinces'. Dawson wrote to him as one gentleman to another: 'I know that I have only to ask for you to acquiesce, and in any case I can rely on your discretion in the matter'. When the matter had been satisfactorily and discreetly concluded, Dawson thanked him: 'I am glad we have been able to arrange matters. "Where there's a will, there's a way". What a pity some authors don't seem to appreciate the force of this little saying.'[43]

Elsewhere, the struggle continued. In June 1912 more than sixty playwrights were amongst the many signatures on a petition sent to the King; its intention was 'to call attention to the grave injury inflicted on the heart of the drama, and the obstacles placed in the way of its further development, by the present administration of the functions of the Censorship of Plays under the Department of your Majesty's Lord Chamberlain'. The petition criticised the formation of the Advisory Board, 'for the existence of which no warrant of any kind can be found in the laws of your Majesty's realm'; its rhetorical claims for the significance and potential of contemporary dramatists were certainly not under-stated:

> Your petitioners submit:
> That during recent years a development has taken place in the British

drama which is proving so fertile that among the subjects of your gracious Majesty there is now a group of native dramatists which, in point of literary culture, dramatic power, and intellectual quality, cannot be matched by any similar group since the days of the unparalleled outburst of drama in the time of Shakespeare. The production and publication of plays if permitted to attain their natural development will cause the British drama to become one of the chief artistic glories of your most gracious Majesty's reign. At present, however, this natural development is being hampered and checked by the methods and principles of administration exercised by officials of your Majesty's Household in the Department of the Lord Chamberlain—methods and principles which had they existed in the days of your Majesty's predecessor, Queen Elizabeth, would have deprived the English-speaking world of some of the chief glories of its literature.[44]

However, the mood in the country was by no means all one way. Even if the playwrights' petition had enjoyed any chance of influencing events, it was counter-balanced by a pre-emptive strike in the form of a letter to the King signed by theatre managers and others in the profession which reasserted the 'necessity for such a censorship as a protection to ourselves and to the public'.[45] Another petition in the same year, signed by editors and publishers, even went so far as to demand a Bill which would impose broader restrictions on 'pernicious and demoralising literature' and would require 'the police to be more vigilant and active in the matter of prosecutions'.[46] This actually represented an attempt to extend control into other literary forms, as the playwright and philosopher Israel Zangwill had previously predicted:

> I am convinced that the question at issue is not merely the abolition of the Censor of Plays, but the introduction of the Censor of Books and of other forms of repression until we are reduced to the level of our Russian ally.[47]

In 1913 Fowell and Palmer expressed similar fears that censorship in the theatre was set to become more rather than less extreme, and that this would be too easily accepted by the majority of people:

> it is quite possible that a movement might be set on foot sufficiently vigorous to secure a stricter censorship of plays, largely on account of the inertia of the majority of playgoers. We are, as a nation, easily trodden on; shamefully indifferent to attacks on our personal liberties.[48]

The authors claimed that though it was 'only in recent days that the censorship has seriously assumed the task of taking charge of the nation's morals', sex rather than religion or politics had now become 'the bogey of the English Censor'. The Lord Chamberlain, they suggested, was part of a national move-

ment 'to exorcise the demon of animality'. They sound distinctly Lawrentian in their attack:

> In no country has the satisfaction of the sensual instincts been degraded into the slimy, loathsome thing it has become in this England of ours . . . we have degraded it into a national obscenity, a thing of dark places, of shame and disease.[49]

Two years later, Lawrence's new novel *The Rainbow* would be seized and suppressed as unhealthy, diseased, decadent, and likely to undermine the British war effort.

Most 'serious' playwriting continued to be identified by its authors and supporters as being absolutely and consciously moral; in criticising certain aspects of society it was attacking hypocrisy and injustice, and it stood on its commitment to social responsibility. Writing in 1912, the critic H.W. Massingham re-asserted the importance of ethical values and principles to modern drama, and the irony of this being censored by Brookfield:

> An entirely fresh spirit is astir in it. And the main direction of this spirit is moral. Our new dramatists are nothing if not moralists . . . Shaw . . . Brieux . . . Tolstoy . . . The most sincere and vital work of these men may be and is turned off the English stage by the author of the worst piece now being played in London.

Massingham not only continued to rehearse the familiar argument that many of the plays which were currently receiving licences were in fact immoral, but also described the censorship as a 'palpably wicked institution', since 'like the licensed brothel, it sets the stamp of the State on evil in the name of the people's good'.[50] In a comparable analogy, Fowell and Palmer cast serious playwrights in the role of doctors, who represented the only real hope of purging a sick society:

> The issue would seem to be: are our social evils going to be made worse by talking of them? If you apply the same question to, say, smallpox, it becomes obviously absurd . . . a nation of people talking of smallpox would very quickly discover a remedy.[51]

In the years immediately before the First World War, a concerted campaign—supported by, among others, the Church, the Public Morality Council and the *Daily Mail*—was mounted to 'clean up' the music-halls, and the freedom of the halls to perform unlicensed plays was partially curtailed. In 1912 the London County Council ruled that sketches to be performed in halls under their jurisdiction required official approval, and the Lord

Chamberlain had little choice but to institute a similar policy for venues licensed by his authority. The Office was reluctant—for practical reasons if for no other—to enter fully into such a commitment, and was desperate to limit it; when, in April 1912, the manager of the Tivoli submitted the words of three songs with what he called 'spoken between' to see if they required licensing, the Lord Chamberlain consulted the Home Office:

> If we accept these as stage plays, all the songs and patter, where two artists are upon the stage, of which there are countless numbers, will have to be submitted to the Lord Chamberlain for licence.
> What do you advise?

The Home Office agreed that it was 'a very awkward situation' and that it would be 'inconvenient in the extreme' if the Lord Chamberlain had to deal with all such material; nevertheless, they thought it 'probable' that if a court were forced to rule, it would decide that such material did come within the Act governing stage plays; the Home Office therefore proposed a classic fudge, almost worthy of a Gilbertian satire:

> I think therefore your best answer . . . is to say that you cannot undertake to give an authoritative and binding opinion as to whether a given produc-tion is or is not a Stage Play, which can only be done by a Court of Law; but that if these three songs are produced as proposed *you will not deem it your duty to take any proceedings* [my emphasis].

If the manager in this instance were to press for a licence to guarantee his own security, the Home Office advised that the Lord Chamberlain should agree to issue one, 'stating that you did so as an exceptional case' and making clear that 'you certainly do not propose to undertake the licensing of ordinary music-hall songs'.[52]

In April 1913 Harcourt finally managed to institute a full Commons debate on censorship, based on his proposition that 'the attempt to maintain by means of antiquated legislation a legal distinction between a Theatre and a Music-hall, and to differentiate between productions called Stage Plays and other dramatic performances, is unworkable'. He described the current situ-ation as one of 'sheer chaos' in which 'rules are altered from day to day', where 'no one knows where they are', and a playwright 'is never able to know what he will be able to produce'. He drew attention to the fact that an unlicensed play could be performed in a theatre to members of anything calling itself a private society, and cited 'what is humorously called a private performance' of *Mrs Warren's Profession*, recently given in Glasgow at 'a frankly bogus club', at which each member could be accompanied by two non-members.[53] As with music-halls, the actual legal situation regarding such societies was completely

unclear. After a licence had been refused for *The Secret Woman* in 1912, two members of the Lord Chamberlain's staff had attended a private matinée at the Kingsway Theatre and reported that the performance had included the banned lines. A lengthy debate ensued, again involving the Home Office, over whether such a performance was really private or whether a prosecution should be brought against it as an unlicensed public performance; eventually the Lord Chamberlain and the Home Office concluded that 'the insufficiency of the existing law' made it, for the time being, too uncertain to risk going to court.

> As is well known, The Home Secretary has promised a bill based on recommendations of the Joint Committee which will remove the defects of the existing law and will enable such outrages as this on public decency to be dealt with.[54]

The Bill never came, but, as a temporary alternative, the Lord Chamberlain came up with a form of words designed to unsettle managers and discourage such performances, without risking a legal confrontation; theatre licensees were simply warned that without the protection of his licence they had no guarantee against a possible prosecution and 'could not be surprised if the criminal law is invoked against them' in respect of performances of unlicensed material judged by him to be coarse or indecent. One wonders whether those involved in theatre would have been surprised by anything which emerged from the Lord Chamberlain's Office.

Opposing Harcourt's motion in 1913 was Ellis Griffiths, the Under-Secretary of State for the Home Department; he proved to be inadequately briefed, and provoked mockery when he apparently assumed that plays at music-halls were licensed in the same way as in theatres. However, speaking, on his own admission, 'as a friend of capitalists', he defended the right of managers to be guaranteed safety from prosecution: 'Why should not the man who invests his capital in a production go to some authority before he incurs all this expenditure?'. He insisted there was no widespread wish for a change in the laws on theatre censorship, that most people in the theatre profession supported the present system, and that 'no legislation on this subject would be justified unless there was a general demand for it'.[55] Yet Harcourt's motion received considerable parliamentary support; censorship, said another MP, was 'a convenience for those who want to sail near the wind',[56] and the wrong people were being punished: 'Pernicious writers exercise their whole ingenuity to dodge the Censor . . . while . . . honest writers are harassed at every step', declared one speaker, and again it was argued that so far from having kept the stage clean, immorality was only too easy to find if you looked, not at plays which had been refused licences, but in the music-halls. [57]

In the autumn of 1913, the *Daily Mail* published a message from the Bishop of London, the chairman of the Public Morality Council:

> I am very glad indeed that *The Daily Mail* has taken up this matter of stage morality. It must be understood that it is in no spirit of prudery that I and the Bishop of Kensington have been acting. But we and all right-minded people in London are determined to prevent in a nominally Christian city a spirit which can only lead to the degradation of its inhabitants . . . Our single object is to secure a cleaner London, for the generation to which we belong as well as for the generation which is to follow us . . . not for one moment do we tolerate or intend to tolerate anything which is degrading.

The Bishop asserted the existence of an unalterable and 'absolute standard of purity', and dismissed the relativism which allowed individuals to question the right of the censor to make decisions on behalf of others. In a statement loaded with ideological assumptions, the Bishop insisted that to deny this truth was to descend 'far below . . . the morality of many wild tribes in Central Africa', and he reasserted the missionary evangelism of the Christian religion: 'If the world has no standard, the Church has a standard; and the Church is strong enough, if it wakes up, to enforce that standard on the world'. [58]

Yet in the middle of its campaign against the supposed sleaziness of music-hall entertainment, the *Daily Mail*, to its credit, published an alternative view. Under the headline 'The Mistakes Of Puritanism', the writer—'An Englishman'—paralleled the arguments of the modern moral reformers with those of Jeremy Collier in the Restoration period, and championed the music-halls precisely for their refusal to try to improve their audience. The Puritan, said the writer, may be motivated by the 'laudable ambition of doing good', but that in itself is a form of coercion and therefore anti-freedom:

> The music-hall cherishes an ambition, equally laudable, of amusing its clients. But, says the Puritan to the music-hall, it is not enough to amuse. You must endeavour . . . to do good also. You must strive to elevate those who find comfort in your plush-covered stalls . . . The music-hall is quite right. It is not its business to elevate or improve. It is the one institution in the country that has bravely declined the duty of moral suasion . . . we can hardly escape being elevated . . . On all sides we hear nothing but this hoarse cry of elevation. The demagogues . . . saints, prophets, or martyrs. They tell you in a dozen strident tones that it is their business to do you good . . . The 'intellectual' theatres echo the same cry.[59]

Clearly, this position can be viewed as an argument for theatre as escapism and distraction, inevitably serving the interests of the status quo and those in power; but arguably, the music-hall's irresponsibility could instead be seen as

a potentially more radical undermining of the establishment than the earnest zeal of the self-styled intellectual theatre. The attack by 'serious' playwrights on society's values and morals was above all a rational, an idealist and a reforming one, and from a modern perspective it is possible that some of the 'frivolous' material may actually appear to be more fundamentally subversive. In any case, the advent of the First World War was bound to shift theatre—and therefore the censorship of theatre—into new positions.

A Clique of Erotic Women

The First World War (Part One)

> The only thing that seems to ban a play under the censorship as we have
> seen it in recent years is that it treats a serious moral problem in a serious
> way . . . If we had had this censorship applied not only to the theatre, but
> to art and literature, much of the greatest work that has been produced in
> this country would have been impossible.[1]

In a sense, any play staged during or very close to a major war becomes *ipso
facto* a war play; however, while the succeeding chapter will concentrate on
plays in which the First World War was also the explicit subject of or background to the drama, I propose first to explore some of the activities of the
Lord Chamberlain and his Office in relation to plays submitted for licence
between 1913 and 1918 which were ostensibly focused elsewhere.

One major breakthrough for the highbrow movement on the eve of war was
the granting of a licence for *Ghosts*, which had hitherto been deemed impossible to allow. 'The case is an important one and the more expert help I can
get the better', wrote Lord Sandhurst in May 1914. Sandhurst was seeking a
way to license Ibsen's play without appearing to undermine his predecessors
who had refused it, and his recently appointed Reader, George Street, was
convinced that the time had come to compromise:

> The violence of the attacks in this country on *Ghosts* twenty years ago seems
> almost incredible now, but I think may be explained by the play's having been
> made a sort of battle ground for a general controversy about the theatre which
> drew its bitterness from the extremists in either camp, the rather preten-
> tiously intellectual in the one and the rather brutally Philistine in the other.

Street offered a broad hint to his superiors that, if only in order to avoid undermining the status of the Office, it was necessary to treat such a well-known
play as a special case:

The play is received with respect and with no attacks when it is performed in a technically private manner. Moreover its free performance everywhere else in Europe would make a refusal of a licence in London slightly ridiculous. It is an acknowledged masterpiece of the modern stage.

The members of the Advisory Board were by no means in agreement that *Ghosts* was a masterpiece. Even the supposed friend of modern thought and ally of contemporary playwrights, Professor Raleigh, appears to have supported the licence reluctantly and for rather perverse reasons:

> One of the hardships that I suffer from the refusal of licences to plays like this, or like Mr. Shaw's *Mrs Warren*, is that they get a fictitious and enduring importance. They become heroic . . . This enrages me. *Ghosts* is almost hysterical. Syphilis in real life is bad enough, but the behaviour of humanity under the scourge is a model of dignity compared with the gibberings of this play. If it had been acted twenty years ago it would be dead now . . . If Ibsen tells a lie, (and *Ghosts*, I think, is a lie) he ought not to be protected. Let him tell it right out, and pay for it.[2]

The main problem with licensing *Ghosts* was that sexual diseases were still held to be unmentionable on the stage; some two months earlier a licence had been refused for the serious and well-intentioned warning play *Damaged Goods*. 'Venereal disease seems to me a subject essentially unfit for description or discussion on the public stage', commented the Examiner in relation to Brieux's play, 'no matter how good the motive for such discussion may be'.[3] For the Lord Chamberlain and his advisers to feel justified in licensing Ibsen's play, it was necessary to practise an intellectual contortion: 'I doubt if people who knew nothing of syphilis would know any more after reading the play', one member of the Board helpfully reassured Sandhurst. But it was Sandhurst's own leap which was most remarkable, for those speeches in the play which referred to the unmentionable disease were dismissed by him as 'the wanderings of a semi-imbecile—the meaning of which I am unable to follow'; indeed, he somehow contrived to convince himself that there was no evidence that at any point the playwright had intended to allude to syphilis.[4] His determination to find a route which would enable him to license this particular play gives the lie to any notion that the identity of a playwright and the international reputation of a text had no relevance to decisions made by the Lord Chamberlain.

As we have already seen, at its simplest level sexual censorship often focused on the issue of the woman's body on stage. It has been argued that the fears and nightmares of war, and the savage destruction of male bodies, contributed to a desperate need for escapist entertainment and a lifting of the restrictions on displaying healthy and arousing female flesh on stage; that may

be so, but the Lord Chamberlain did not abandon his traditional role. In 1915 the Office recommended that the Bath police should check on the state of dress in a revue with the disturbing title of *Very Mixed Bathing*, which apparently involved a bathing machine and spectators looking into it.[5] In 1916 the censors worried about whether to ask the Manchester police to investigate what the notoriously provocative French singer and dancer Gaby Delys was actually doing while singing a song called 'Get out of Hot Water' in her bath, within a performance for which they had already licensed the script. For strategic reasons they seem to have decided to leave well alone:

> May I venture to suggest that this might be rather a dangerous procedure, for as you know the Manchester people are distinctly squeamish, and it would be rather awkward if, after you have licensed the piece, you received a report saying that the whole production was disgraceful, for of course it is impossible to know who would be sent. It might be an ordinary constable who, for the occasion might think himself very important.[6]

In a 1915 Cochrane revue in London called *More*, the Office complained about the low cut of an actress's dress and insisted in a letter to the manager that it be raised 'to remove the impression of indelicacy';[7] meanwhile, in another revue, also produced by Cochrane under the title *Odds and Ends*, the Office refused to allow an actress to try to fool an audience into thinking she was removing her clothes behind a screen, even though she subsequently appeared fully clothed. Interestingly, the breaking of the fourth wall was seen by the Office to exacerbate the problem: 'she advances down the stage to the footlights and pointing to her drawers she whispers to the audience "Will you please excuse me as I have to take ziz off" . . . the fact of her talking to the audience gives the impression that she is undressing for their delectation'.[8] As part of its campaign to improve the morality of music-halls, the *Daily Mail* had criticised the use of women of the wrong shape, attacking 'the scanty attire of the performers, whose physique in some cases was an artistic offence'.[9] The Lord Chamberlain, too, sometimes insisted on drawings of costumes being submitted to him, and took into account the shape of the performer. On one occasion, for example, he permitted an opaque black suit of tights to be worn by a woman playing Mephistophilis 'as the lady's figure is graceful and not too exuberant'; he suggested that 'on a person of more massive proportions it would be impossible'.[10]

The Lord Chamberlain's Office was not entirely dominated by issues of sexual morality, and the most pious and conventional scriptural plays were often as unacceptable as the most decadent. In 1911 Lady Gregory's *The Birth of Christ—a Nativity Play* had been refused a licence on the recommendation of the Archbishop of Canterbury. Again, it was the possible effect and impli-

cations of the performance rather than the intention or attitude of the writer which caused concern; the Archbishop was worried

> not because there is anything irreverent in the play: quite the contrary: it is conceived in a reverent spirit . . . it is perfectly free from anything that is wrong or harmful. But that is a very different thing from saying that its performance would be harmless. If once you admit the performance of this, how can you prevent other plays dealing with the same profoundly serious incident in the world's history?

He noted rather patronisingly that 'probably the play was written for simple village folk like those at Ammergau [sic], and that is totally different from its representation on the London stage'.[11] For a human actor to represent the Divine was tantamount to blasphemy—especially as it was impossible to dictate who would be playing the parts; as one critic, perhaps ironically, observed:

> We could not expect all the actors chosen to represent Christ to be gentlemen of fine sensibility, high character, and sincere feeling for art . . . it is hardly pleasant to think of the character in the hands of some members of the profession. One can imagine a feeling of revulsion if any of the actresses who have made history—in the Divorce Court—were chosen for the part of the Virgin Mary.[12]

In 1913 even the offstage voice of Christ speaking two lines from the Gospels was removed from one play, and the following year the Office only licensed *The Carpenter*—written by the Reverend A.J. Waldron—on condition that the central character was not allowed to look like Christ, and that the sign of the cross was not made on stage.[13] In a 1915 translation of Andreiev's *A Life of Man* for Edinburgh, the Office was anxious about how the supernatural Being in Grey might be interpreted; the Reader conveniently chose to assume that it stood for Fate, but noted that 'obviously it might be taken to stand for God and so offend the orthodox, especially as prayers are said by the man and his wife turning towards the corner where he stands'. However, the Reader was confident that such a 'long and dismal allegory' as Andreiev's was unlikely to attract anything but 'a special audience of so-called intellectuals', and could therefore be allowed. 'Had it any attraction for the general public I might hesitate', wrote Street. Even so, the licence was granted with the proviso that the prayers should not be addressed towards the mysterious figure.[14]

As already mentioned, according to the Lord Chamberlain's interpretation of the 1843 Act, a script could only be licensed once there was a specific venue planning to stage it, but once approved it could subsequently be performed

anywhere, unless there were special grounds for withdrawing the licence. This created a problem for some proposed productions supported by the Church. In 1915 a licence was sought for a dramatisation of the events of Christ's Passion to be performed in Westminster Cathedral Hall; the script was written, said the Reader, 'with dignified eloquence and in perfect Catholic taste', and, to avoid having an actor represent the Son of God, the events were described by eyewitnesses rather than depicted on stage. However, the Virgin Mary was to appear, and this, said the Reader, would normally render the play automatically 'unfit for stage representation'.[15] Sandhurst wanted to find a way to allow this production to take place without allowing the script to become freely available, and in recent years he had from time to time pursued a strategy which went largely unchallenged, even though it contradicted normal practice. Several religious plays had been licensed for specific venues only, with a catch-all endorsement attached, specifying that the play 'shall not be produced anywhere in Great Britain, except under conditions that shall be approved by the Lord Chamberlain'. In 1913, Tree, with the support of the Bishop of London, had persuaded Sandhurst to allow his production of *Joseph and his Brethren*, a play by Louis N. Parker, to be staged at His Majesty's Theatre. The title was discreetly changed to *The Deliverer*, and Tree agreed that the licence should apply only to his production, which then went ahead with the blessing of the Lord Chamberlain and the Archbishop of Canterbury. On a similar basis, the Lord Chamberlain allowed *Job* to be staged at Blackfriar's Hall, Norwich, and *Joseph in Canaan* at the Theatre Royal in Glasgow, each with the proviso that they could not be performed elsewhere without his permission.[16]

Would Sandhurst's tactic have stood up to a challenge in the courts? The opinion on which the Lord Chamberlain relied was offered in relation to the 1913 Covent Garden production of *Parsifal*; on that occasion, Sandhurst had sought the advice of the Home Office, which confirmed that the Lord Chamberlain retained the right to 'prohibit a subsequent performance at any other theatre in any circumstances which gave reasonable ground for apprehending that the performance would violate <u>decorum.</u> etc.'. It therefore followed that he could effectively prevent productions of a script he had previously licensed whenever he wished to do so. 'This would of course be a delicate task', warned the Home Office, 'but the Lord Chamberlain is used to dealing with delicate questions'.[17] It was certainly a useful tactic to have available, and one with potentially far-reaching and important political implications, as Dawson realised:

> I think it is an important addition to our reasons for licensing the play, as it obviates the chance of a low class theatre giving the play in objectionable surroundings. It practically keeps the performance in our hands, a powerful weapon.[18]

If handled with discretion, this opened up whole new possibilities for licensing all sorts of plays. Only the previous year, the Office had refused to license a risqué French comedy which Dawson himself claimed to have seen so many times in Paris that he almost knew the script off by heart, but which he did not think suitable for everyone to see:

> Were the Lord Chamberlain only licensing for one particular class and opinion I should say license it, and no doubt that class will complain if a licence is refused, but having in view the diversity of opinions we must consider, I am very doubtful what to say.[19]

The option of licensing the script only for a specific audience or venue might have changed the decision to turn it down.

Explicit political censorship took place on a variety of fronts, before as well as after war broke out. In 1912 a licence was refused for *The Coronation*, which had been presented privately by the International Suffrage Shop. 'The central theme running through the piece, appears to be the wholesale robbing of the Rich to benefit the Poor', wrote one of the Lord Chamberlain's staff, and Brookfield described it as 'an inflammatory pamphlet in dialogue form—anti-military, indeed anti-most things, except Univeral Suffrage'. Its politics certainly made it unsafe for the British stage:

> A most unpleasant play full of socialistic ideas and sentiments tending to class hatred. A dangerous play to produce at any time, and especially now when strikes and labour unrest are rampant everywhere, as it holds to ridicule all law and order.[20]

In 1913 a proposal by a character to blow up Buckingham Palace and the Houses of Parliament was cut from another play, and a whole genre of melo-dramas identifying Germany as an actual or potential military enemy had to be amended so that no specific nation was identified and hatred of the Germans not encouraged.[21] 'It is unfortunate that at this critical moment authors choose this risky subject, through short sightedness I feel sure', wrote Dawson in 1912. Among the sections removed from *At the Point of a Pistol* were the following lines, spoken by the villain:

> Faithfulness of the Fatherland is hatred of England. That axiom is branded deep in every German heart . . . it may mean the digging of England's grave and the death of all her schemes. Here's to that happy ending.[22]

Repeatedly the Office reminded managers that avoiding direct textual refer-ences to Germany was not in itself sufficient; they always insisted 'that in

designing the uniforms worn by the Foreign Officers care will be taken to avoid uniforms resembling those of any Foreign Powers'. The same principle applied to the names used for characters.

In 1912 a question was asked in Parliament about whether the Home Office had 'any power to check the use in plays or songs in theatres or music-halls of language of insult to princes and chiefs in India in alliance with the British Government'; the question had been provoked by newspaper reports of *The Sunshine Girl*, and Dawson insisted in response that lines had been interpolated in performance after the licence had been issued, and that these would be removed.[23] The need to avoid offending friendly rulers in India was a very serious issue for the government, since the possibility of exploiting the exotic appeal of the sub-continent to attract audiences was not missed by managers and promoters. At the end of 1913 an enormous row took place over *Romance of India*, a spectacular pageant which was scheduled for presentation at Earl's Court on Boxing Day. The entertainment was to feature not only 'carefully trained native performers, elephants, camels, horses, and a Bengal tiger', but also a staging of traditional Indian religious ceremonies. The India Office expressed concern about the political impact of such an event on Indian sensitivities, especially after a check by the Metropolitan police revealed that no Indians were connected with the proposed production, and that the Hindustani Spectacle Syndicate Limited, which had hired the hall for the occasion, was, despite its name, 'composed entirely of English gentlemen'. According to a preview of the event published in one newspaper:

> The key note of the scenario is the triumph of 'conquest', gradually translated into the beneficent influence of British Rule over the Evil Genius of India, as represented by the crueller forms of native religious observance, by barbarous customs, fanaticism, and military revolt.

Such publicity attracted much attention, and the India Office and the Lord Chamberlain received numerous letters and petitions complaining that the performance would not only be 'most painful to Hindus and other Indian residents within the United Kingdom' but was 'calculated to create ill feeling among his most gracious Majesty the King's loyal subjects in India'. After discussions with the India Office and others, the licence was refused by the Lord Chamberlain on the grounds that

> The scenario contained a series of scenes in which Indian Nations and Indian Religion were constantly shown as barbarous and degraded and were overcome by the enlightened western forces and religion, and that this would greatly offend not only a large and important community, living in London, but also their friends in India, with whom they are in constant and intimate correspondence.[24]

It would be reassuring to think that such a response might have reflected a degree of cultural sensitivity, but in fact it was entirely based on political and strategic imperatives, and served British interests. At exactly the same time as *Romance of India* was being discussed, the Lord Chamberlain received via the Foreign Office a letter of complaint from the Chinese Embassy about a melodrama set in Hong Kong which was being performed at the Strand Theatre. The letter argued that *Mr Wu* 'grossly misrepresents Chinese practice and opinion' and was 'calculated injuriously to effect the good relations and mutual esteem now happily attaining between English and Chinese both in London and the East'. The play showed a world of sex, drugs, poison and revenge, and it was the likelihood of audiences accepting the stereotypes as authentic which worried the Embassy, which complained after receiving protests from the Chinese Student Union in London. The Embassy itemised these complaints and the potential danger of such stereotyping:

1) The act of revenge is not only non-Chinese but also un-Chinese.

2) It may lead the English people to think that the Chinese students now in their midst may turn out so many 'Mr. Wus'.

3) Just as the English people are beginning to befriend us this play will seriously dampen their ardour.

4) The play may therefore prejudice the present friendly relationship existing between the English and Chinese in this country.

5) The play also contains this moral: don't teach the Chinese, for if you add Western education to his natural oriental cunning you make him a veritable demon.

Citing both *The Mikado*, from which a licence had been famously withdrawn for fear of offending the Japanese, and *Romance of India*, the Embassy requested that the licence be cancelled. However, in this case the Foreign Office informed the Lord Chamberlain that 'no political considerations are involved', and he therefore chose not to interfere with the performance. The implication is clear: there was no need to be as sensitive to the feelings of the Chinese as towards races still living as subjects within the Empire, because there were fewer political ramifications to be concerned about.[25]

Frequently, sex and politics were interwoven. In 1913 a licence was witheld from *The Tsaritza*, a Hungarian play already performed in much of Europe, which dramatised the life of the Empress Catherine of Russia. It was, said the Reader, 'a vigorous if crude illustration of the temperament and moods of an imperious Queen who in her middle age periodically becomes a slave to her sexual passions'. Even while recommending the play for licence, he acknowledged that it might antagonise Russians as 'a rather bald travesty . . . of their Court in the 18th Century'. The Lord Chamberlain was persuaded not to grant a licence by the direct intervention of the Russian Embassy:

> Please do not forget that the Empress Catherine, whatever her morals may
> have been, is still considered by the whole country as the greatest Sovereign
> Russia has ever had with Peter the Great . . . I feel strongly that a play like
> this licensed by Lord Chamberlain, in the present political conjuncture,
> would be resented, I fear gravely.

It is hard to know exactly what was being implied by the phrase 'in the present
political conjuncture', but as diplomatic discussions and a need to secure solid
alliances must have been an important part of the preparations for the increasingly inevitable European conflagration, it was certainly not a time to risk
upsetting the Russian Court:

> The presence in London of the Empress Marie, renders the matter
> still more delicate . . . The production is sure to offend seriously all
> Russian circles here and in Russia as well. I should be extremely sorry
> for it.[26]

Meanwhile, the Embassy, clearly familiar with practical strategies of censorship, even helpfully suggested how the script might be changed: 'Could it not
be more Oriental, some Chinese or other country?'

Surprisingly, the Lord Chamberlain was less amenable to Russian reservations about Bernard Shaw's *Catherine the Great*, and a licence was issued
in the same year as the one in which *The Tsaritza* was turned down. Dawson
again sent a copy of the script to the Russian Embassy, inviting comments:
'You will know as well as I do, what Mr. Shaw is', wrote the Comptroller,
'How he turns everything into ridicule'. Again, the Ambassador opposed the
performance: 'I am afraid the moment is not well chosen for the production
of the play—in many ways. As you say, I know what the author is.' But on
this occasion, Sandhurst—perhaps wishing to avoid yet another run-in with
one of his chief tormentors—accepted his Reader's advice that Shaw's work
was in effect a pantomime which could not be taken seriously, and which
therefore cast no aspersions on the moral character of its central figure. It was,
he ruled, a 'pseudo-historical extravaganza' rather than 'a serious drama'.[27]
Two years later, however, a licence was withheld from another play about
Catherine which showed her being attracted to a handsome young servant
and inviting him to share a pancake breakfast with her. Ironically, Miles
Malleson's *A Thumbnail Sketch of Catherine the Great of Russia* was intended
for performance at a garden party organised by Lady Paget, as part of the
celebrations of Russia Day and in support of an important wartime ally;
Bendall recommended the play for licensing:

> It is obvious that the young man is destined for the imperial embraces, but
> nothing in that way is done beyond her stroking his arm . . . and his kissing

her hand. Given Catherine's life, I think it would be quite absurd for anyone to object to this very mild intimation of his amatory element.

But Sandhurst sent the script to the Russian Embassy, and it again insisted that 'any equivocal reference to Catherine the II's faiblesses' must be avoided; its concern and tact over a single and celebratory matinée performance is remarkable, but it was the nature of the audience likely to be invited to. Lady Paget's garden party which was part of the problem:

> If the play had to be performed in the usual way before the usual public, I could and would have said nothing. But where I cannot agree with Mr Street's opinion is when he writes 'especially as the play is to be done at Lady Paget's matinee'.
>
> To tell you frankly the truth, I think that is the very occasion, on which any equivocal reference to Catherine the II's faiblesses ought to have been avoided. I do not wish to create any difficulties, and especially to put any obstacles to Lady Paget's most friendly and energetic endeavours for the Russia day . . . [but] I think I ought to put the condition that every effort must be made that the 'acting' should mitigate the impression of a love affair . . . She should remain the Empress throughout, whether the young man admires her as a woman or not, and every word not absolutely necessary for the play omitted or corrected.
>
> I think it can be done and I believe it of the utmost importance. Just think of the audience.

Before meeting Lady Paget and the playwright to discuss the changes, and having ensured they were 'willing to cut out everything I object to', Dawson wrote to the Embassy again to check whether it would be sufficient 'to make a clean sweep from the play of all allusion or hint of tendresses and amour on the part of the Empress'. The Ambassador, however, wished to go further than this, having all explicit references to Catherine removed, the young man transformed into an old one, and the pancake breakfast cancelled. In the event, the application for a licence was withdrawn, and the garden party presumably went ahead without its dramatic interlude.[28]

One of the most talked about social and political issues in the years before 1914 was the so-called white slave trade. In 1912 the government finally passed controversial legislation to try to address the issue, introducing measures which controversially included the possible use of flogging against both men and women. The subject was too potentially melodramatic for playwrights to avoid it, and though plays were bound to be ostensibly unambiguous in reviling the exploiters and pitying the female victims, box office considerations meant the action was likely to concentrate on sometimes

graphic depictions of the very aspects that were supposedly being condemned. *How Girls Are Brought to Ruin*, *The Sins of London*, (both 1910), *White Slave Trade* (1912) and *The White Slave Traffic* (1913) were amongst the plays licensed for performance which brought considerable criticism of the Lord Chamberlain, even though they were all absolutely and explicitly moral in their official messages and conclusions. As one Reader commented: 'I think it is a pity that managers should try to make capital out of such themes and titles as The White Slave Traffic, but it is a question of taste rather than of morals'.[29] On the other hand, a licence was refused for *Champions of Morality*, an attack on the moral hypocrisy of the leading members of a Vigilance Society, who are revealed to have been secretly visiting a courtesan; the fact that the setting was Germany did not alleviate the possibility that 'such trash' might cause embarrassment and 'have a harmful influence if played before the Public'.[30] In 1913 a licence was also refused for a white slave traffic play, *Abode of Love*, in which a clergyman is shown buying an innocent young woman from her mother, who wishes to see her ruined. 'This violent and foolish piece is so overdone in its attack upon vice that it would be likely to do much more harm than good', argued the Reader; he complained that, whatever its professed message, the play would merely produce 'disgust instead of rousing the righteous indignation at which it presumably aims'. One adviser commented, 'I cannot understand how any sane person can have written such trash', and it was clearly not a world into which Sir Douglas Dawson wished to delve: 'It makes one blush to think a gentleman should be called upon to license such filthy rubbish', he complained.[31] A similar play in 1914 was *Where Are You Going To*, which was initially recommended but subsequently turned down. The Reader described it as a 'glorified penny-dreadful', and 'an earnest but wildly-directed attack upon the methods and possibilities of the White Slave Traffic'; it was, he said, 'not less painful than well-meaning, especially in its highly imaginative sketch of the lurid proceedings in a procuress's prison'. Though he declared his own distaste for such plays, the Reader felt it should be licensed, 'seeing that in its ladylike and exaggerated way it is sincerely meant as a warning exposure of a real, if rare, social evil'. However, with the Advisory Board split, Lord Sandhurst ruled against it.[32]

Of course, none of these action-packed melodramas engaged very seriously with the economics or politics of prostitution in the way *Mrs Warren's Profession* attempted to do. Shaw's play had been banned from public performance since the 1890s, but it regularly resurfaced in the Lord Chamberlain's Office, and Shaw continued to make perhaps extravagant claims for the significance of its suppression:

> How badly the play was needed was shown by the hysterical unpreparedness of the public for the White Slave agitation, and the useless and savage

legislation which followed . . . Had *Mrs Warren's Profession* been allowed to take its proper place on the stage when I wrote it, that blunder and all those hysterics might have been averted.

In 1916 Plymouth Repertory Theatre tactfully applauded the generally 'enlightened censorship' of the current regime before suggesting that now was the time to allow Shaw's play to be performed:

> it is essentially a play for women, to whom it conveys a great moral lesson, and as now, with the bulk of our manhood on war service, the theatre is largely patronised by women, this seems to me an appropriate time to ask for further consideration of a play that is sincere in purpose and moral in tendency.

However, the Lord Chamberlain's Office refused to acknowledge that there was any reason for reconsidering the play, reasserting the conviction that 'such a discussion and such a character are not fitted for casual audiences of various ages'. It admitted the importance of the issue dealt with, and that its evils might properly be aired at length in the press, but continued to maintain that 'the theatre is not the place, except before an audience well knowing what it is to expect and of a special kind, as is the Stage Society'. Irony and paradox rarely recommended themselves to the guardians of theatre, who believed they were protecting the minds of people who could only take what they saw at face value: 'The more cleverly Mrs Warren defends prostitution the more objectionable does it seem to me that she should be allowed to do so on the public stage'.

Shaw now tried a different tactic, querying why the censorship was still agitated about a play whose moment had passed; in his letter to the Lord Chamberlain's Office he posed, instead, a question of principle:

> The statement that you do not see a way to alter a decision that you never made is only a form: Heaven forbid I should hold you responsible for the things that were done by your predecessors in those dark days! . . . What I do want to know is whether there is any provision in the office rules for reconsidering a decision which was arrived at in view of the state of public opinion on matters subject to change . . . anything like a rule of once stopped always stopped would be outrageous.

The Office had declined to reconsider the play when it had been resubmitted in 1916, and had consequently returned the money which the would-be manager had sent as the requisite fee for having the play re-read. Openly revelling in his use of *Mrs Warren's Profession* as 'a stick to beat your department with', Shaw mocked this decision:

> I contend that your Reader should have read the play again; pocketed my
> two guineas; and, if he felt still in the eighteen-nineties about it, reported
> against licensing it exactly as if it were a new play . . . I of course do not
> contend that it would be reasonable to send the play in every month—
> though for the life of me I do not see why the Reader should object at two
> guineas a time—but a reasonable interval has passed in this instance since
> the last attempt.

When the Lord Chamberlain replied that he had no need to re-read the play
before making his decision, Shaw—modest as always in his comparison—
commented that he himself needed to re-read biblical texts on a regular basis
because 'though the New Testament will not change, my perception of it will
change'. Few other playwrights who suffered at the hands of the censorship
managed to give the appearance of enjoying their fights quite so much. Shaw
even offered to guarantee paying an annual fee if the Office would accept his
contention that *Mrs Warren's Profession* 'should be read carefully through
every year by your whole staff, including Col. Sir Douglas Dawson'.
Abandoning his tactic of suggesting the play no longer mattered, he reverted
to insisting on its continuing topicality and relevance: 'Mrs Warren is having
the time of her life with our men in training and on leave from the front'.

Mrs Warren's Profession was re-submitted several times in 1917, once
accompanied by a five-page petition generally asserting the educational function of theatre and specifically supporting the licensing of 'a dramatic work
of acknowledged excellence' which was addressing an issue 'of extreme
gravity'. In a letter apparently written to his prospective manager, but which
was doubtless intended to reach Lord Sandhurst's attention, Shaw dared to
claim that vested interests would probably continue to prevent it:

> I greatly doubt whether it will ever be licensed in this country, because it
> has against it the huge commercial interests in prostitution, which are not
> exposed by . . . plays which deal with sexual vice in a frankly pornographic
> manner, and are licensed without demur . . . whereas these latter act as
> aphrodisiacs and actually stimulate the trade in women, my play makes it
> extremely repulsive . . . I think a really good performance of *Mrs Warren's
> Profession* would keep its audience out of the hands of the women of the
> street for a fortnight at least. And that is precisely why it encounters an
> opposition unknown in the case of plays which stimulate the sex illusion.

In his attempt to needle and perhaps shame the Lord Chamberlain, Shaw's
letter went so far as to imply that the censors were effectively in league with
the brothel owners:

> The Lord Chamberlain's Office . . . will allow the prostitute and the

procuress and the brothel to supply the sensations of a hundred melodramas; but it will always ward off the one touch at which the attraction
of these things withers . . . you must find some piece that will not threaten
the profits of the Euston and Marleybone Roads.

Dawson was finally provoked:

> I consider the statements marked in Mr Shaw's circular to be not only false
> but libellous. He accuses the Department of working with the brothel
> manager, whose trade is so prosperous it is too powerful and presumably
> bribes too high to be restrained.

He declared that he was 'more than ever against a licence being granted this
play' and that 'all Mr B. Shaw's abuse of our Department won't alter that fact
or my opinion'. Edwin Heys—the manager to whom Shaw had sent the
letter—wrote again to the Lord Chamberlain in November 1917, claiming
widespread support from 'a great weight of influential authority' for a licence
being granted. This included, he said, '3 Bishops, 12 important Army
Officers, 37 Medical Officers and Physicians, 44 Privy counsellors and MPs.,
Most of the leading men and women in the Theatrical profession, Practically
every living author of note, and Many other distinguished men and women'.
Again, the argument was that the play might help to cure a sickness. The Lord
Chamberlain's Reader, however, still found himself unable to 'imagine any
preventive or curative result likely to be effected by this particularly nasty
medicine', and confirmed that 'the dose is accordingly not recommended for
licence'.[33]

One of the reasons why advocates of *Mrs Warren's Profession* had felt they
enjoyed a stronger than usual chance of success in the autumn of 1917 was
the controversial decision earlier that year to license a translation of Brieux's
Damaged Goods, a play which had previously been turned down. The entire
focus of Brieux's drama is on the danger and hideous effects of syphilis, and
it was eventually licensed—in the face of some bitter opposition—precisely
because the government was persuaded to accept the argument that the play
might help to educate and modify people's behaviour. However, the Lord
Chamberlain's Office was determined to prevent this decision from opening
any floodgates:

> The recent removal of the 'ban' from *Damaged Goods* affords in my
> opinion no reason for its removal from *Mrs Warren's Profession*. The
> former Play, disagreeable though it is, was reluctantly licensed on the
> grounds of its possible usefulness for 'propaganda'. The latter's offen-
> siveness is not redeemed by any kindred 'propaganda' . . . It teaches, so
> far as I can see, no valuable lesson.[34]

Damaged Goods had been permitted because its lesson had become an urgent one that needed to be communicated and because, as the Archbishop of Canterbury put it, 'its production, <u>and this is most important</u>, was supported by a weighty body of opinion on the part of men entitled to be listened to'.[35] However, problems about how to draw the line between exploitation and useful propaganda were bound to follow, and emerged in August 1917 when the Lord Chamberlain reluctantly approved a licence for a play called *Tainted Woman*:

> This is one of the many plays of its offensive if well meaning kind, for which a licence is now sought as a matter of course on the strength of successful appeal on behalf of *Damaged Goods* by distinguished clerical and medical authorities . . . its subject, which alone would formerly have barred it from our stage, is the havoc, physical as well as moral, wrought by what its author calls syphylys . . .
>
> To my taste *The Tainted Woman* . . . is too disagreeable . . . for presentation . . . as propaganda, however, it may—though I doubt it—do good by warning playgoers not to run the risk of catching 'syphylys' so it must be recommended for licence.[36]

Similarly, in 1918 the Office passed a sketch avowedly designed by its author to 'make Parents realise the deadly danger of the greatest Social Evil'. The focus of *Her Escape* was a young girl about to marry a dissolute roué, whose mother keeps her in complete ignorance of the dangers by refusing to answer her questions, and telling her she is 'unladylike' for asking them; the daughter is saved only by a warning from her fiancé's mistress. The Reader felt bound to recommend licensing the script 'on the "propaganda" theory, which presumably holds good for music-halls as well as theatres'.[37]

On the other hand, when Frederick Bowman submitted an old-fashioned blood-and-thunder melodrama about syphilis in August 1917 under the title *Is Vice Worthwhile?*, the Lord Chamberlain turned it down. Bowman's publicity described him as the writer of 'the Sensational Sketch *Enslaved By A Mormon*' and of 'the enthralling Drama *The Confession*', which featured 'merciless flogging of the unfortunate Ethel'. He also announced himself as the 'Winner of THE CINEMA CERTIFICATE OF MERIT for novel publicity methods'. Bowman claimed that his latest play dealt 'in trenchant style with the WRECKAGE OF SOULS through ignorance' and that it was equally well-intentioned as those which had been recently allowed; the Office, not unreasonably, suspected Bowman of trying to cash in and exploit the situation. 'I suspect the author of having a screw loose', wrote Sir Douglas Dawson. But Bowman was not easily put off, and the example is an interesting one because it exposes the perennial difficulty faced by even relatively liberal censors of how to draw a legitimate and defensible distinction between

the well-intentioned and the exploitative. Such difficulties are perhaps especially acute where the exploitative denies itself and demands to be treated as something else. Bowman wrote a lengthy and passionate letter to the Office expressing shock that his play had been turned down, and feigning incomprehension and distress: 'Ever since I saw *Damaged Goods* I have been working day and night on this script, and it is awful to think that all that labour and anxiety goes for nothing', he lamented, and he challenged the Office directly:

> As I now write I have a copy of *Damaged Goods* and *Ghosts* by my side, and though I have searched my own script with the utmost care, I can discover no passage or episode which is more out-spoken or more likely to give offence . . . If you can point out any such passage or incident, I am willing . . . to at once delete it . . . the plot has merely been adapted to meet the present-day tendency of the public to tackle moral questions in a straightforward and plain-spoken way. The moral is good—that vice brings ruin, and that girls should not barter their souls for money, and whereas everyone who is evil in the play comes to destruction, the ones who are virtuous rise to happiness.
>
> If this play incited to vice, I could understand the script being banned, but it does NOT. And if all stage discussions of moral problems must be taboo, the licensing of so many other dramas like *Damaged Goods*, *Ghosts* and *The Blindness of Virtue* must naturally make authors, as a body, wonder why one script is banned while another on a similar subject gets passed.

Bowman offered to change the title or to cut any lines deemed offensive by the Lord Chamberlain. He was even willing to 'delete the comedy element, and run the play as a solid denunciation of the social evil on the same lines as *Damaged Goods*', if humour was thought inappropriate to such a serious issue: 'In short, I don't care what you ask me to do as long as you give the script a fair chance'. Audaciously, Bowman claimed to have been 'profoundly impressed by the value of the moral lesson' in Brieux's play. He then professed that his own mission was to make the same message more widely accessible to those who would never have gone to see such a highbrow performance: 'it is in an effort to reach a section of the community to whom an entirely "talky" play on the subject would NOT appeal that I have written this melodrama'. The Lord Chamberlain, however, refused to negotiate.[38]

After the licensing of *Damaged Goods*, it was unclear whether automatic taboos could still be sustained in relation to other moral and sexual questions simply on account of their subject matter. In July 1918 *His Childless Wife* was submitted, a play intended, in Street's words, 'to denounce the evil of women refusing motherhood and escaping it by illegal operations'. Given the seriousness of this play and the fact that 'the evil it attacks certainly exists', Street recommended licensing it; he noted that 'since the production of *Damaged*

Goods and other Plays dealing plainly with venereal disease I think it would be inconsistent to refuse this'. Some of the Advisory Board agreed that 'after *Damaged Goods* it would appear that no subject is to be considered in future unfit for stage treatment', and all acknowledged *His Childless Wife* to be a serious and sincere play. Yet there were reservations about opening up the debate on abortion, and the possibility was raised that perhaps the play could be licensed 'for adults only'. On Dawson's advice, and because 'the question herein raised is so important, and concerns so intimately the principle on which we work in future', Sandhurst called a special meeting of the Board. Predictably, it was Dawson who was most strongly against any loosening of policy, and he made an impassioned declaration of his position:

> This play is written seriously and with dignity. There is not an atom of indecency about it. But, to my mind, we take a very grave responsibility on ourselves in considering whether we should advise the Lord Chamberlain to license it for public production . . . it resolves itself into a question of whether we are now going to alter our policy entirely, and license plays which, under the guise of propaganda deal with procuring abortion, venereal disease, and such like horrors. Personally I am against it, and shall always be so, otherwise why have a censor. His duties to my mind extend far beyond suppressing indecency. It was with this idea that clean minded people in Paris asked for a Censor. The trouble is that yielding to the persuasion of high placed eclesiastics [*sic*] and a certain clique of erotic women we have already permitted the principle, and by so doing have tied our hands. If we license this play what argument remains against licensing *Waste*.

Dawson's logic prevailed, and the licence was refused.[39]

If *His Childless Wife* had been intended as a warning against mothers resisting their supposedly natural duty to bear as many children as possible, a couple of months later the Office considered another play by Brieux which took a very different stance on the same issue. *Maternity* focused on a woman's grievance at what she considers the excessive demands of her husband to continue having children. In Mrs Shaw's translation, *Maternity* had been rejected for licence in 1907, and she had claimed the refusal was accompanied by the instruction—presumably Redford's—to 'inform whoever is responsible for this play that it will <u>never</u> be licensed in England'. In his report on the play, written more than a decade later in September 1918, Street described the play as 'far less revolting' than *Damaged Goods*; 'On the other hand', he continued, 'I do not think this play can be justified as useful propaganda'. Indeed, it could even have been interpreted as a defence of the principle of abortion—in spite of the fact that the young woman who chooses this route dies. Again, the real battle in the Lord Chamberlain's Office was

about whether or not, in the new post-war world, the time had come to relax some of the rigorous rules and principles of a previous era, and to permit significant social debates of the day to find a voice on the stage. Buckmaster was in favour of doing so:

> I find it difficult to know why this play should not be produced . . . The artificial limitation of families is one of the familiar subjects at meetings and conferences of all classes of people who discuss social welfare and their proceedings are reported without any attempt at evasion in the daily press . . . it cannot honestly shock anyone nor can it make vice familiar or lower the standard of conduct or morals.

But Dawson rarely, if ever, accepted the need for change or the arrival of a new era; in one of the fullest statements of the principles governing his views about theatre and audiences, he took up a much more hard-line stance:

> I am wholly in favour of elasticity in our methods, each case to be judged on its merits, no red tape and hard and fast refusals. But, as in every other problem, a dividing line on which the policy is based seems to me to be necessary.
>
> Thus to my mind our policy is broadly speaking to taboo indecency, blasphemy, and lèse majesté.
>
> Bernard Shaw may say what he likes with regard to the stage license to portray any and every subject which are universally known to be part of the daily life. There are certain subjects which in my opinion should only be dealt with by the ecclesiastic or the medical profession. I refer to subjects on which we literally turn the key. In a civilised world we do not discuss openly the details of sexual intercourse, of visits to the W.C., and I would add to these such subjects as venereal disease and procuring abortion.
>
> I believe still in keeping such subjects for discussion in privacy with the priest or the doctor. I do not believe in the value of the stage for propaganda purposes on such subjects. The class attracted by such plays is not that which it is wished to convince, morbid and erotic natures such as those who advocate the production of such plays are drawn by them, natures that have already eaten the apple; but not those to whom the lesson would be of value.

As always, Dawson was confident that his view would be widely accepted— at least by people who mattered:

> I believe that if a plebiscite could be taken of the educated public, the proportion in favour of production of such plays on the stage would be

infinitesimal, while the enormous majority would say what use to us is a Censor who allows such uncleanliness to be discussed in public.

In the face of such conflicting views on *Maternity*, Sandhurst consulted the Archbishop of Canterbury. The Archbishop accepted that Brieux's play was not 'coarse, or demoralising in tendency' and that since the character who undergoes an illegal operation to terminate her pregnancy dies, the play could hardly be seen as 'encouraging resort to abortionists'; yet in a development which seemed to mark a further stage on the route which censorship so often follows, he declared himself against the play because of the absence of positive propaganda: 'I fail to see what good purpose, social or moral or intellectual or educational its production in England at present would promote', wrote the Archbishop. 'What is the <u>object</u> or the <u>moral</u> of this play?' In other words, the control of propaganda in the theatre would not necessarily limit itself to rejecting something for teaching 'bad' lessons but must also take into account the failure to teach good ones. The Archbishop was concerned about the possible effect of Brieux's play in a contemporary context:

> What it does is to press the 'lesson', such as it is, that the production of many children is cruel to the wife, selfish on the husband's part and, in present economic conditions incapable of working well except among rich people. All these allegations are open to challenge and there is no real argument. But, anyhow, is that the lesson which wise people will say England needs to learn just now? Surely not.

Sandhurst had previously seemed inclined to favour *Maternity*, but he now accepted the Archbishop's advice and refused to license it. Before 1914 the censors had at least paid lip-service to the principle of keeping explicit propaganda out of the theatre. The First World War gave propaganda a good name.[40]

In 1912 playwrights had complained to the King that since the 1909 enquiry the Lord Chamberlain had 'exercised his powers of refusing to license plays far more oppressively than before'. Six years later, the censorship was perhaps becoming more heavy-handed, and this was reflected in the resignation from the Advisory Board of Professor Walter Raleigh. In May 1918 Raleigh informed Sandhurst that he could 'not see what is the use of men of letters on the Committee', and the Lord Chamberlain made no attempt at all to dissuade him from resigning: 'I have felt for some time that the duties were irksome to you', he wrote. In response to Raleigh's questioning of why witty plays should be banned 'when so much trash is daily acted', he rehearsed a familiar argument which hardly boded well for serious playwrights:

I sometimes think that in some cases the well written plays may in some respects be worse than those of a very light nature, the jokes—if they are jokes—causing a laugh and passing while the effect of the more thoughtful plays may be more lasting.

Though Raleigh's decision was evidently based on a cumulative experience, the play which finally provoked his resignation was a satire called *Angelo the Ninth*, which mocked both 'the typical Socialist demagogue who hates royalty but loves notice from a King' and the monarch who enjoys travelling in disguise so he can enjoy 'the illicit pleasures denied to him' at home. There are no prizes for guessing which of these two parts of the storyline worried the Lord Chamberlain's Office, and perhaps the Reader's reservations are understandable, given the significance in European and political history of the month of October 1917, when the play was first submitted. Indeed, it was probably inevitable that he should query 'whether this is the time for attacks upon royal voluptuaries and their political panders'. He concluded: 'Personally I have enjoyed reading the naughty humour: but for public performance it is NOT Recommended for Licence'. In May 1918 a revised version was submitted; the Reader confirmed that 'the Gallic salt still seems to me too strong . . . for the British palate', and Sir Squire Bancroft on the Advisory Board agreed that 'these are not the times to grant licences to such plays'. However, while recognising that 'the times are difficult', Buckmaster issued a warning:

> all forms of censorship grow daily more unpopular and to refuse a licence merely because some member of a Royal House was presented under ridiculous or even scandalous conditions might provoke more mischief than the performance could create.

Buckmaster was 'not prepared to dissent from the views expressed' by those who thought the play too dangerous to allow; but Raleigh relished the intellectual playfulness of the script in comparison with what he called 'the tedious itch of lubricity' dominating contemporary theatre. Isolated yet again, he resigned on the grounds that an exaggerated caution and sensitivity had taken over the censorship and that the quality and aesthetics of a play had become irrelevant. 'Are wit and satire to be permitted on the English stage?', he asked rhetorically. Raleigh scorned the idea that 'the loyalty of the people of this country to the throne can be either impaired or shocked by the wit of this play', arguing that to ban such a play was a sign of weakness rather than strength:

> Medieval satire often played very outrageously on monks and priests, and on the mysteries of the Catholic Church. It was listened to tolerantly by

bishops and abbots. The Church was too strong to resent it. I think the Monarchy, in this country and empire, is in much the same position.[41]

Presumably others did not share his confidence in the inviolability of the status quo.

The Hidden Hand

The First World War (Part Two)

Stage and Propaganda

The West End just now is doing fine work in the way of war propaganda
. . . No Englishman could witness any of these entertainments and fail to
feel refreshed and invigorated and more determined than ever to bring
about the defeat of Germany.[1]

In *The Great War and Modern Memory*, Paul Fussell explores the theatricali-
sation of the war itself, showing how it was conceived both consciously and
unconsciously in terms of costume and set, and how the trappings and situations of stage plays were sometimes employed at the front, along with
heightened or even comic dialogue, to try to contain the enormities with which
soldiers were confronted. Drawing on personal accounts and diaries, he
suggests that individuals finding themselves in the midst of unspeakable
horrors often coped by making an instinctive separation between the self and
the melodramatic role they were forced to play, a role which was simultaneously performed to the hilt and observed with detachment.[2] Fussell also draws
attention to the significant participation of the theatre itself in the wartime
situation; this took many forms, from the construction of imitation trenches
in Kensington Gardens and a ruined village in Trafalgar Square to the revues,
concerts and shows performed at the front, or the speaking of lines from *Henry
V* while going into battle. It is well known that even the film purportedly documenting the Battle of the Somme achieved its most memorable images
through soldiers re-enacting an assault for the benefit of the camera—something not revealed to the massive cinema audiences in Britain who in 1916
watched it as reality.[3] Fussell further indicates that soldiers home on leave
constituted a very important component of the audiences attending theatres
in England; one might speculate about what kinds of performance they would
have wanted to see between periods in the trenches, but more significant here
is the implication for the censorship in terms of what the authorities would
not want them to see. It would certainly have been considered unhelpful to

national morale for even non-combatants to watch anything which undermined the mythic image of a heroic, well-led, united and effective British army
on its way to defeating an evil enemy; for any such thing to be witnessed by
those who would subsequently be returning to the front might have been
disastrous.

At the start of the First World War, the British government passed the
Defence of the Realm Act (DORA), giving itself extensive powers to silence
anything it considered liable to hinder the war against Germany. As the historian Samuel Hynes explains in *A War Imagined*, this Act 'gave the State
unlimited power to control the instruments of communication and the trans-
mission of information'. Theatre was obviously one such instrument. In
developing the scope of its control, the government soon assumed the right
'to prevent the spread of reports likely to cause disaffection or alarm', and by
1916 had, according to Hynes, effectively outlawed 'any expression of
opposition to, or criticism of, the war in any art form'.[4] But effective censorship—especially in wartime—is not only about what you prevent people from
imagining, but also about what you can persuade them is real. Barrie, Bennett,
Galsworthy, Zangwill, Archer, Granville Barker, Jones and Pinero had all
previously clashed with the authorities who presumed to limit their imaginations; all now more or less cheerfully committed themselves to supporting the
British propaganda machine against the Germans. Like other oppositional
forces—the suffragette movement for example—they apparently accepted the
need to encourage national unity. Even Shaw, explaining why he had
remained 'loyally silent' on the subject of the war and the incompetent way it
was being run, declared that 'truth telling is not compatible with the defence
of the realm'. Writing in 1919 under the title 'How War Muzzles the Dramatic
Poet', he explained why self-censorship was inevitable during wartime:

> You cannot make war on war and on your neighbour at the same time.
> War cannot bear the terrible castigation of comedy, the ruthless light of
> laughter that glares on the stage. When men are heroically dying for their
> country, it is not the time to shew their lovers and wives and fathers and
> mothers how they are being sacrificed to the blunders of boobies, the
> cupidity of capitalism, the ambition of conquerors, the electioneering of
> demagogues, the Pharisaism of patriots, the lusts and lies and rancors and
> bloodthirsts that love war because it opens their prison doors, and sets
> them in the thrones of power and popularity.[5]

If even Shaw adopted that position, one might wonder how far an official
censor would even be required during the war.

The use of the theatre for positive propaganda, reinforcing and manipulating public opinion about the war and the Germans was extensive—if
frequently unsubtle. According to L.J. Collins in her recent study of British

theatre between 1914 and 1918, over 200 war plays were licensed by the Lord
Chamberlain in the first two years of the war, many of them spy stories based
on British heroics and German treachery. International allies must never be
upset, but anything derogatory could be said about enemies. Collins argues
that because its audiences encompassed such a diverse range of social backgrounds, the theatre 'provided a perfect setting for engineering a corporate
sense of patriotic identity' and was ideally suited to the task of helping 'to fuel
the fires of patriotism set alight by the media'.[6] Plays written to encourage
members of the audience to volunteer—or to persuade their loved ones to volunteer—were an early manifestation of this directness. At the performance of
England Expects by Seymour Hicks and Edward Knoblock in September 1914,
recruiting officers were placed in the theatre; at the climax, the music swelled,
a screen showed cinematic pictures of the Prince of Wales and of the army
on drilling exercises, and 'plants' hidden among the audience came onto the
stage to volunteer, encouraging others to follow them. Crucial to the effect of
the play was its demonstration of the recovery through war of a united national
identity which would close the fissures which had been opening in society:

> EUSTACE: Cook's sons, Duke's sons, sons of a belted Earl. They are all
> one now. There is no such thing as mass and class. We're brothers fighting
> shoulder to shoulder, and we are going to come out top dog and smash
> Germany to hell if it takes us thirty years to do it. (*Raising his glass*)
> Gentlemen, the King.

Ironically, given the play's theme, 'Eustace' was a substitute for the identity
originally given to the character, which the censorship had refused: 'a name
less connected with the peerage than the Hon. Maurice Baring should be
chosen', it was insisted.[7]

No play questioning the necessity of the war or the evil of the Germans
was likely even to find its way as far as the Lord Chamberlain. In 1914 all
copies of Fenner Brockway's *The Devil's Business*—a sharp attack on the
armaments trade—were seized by the police and most of them destroyed, but
it seems unlikely the writer had ever envisaged his play could be publicly
staged. The Office was on the look-out for any hint of an inappropriate shade
or tone, and was quite prepared to be pro-active; in November 1914, it inter-
cepted a planned production of a script which had been licensed some years
earlier: 'The theme of the play, Anglo-French rivalry of 100 years ago, was
unimportant at the time the play was licensed in 1900, but it is liable to give
offence if emphasised at the present time'. The producer replied that the
rivalry was being modified to make it Anglo-German instead, and expressed
some anxiety at the suggestion that performances might now be banned: 'I
paid a big price for the rights of the play, and look upon it as a valuable asset'.[8]
Before approving the play's revival, Lord Sandhurst insisted on seeing copies

of posters and promotional material for the production. These were aspects of performance for which he had usually denied all responsibility, but, presumably in part because of an increasing public acceptance of the need for censorship throughout public life, he now began to intervene more and more. When a touring production of a comedy called *Tantalising Tommy* was announced for Windsor in the autumn of 1915, he refused to allow an advertising image which depicted a woman in pyjamas, smoking as she reclines at her ease against cushions, with a tiny soldier sitting astride her ankle. The caption claimed that this was a comedy which 'will tickle you to death'; one feels it would have taken a very brave man even to think of tickling Sir Douglas Dawson—especially in the middle of a war and in Windsor High Street. He was adamant that the posters and the image should be removed: 'I am desired by the Lord Chamberlain to say that unless the posters in question are removed in their entirety . . . he will forbid the representation'.[9]

There were few difficulties in the early months of the war about licensing a succession of more or less ludicrous plays about the downfall of wicked German spies, though the Office remained vigilant for any details which might be damaging to British morale. The problem here was that just as all good boys' sporting stories had to show their heroes coming from behind to defeat strong opponents, so if a spy was going to be worth defeating, then the Germans had first to enjoy their moments of triumph in which the British are tricked. The Lord Chamberlain tried to make sure that at least *important* British people were never duped by Germans. In November 1914 the Reader had reservations about *Honour Gains the Day*; 'the essential idea is not different from others which have been passed', he wrote, 'but the chief character and the setting of the Play make it inadvisable in my opinion to pass it in its present form'. Though of course the right side wins in the end, the plot in this case depended on a high-ranking captain in the Intelligence Department of the British Admiralty being overheard in his office by a female German spy as he foolishly talks aloud to himself about plans and secret codes for the forthcoming naval battle. Given the classic gender set up here, it is tempting to speculate that perhaps the original plot line might already have been censored before the play was submitted, or that it could have been read as a code for a rather more plausible way of conceding crucial information to the enemy; either way, it was hardly advisable that audiences should imagine a captain in the Intelligence Department talking to himself—and certainly not making such a mistake:

> The objection is that a high official in the Admiralty is made the foolish victim of a designing woman-spy, and it is undesirable to suggest the possibility of such a thing. If the play were shifted to a humbler sphere, to a coast-guard station, for instance, I think it might pass.[10]

More surprisingly, for some time the Office largely kept to its policy of not allowing the offensive portrayal of actual foreign statesmen, even in the case of the Germans. In January 1915, the main characters in a spoof spy comedy called *The Master Hun* were Votiskname and Von O'Clock; the latter supplies his leader with stolen secret documents which supposedly contain crucial information to win the war for the Germans, but which turn out to be nothing more than the plans for a new cabdrivers' shelter; meanwhile, the Master Hun himself is defeated by a boy scout with a broomstick. Street described the play as 'the work of a lunatic', but still insisted on maintaining an existing rule that the actor playing the Master Hun 'must not be made up as the Kaiser'.[11] Of course, the dilemma was created by the fact that the Kaiser was not only the enemy but also Queen Victoria's grandson (and therefore linked to the current monarchy). In *The Glorious Day*, in February 1915, the Office again insisted that 'characters representing the Emperor and the Crown Prince in the last scene are not made up to represent the German Emperor and the Crown Prince of Germany', and in *Somewhere in France* in April that 'the stranger shall not be made up to represent the German Emperor'.[12] In May the Prologue to Stephen Phillips's *Armageddon* was set in Hades, with Satan and his henchman discussing in pseudo-Miltonic verse their plans to consume the Earth in violent battle. This they decide to do by sending back the spirit of Attila in human form to lead the destruction, but the Lord Chamberlain was insistent that it should be implicit rather than explicit that the German Emperor be signalled as Attila's host: 'It is not definitely stated into what human frame he should enter, but of course, the Kaiser is understood: however, that is left vague of any possible offence'.[13]

By August, however, the policy had changed. *Gott Strafe England* was a short piece for one actor who presents a series of characters including Sir Francis Drake, Lord Kitchener and the Kaiser, the latter waking from a dream to hear that Berlin has been captured by the allies. While the Reader found that the announcement of such a 'premature triumph of our arms is irritating while Berlin is still so far off' he concluded that there were now no grounds for censorship: 'A few weeks ago this would have been forbidden under the rule prohibiting the introduction of the German Emperor . . . but the Lord Chamberlain has waived that rule'. Dawson sent a telegram to check with the Lord Chamberlain:

> A play has come up with German Emperor in it, no attempt at disguising the personality . . . naturally depicting the War Lord in a very unfavourable light . . .
>
> I knew we had forbidden German Emperor, but heard a rumour this had been relaxed. Will you let me know what you want done in this instance.

He was informed that there had been some relaxation—'for I did not think

we need be too particular'—but that an 'actual copy of Kaiser' had not yet been allowed. The manager of the theatre where the sketch was to be performed was advised that he must take care to avoid 'business or language to excite public feeling'.[14]

The flood of patriotic plays full of evil Germans and heroic Brits caused concern in the Office for other reasons too. In January 1915 Street commented that

> Unless the war were vetoed altogether as a subject, which is impossible, it is impossible to prevent the melodramatists being silly and ignorant in their treatment of it, however, it is difficult to forbid the production of a play written in good faith, apparently, on grounds of incorrectness.

Street was agonising in response to *War and a Woman*, and his concern was primarily about the excessive violence of the German army—not because he doubted the truth of what was being shown but because he feared the effect on audiences of

> a great deal of German brutality, as the knocking down of a woman, the kicking of a child's cradle, the pulling down of portraits of King George and King Albert, and worst of all, the tying up of the heroine on the door to prevent the English firing. It is a question of how far the feelings of an audience should be harrowed in this way. But it cannot be said that such incidents are a 1000th part as bad as things the Germans are known to have done, and brutalities as bad are commonly permitted in melodramas.[15]

In *For England, Home and Beauty* in May 1915, the Reader was mildly worried by a scene in which a German general throws water in the face of an injured British prisoner—'but I think it is no worse than things we know to have happened'—and by a comedy scene in which two characters swap their clothes: 'This involves the woman being in khaki and is therefore perhaps objectionable, though I think it is insignificant', he wrote. Of more concern was the climax in which British nurses at the front are so appalled by the atrocities they have witnessed that they abandon their medical duties and join in with the fighting:

> The nurses remove their Red Cross badges before becoming combatants, but even so, it is, I think, doubtful if it should pass. It could not happen in reality, and though there is no harm in the spirit of it, it represents nurses as acting contrary to the rules of war.

Faced with another in a chain of melodramas which were short on facts but

long on action and patriotism, Street used this play as an example to try to define some rules for himself as to where he should draw lines:

> These plays are so much alike that it is almost impossible to distinguish between them, but I conceive the essential points to consider are that any barbarity exhibited should not be too horrible or disgusting and that the King's uniform should not be made ridiculous. The latter point is the more difficult, because the comic relief man generally enlists and continues to be comic relief: I take that to be unobjectionable provided he is made a decent fellow and does nothing derogatory to the character of a soldier. [16]

Of course, the reputation of the British army was to be protected absolutely. In January 1915 a play described by Street as 'perhaps the stupidest production I have read' included amongst its otherwise insignificant and largely harmless fun, a disreputable character in a British army uniform:

> The man is a thorough rogue and therefore, since it has been agreed that soldiers must not be exhibited in this light—and he is ridiculous as well as sordid—I recommend that it be required that he shall not be in khaki and that all references to his being a soldier shall be omitted. [17]

In March, a 'foolish piece' called *Cheer Up* showed a colonel who is suffering from melancholia being persuaded to appear in a clown's costume in a cabaret; the objection was that he wore this over the military uniform which was subsequently revealed. 'I don't quite like the idea of a clown's dress covering the King in uniform' wrote Dawson, and the Office insisted that he must not remove the clown costume. [18]

Again, in a 'farcical, though inoffensive' piece such as *Kiss Me Sergeant* in July 1915, Street suggested that 'the hero ought not to wear khaki' and objected to the fact that 'a man previously in a bathing dress wraps himself in the Union Jack'. [19] The Office was more lenient with *The Gates of Mercy*, a 'silly melodrama' set partly at the front. 'Though the military part is foolish, it is well meant', wrote Street:

> It may be undesirable that an English Officer should be represented as showing the white feather, but then he was mad, which might happen to anyone. A comic man becomes a soldier, but as he is not made particularly ridiculous afterwards, I do not think that matters. [20]

Perhaps more serious were the implications of *His Mother's Son, V.C.*, a war play set in Ireland and submitted in December 1915. Street found it 'difficult to make head or tail of this play and its story almost defies analysis', but one aspect was unacceptable:

> It may be thought hardly worthwhile to spin such meaningless and
> insignificant rubbish . . . But however preposterous the play may be it is
> unwise to license one representing British soldiers, one of them a V.C.,
> spreading seditious pamphlets among their comrades—which is the main
> plot of the play.

Modifications were duly made.[21]

Supposedly factual accounts and details of German atrocities in Belgium
had been published in Britain as early as September 1914. In February 1915
The Official Book of the German Atrocities was published, and in May an extensive report was produced by the Committee of Alleged German Outrages,
under the chairmanship and authority of Viscount Bryce. According to
Hynes, the effect on British attitudes was considerable: 'henceforth it became
quite acceptable to express a desire for the annihilation of Germans, the
bombing of German civilians, the gassing of German troops'.[22] Versions—or
equivalents—of some of the atrocities detailed soon began to feature in
playscripts submitted to the Lord Chamberlain, and this led to serious debates
regarding the advisability or otherwise of presenting violence and brutality in
dramatic form for propaganda purposes. In April 1915 Street was cautious
about some aspects of *The Nun and the Hun*:

> The objections to this play are its title and certain passages of excessive
> brutality, made worse by the objects of it being nuns. Otherwise it is on a
> par with other such melodramas which have been passed. It is to be hoped,
> however, that the stage is nearly surfeited with such stuff.

Again, it was not just the play itself but the promotional material that he was
concerned about.

> I do not think that at a time when people's minds are excited by hideous
> stories, some at least true, of the treatment of Belgian nuns by Germans
> it is desirable to have posters etc., suggesting these horrors.

But the detail of the horrors depicted on stage was the main concern, and
Street's instinct was to be protective of audiences; specifically, he disliked the
idea of hearing from offstage the shrieks of a woman being whipped. There
were mixed feelings in the Office, and an alternative argument was advanced,
proposing the need to educate and remind audiences about the extent of
German depravity, rather than to shield them:

> Mr Street says that he does not think it is desirable to have these horrors
> brought to people's minds. On the other hand, if it is not allowed to
> go too far, I think that what our soldiers are fighting to redeem

should be brought home to the people of England, who do not view the War in its terrible reality.

Eventually, a series of cuts was made and the title was altered to *In the Hands of the Huns*. Street had also objected to 'a repulsive scene of German brutality' in which a young Frenchwoman, who refuses to give information, is tortured by German officers and burnt by a hot iron. Such cruelty would not have been allowed in a contemporary play before the war; so far from becoming just a medium for escapist comedy, the stage, too, was becoming brutalised:

> In my opinion, this extreme form of working on the feelings of the audi- ence is most unwholesome, and I am not sure if anything quite so bad has been permitted. However, as it is done 'off', and is consistent with the rest of this brutal play it may not be worthwhile to prohibit it.[23]

For the Lord Chamberlain's Office, it was hard to decide how far this greater licence to show such horrors should be allowed to go. In April 1915 the Reader noted of *There Was a King in Flanders*—'a fine and stirring little play' about an English nurse helping a Belgian soldier who has killed a German—that 'the author should be told that this exhibition of wounds is too dreadful for the stage and must be modified'; the endorsement on the licence insisted that 'there should be no <u>gross</u> exposure of bloody wounds'.[24] Yet there were obvious problems for any play which showed German soldiers in anything other than a brutal light. In June 1915 *Marie Odile* showed an inno- cent novice in a convent in Alsace in the 1870s having the child of a German soldier; for once he is not depicted as inhuman or uncivilised and only becomes her lover after she asks him to stay. The Reader described the play as 'a pretty idyll with a sad ending', commenting that it seemed 'a curious play to be produced at the present time, since the soldier is quite a sympathetic character'. However, he was reassured by a note from the author promising 'that all references to Germany and German soldiers will be struck out and the war, soldiers and country made indefinite'. Nevertheless, there were complaints made to the Foreign Office about allowing a sympathetic portrayal of a soldier who was 'unmistakeably a German', even though nothing remained which necessarily identified him as such:

> It would at any time be a most undesirable production, but that a play of this character should be acted at present in London is a scandal . . . the hero is a German, and I am sure many people come away with a senti- mental feeling that after all the Germans cannot be so black as they are painted.
>
> From a Catholic point of view the play is an outrage; and when you remember how Catholics, especially our Belgian and French allies, have

been wounded in their deepest feelings by the German barbarians, it seems a direct insult that such a play should be going on in our midst.[25]

There were other complaints about this play, and though the Lord Chamberlain refused to accede to demands that he should cancel the licence he had issued, pressure was almost certainly put on the management to ensure that the production was soon withdrawn. When another war play actually under the title of *The Nun* was submitted later in the year, the Lord Chamberlain was more careful about Catholic sensitivities, and Dawson wrote to the manager citing three objectionable features requiring modification:

1) A violated nun who murders her seducer.
2) A British General who strikes a prisoner across the face.
3) A French Officer who gets drunk.

The licence was granted when those elements had all been removed.[26]

Perhaps at no other time in the century were national and international politics bound together quite so publicly and overtly with sexual morality; to the self-appointed guardians of the pure and sacred flame of virtue, the supposed decadence and licentiousness of the period before the war were as threatening to British civilisation as were the Germans. There was, indeed, more than one war to fight: 'It is just as important to civilization that Literary England should be cleansed of sex-mongers and pedlars of the perverse, as that Flanders should be cleared of Germans', declared Lord Alfred Douglas in 1915. He was responding to a newspaper article which declared:

When we hear of German brutality in Belgium . . . there should be no matter of surprise. For years the Germans have cultivated a wholesome brutality as part of their military training, and latterly this brutality has found national vent in sexual perversion. Such things do not make men gentle, humane or noble.[27]

Sometimes, the twin enemies of the country were identified as two parts of the same threat: 'The tendency in Germany is to abolish civilisation as we know it, to substitute Sodom or Gomorrah for the new Jerusalem, and to infect clean nations with Hunnish erotomania'.[28] To those who were shocked by the decline in power of the British Empire, the infection ran through every aspect of British life; disease was a key metaphor, repeatedly invoked by those who attacked the supposed sickness of contemporary society and culture. They welcomed the outbreak of war in 1914 as a 'violent tonic' which 'teaches us self-sacrifice' while 'welding us once more into a social unit', and even saw its

primary aim as being to destroy the virus which had spread through British culture like an epidemic:

> It was high time that war should come with its purifying fire. In some fifty years so-called Art had grown in Europe like unto a puffed-out and unhealthy fungus of enormous size, without beauty, without delicacy, and without health. A wave of diseased degeneracy had submerged Philosophy, Literature, Music and Art.

Its origins were apparently in Berlin and Vienna, but it had taken root closer to home.

> We find, perhaps, in the German philosophers and musicians the first crystallised expression of this viciousness, but unfortunately we . . . cannot pretend that we are exempt. The morbid invention of the artistic mind is seen everywhere. We have Oscar Wilde, Aubrey Beardsley, and others. The futurists, the cubists, the whole school of decadent novelists.[29]

In this analysis, the war was 'the sovereign disinfectant' and its blood 'the Condy's fluid that cleans out the stagnant pools and clotted channels of the intellect', which would enable Britain to recover its greatness as it awoke from its 'opium-dream of comfort' and 'the lethargy of our dilettantism'.[30] At the start of James Barrie's 1914 play *Der Tag*, the German Emperor confidently announces that

> Britain has grown dull and sluggish: a belly of a land, she lies overfed, no dreams within her such as keep Powers alive; and timid too—without red blood in her, but in its stead a thick yellowish fluid . . . Britain's part in the world's making is done: 'I was,' her epitaph.

But the Emperor's arrogance is confounded towards the end of the play, when the personification of Culture visits the German Kaiser to bid him farewell. She reveals to him the unanticipated and unwelcome result of his aggression: 'England, O Emperor, was grown degenerate, but you have made her great again'.[31]

It was no arbitrary choice that it should be Culture whom Barrie imagines visiting the Kaiser 'with this gaping wound in my breast', for culture was one of the battlefields where the war was fought. As Hynes shows, there was a concerted movement to delete German art from British culture, particularly where its manifestations were located in modernism; 'war and Schönberg were essentially the same', says Hynes. But there were also attempts to remove all German composers, conductors and musicians from classical concerts. In literature, Sir Arthur Quiller-Couch, Professor of English at Cambridge

University, insisted in 1914 that Germans were 'congenitally unfitted to read our poetry' because of 'the very structure of their vocal organs', and Hynes convincingly argues that the war 'had simply given the majority of Englishmen an opportunity to be what they had always been—xenophobic, homophobic, and art-hating—and to call it patriotism'.[32] As we shall see, the apotheosis of this conjoining of nationalism and sexual politics was reached with the 1918 Old Bailey prosecution focused on Oscar Wilde's *Salomé*, and the confrontation between, on the one hand, its director J.T. Grein and its star Maud Allan, and, on the other, their accuser, the MP Noel Pemberton-Billing. Extreme and in some ways unique though that case may have been, it was no isolated incident.

The theatrical presentation of sexual immorality or impropriety in war situations was a matter of particular concern for guardians of the theatre. Following a complaint in 1915 by the Newcastle and Gateshead Vigilance Society, for example, the Lord Chamberlain ordered the removal of a scene from *The Glorious Day* in which a young unmarried woman accuses a British soldier of being the father of her child.[33] In April 1915 *Outraged Women* was refused a licence; though Street recognised that it was intended to whip up hatred of the Germans, it had another dimension:

> The play is described as a 'recruiting sketch', but its direct object is to plead for the destruction of infants born of rape committed by German soldiers . . . in my opinion the stage is entirely unfitted as a place for the discussion of this dreadful and difficult question, even apart from the violent and (as most people would think) wicked solution propounded by the author.

The other reader, Bendall, agreed; 'I might safely have stopped at its title', he commented, adding that 'I cannot imagine any healthy point of view from which *Outraged Women* would seem desirable, or even permissible on the stage'. The author complained that the issue was a serious one receiving widespread coverage in newspapers: 'I fail to see why one of the most serious problems of the War should not be dealt with in a dramatic playlet'. But the Office refused to consider even the possibility of modifications because the subject was 'eminently unsuitable, even when most delicately treated, for representation upon the Stage'.[34]

In the autumn of 1915, the Office was drawn into a prolonged conflict over a touring melodrama with the controversial title *The Unmarried Mother*, which it had licensed in June. Street had described it then as 'a singularly crude and foolish melodrama, badly written with the best intentions', and it told the sentimental story of a servant who loses her position when she becomes pregnant by a lover who has been called back to the front before they can get married. The play has a happy ending, in which he returns to her, wounded, but having earned a Victoria Cross. It might have seemed a

triumphant tale of love and loyalty. But for those determined to reinstate a supposedly pure pre-Edwardian morality, the fear that basic family structures were being seriously undermined by the rising number of 'war babies' was a significant problem, which this play did nothing to help. The play provoked outrage among the authorities in Liverpool—not least for its poster, which showed a girl holding a baby and asking the onlooker: 'Am I very wicked to have a baby without being married?'. For many, this was not a question which audiences or even passers by should be invited to think about, for there was only one acceptable answer. A JP from Birkenhead (who had not seen the play) wrote to the Lord Chamberlain to tell him off in a gloriously Beachcomberish tone:

> I find in 'Whitaker' that in your Lordship's Department is vested the responsibility of censorship for the plays that are allowed to be presented to the public; I venture to speak in the name of all the good women of Liverpool and Birkenhead in protesting . . .
>
> Your Lordship's Department is an integral part of the Government and has been placed in charge of the moral standard of the country, so far as the drama is concerned. I maintain that in passing *The Unmarried Mother* for performance it has placed the Government on the wrong side of the fence with respect to War babies . . . it has allowed a most questionable propaganda to be issued upon the most effective platform in the country—the theatre stage.
>
> The good women of Birkenhead and Liverpool have been holding mass meetings, crammed to the doors, and have enrolled thousands of their young sisters in a 'League of Honour'. Good women patrol the streets at night, and do their best to restrain the girls from what is wrong; it is by no means a pleasant task.
>
> Allow me to say, my Lord, in the name of every right minded man and woman in England, that a public explanation is due from your Department.

So important did the writer consider the issue, that he also took it upon himself to appeal directly, and very personally, to the King:

> Sire,
> It is impossible for any man to write, on a more serious subject than I have in hand.
>
> Thousands of young men and women, the hope of England, are every week, seeing this play. The morality of the country is being undermined. The Lord Chamberlain . . . forgets the awful misery it will entail not only upon the girls themselves, but upon their families. Any man who has daughters can understand that. I have but one daughter; if by any conceiv-

able misfortune she saw this play, and followed its wild and immoral teaching, death would indeed be a welcome friend to her father and mother. Without doubt, thousands will have to tread this fearful Via Dolorosa. I am urging the bench in Liverpool and Birkenhead and Manchester to urge the suppression of the play. Will not Your Majesty speak to the Lord Chamberlain on the subject?

The JP subsequently wrote again to the Lord Chamberlain 'to inform you that I have reported your conduct in this matter to His Majesty the King', and persuaded the Archbishop of York to contact the Lord Chamberlain twice in order to complain about the play. The Archbishop was himself a member of an official committee investigating 'the possible danger of illegitimate births owing to the present War conditions', and he told Lord Sandhurst that he thought it 'most unfortunate that a play should be publicly acted which condones if it does not advocate at a very specially critical time a course of conduct which every patriotic citizen would deplore'. He was, he said, deeply opposed to the public presentation of 'anything which would strengthen the temptations to which many soldiers quartered in our camps and billets and the young women among whom they are quartered are subject and which would seem to justify a course of conduct which would be deplorable in the national interest'. Though complaints from other cities followed, the Lord Chamberlain was always reluctant to withdraw licences he had previously issued, and in this case Bendall insisted that 'after rereading I still cannot see that this crude story, which is neither indecent nor objectionable in its moral need be banned'. Lord Sandhurst promised to 'watch such pieces carefully' in future, and reminded the JP of Birkenhead that they had the authority themselves to prevent performance at a local level.[35]

Wartime promiscuity continued to be a topic of great concern to the authorities, and was perceived as something which, whether or not it was deliberately instigated by Germans and their stooges, had the capacity to help destroy the British nation. *Damaged Goods*, Brieux's warning about the dangers of syphilis, had been automatically banned in 1914; 'I do not think that the public theatre is the best place for the delivery of this sermon', one member of the Advisory Board had commented, and another agreed that the subject was 'better suited to the lecture room of a hospital than the stage of a theatre'.[36] By 1917, however, the need to try to control the spread of the disease was paramount, and had become a matter of public debate outside the theatre and a significant issue for the government; one in five of the four million soldiers who had returned from France had brought back syphilis, and infant deaths from the disease rose sharply in 1917.[37] Could the theatre, increasingly accepted as an effective medium for explicit and overt propaganda, play its part in discouraging the spread of the disease? Brieux's play was officially reconsidered and passed, specifically for its 'practical addition

to the propaganda'. The play gained at least the tacit support of the Archbishop of Canterbury:

> I could not go so far as to urge you to give sanction to its performance; but on the other hand I am inclined on the whole to believe that you would be taking a mistaken line if you were to veto it at a moment when the subject with which it deals is being freely discussed everywhere, the barriers which used to shut it off from the public gaze and talk being rudely broken down.[38]

The decision to license *Damaged Goods* in 1917—with all proceeds from performances going to the National Council for Combating Venereal Disease—was presented not as a caving in to immorality, but rather as a direct and conscious attempt to use the theatre for positive wartime propaganda. It did, however, create a potentially awkward precedent, and admitted the existence of something which, by previously banning it from the theatre, the authorities had more or less denied. Did this mark a new willingness to accept that more 'truth' could be put on the stage? Certainly Collins argues that playwrights were increasingly allowed 'a greater degree of realism' in depicting reality as the war progressed.[39]

Yet Brieux's play had been allowed not because it was 'true' but in desperation and because it was hoped that it would have a useful and even measurable effect. Freedom for the theatre remained extremely limited.

In 1916, Miles Malleson published two war plays; in *Black 'Ell*, a young man returns to his family and his fiancée from the front, a hero for his part in clearing a German trench and killing soldiers. But he is haunted by the memory of what he has seen and done, and speaks passionately against the war and its advocates, insisting on the essential similarities between ordinary soldiers on either side. It is impossible to imagine that such a play could have been performed in 1916, and probably no manager would even have wasted time submitting it; in fact, it was that rare thing, a play which was too dangerous to be read, as Street explained when it was eventually sent in for licensing a full decade later:

> When this play, with 'D Company' by the same author, was published in 1916 the volume was confiscated and destroyed by the authorities under the Defence of the Realm Act as a calumny on the British soldier . . . I can quite understand the book being confiscated in 1916 and of course a licence for the play would have been out of the question. Obviously it would have tended to discourage recruiting.

Eight years after the war had ended, the Office was willing to concede that it

might be 'an undue restriction of the freedom of the theatre' to retain the ban, given that 'the views expressed have become a commonplace in many quarters'.[40]

There had in fact been questions in Parliament in 1916 about the suppression of *Black 'Ell*, and Hynes sees this as a clear indication of the power attributed uniquely to theatre, and as a significant moment in the development of wartime censorship:

> One must wonder what War Office reasoning allowed polemical pamphlets to appear unhampered, but seized and destroyed plays. A distrust of the imagination, perhaps, a fear of the power of literature that was greater than fear of argument? Whatever the official motives, something important happened with the publication and suppression of *Two Short Plays*: opposition to the war became literary, and literature became a threat to authority.[41]

Hynes dates the development of significant protests against the war to 1917, but inevitably these also led to counter-protests:

> Opposition to the war was more widespread and more articulate in the last year of the war than it had ever been before . . . as the voices of opposition swelled, the voices of censure and suppression grew more clamorous too . . . Pacifists were refusing to serve in the army . . . advocates of a negotiated peace were weakening the nation's resolve to fight on to total victory; and a permissive, un-English decadence in high places was corrupting English society . . . So the war against dissent went on, and grew fiercer, more vindictive, and more punitive.[42]

The war against dissent was inevitably reflected in what was and was not allowed in the theatre. Henry Arthur Jones wrote an attack directed against those 'still seeking to bring about the tragedy of an ignominious peace'. Set in the village of Market Pewbury, *The Pacifists* was described by the Lord Chamberlain's Reader as a 'rollicking satire'.[43] Meanwhile, in another play also called *The Pacifist*—its alternative title was *The Peace-Monger*—the central character is a supposed pacifist who is secretly in league with the Germans, and who

> uses his position in the Port of London Authority to give information to the Germans about transports and to facilitate air raids by signalling. He has also, apparently, blown up a transport himself by putting a bomb on it. His object in these activities is to compel England to make peace.

Of course, he is detected and poisoned by the heroine and the resolution is a

happy one. The easy (and predictable) bias of the Lord Chamberlain's Office is apparent from the Reader's comment on the script: 'The Play seems unfair to the pacifists. But I see nothing to object to.'[44]

The central character in *The Pacifist* was also described by the Reader as 'impossible, I hope', but in fact he was an early model for a figure who began to appear regularly, both on and off stage. As it began to seem possible, and even likely, that Britain would lose the war, a new scapegoat was identified, and the conviction that there was a sizeable number of British citizens deliberately or unwittingly working for a German victory became widely articulated and believed. The never-ending anti-German propaganda therefore began to take as one of its main focuses the Germans, or German sympathisers, who were supposedly living in Britain, and who were secretly undermining the British war effort through deliberate sabotage and by providing the 'hidden hand' to help the enemy. Such sabotage was credited with taking many forms, but the fact that the traitors were often high-ranking (if fictional) public figures was a reflection of quite widely held views. In *Beware Germans* in 1918, the main villain was a German spy who is not only the manager of a large company, but also a magistrate and a knight. Though the Reader described the plot of this melodrama as 'farcical' in its details, he recorded that it was 'seriously patriotic in purpose', and that 'it can only afford useful lessons'. The manager is secretly provoking a strike by the workers in the hope of instigating a revolution, and simultaneously attempting to use the widow of his dead son to help his secret military operations:

> One of his plots is to forward her engagement to an Air-Service Lieutenant, in order that she may steal the plans of a wonderful bombing-machine which he has invented. Another is to forward an air-raid on the East Coast where they live: and a third concerns the possession of a mysterious 'blank book' similar in purpose to that discussed in a recent trial.[45]

The 'recent trial' to which the Lord Chamberlain's Reader was referring in the above example was a real one, at which the existence of a mysterious book containing a list of people in Britain who were secretly in thrall to the enemy had been much discussed. The trial had arisen out of the proposed production in 1918 of Oscar Wilde's *Salomé*, but since two book-length accounts of that trial and the circumstances surrounding it have been written in relatively recent times, there is no need here to reproduce the details of the trial itself.[46] Understandably, however, neither of these accounts sets it fully in the context of theatre censorship, and even though the Office was not directly involved it was certainly implicated in the judge's ruling and final statement. Moreover, it could be argued that the silence of the Lord Chamberlain's Office during the trial itself speaks volumes; certainly, it is interesting to speculate why a representative of the Office was apparently not invited to give an opinion on

the play, and to wonder what the effect might have been if the relevant correspondence between the Lord Chamberlain and his advisers had been
presented in court—or even in the press. However, they remained bystanders
to a remarkable campaign orchestrated by the independent and right-wing
radical MP Noel Pemberton-Billing—a man described in one account as 'the
Goering we just missed', and who, in a typically anti-Semitic remark,
described Yiddish as 'German written in Hebrew characters'.[47]

As we have already seen, sexual decadence was one of the corruptions from
which pre-war Britain had supposedly been suffering, and which it was hoped
the war would exorcise. Though such decadence might take many forms, it
was 'perversion'—or homosexual practices—which were seen to be the most
extreme and the most undermining of the British way of life, and much of this
was traced directly back to Oscar Wilde. By 1918, the methods by which
Germans were believed to be infiltrating and weakening the moral fibre of the
British nation as they worked for its downfall were thought by many to include
sexual seduction and blackmail—especially of homosexuals. The basic
assumption informing Billing's case in the trial of *Salomé* was that there was
a demonstrable link connecting homosexuality, decadent aesthetics, foreign
spies and treachery, and in combination these were costing Britain the war.

Having been refused a licence for public performance many years earlier,
Salomé—Wilde's play rather than the opera, which, as we know, had been
licensed in 1910—was resubmitted in March 1918 for a proposed production at the Prince of Wales's Theatre under the direction of the Dutch-born
theatre director J.T. Grein. Grein was a well-known figure in national and
international artistic circles, having founded the Independent Theatre in 1891
in order to put on a private production of Ibsen's banned play *Ghosts*. He had
been a naturalised British subject since the 1890s, and had for many years
worked as a theatre critic for the *Sunday Times*. However, it was precisely
'naturalised' British subjects—and the question of whether they could be
trusted—which was now the subject of public debate and prejudice. Although
Grein was not German, he had a number of associations with that country.
Between 1899 and 1906 he had founded and run a German Theatre Society
in London—a project which reflected, as his wife later explained, Grein's
'cherished dreams of tightening the bonds between nations by the interchange
of dramatic art and of widening the outlook of our English dramatists and
managers'.[48] In 1918 such ideals and enthusiasms were sufficient in themselves to condemn him in the eyes of nationalists. Moreover, Grein had been
involved in touring plays through Europe, and in 1907 had set up a visit to
Berlin for Tree and his company, which had encouraged the Kaiser to talk of
theatre 'as a mediator between nations'. Indeed, Grein himself had been the
recipient of official honours from the German Emperor. All of these activities were used as circumstantial evidence against him in court.

In view of what was said about Wilde's play during and after the trial, it is

crucial to recognise that, when it was submitted to the Lord Chamberlain in March 1918, both the Lord Chamberlain's Examiners recommended the play for licence—albeit with some reluctance. Street noted that the rule forbidding scriptural characters on stage had been relaxed since Wilde's play had been previously banned, that Salomé's language, while 'likely to shock', contained nothing actually indecent, and that the climax could be staged (as in the opera at Covent Garden) without showing a severed head. He concluded that, since the play had now been widely performed in other countries, and since the dance which constituted 'the crudest part of it' had been allowed in Britain, there was no reason to refuse a licence—especially since 'I do not think that the more ignorant sort of audience is likely to be attracted'. Two of the three members of the Advisory Board who were consulted agreed with these views, and the third was prepared to yield to the majority view. It seems probable the Lord Chamberlain would have allowed a licence to be granted, perhaps after witnessing a private performance to reassure himself. But before a decision was announced, the issue was forcibly taken up elsewhere.[49]

Noel Pemberton-Billing was the leading exponent and publicist of the argument that the reason Britain had not yet won the war was that the country was riddled with German sympathisers, occupying prominent positions up to the highest level of society. In 1916 Billing had founded a newspaper which he called *The Imperialist*, and in 1917 he launched a society called 'The Vigilantes', dedicated to 'the promotion of purity in public life'.[50] Billing maintained that, central to the war itself, was the battle for a British civilisation and morality against the decadent and perverse Germanic culture which sought to destroy such purity. By 1918 he had changed the name of his newspaper to *The Vigilante*, and among the enemies whom he constantly attacked here (as in Parliament) were the so-called aliens within—the 'hidden hand'. Billing demanded that all such aliens should be interned, and claimed to have evidence that 'in the cabinet noir of a certain German Prince' there existed a book containing a secret list of 47,000 British people, over whom the Germans, working with their 'usual efficiency' and 'making use of the most productive and cheapest methods', had obtained control—namely, sexual blackmail. The book had been

> compiled by the secret service from the reports of German agents who have infested this country for the past twenty years; agents so vile, and spreading debauchery of such lasciviousness as only German minds could conceive and only German bodies execute.

It supposedly contained 'general instructions regarding the propagation of evils which all decent men thought had perished with Sodom and Lesbia', and Billing had little doubt that this 'demoniacal plan' was the Germans' most powerful weapon:

> All the horrors of shells and gas and pestilence introduced by the Germans
> in their open warfare would have but a fraction of the effect in extermi-
> nating the manhood of Britain as the plan by which they have already
> destroyed the first 47,000.

The Germans, said Billing, had taken particular advantage of 'the sexual pecu-
liarities of members of the peerage', but included on the list, which he claimed
to have seen, were 'Privy Councillors . . . Wives of Cabinet Ministers, dancing
girls, even Cabinet Ministers themselves . . . diplomats, poets, bankers,
editors, newspaper proprietors, and members of His Majesty's household'.
Indeed, 'no one in the social scale was exempted from contamination by this
perfect system'. There were also, he claimed, 'lists of public houses and bars
. . . which had been successfully demoralised', notably 'incestuous bars'
which the Germans had 'established in Portsmouth and Chatham', and in
which 'the stamina of British Sailors was undermined'. In order to capture
the minds and bodies of those who did not frequent such places, 'comfort-
able flats were taken and furnished in an erotic manner', while 'even the
loiterer in the streets was not immune', since 'agents of the Kaiser were
stationed at such points as Marble Arch and Hyde Park Corner'. Women were
identified as having been particularly vulnerable targets for the Germans:
'Wives of men in supreme positions were entangled. In Lesbian ecstasy the
most sacred secrets of State were betrayed.'[51]

In February 1918 Billing's newspaper referred briefly to the proposed
private performances of Grein's production of *Salomé*, in which the interna-
tionally recognised dancer Maud Allan was to have her first major speaking
role in the title part. There had long been rumours and gossip concerning
Allan's possible sexual liaisons with leading British politicians, establishment
figures, and even members of the royal family. Her rather exotic and
dangerous theatrical reputation in Britain was built largely on her dance of
The Vision of Salomé at the Palace Theatre in 1908, when some reviewers were
convinced that she appeared naked, even when they were assured this had not
been the case. In 1913 the *Daily Mail* had blamed that performance for having
'opened the floodgates' to the decline in music-hall morality, as other
performers sought to imitate her approach.[52] Now, under the deliberately
provocative headline 'The Cult of the Clitoris', Billing suggested an essential
link between the members of the private society who would be willing to
witness the performance of Wilde's play and the traitors seeking to help
Germany to defeat Britain: 'If Scotland Yard were to seize the list of these
members', he declared, 'I have no doubt they would secure the names of
several of the first 47,000'. [53]

Probably falling into a trap Billing had deliberately set in order to generate
publicity for his cause, Allan and Grein brought a legal action against him;
their counsel argued that, by implication, Allan was being accused of

lesbianism—'and a more horrible libel to publish of any woman . . . it is impossible to find'. But Billing, vigorously conducting his own defence, insisted it was really Wilde's play which was on trial: 'The issue we are really trying is not whether I have libelled Maud Allan or not . . . the issue is whether *Salomé* is a decent or an indecent play'. He called as witnesses doctors who described the play as 'a melodrama of disease' with the potential 'to light up dormant perversion in men who did not even know they possessed it'; it was, they said, a performance which was not only 'calculated to deprave', but which would do 'more harm . . . to all who see it . . . than a German army itself'. Billing used the trial as an opportunity to attack Wilde and those who championed his work or defended his lifestyle. Written by 'a moral pervert' and offering a picture of 'degenerate sexual lust, sexual crime, and unnatural passions', *Salomé*, he declared, was bound to appeal to the very people whom the German authorities were blackmailing and pressurising as the enemies of Britain. He claimed that the play's first performance had been in Berlin, and attacked Allan for her 'German associations' and Grein as someone 'of alien origin'. Contemptuously dismissing the latter's argument in court that 'war and art have nothing to do with one another', Billing demanded that good art must also be useful propaganda, and questioned how this production would serve the national need:

> Can you tell me why you consider it in the interests of our nation that this should be produced when we are in the middle of a great War? . . . Does this play assist us to concentrate on the great national problem which presents itself to every Britisher today? . . . Do you suggest that this play brings either solace or comfort to the wives, daughters, and sisters of 3,000,000 men in France?

He insisted that 'either knowingly or unknowingly', Grein was 'ministering to the moral perverts of this country', and that the intention to tour *Salomé* to neutral countries as an example of British culture was calculated to help secure the decline of the nation:

> They have chosen, at a moment when our very national existence is at stake, to select the most depraved of the many depraved works of a man who suffered the extreme penalty at the hands of the law for the practising of this unnatural vice . . . they choose this moment to present it to a nation in sorrow as a solace for the tragedy of this War.

The trial received the widest possible publicity and dominated public debate; the eventual acquittal of Billing at the Old Bailey in June 1918 had devastating implications, not only for Wilde's play, which remained beyond public performance until the 1930s, but for its effect on Grein's career—he

immediately lost his job with the *Sunday Times*—and for others implicated in Billing's attack. In his summing up after the verdict, the incompetent Judge Darling also had some damning words for this particular play; completely erroneously—but no one corrected him—he insisted *Salomé* was a play which it was 'perfectly clear the Censor would not permit to be played in public'. In fact, when the play was resubmitted in 1927, Lord Buckmaster recalled that it was he who had 'strongly advised Lord Sandhurst' in 1918 that 'while the proceedings were pending it was impossible to grant a licence'; he specifically noted that the eventual refusal of the licence 'was not due to an adverse judgement on the play itself'.[54]

Judge Darling, however, also took it upon himself to criticise the practice of permitting private clubs to stage unlicensed plays:

> Somehow or other, people who cannot get the leave of the Censor to produce plays in the ordinary way are able, as the law stands, to produce them . . . in some way which apparently cannot be stopped. Now it is perfectly plain that this play, as anyone who has read it must see, is a play which never ought to be produced either in public or in private.[55]

Darling strongly advocated that the law should be altered to prevent such performances taking place at all, and widened his criticism of the laxity of the censorship by suggesting the authorities should 'exercise their powers most stringently' in order especially 'to prevent improper dances being danced or such costumes as I am certain are worn upon the stage now to be worn'. Referring specifically to Maud Allan's dance as Salomé, he described it as 'a perfect scandal to my thinking that it should be possible for people to do such things in public and upon the stage'.

In 1918, not only theatre, but society itself, seems to have been ready to inhabit the land of melodrama, to an extent which is hard to comprehend. As Hynes comments:

> The idea of an army defeated by performances of *Salomé* is hard to take seriously; so is the idea of a covert force of deviants turning English soldiers into cowards and English politicians into collaborators. But these notions were taken seriously—by an English jury, and by the general public.[56]

Indeed they were, as an article by one of Billing's supporters which was published in a national newspaper at the time of the trial makes clear; employing what he said was a central European term for homosexuals, Arnold White quoted from 'the Urning Bible', and employed a particularly unpleasant metaphor to describe the Germans as 'the intestinal worms of central Europe', entering the human body as parasites. Crucially, this was not only a means of winning the war, but an end in itself:

In England we call the victims of this vice 'degenerates'—the German scientific view is that 'homosexuality is in no way a sign of "degeneration."' . . . The British, French and American conception of national life is that the home is the unit of the nation—father, mother, and child— Monsieur, Madame, et bébé . . . So long as the homes of the Anglo-Saxon and Kelt exist, men must go on fighting unless the planet is to be a storehouse of wealth and vice for the Urnings . . . Every father and mother in the British Empire should know why Mr Billing and the rest of us have humbly laboured to inspire, strengthen and convince the nation why Germans are to be hated . . . The legalisation of unnatural offences is a broadstone of Empire to the Huns.

Bizarrely, the first outcome of the defeat of the Germans would be the guarantee that 'the filth of Oscar Wilde shall no longer defile our family life through the secret or public stage'.[57] The real war, it appears, was the one to be waged against homosexuality; fighting the Germans was, in effect, just a means to that end.

Even as Billing was being acquitted, the Lord Chamberlain was dealing with a war play actually called *The Hidden Hand*, in which Germans were once again shown to be occupying positions of high authority in the British establishment. Though he thought it 'better written than most popular plays', Street worried that the theme was 'calculated to increase vague popular suspicion about German agency in high places, which is not a useful thing'. The villain is a German Jew called Rosenbaum, first seen in a Prologue, having a private meeting with the Kaiser before the war. He then disguises his identity and allegiance by changing his name to Strathconnel, and becomes not only a successful British business entrepreneur, but also a Privy Councillor, an MP and a Baronet. From this position of power, he is shown promoting industrial conflict by secretly supporting a strike in his own shipping works while simultaneously preventing the directors from conceding to the strikers' demands. He also tries to persuade a Foreign Office clerk to give him official secrets, and his plans to signal to zeppelins to destroy the fleet and to spread disease across the country are thwarted only by the heroism of a wounded padre (St George, no less, with 'something supernatural about him'), and by the fiancée of a British naval officer.

The conclusion to Street's report gives an indication of the sense of paranoia and of the fear of a developing witch hunt:

I think this Play with its suggestion of a man in high position and wide influence working for Germany, unwholesome in its effect. But I do not see that it can very well be disallowed. (The author in that case would certainly, by the way, see the 'hidden hand' in this Office!)

Street recommended a series of modifications, which included removing the suggestion that Rosenbaum becomes a Privy Councillor:

> Whether or not the author intends to point at an actual person, this may be going too far. The author probably felt that he <u>might</u> go too far, as he has himself cut out references to Cabinet Ministers.

Street also objected to a line suggesting that Rosenbaum was 'in the confidence of leading men of both parties', and to his claim that he even has a portrait of the King 'presented to me by his Gracious Majesty Himself'. This was potentially explosive stuff, and the manager of Liverpool's Royal Court Theatre, where *The Hidden Hand* was to be staged as 'a purely propaganda play', admonished the Lord Chamberlain for his hesitation over the issuing of a licence:

> It is common knowledge that Naturalised Germans <u>have</u> occupied positions similar to those to which you take objection. The whole point of this play lies in the fact that Rosenbaum is a man of high position which gives him facilities for acting as he does and mis-uses it to the detriment of our country.

He reluctantly agreed to make some changes, but the Lord Chamberlain's objections were leaked to a press sympathetic to the play's message. As one national newspaper reported:

> A good deal of difficulty was experienced getting the Lord Chamberlain to pass *The Hidden Hand*. First of all he objected to the naturalised villain being a P.C.—and his objection prevailed. Then he didn't like him being an MP. But when the Lord Sandhurst was informed that members of the House of Commons had actually taken part in the filming of the play that objection went by the board.

The manager also informed the Lord Chamberlain that Mr Ben Tillett, the Labour MP for Salford (whom he described as the 'Director of Theatrical Propaganda for the Ministry of Information'), had stated his intention to make use of this play; he also sought special permission to retain the word 'bloody'— a word still not generally passed—'as an adjective to the word "Germans"', declaring that 'the phrase will be most effective from a propaganda point of view'. Indeed, he described its effect at a previous performance, which had been watched by a number of well-known public figures, including Horatio Bottomley, the former MP now editing a jingoistic newspaper called *John Bull*:

The distinguished audience included The Lord and Lady Mayoress, Brigadier General Edwin Commanding Mersey defences, and the phrase as rendered elicited a burst of cheering lasting some minutes, the audience thoroughly appreciating this way of speaking of the enemy. Mr Horatio Bottomley happened to be in the theatre, and at the fall of the curtain, he was prompted to rise and address the audience eulogizing the play as the finest war play ever written and hoping it would be utilised throughout the land so that we should obtain the benefit of the message it conveyed.[58]

Certainly no play title could have chimed more effectively with public concerns. The *National News* confirmed its topicality in July 1918, reporting that the play was 'based on a subject of vital National importance' and that its production served 'the excellent purpose of bringing vividly before the public the possibilities that lie in the policy of regarding a naturalised German as friendly until he is proved otherwise'. In the same issue they ran a news story under the headline '"HIDDEN HAND" CRUSADE', describing massive public protests in favour of removing the freedom of the '12,600 uninterned male alien enemies' currently living in Britain.[59]

A couple of months can be a long time in political theatre. By September, one producer, who was planning to stage an anti-German play which had already been licensed, was worried enough to ask the Lord Chamberlain whether it was safe to proceed with the production:

> In the event of the Capitulation of Germany—or even of an Armistice—
> is it likely that the performance of the play will be prohibited? Or that we
> shall be directed to modify and considerably alter the play?

However, the British government's policy appeared to favour the absolute destruction of its enemy rather than a reconciliation, and the Reader's response reflected this: 'I think that the possibility of the licence for this and other anti-Kaiser dramas being cancelled when Germany capitulates is one which may be safely ignored'.[60]

Meanwhile, the British authorities were still concerned about how their own army personnel were depicted. In November, 1918 lines cut from *A Spy in the Ranks* included a British army officer complaining that 'it's a bit beastly now we Officers of the old army have to rub shoulders with some of the Officers of today'; such an admission of class conflict within the army was 'precisely what was objected by the Military Authority'. Even after the removal of this and similar passages, there were still objections to the play, and during its run in London the Office received a strong letter of complaint from a major assistant provost marshall about the dangers of portraying a villainous British officer on the stage:

> My attention was drawn to this play by several Officers, and I witnessed the performance twice ... in order to decide whether I should take proceedings under the Uniforms Act, 1914, against the actor playing the part of the villain for bringing contempt on His Majesty's Uniform.
>
> Although I decided not to take proceedings under this Act, it appeared to me, as it did to other Officers and to Warrant Officers and Non Commissioned Officers, that it was prejudicial to Military discipline for an actor wearing an Officer's uniform to be hissed at from the gallery in which were soldiers as well as civilians. This army 'captain' appears as a thorough blackguard in the play.

Had he noticed, one wonders, that the villain was actually a spy impersonating a British officer, rather than the real thing? After a subsequent intervention from the Lord Chamberlain, the character's name was changed to Oppenheim, and, to make sure no one could miss it, he was given a new speech which left little room for ambiguity or misinterpretation:

> Curses; still if they only knew, only knew the truth, that I was no more an Englishman than they were Germans; no my father, my mother, were German, both clever Germans and brought me up to serve my Kaiser as they served their Country; I have lived here all my life, but I serve my German land; here I am disguised as an Englishman, here I can find out so much and send it across to my friends, and serve my Country.[61]

Much more problematic in terms of its perceived potential as ambiguous propaganda was the last wartime play to cause serious disagreement within the Lord Chamberlain's Office, *Friendly Enemies*. The play was already running successfully in New York, and was submitted to the Lord Chamberlain at the end of 1918 for performance at the Haymarket in January 1919. But before the script arrived, the Lord Chamberlain had received a warning issued by the War Office, following a visit by an American intelligence officer:

> Lieutenant Collins stated that the play is an ingenious piece of German propaganda. He also stated that the author of the play is a German Jew, that it was produced in America by a Hungarian and that the leading actors were Germans.

Friendly Enemies focused on two successful German-born businessmen in New York, one of whom has become thoroughly American and has abandoned any allegiance to his place of birth; but the other remains a 'typical, stubborn, hide-bound Teuton', who trusts absolutely in the virtue of Germany and the Kaiser, and is persuaded by a German spy to donate a lot

of money, supposedly to help counter anti-German propaganda in America.
In fact, this money is used to help blow up an American naval ship carrying
his own son. Inevitably, the German is immediately and totally converted. He
now denounces Germany and the Kaiser, helps to trap the spy, and ends the
play belting out 'My Country, 'Tis of Thee' instead of the German folk song
he had sung in the first scene. So where, one might ask, could the political
objection to such an absolute conversion be hidden? Step forward the Lord
Chamberlain's senior Reader, Ernest Bendall:

> The play has for its moral the suggestion that our German enemy, espe-
> cially when he realises he is beaten, is at bottom a very good fellow after
> all . . . However favourably this may have appeared to New York with its
> largely German population it will not do for London at all. Hence *Friendly
> Enemies* which is of German authorship, and is a piece of subtle propa-
> ganda with commercial post-war reconciliation for its object is not
> recommended for licence.

Street disagreed with his fellow examiner, pointing out that it would be hard
to ban, and that 'it certainly would be an intolerant attitude to lay it down that
a play must not suggest that any German could possible be a good or lovable
person'. Yet he was prepared to accept that it must be a peculiarly subtle piece
of propaganda, even if the play itself contained no evidence of this; he looked
for justifications to ban it:

> A refusal of a licence must therefore be based on the a priori knowledge
> that it is intended as propaganda. I do not doubt this: the object no doubt
> is to conciliate opinion in favour of a reformed and converted Germany.
> A refusal might also be based, perhaps, on the possibility of a disturbance
> in the theatre when the pro-German asserts his original views, but such
> views have been expressed (by the villain) in many War plays.

Sir Douglas Dawson, with what he called 'my experience of tortuous methods
of the Teuton', believed that 'the very name of the play shows up its aim'. He
was adamant that it was dangerous propaganda, and that a licence must
accordingly be refused:

> Knowing how credulous is the British public . . . I feel convinced the
> German knows it too, and is already working underground to try and dissi-
> pate the feelings of horror created all over the world by their policy . . .
> the Stage is a powerful medium of propaganda, and the German knows
> it.

But for once Sandhurst over-ruled him, taking the advice of members of his

Advisory Board who could find no such propaganda in the play. One, Henry Higgins, reasonably declared:

> I cannot myself understand by what process of reasoning the conclusion can be arrived at that this play, which is really a consistent denunciation and exposure of German frightfullness, can be looked upon as a subtle form of pro-German propaganda. It is rather an appeal to Germans to realise the odiousness of the methods of those who until recently were their rulers and their guides.

Reflecting the paranoia and the ideological contortions of the period, he even suggested that if they suppressed the play then some people 'might plausibly plead that the hidden hand has been at work to suppress a useful piece of pro-Ally propaganda!'. Lord Buckmaster was similarly bemused by Dawson's argument:

> I gather from the papers before me that this play is suggested to be a piece of enemy propaganda and ought to be stopped in the national interest . . . I have utterly failed to discover anything that supports the suggestion . . . I feel no more friendly to the Germans after its perusal than before. I see no palliation of their brutality I see no excuse for their treachery and cruelty; on the contrary I see an organised system of atrocities exposed with spies and agents acting for the German Government.

Buckmaster, like Raleigh, was becoming more generally uneasy about the direction in which the censorship seemed to be going:

> I ask myself what it is that is feared from the dramatic representation . . . to this question I can find no answer.
>   If the British public cannot be trusted with the chance of seeing such a performance—a chance of which I do not believe they will avail themselves—they can hardly be trusted to walk alone.

Eventually, the Office decided that although the play itself could be licensed, the title sounded dangerously propagandist; it was performed as *Uncle Sam*.[62]

By 1919, there was perhaps a mood of embarrassment about some of the anti-German excesses which had become normalised in the theatre, and the Lord Chamberlain's Office refused to license *The World's Enemy*, which showed the Kaiser hiding in a neutral country, with Faust as his aid and confidant. The plot involved an English agent and an American journalist trying to get the Kaiser to England to stand trial for murder, and their attempts to use a former mistress to seduce him.

This play is an attempt to exploit the general hatred of the Kaiser, and it
pursues its object with extreme vulgarity and a very mean sort of malig-
nity . . . There is a long scene of him inflicting unwelcome caresses on her,
bullying his servant, eating voraciously and so on—the intention being to
make him as repulsive as possible . . . Eventually the Kaiser is arrested by
the British and led off screaming wildly.

Both Examiners found this to be in 'monumental bad taste' and 'revolting to
any sense of national dignity or magnanimity', and it was time to recall again
the common ancestry shared by the Kaiser and the British monarch.[63]
Probably more to the point, by 1919 there was a new international enemy
challenging the British way of life. In a changing Europe in which the principle of monarchy itself was under threat from revolution and communism,
alliances might also have to change—and to do so rapidly. The next war might
be fought not just between nations but also between classes, and the Lord
Chamberlain might find it harder to ensure that the theatre continued to play
its part in uniting the country against an agreed common foe.

SECTION TWO
1919–1932

CHAPTER SIX

The Dead Men
Principles and Practice

> While it is a task that demands great discrimination and great industry, it is also one which, being entirely negative, men of ability and energy will not often perform . . . the censor lives in an office, not in the world; everything he reads is, for him, something to be censored, and the onus on every writer is to prove that what he has written ought to be published.[1]

> The Lord Chamberlain has no objection to his official title being substituted for the word God.[2]

The restrictions under which the censorship forced theatre managers and writers to labour during the period between 1919 and 1932 strike us today as appalling. The final four chapters of this volume will focus on detailed examples of censorship in relation to the specific themes and issues which recurred most regularly and significantly. First, however, it is necessary to establish a historical context, and sketch in some other details in the pattern.

It is easy to assume that the Lord Chamberlain was the architect of an authoritarian and repressive control. But the processes by which theatre was censored were complex, and the principles and policies of his Office were far from extreme when compared with the expectations of some of his powerful critics. Writing for publication in 1925, his Reader since 1914, George Street, claimed that the censorship had become increasingly liberal in recent years; he expressed his full support for this shift, and even dared to suggest that perhaps those theatregoers who were likely to be disturbed by what was permitted 'might often make more enquiry before they go the theatre and choose a play suited to their tastes'. His own instincts about what should be allowed were far from reactionary:

> I think it impossible and undesirable to exclude from the theatre that greater freedom in facing problems and viewing situations, that greater

frankness in reproducing speech and manners which began some forty years ago.

However, Street insisted that the balance had changed in spite of powerful opposition from those who believed that visits to the theatre should be immune from any possibility of shock; he had no doubt that 'the greater pressure now is not from intellectuals who demand a broader freedom, but from those who demand a far stricter censorship'.

Street became the sole Examiner and Reader following the death of Ernest Bendall in 1920, and though he had no ultimate authority, his recommendations to the Lord Chamberlain were usually trusted and accepted. *The Times*—in what was perhaps a somewhat cynical but perceptive article about censorship—suggested that the focus of attention for any censor tends to be the wish to please those in authority above him: 'his first principle is to leave nothing in that may cause any offence to his superiors. He thinks of them rather than of the public.'[3] Certainly, Street was fully aware of the need to ensure that the opinions he offered were broadly in line with the principles of the Lord Chamberlain, and with the external climate; yet he, at least, was no puritan. Street had written plays himself, and he summarised the responsibility of the censorship as being 'to hold a really enlightened balance', and to try to distinguish between the serious artist and the exploiter. His aim, he said, was to support 'genuinely artistic or even didactic efforts' and 'to curb sharply the efforts to attract by pruriency or mere salacity or intolerable vulgarity'.[4] Inevitably, such generalised principles remain open to different interpretations, but in view of the assumptions that are too often made about the blinkered attitude of the censors, it is worth noting that Street had championed Ibsen's plays long before they were accepted, and as early as 1905 had openly described Oscar Wilde as 'a genius whose ruin was one of the saddest tragedies in my lifetime'.[5] In the 1890s he had even edited a two-volume collection of the plays of William Congreve, and while Congreve's reputation was not quite as low as that of some other Restoration dramatists, Street's general celebration of the genre—and especially his longing for it to be rediscovered through performance—would hardly have endeared him to those who believed the theatre must be a centre of moral orthodoxy. 'Grossness of language', he wrote in relation to Restoration plays, was not something absolute, but 'a matter of time and place'. His introduction to Congreve's work pointedly refused to accept the responsibility of the theatre to recommend and instruct, advocating rather 'the suspension of moral prepossessions' by those who encountered it, and condemning the naivety of confusing the voices of Congreve's characters with the opinions of the author. He urged readers and audiences not to forget they were 'in a court of art and not in a court of law'.[6] Thirty years later, debating the censorship of Somerset Maugham's *Sacred Flame*, Street was still urgently reminding his colleagues

of the important truth that 'a dramatist is not to be regarded as a propagan-dist of the views of his characters'.[7]

Legislators almost always claim (and doubtless often believe, with Street) that they are striking a balance between two extremes, failing to recognise that they themselves are positioning the fulcrum. 'It is not in the province of the Censor to exclude the expression of political opinion from plays *if kept within decent limits*', wrote Street in 1924, for example (my italics).[8] But it is clear that during the 1920s, the Office was the frequent recipient of complaints from prominent public figures and from organisations with influential members, and was the target of concerted attacks and campaigns in the press; most of its critics were indeed advocating much stronger censorship, above all over issues of sexual morality. 'From the number of representations that have been made to me from various quarters', wrote Lord Cromer, the Lord Chamberlain in 1924, 'I should not be surprised if the brewing storm about censorship was to burst before long'; he added that 'the criticism is not on account of the plays that are stopped but on account of those that are passed'.[9] Under attack in the House of Lords in a 1926 debate, Cromer compared the numbers of plays refused licences over recent years to demonstrate that, far from going soft, censorship was being applied with 'increased severity'; this might at first seem to contradict Street's claim that it had become more lenient, but the apparent inconsistency reflects the fact that more playwrights and managers were demanding greater liberties, and it was in consequence of this that more plays were being turned down. For many MPs this was not enough, and the debate complained that 'many plays have escaped his net which ought not to be presented', and urged the Lord Chamberlain 'to be, if possible, even more severe and careful'.[10]

Amongst those who acted as official advisers to the Lord Chamberlain in the period between 1918 and 1932 there was a considerable divergence of opinion. One of the most respected members of the Advisory Board was still Lord Buckmaster, a former Chancellor and Liberal MP, who was perhaps best known for having actively campaigned against capital punishment and in favour of birth control and changes in the divorce law. Like Street's, his view on the function of theatre appears relatively enlightened: 'I think the pulpit and the stage should not be confused', he wrote, and he was adamant that censorship must always 'be capable of justification on ascertained prin-ciples'. Yet the grounds on which he was prepared to advise rejection still reveal a strong bias in his world-view; a play should be licensed, he said, 'unless it is of a brutalising and degrading character, shocks or pains the moral or reli-gious feelings of reasonable men and women, is likely to disturb international relations, subjects Members of the Royal Family to ridicule or contempt, or promotes public disorder'. He later recommended extending the same protec-tion granted to royalty 'to all people occupying eminent public positions'.[11]

The most regular and extreme reactionary voice in the Lord Chamberlain's

ear continued to be that of Sir Douglas Dawson. In 1920 Dawson became State Chamberlain, and was succeeded as Comptroller by Sir George Crichton, another old Etonian and Colonel of the Coldstream Guards. On the whole, Crichton took a much less forceful position than his predecessor, seeing his role more as that of co-ordinator than advocate; however, no one seems to have been able to tell Dawson that he no longer had an official voice, and he remained, *de facto*, a committed and sometimes belligerent adviser for another decade. Dawson was particularly opposed to anything he considered subversive of the existing order, and was easily shocked by the cynicism towards traditional values and the status quo expressed by playwrights such as Coward and Maugham. It was a *sine qua non* for him that criticism of the monarchy, the Empire, the aristocracy, or the British or even the French armies, was utterly beyond the pale. Nevertheless, even he acknowledged that it was 'no part of the censor's duty to teach morality', but rather that 'his role consists of safeguarding public susceptibility from being outraged'.[12] Yet Dawson had little time for the expression of modern thought or ideas on the stage. When Street recommended *The Suppressed Wish* in 1924, Dawson sarcastically commented: 'I do not share Mr Street's opinion that this play is amusing. I find it boring . . . But then I am lacking in education for I never read Freud, and am ignorant of his theories regarding "dreams", "suppressed wishes" and " . . . staircases" '. [13]

What, then, of the Lord Chamberlain himself? After the death in office of Lord Sandhurst, a Liberal Peer, the post was briefly held in 1922 by the Duke of Atholl, a former Conservative MP and Lord High Commissioner to the General Assembly of the Church of Scotland; but from 1922 until the late 1930s the man who, by what *The Times* described as 'an odd historical anomaly', officially controlled what could be staged for public audiences was the Earl of Cromer.[14] Before taking up his duties as Lord Chamberlain, Cromer had most recently served as Chief of Staff to the King and the Prince of Wales on their visits to India and the East, but it was probably his years of experience in the Foreign Office—and especially the Diplomatic Service— which were widely seen to be most relevant to his duties as a censor; much of his work in this field indeed shows him to have been an adept politician, compromising and avoiding confrontations whenever possible, and constantly weaving a path between different pressures. For anything significantly connected with the British monarchy (and much else besides) he consulted the King; for religious decisions he turned to the Archbishop of Canterbury; the opinions of government departments, foreign embassies and important public figures were all sought and listened to whenever he deemed it necessary or appropriate. For Cromer, the real art of censorship was that as much of it as possible should remain unseen and therefore unacknowledged. Sometimes a relatively innocuous play would be refused a licence in order to discourage others on the same theme; sometimes he would politely

but deliberately request such widespread and detailed changes that a play was almost certain to be withdrawn without his having to ban it. Often discussions between Cromer or his representative and a theatre manager negotiated changes which would be incorporated within a new and clean script, which could then be licensed without any endorsements or evidence of censorship. On occasions, he even encouraged managers to send in scripts informally, in order to test whether it was worth their while submitting them officially; sometimes ideas were discussed before a play had been translated into English (or even before it had been written) in order to determine if it was likely to prove acceptable. Such practices disguised the true extent of theatre censorship.

Cromer's unusually long career as Lord Chamberlain was partly the result of this appointment becoming 'non-political', so that its occupant no longer changed with the government. However, he also showed the politician's ability to be different things to different people, and to ensure that, wherever possible, blame and criticism were diverted elsewhere. One tactic which he developed in order to try to absolve himself from liability was to devolve to managements the general responsibility for ensuring that audiences were not shocked or upset. Thus in the case of a play about the French Revolution, performed in 1927, his endorsement on the licence insisted that the management must 'ensure that the killing of Marat in his bath will not be acted in such a way as to cause offence *to any member of the audience*' (my italics).[15] Such vague and almost impossibly far-reaching requirements gave the Lord Chamberlain a get-out clause in the event of complaints. However, the passing of responsibility was not always successful. On one occasion he allowed a particular scene in a revue 'on the clear understanding that should his Lordship receive any complaint which proves to be well-founded, he may call upon you to omit the Scene altogether'. His letter was leaked into the hands of a hostile press, and the *Daily Graphic*, a frequent critic of the weakness and inadequacy of the censorship, sought to embarrass him:

> Anybody who knows anything about the theatre laughs at the censorship always, but this new idea of the Lord Chamberlain's, that he does not mind a thing if the papers do not, is surely a confession of the most extraordinary weakness.[16]

It is to Cromer's credit that almost as soon as he took up his position he began trying to recruit a woman to his Advisory Board. 'I feel that in these days women should have opportunities of representation', he wrote in 1924, and he invited suggestions as to who might be suitable. 'It is very difficult to think of anyone who has both the time and the brains', replied an MP at the Colonial Office, and Cromer temporarily abandoned the idea on the advice of the Home Secretary and 'for the simple reason that the question of selecting the right woman presented almost insuperable difficulties'.[17] However, during

the parliamentary debate on censorship in 1926, Lord Newton proposed that, in the light of contemporary patterns of theatre attendance, having a woman's opinion was a more or less necessary evil:

> As everybody knows, there are far more women who waste their time and their money in going to the play than men. You can see hundreds of these misguided women waiting for hours and hours in all kinds of weather on the pavement in order to witness some perfectly imbecile piece . . . My suggestion is that a woman should be put upon this Committee—a really sensible woman, not the kind of woman who would stand twelve or possibly twenty-four hours waiting on the pavement.[18]

This was the invitation Cromer needed to enable him to overcome the reluctance and conservatism expressed by Sir Douglas Dawson. The latter described himself as 'sceptical' of such an innovation, because of his 'impression of the psychology of . . . the "female woman's" mind'. Cromer, however, faced him down, insisting 'that as the majority of playgoers are women, it is really unfair that the woman's point of view should not be voiced'. Seeking, as usual, to appease rather than to confront, Cromer diplomatically allowed Dawson to think that he had felt 'obliged' to consider Newton's proposal, and that he was probably engaged in a cosmetic and defensive exercise: 'I do not know whether we shall gain very much by having a woman on the Board, but public opinion will probably think so', he wrote. One of the likely names he now put forward was that of Lady Violet Bonham Carter, the daughter of the ex-Prime Minister H.H. Asquith, and herself an active and campaigning liberal, and the recent President of the Women's Liberation Federation. Dawson could not approve of someone with her background becoming involved, or being privy to the discussions which took place. He warned Cromer of the danger of allowing people with such unorthodox views and backgrounds to, as he put it, 'have a finger in the pie', and advised that he 'would be very chary of admitting one from that "milieu" behind the scenes'. Dawson had not forgotten the origins of what he clearly saw as the misplaced and vindictive attack on the Office of 1909: 'Remember the Joint Committee appointed by her father to enquire into the working of the Censorship, without one word to the Lord Chamberlain'.

Cromer professed to recognise Dawson's doubts—'I quite agree about the danger of that "milieu", and I had quite forgotten that it was her father who was responsible for setting up the Royal Commission'—but he invited her anyway. It is interesting, too, to note the reason for Cromer's rejection of the alternative suggestion of Henry Irving's daughter-in-law, Miss Dorothea Baird; her inclination for 'good works', he feared, 'may perhaps have developed too strongly any puritanical strain there may be in her character'. Clearly, Cromer was not interested in strengthening the reactionary wing of his

Advisory Board. He tactfully suggested to Dawson that as she was 'a busy woman of many occupations', he was not really expecting Lady Violet Bonham Carter to accept. But, as he had hoped, she did.[19]

Predictably, much of the censorship practised during the 1920s and early 1930s seems now to have been focused on inconsequentials. References to Beecham's Pills or to smelly feet were generally cut (indeed, smells of any kind disturbed the censors) and any hint of a raspberry being blown was automatically removed. They cut the word 'Bulgaria' from a revue because it 'stands for an unmentionable one', 'blurry' because in a west country accent 'it can easily be pronounced to sound like "bloody"', and the substitution of 'cod's' for 'sod's' in O'Casey's *Shadow of a Gunman* because 'the two words are so similar as to be indistinguishable in speech'.[20] They even insisted on changing the identity number of a convict uniform in an otherwise unremarkable farce:

> The number 69 has, I believe an esoterically bad meaning—too esoteric for the ordinary public and certainly not meant by the author. I do not know if it is worth pointing out, but some critic is likely to talk of 'the innocent Censor'.[21]

However, while it was relatively easy to adopt simple and absolute rules over such trivialities, consistency on bigger issues was difficult to maintain. In 1927 a policy was introduced 'with the aim of reducing bad language on the stage'.[22] But even that aim marked a tacit acceptance that some 'bad language' was permissible; the issue was where and when to draw a line. In April, referring to 'a needless bloody', Street noted that 'it is difficult to censor this consistently, but the word is becoming too frequent'.[23] Of a war play the following month, he commented that the language of a character being shelled 'involves a bloody or two, but he is an ordinary soldier under fire'; it was allowed to stand.[24] Similarly, licence was shown in 1929 in the case of *Journey's End*; 'The Gods I think may be left unchallenged', decided Cromer, 'and also the bloodies except for those . . . where their use in conjunction with the name of God renders them more offensive'. Again, in *The Life and Misdoings of Charley Peace*, the 'bloodies' survived, because they were employed 'by a north-country labourer of the roughest type'. As one of the Lord Chamberlain's officials pointed out: 'As is generally known, the language of the common northerner is liberally punctuated by strong adjectives, and for this reason there could be no possible objection to the expression'.[25] Yet swearing was banned the following year from what Street called 'a well-intentioned anti-war play' as being 'objectionable on the lips of a young woman'.[26] The word 'bastard' was generally disallowed, and 'pox', 'whore-begotten', 'belching', and 'body odours' were all removed from a 1930 play set in

Newgate prison.[27] The sexual use of the word 'had' was a particular *bête noir* of Lord Cromer; in 1930 'I have had her a dozen times' was typically changed to the more romantic 'She has been in my arms dozens of times'.[28] Sometimes it was a question of quantity, as when the Reader noted: 'I have not marked the damns and blasts and hells as they are not banned words, but there are too many of them, too close together'. On that particular occasion, the Lord Chamberlain generously ruled that 'the producer may have a say as to which words he prefers to retain for dramatic necessity'.[29] Inappropriate references to the Deity—such as 'God, what ankles'—were usually removed;[30] however, on one occasion, when Street proposed preventing a young woman from saying 'Good God' because it was 'not very nice', the Comptroller pointed out that the play had been written by a Parson and that it might therefore seem 'rather ironical to delete the word "God"'.[31]

In day-to-day practice, the censors waged a perpetual struggle to match individual plays against general principles; was the depiction of evil acceptable provided virtue triumphed and wrongdoers were punished? Could an immoral line be placed in the mouth of a character whose behaviour is clearly condemned? 'I am never quite clear on what ground a play can be refused a licence when it deals with a vicious incident', admitted Buckmaster during one of the recurring debates on such issues. He pondered whether the crucial factor was that 'vice should never be made attractive and triumphant'.[32] Buckmaster also tried to draw a distinction between the subject of a play and the way in which that subject was treated, concluding that it was generally 'the presentation rather than the plot that is the most obvious cause of offence'.[33] But Dawson disagreed, and the conflict was never resolved. 'It appears to me', wrote another member of the Advisory Board when seeking to establish some firm boundaries, 'that as a general rule subjects that are not usually discussed by a mixed company of ordinary men and women are not suitable for stage treatment'; he went on to cite 'venereal disease, unnatural vices, abortion, incest +c' as examples of what was unsuitable. In practice, however, the outlawing even of these subjects was conditional rather than absolute.[34]

The Office tried to base its decisions, not only on what was immediately apparent in the words of a script, but also on how it anticipated something might appear in performance; however, it was always easy for opponents of censorship to accuse the Lord Chamberlain of having imagined meanings and possibilities which had never been intended. To be sure of the attitude not only of the playwright, but also of a hypothetical production and different audiences, was impossible. In the early 1930s, a stage adaptation of Evelyn Waugh's *Vile Bodies* was repeatedly rejected on the grounds of its immorality, but the play's defenders claimed that its very purpose was to satirise and denigrate the immorality it depicted. The script was licensed only after a narrator had been inserted at the beginning of each scene to state in explicit and apparently didactic terms the moral of what the audience was about to see; but of

course, even such statements are themselves liable to become ambiguous in performance. As Street noted, 'I do not think much of this as the audience might take his remarks as ironical'. Reading the script now it is hard to imagine that they would have done anything else.[35]

As we know, greater freedom had traditionally been extended to foreign plays, especially if performed in their original language.

> The mere fact that a play is in a foreign language is in itself sufficient to exclude most young people and in addition everyone knows that things can be said in French that could not be tolerated in English.[36]

One example of this freedom being exercised occurred in relation to Pirandello's *Sei personaggi in cerca d'autore*, which Cromer licensed in Italian in 1925, soon after the English translation had been rejected: 'People who speak Italian and are interested in Italian literature would be disappointed if they could not see this famous play and the same can be said of the Italian Colony'.[37] The English translation, which had been turned down because of the incestuous implications of the plot, was granted a licence only in 1928, and after a considerable struggle, when Sir Barry Jackson persuaded Lord Cromer to watch a private performance at the Arts Theatre to prove to him that it was not causing offence. However, there were limits to the freedom even for foreign plays in their own language; in 1928, for example, 'sodomie', 'urines' and 'excréments' were removed from *Knock* by Jules Romains. 'I think it would be an unfortunate precedent to admit the speaking of these three words on the stage merely because they are said in French', observed Cromer.[38] Probably the fact that these words were almost indistinguishable from their English equivalents was also an important factor. Again, when *Maya*, a serious portrayal of the life of a prostitute, was to be performed in French for a single matinée in 1929, the fear of creating a precedent was too great:

> Since the play is clearly impossible for licensing in English, as too grossly offending English feeling in the picture of a prostitute's promiscuity, and since it has been done 'privately' in English and no doubt would be done publicly if allowed, the case is altered. A permission to do it in French would be cited as inconsistent with the refusal of it in English.[39]

Cromer declared himself generally 'not disposed to encourage translations or adaptations from French plays', but by the mid-1920s the danger was originating elsewhere: 'Formerly the bulk of doubtful plays, or indeed plays that were beyond any doubt, hailed from France', wrote the Lord Chamberlain in 1926; 'latterly it is America that has provided this form of drama'.[40] Indeed, Cromer even contacted the British Embassy in Washington to ask whether

there was 'anyone in New York to whom you could refer me for private and unofficial advice' about dubious material being performed in the United States which managers might be planning to export to England. 'It should be an Englishman conversant with English tastes', wrote Cromer, 'and of a discriminating mind'. The Embassy was understandably reluctant to be seen to be getting involved, and pointed out the risk of 'unpleasantness or even retaliation' if it was accused of trying to censor plays which had been allowed in America; nevertheless, it promised the Lord Chamberlain in March 1926 that it was 'on the watch' for a suitable agent.[41]

Of the pressures on Lord Cromer to be more rigorous and draconian, one of the most forceful and determined was still that exerted through the Public Morality Council. The Council's secretary regularly bombarded the Office with both general and detailed complaints and demands, backed up by documentary evidence and letters of support, and frequently accompanied by requests that he should receive a deputation. With so many high-ranking churchmen and public figures among its active committee, the complaints of the Council were not easy to dismiss. Its Chair, the Bishop of London, proudly declared in Parliament that he had 'been a trouble to successive Lords Chamberlain' and that many plays had been modified as a result of the society's representations.[42] There is some truth in these claims, but the overall impact of the Council is hard to assess because much of its effect was cumulative rather than direct. Yet it is important to note Cromer's refusal to capitulate to it. Soon after he took up his post, a large delegation tried to convince the new Lord Chamberlain that he should be much more assiduous in controlling not just actual words and images, but 'the atmosphere' of plays. Cromer put the Council carefully in its place, reminding it that his duty was to balance the views of the whole community, and that this included those voices which spoke loudly against all censorship, in any circumstances. Even more pointedly, he observed that some of the policies of his predecessors had exceeded what was officially allowed by law, and that this risked provoking a confrontation which might lead to the end of theatre censorship:

> He mentioned that Clause 14 of the Theatres Act of 1843 contained the only statutory regulations upon which the Lord Chamberlain could act. There were also certain Rules and Regulations, drawn up by previous Lord Chamberlain [sic], which really go beyond the Act, so that he really went further than the statutory powers allowed, and if any drastic action were taken, somebody might raise a point on this . . .
>
> The Lord Chamberlain asked the deputation to leave the whole matter in his hands, and he would do what he could to meet their views, but he made it quite clear that he must be guided by the impulse of public opinion, otherwise there was a danger of the censors being abolished altogether.[43]

While Cromer was doubtless keen to stake out his authority at the start of his term of office, and to prove to the Council that he would be no push-over, his fears were not necessarily spurious or without foundation. After less than a year in Office, Cromer advised the King that the system of censorship was problematic, and becoming 'more difficult with the growing tendencies of this free-thinking age'; despite this, he made it clear that the last thing he wanted was any further legislation, which would inevitably 'give rise to all sorts of difficulties including a clamour, in some quarters, for the entire abolition of censorship'. He also warned the Home Secretary, Joynson Hicks, that the government must expect 'periodical agitations' from both sides of the divide, and 'an open clash of ideas between the free-thinkers and reactionaries'. Seeking to take the opportunity to strengthen his own position and ensure himself against political sniping, Cromer even invited the government to consider whether it would prefer to establish an alternative means of controlling theatres. Not unexpectedly, Hicks admitted that the government was too wary of stirring up problems to tamper with the system. As Cromer informed the King, censorship had become 'so thorny a question that no-one is particularly anxious to take the responsibility out of the hands of the Lord Chamberlain, and to tackle it themselves'.[44]

One area where the Public Morality Council became very agitated during the mid-1920s was the apparent willingness of the theatre to normalise adulterous and non-conventional relationships, by making them the focus of so much drama, and failing automatically to condemn them. In the summer of 1925, several newspapers gave great publicity to a church sermon by the Reverend J. Stuart Holden, which attacked the 'glorification of the dustbin and the cesspool' and the 'grinning menace' of contemporary theatre. The attack was indeed an outspoken one, which continued to insist on the importance of theatre in shaping society and behaviour:

> If these plays bear any relation to English life today we are hastening toward some inevitable catastrophe, for they are dramas of the open drain.
>
> They portray various sets of people, chiefly of the wealthy class, who exhibit open and cynical disregard of all moral prohibitions and sanctions . . .
>
> We should not think of tolerating an open sewer in our city, belching out its deadly bacteria of typhoid and typhus.
>
> Why should they be permitted to fasten on the rising generation of our young men and women with all the clever sententiousness of smart worldly wisdom the moral standards of the jungle and the gutter.
>
> If these dramatists are right: if there is any considerable section of society which actually lives as these stridently vulgar and unclean-minded people on the stage do, pursuing sexual satisfaction without regard to

the laws of God or the rights of men, then society is going to have a rude awakening.

Dr Holden even revived familiar wartime invective in accusing the Lord Chamberlain of betraying his country:

> There exists, for the preservation of our land from this impudent evil that stalks unrebuked and from its degrading consequences, a law of censorship.
>
> Why is it not put into operation? What hidden hand is protecting these purveyors of pornography?..
>
> Why does the Censor not act? . . . I indict him for grave dereliction of duty, and call for his examination and dismissal.

Two days later, the newspaper carried a headline announcing: 'LONDON CONFERENCE ON MORBID PLAYS'.[45] So widespread and angry were the attacks at this time—or so successful the propaganda of the moralists—that the Lord Chamberlain warned the Home Office of 'threatened militant action at certain theatres', and identified at least five specific London productions where he anticipated significant protests and threats to public order might take place.[46] Since the law stipulated that the Lord Chamberlain should refuse a licence to any play he considered likely to lead to a breach of the peace, threats to interrupt and disrupt performances were no doubt a carefully orchestrated and strategic tactic, designed to increase the pressure on him.

Introducing a parliamentary debate on theatre censorship the following year, Lord Morris cited play after play and criticism after criticism of the Lord Chamberlain's leniency (though his confident rhetoric was somewhat undermined when he mistook the title of a play for the title of a non-existent newspaper). Morris demanded that the Lord Chamberlain should be much more uncompromising and pro-active in suppressing people's appetites: 'The public are asking for filth, and the younger generation are knocking at the door of the dustbin', he declared. Morris also argued that it would be better not to have a censor at all than to continue with the present misguided liberalism, since anything licensed was imbued with what he called 'the imprimatur of the Lord Chamberlain'—and effectively, that of the Crown. Lord Braye announced himself as 'one of those people who believe that all plays are mostly detrimental', arguing that, with a few exceptions, all plays were immoral, since they presented 'the uncontrolled passions, of men and women'; the problem, he maintained, was not peculiar to modern playwrights, since 'from the days of Sophocles and Euripides that has been the theme of every play that has been written by every play-writer'. He did, however, retain a particular contempt for Restoration dramatists, such as Congreve and Wycherley, and

the fact that they had recently been 'unearthed and brought before the public as great playwrights' was a sure sign of a new low being reached. Braye described the theatre as 'the barometer by which you can read the exact degree of national morality'; and at present 'all right minded persons agree that it has come down very nearly to zero'.

The extreme positions adopted by the moralists hardly helped their cause, and the Lord Chamberlain's record was forcefully defended by Lord Buckmaster, who sought to alert his audience to the dangers of imposing too heavy a censorship on artists. He employed a well-judged example: 'Is there any play that ever was written', he asked, 'that possesses more sumptuous immorality than *Anthony and Cleopatra*?'. He pointed out that Shakespeare had not even bothered to include lines condemning the morality of his protagonists, as most modern writers would probably feel obliged to do; 'You cannot say that because a play deals with an immoral situation, or because it deals with it without reproving the immorality, therefore it should not be performed', he argued. Buckmaster also focused on the class bias inherent in recent attacks on modern plays, suggesting that they were causing a disturbance only because they revealed immorality 'among people who are well-to-do and who, for want of a better word, are sometimes called the "upper class"'. He pointed out to the House that 'the vices of the poorer people have never been excluded from the stage', and there could be no legitimate reason for allowing one and not the other. While applauding this stance, it is hard not to think that it was partially informed by a fear that such a bias might prove counter-productive and even dangerous:

> No worse service could be done to the censorship of the stage, or to society, than to lead the public to believe that a kind of screen was going to be put up and that people who lived behind that screen were not to have their lives caricatured or represented on the stage, while the people on the other side could.[47]

As we know, many of the difficulties for the censors arose from the obvious fact that the script of a play is only the starting point for a performance. Complaining to the Office in 1927 about the vulgarity of a musical farce which had been licensed, a police report from Birmingham commented as follows:

> The principal comedienne is Miss Nellie Wallace, who for many years past has had a reputation for songs of a suggestive type and very obvious double entendres. There are in this performance several extremely obvious allusions to sexual relationships between men and woman. . . . The emphasis which is being given to particular lines undoubtedly places a construction which could never have been anticipated by the Lord Chamberlain's Department when the script was licensed.

The report gave an example:

> He tells her that he cannot understand why she is not married or even
> engaged. She makes a remark, 'well, I haven't been neglected', at the same
> time making a grimace which makes the intention obvious. This remark
> is in the script.

Street pointed out that 'the standard of the Birmingham Police in the matter
of morality and suggestiveness is stricter than that of the rest of the country',
but Cromer insisted that 'the Birmingham Police should be thanked', while
those responsible for the production must be given 'a good dressing down'
and warned that the Home Office was considering the possibility of a prosecution.[48] In fact, the Lord Chamberlain and his advisers were certainly well
aware of the possible gaps between a script as licensed and as presented, and
where stage directions were included in a script, they were not infrequently
the subject of censorship. Buckmaster, seeking to absolve the Lord
Chamberlain from responsibility for what was actually staged, told the House
of Lords that often 'offence does not lie in the thing that is performed but in
the way it is performed'. Yet while we might take this as a self-evident truth
about the nature of performance and interpretation, Buckmaster's view was
also informed by class prejudice and assumptions:

> It is not the dialogue that makes the play indecent; it is the way that dialogue
> is interpreted on the stage . . . If it is done by a high-minded woman, as I
> beg your Lordships to believe our best actresses are, it will cause no offence
> whatever. If it is done by a lower-class woman with salacious impulses it
> will offend people of decent minds.[49]

One of the specific questions Lord Cromer was asked to address during
the parliamentary debate was whether he would object if the responsibility for
granting annual venue licences to London theatres were to be vested in future
in the London County Council rather than in his Office. The significance of
this was that many—including the Public Morality Council—believed that
more pressure could be brought on theatre managers if they were compelled
to live under a real threat of not having their annual performance licence
renewed. Indeed, this was the system which operated outside London, and
local watch and vigilante committees were seen to provide an additional and
often a much stricter check on managers' freedom. Not without some reason,
the Public Morality Council viewed the relationship between the Lord
Chamberlain and London managers as one of cosy gentlemen's agreements,
and believed that the London County Council might be more susceptible to
the kind of pressure successfully exerted elsewhere. In March 1926 the Home
Office hinted to the Lord Chamberlain that comparable safeguards to those

which existed outside London could 'supplement in a valuable way the authority of the Lord Chamberlain'; it asked him to detail the equivalent 'machinery' he employed to inspect performances in theatres under his jurisdiction. Forced onto the defensive, his Comptroller rather implausibly claimed that 'all questionable plays are visited, either in rehearsal or on the first night by one of the staff of this Department'. The Home Secretary was not convinced, and told Cromer that he was under pressure to transfer the licensing of all London theatres to the London County Council, with a committee set up to hear the annual applications in public. For Cromer, the oil which greased the machinery of censorship and ensured its reasonably smooth running was precisely the informal relationships and agreements he entered into with managers, and he successfully resisted a change which he warned the Home Office would 'exasperate the West End Theatre Managers and make them less tractable in their relations with the Lord Chamberlain's Department'. As a concession, he agreed that in future he would renew all licences on specific days, on which he would also receive and consider public protests about specific theatres.[50]

A further problem for the Lord Chamberlain was that unscrupulous managers or actors would change or add to the approved script, taking the gamble that this might go undetected. The Lord Chamberlain told the Home Office that such devious practices were more likely to take place outside London, where it was harder for him to maintain control. 'It is almost impossible, once a play has left London, to check how it is played in the Provinces', wrote his Comptroller following one complaint, 'and we know only too well that full advantage is taken of this fact by Managers and Touring Companies'.[51] In 1923 the Home Secretary had, at Cromer's request, written to all chief constables, acknowledging that it was 'impossible for the Lord Chamberlain to watch all plays that are being performed throughout the country', and asking them to report on 'any cases in which objectionable scenes or actions are introduced into a licensed play'.[52] Some forces took this responsibility very seriously, regularly inspecting and making detailed reports on performances, and checking these against the original script. The problem was perhaps especially acute in revues, where whole sketches might be cut or added, or where a new scene might be illegally played under an old title. It is impossible to estimate how widespread was the practice of illegally altering material, but the successful prosecutions against actors, managers and licensees which occurred fairly regularly may well have been no more than the tip of an iceberg. While we will never know exactly what happened on the ground, any analysis of censorship must at least avoid assuming that the Lord Chamberlain's rulings were always observed in practice, or that his control was as effective as might appear from the licences and their endorsements. Comedians were seen as particularly likely to add topical gags or engage with an audience through improvised repartee, and for much of the time a blind

eye was turned to the practice. 'As far as I can remember', recorded a surprisingly vague report by one of the Lord Chamberlain's staff who had been sent to inspect a performance, 'the licensed script was generally followed'; but the official noted 'the addition of some comedian's "back-chat", *which is not unusual*' (my italics).[53]

Legal prosecutions for performing unlicensed material in public were not particularly uncommon. Indeed, in 1925 the House of Lords approved an amendment to the Criminal Justice Act, which was intended to help secure more prosecutions. Previously, the law had specified that in the event of a successful prosecution against a performer, the venue itself should automatically lose its performance licence; this was now acknowledged as being unfair to managers—who in the case of touring shows might never have been supplied with a complete script—and juries had therefore become reluctant to convict a performer for fear of punishing an innocent manager. The new amendment made the withdrawal of the theatre's licence discretionary. In practice, though, the Home Office and the Lord Chamberlain continued to be extremely wary of the risk of unsuccessful prosecutions, fearing the loss of authority that would result:

> The general opinion of the Lord Chamberlain is that it is more politic only to prosecute in an absolutely clear case, where there will be little or no possibility of a conviction not being obtained, as to bring a case which might be dismissed by the magistrates on the grounds of insufficient evidence might do more harm than good.[54]

According to Cromer, there were also differences in taste in different parts of the country: 'It is hopeless to try and cure vulgarity in the Provinces', he wrote in connection with a play licensed for Musselburgh Town Hall.[55] A contrary perspective was offered by the Chief Constable of Newcastle, who accused the Lord Chamberlain of failing to appreciate the different expectations of London audiences and those elsewhere:

> I am an old Metropolitan Police Officer and know what the public may tolerate in the centre of London and in the provinces respectively . . . Yet it seems to me that the class of show passed for London is also made applicable to the provinces.[56]

What is evident is that—as Street's comments in relation to Birmingham show—some police and regional authorities were known to be much stricter than others. It was, again, the Chief Constable of Newcastle who on one occasion complained to the Lord Chamberlain that 'the word "Oh" was substituted for "Ah"'; no wonder the show's producer was quoted as saying that Newcastle had become '750 per cent more narrow-minded than Birmingham'.

Following complaints from other cities about this same touring revue, police in Exeter responded to the request by the Lord Chamberlain to supply a detailed report on any alterations from the script which were being played:

> The production was in accordance with the certified copy, with the following exceptions:- Scene 5; the French girl instead of saying she had lost her 'Bow Wow' she used the words 'Pussy Cat'. Scene 15; The Comedian in the Gallery instead of using the words 'Gawds' said 'Lords'.

The Exeter police reported that they had immediately challenged the producer over these discrepancies; it is hard to judge at this distance who was fooling whom:

> I told her that the words 'Pussy Cat' instead of 'Bow Wow' in Scene 6 had been used, and she stated that the words were altered as the girl was able to pronounce the substituted words better than the original. With reference to Scene 15; she stated that owing to Exeter being a Cathedral City the word 'Lords' was substituted for fear some person might object to the original word if used. [57]

Another grievance of those demanding stricter control of the stage was the degree of freedom granted to private theatre clubs, an outlet for some of the more 'highbrow' and challenging plays since the 1890s. The 1909 Committee report had warned of the danger that 'freedom designed for the "drama of ideas" may be made an opportunity for a drama of indecencies', and as the number of clubs and performances rose, it must have appeared increasingly anomalous that plays which had been officially deemed unsuitable for public performance (or which had never been submitted for licence) were being openly performed to anyone who paid a relatively negligible membership fee.[58] In fact, there was uncertainty at the highest levels about the legal situation, and how the 1843 Act should be interpreted. In January 1925 the Comptroller asked the Home Office to rule on whether the Act was being broken if a theatre staged an unlicensed play without charging its audience for admission; he was told in reply that, although it had previously been assumed that if no charge was made then there was no acting 'for hire' and that therefore no offence had taken place, it was now felt that this seemed 'to narrow unduly the scope' of the Act. Advice was sought from the Law Officers of the Crown, who took fully twelve months to confirm that in their view it was indeed 'only a production or performance for hire which the Lord Chamberlain can effectively prohibit'.[59] Yet the government was keen to appease its most censorious supporters by clamping down on the freedom of clubs, and in 1926 the Home Office pointedly asked the Lord Chamberlain to reconsider whether he should be taking steps to prevent private produc-

tions of plays which had actually been refused licences. Cromer opposed this, fearing the inevitable confrontation would ultimately have the opposite effect to what was intended; at a meeting with Joynson Hicks, the Home Secretary, in April 1926, Cromer urged upon him 'the undesirability of direct interference on the part of the Lord Chamberlain'. He insisted that 'these performances serve their purpose', and warned of 'the wide-spread resentment that would doubtless result' if a new policy were introduced. However, though Cromer's instincts were probably much more libertarian than those of the government, his persuasive letter to the Home Secretary argued his stance from a purely pragmatic standpoint:

> I think it would gravely prejudice maintenance of Censorship of Stage Plays if an absolute prohibition were imposed upon the production by private dramatic societies of plays that have either not been submitted for licence, or that have been banned. This is a sort of safety valve which has its uses in enabling what is called 'pioneer work' to be carried out on the stage. If this were put a stop to, I think there would be a considerable outcry among authors, literary people and theatre people about our reactionary methods, autocratic interference by the bureaucracy, and all that sort of thing, which would be difficult to justify as not curtailing the liberty so dear to the subjects of this country.

Cromer came up with a more tactical approach to reach a similar end; he drew up a code of practice to be observed by play-producing societies which would effectively ensure they were indeed 'brought into line' and 'drastically regulated', but in ways which would deflect any criticism away from him or his Office. He did this by dealing not directly with the societies themselves but with the Society of West End Managers, whose members would be those allowing private societies to use their theatres on Sundays. Cromer was keen to avoid any confrontation which might lead to a challenge to his own authority, and, as he explained to the Home Secretary, it would 'make the whole difference if this prohibition of unlicensed plays were to come direct from the Lord Chamberlain or from the West End Theatre Managers themselves'. His preferred alternative was to use the managers as censors:

> I am inclined to the conclusion that the most politic thing to do would be for the Lord Chamberlain to use the West End Theatre Managers Association as a buffer state, that is to say, to impose upon the theatre licensees certain conditions (not regulations) under which Sunday performances may be permitted . . . it would then rest with the Association to turn to the Dramatic Societies armed with these conditions and to insist on their observance.

He was confident this would 'help to bring about the results we wish to see effected without any public odium being cast on the Lord Chamberlain's Department'.[60]

Cromer immediately entered into negotiations with the President of the Society of West End Managers and with the Director of Public Prosecutions, to produce a series of rules which would ensure that managers allowing their theatres to be used by societies would, in effect, become censors. His tactic was to warn managers that, although there would be no new legislation, he would be 'unable to regard performances of Stage Plays on Sundays given by Dramatic and other Societies or Bodies as permissible in such theatres unless certain conditions are strictly observed'. These conditions included requirements that tickets were only to be sold before the day of the performance to people who had been members for 'a reasonable length of time', though Cromer was warned that, legally, nothing could be done to prevent members selling their tickets to non-members. Yet the most significant stipulation was that no payments must be made to actors, since such payments would constitute 'acting for hire' and render the performance a public one.[61] Such non-payment was bound to impose a considerable restriction on the scope and ambition of most club performances, and it is hardly surprising that reviews so often speak of them as under-prepared. As the leading actress in one controversial play said after its private performance: 'Last night's presentation was not a performance so much as a sketch of what we could do with it. We had only a short time for rehearsals, and could not put our best into it.'[62] Probably more important even than the letter of the new code was its spirit, and the signal to West End managers was unmistakable; if they wanted to keep on the right side of the Lord Chamberlain—and they mostly did— then they must guard carefully what went on in their theatres, even when they hired them out. One senior manager advised Cromer that the introduction of such regulations 'would probably have the effect of stopping the production of unlicensed plays, as Managers would not let their theatres for such performances'.[63] Cromer knew that managers wanted to keep in his good books, and his careful strategy was informed by the principle that the most effective way to censor was to convince someone else that it was in their interests to exert control, and to remain in the background himself.

The new system introduced in 1926 was intended as an experiment, with an implicit threat to be understood that tougher measures might be implemented if necessary. The record of a meeting in May 1926 between the Lord Chamberlain and Mr Walter Payne, the President of the Society of West End Managers, noted that 'it was agreed that if after trial these conditions did not prove effective the whole matter would have to be re-considered afresh'.[64] Three years later, following a storm of mostly negative publicity about the private performance of a banned play, *The Shanghai Gesture*, Cromer was again asked by the Home Office whether what had occurred would 'justify

any reconsideration of the position' he had previously championed. While acknowledging 'an increasing tendency to stage plays privately after they had been refused licences for public performance', Cromer maintained his position, as the reply to the Home Office by his Assistant Comptroller spelled out very clearly:

> Lord Cromer asks me to say that he quite well remembers that when the conditions governing performances by Dramatic Societies were under discussion in 1926 there was a proposal that there should be a definite prohibition against the presentation of plays which had been refused a licence, but the Lord Chamberlain's view at that time was, and still is, that it would be very unwise to make any such rule . . .
>
> If such plays were prohibited from being shown even privately, there would always be a certain number of people who would continually agitate for their reconsideration, and keep reiterating that they were plays of more than ordinary merit which had been, in their opinion, unreasonably banned . . .
>
> In this case, the press practically unanimously condemned the play and supported the official decision to refuse it a licence; in consequence, we shall hear nothing more about it . . .
>
> The Lord Chamberlain considers that it would not only be unreasonable, but impolitic, to alter the conditions governing Sunday performances, so as to prohibit the performance of a banned play under private auspices . . . These private productions more often than not vindicate in the public mind the action taken by the Lord Chamberlain in having banned them for public performance, and thereby all further press agitation is arrested.

He was still confident that managers and societies were not likely to be tempted to go too far with their freedom for fear it would be taken away from them.

> The Lord Chamberlain does not think that the Home Secretary need be apprehensive that any definitely obscene, or grossly immoral play is likely to be produced by one of these private Dramatic Societies as this would be detrimental to their own interests. [65]

While any discussion of theatre censorship must acknowledge the loophole which allowed private clubs to enjoy a degree of freedom, it would be wrong to ignore the limitations under which they operated. The Gate Theatre Studio, under the direction of Peter Godfrey, did manage to present advanced (mostly foreign) plays, not just on Sundays, but regularly, operating under club conditions in order to avoid censorship; however, the financial restrictions on such theatres were not insignificant, and the Lord Chamberlain was

only too ready to jump on anyone who broke the rules. In 1928, for example, Godfrey and his assistant director were both successfully prosecuted when plain-clothes police officers secretly and illegally bought tickets for a performance of Kaiser's *From Morn to Midnight*, despite not being members. The claim of the defence that, because the actors were unpaid the play could not be said to be 'acted or presented <u>for hire</u>', was not accepted as relevant.[66]

In September 1932 the Kingsway Theatre, under Gertrude Kingston, took the unusual step of sending back to the Lord Chamberlain its annual venue licence. Kingston announced that the theatre would henceforth operate free of his control, and planned 'to produce such plays as the censor cannot or will not pass ... just as if they were produced by a commercial management'. Among the plays they planned to stage was the hugely controversial *Green Pastures*, an American play which focused on Creation, 'as seen in the mind of a Negro preacher', and which had recently been refused a licence. As *The Stage* put it when it announced the theatre's provocative plan:

> Conceivably the Lord Chamberlain might consider it to be indecorous for many thousands of people to see the Almighty personified as a garrulous Negro in a tight frock coat and baggy trousers and sporting a pair of enormous wings.[67]

The MP for Chislehurst, Waldron Smithers, was so incensed at the blatant attempt to bypass the Lord Chamberlain's control by opting out of the system, that he immediately began writing letters to the Home Office demanding action 'in the national interest' against the Kingsway and its management:

> I hate to see any opportunity given to the Socialistic tendency to undermine our English traditions by a mistaken sense of liberty, which in fact, in my opinion, is only licence. As I believe that liberty can only come through discipline, I venture to hope that a salutary discipline will continue to be exercised.

The Office hoped that the experiment would 'die a natural death', which, it insisted, 'would undoubtedly be the best solution'. But to be on the safe side, a secret meeting between the Director of Public Prosecutions, representatives of the Home Office, and Lord Cromer agreed that a detective should infiltrate the Kingsway club as a member in order to spy on its activities. Perhaps the Kingsway was on its guard or perhaps it was tipped off, but just over a week later the Director of Public Prosecutions reported the failure of this measure to the Home Office with some embarrassment; Inspector Allen—who 'would not from his appearance be taken to be a police officer'—had been unable to join as he could find no proposer or seconder. Unfortunately, the Kingsway's challenge soon collapsed—primarily for financial reasons.

Apparently playing to only 24 per cent of capacity, by the end of November it had reverted to operating under the Lord Chamberlain's licence as a public venue, and was thus bound again to perform only plays he had approved. The Assistant Comptroller described this to the Home Office as 'a satisfactory ending to the venture', and Cromer expressed pleasure 'that the movement for unlicensed plays has met with no support'.[68]

A separate legal issue was the problem of defining exactly how far the Lord Chamberlain's responsibilities extended. His licence was issued specifically to cover stage plays, but what came within that definition was never completely fixed. Cromer was determined to limit it. 'If there is any trouble over the performing dogs scene', he insisted in 1927, 'this must be dealt with separately as it is not covered by a stage play licence'.[69] On another occasion, when Street queried who took responsibility 'for the proper treatment of the elephant', Cromer insisted: 'I refuse to have anything to do with the licence for performing animals'.[70] There were other uncertainties about what was and was not a play. When revues had been introduced to West End theatres, Cromer had decided that their scripts did require licences, on the grounds that they possessed 'a certain unity', being often written by one writer and designed by one designer.[71] However, in 1925 he received a report that an unlicensed scene was being performed within a revue in Exeter; when challenged, the management claimed that the particular scene in question was not a stage play, and Cromer sought advice from the Home Office:

> Is there any standing definition of what constitutes a 'sketch' requiring a LC Licence and a Musical Hall 'turn' skit which does not.
> The Exeter Police call this a 'sketch' while the manager . . . pretends it is not . . .
> Please go carefully into the whole thing and if necessary consult the Home Office.

He was advised that, although the scene was probably 'not a stage play within the meaning of the Theatre Act', it was 'impossible to be sure that a court might not hold a different view'. The advice concluded:

> I see no reason why His Lordship should not agree to license this one *ex abundante cautelâ* explaining to the applicant that . . . whether the duologue is a stage play is not free from doubt. I should not recommend a prosecution.

Cromer took no action against the company for playing an unlicensed script, but duly licensed it when they subsequently submitted it.[72] In 1929 he again contacted the Home Office to ask whether it considered licensing was required for the newly fashionable form of entertainment known as a road show, which

typically consisted of a series of variety turns under a collective title but without a plot, and with a finale involving all the performers. Again the Home Office was uncertain, but suggested that perhaps if the individual acts were not stage plays then the whole entertainment was probably not one either, and the Lord Chamberlain could be absolved from responsibility.[73]

In 1932 Cromer made a concerted effort to avoid responsibility for certain kinds of material in revues, especially the living statuaries featuring scantily clad women in supposedly artistic poses, which certain managers and 'illusionists' were beginning to reintroduce. Cromer's strategy was to withdraw his licence from those specific scenes, defining them as outside his jurisdiction because they were not stage plays; however, he was not able to maintain this policy for long and was obliged to include them again within his licence.[74] In the same year, his Comptroller queried with the Home Office whether a new form of entertainment now being introduced under the term 'revudeville' could be excluded since it lacked the unifying features of an ordinary revue and was simply 'a continuous performance of music-hall turns, interspersed with a few sketches, the chief novelty being the non-stop element'. The Home Office advised that the performance 'as a whole does not appear to be a Stage Play', but keen to cover itself, as always, recommended that separate licences should be issued for sketches or individual items where appropriate.[75] It was more confident in ruling on another occasion that adding sound to a film did not turn it into a stage play. However, the important general point to note is that legal definitions and the precise boundaries of stage censorship often remained surprisingly unclear, without test cases to establish rulings; the Lord Chamberlain and the Home Office were reluctant to take risks over what a court would decide, and Cromer and his staff frequently relied on bluffing—hiding their uncertainties, and relying on not being challenged.

After his death in 1953, Lord Cromer's obituary described him as having been 'on excellent terms with the theatre profession', and he had, indeed, been Chairman of both the King's Pension Fund for Actors and Actresses, and the International Advisory Council of the Entertainments National Service Association (ENSA). His retirement was marked by the Association of London Theatre Managers expressing 'abiding gratitude for the courtesy and patience in which you have never failed, and for the sagacity which you have so constantly exhibited', and the journalist, theatre critic and sometime scourge of the censorship Hannen Swaffer insisted: 'I have never heard anyone speak unkindly of the Earl of Cromer'. He claimed that even managers who found themselves in conflict with Cromer 'all say how nice he is about it'.[76] But of course we need to remember that it was usually counter-productive for a manager to allow any frustration with the Lord Chamberlain's Office to surface; it was normally more sensible to play by the rules—even if it was hard to know what they were, or if they had changed without warning and for

no apparent reason. Challenging Cromer directly was liable to antagonise him or push him into a corner, and there was more chance of gaining concessions by accepting his authority, and expressing full support for his decisions and gratitude for the occasional favour extracted through private agreements. Doubtless many managers indeed saw him as an ally—not least against puritanical watch-groups and above all the Public Morality Council—but even if we leave out the playwrights who suffered at his hands, the legitimacy of the system and the way it operated were certainly not recognised by all theatre managers. In April 1926 Arthur Bourchier, a leading actor/manager, declared that 'the situation would be absurd if it were not dangerously crippling to dramatic art'; he suggested that the powers invested in the Advisory Board left the theatre susceptible to 'privately used animosity', and queried the qualifications of what he called the 'ghostly counsel' who wielded such power. 'Why', he asked, 'should Dramatic Art be governed by laws made in order to hide the moral turpitude of people in high places'. The Home Secretary was sufficiently perturbed by Bourchier's public attack to send a copy of the speech to the Lord Chamberlain for comment, and Cromer's response was to defend himself by launching a character assassination with a vehemence which suggests he had indeed been stung. Bourchier, said Cromer, enjoyed 'a certain position in the public mind' but this did not mean he held 'a corresponding position of esteem or high standing among his leading colleagues'. Indeed, said Cromer patronisingly, 'it must be distressing for him not to be taken more seriously by those of his theatrical and political friends who know him best'. Cromer claimed that Bourchier's antagonism was rooted in his failure to achieve the knighthood he coveted, because of the 'irregularity in his private life'. This had made him resentful of all authority, especially if it were connected with the Crown or the Conservative Party, and he had become, said the Lord Chamberlain, 'a disappointed and embittered man', who had 'turned his mind to other avenues for advancement and personal achievement by the adoption of socialist and communist doctrines'. In other words, according to Cromer, Bourchier's opposition to censorship had little to do with art and everything to do with the politics of envy and personal gain. 'Let me please add', concluded the Lord Chamberlain in a sentence which reveals his mastery of the hypocrisy so useful to diplomats, 'that personally I am on very good terms with Mr Bourchier'.[77]

In the same year as Bourchier made his criticisms, another well-known manager, Basil Dean, articulated a similar resentment of the obstacles being put in the way of new writers; like Bourchier, he believed that the serious artist was being effectively crippled by a system designed to deal with the trivial, and he pronounced it 'a great slur on the Theatre in this country that plays of a high literary standard and written in all seriousness of purpose should be denied production in England and should consequently have to be produced for the first time in America'.[78] Another leading West End actor/manager who

occasionally allowed his frustration with censorship to boil over was Leon Lion. In 1927, for example, Lion was infuriated by the refusal of a licence for a French play he was planning to stage, and expressed his outrage to a senior member of the Lord Chamberlain's staff :

> He appeared to be considerably upset on being told that he must submit a revised version, and said that he had never had such a request before. He asked me on what grounds you refused to license the present version and worked himself up into an excited tirade against the Censorship. He was distinctly rude and objectionable, but subsequently apologised for losing his temper . . .
>
> I thought it best to let you know his attitude at once as he may possibly invoke the aid of the press to advertise the play.[79]

At this time, Cromer was bearing the brunt of journalistic mockery over his repeated interventions on the length of sleeves to be permitted in a pyjama costume worn by the *femme fatale* in *Potiphar's Wife*, and his banning of a passage from the Bible in the same play.[80] But he affected not to be impressed by Lion's outburst, asserting his authority in the tone of a parent dealing with a naughty child:

> Mr Lion is at liberty to invoke the press as much as he likes. Bad temper won't help him to overcome the objections of Censorship.
>
> If he does not choose to do as he is told he will not get a licence for this play.

Lion continued to question the Lord Chamberlain's decision, though he suppressed his anger sufficiently to avoid open defiance, and reluctantly undertook to observe the changes demanded:

> I trust, however, that Your Lordship will understand that this undertaking does not mean my acquiescence in the reasonableness of the revisions demanded . . . and I should be obliged if Your Lordship will give me an early opportunity of hearing from you direct, precisely what are the 'niceties' to which present day drama is to be confined, and whether such words as 'kidney', 'stone', and 'hip' are to be permanently upon the British Theatres Index Expurgatorius.
>
> I appreciate the difficulties of Your Lordship's Office, and I respect its authority when justly exercised, but . . . I am sure the health of the theatre and the respect for authority must be weakened by any fearful and unreasonable exercising of your censoring powers.[81]

As was his wont, Cromer arranged to meet Lion privately to discuss the matter.

There were other managers, too, who would not have recognised Swaffer's praise for Cromer's 'tact and finesse', even if (for strategic reasons) they often swallowed their discontent.[82] One manager who refused to restrain or suppress his views, and who was in almost continuous conflict with Cromer during the late 1920s and early 1930s, was Terence Gray, whose potentially innovative practices and repertoire at the Festival Theatre in Cambridge were to a great extent destroyed by censorship. From 1926, when he became its Director, until he abandoned not only Cambridge but also theatre and Britain in 1932, Gray fought a prolonged war with what he called 'this Nursery Governess of ours', whose principles 'might have been taken out of a thirteenth-century book of rules for the managing of a nunnery'. Neither Gray's ability to mask his feelings in a language of gentlemanly politeness, nor the pleasure he may have extracted from needling the Lord Chamberlain with finely polished and sharpened barbs hidden behind English politeness, should blind us to the bitterness of the antagonism—or to what is represented by Gray's eventual capitulation. 'The best modern drama of Europe is almost closed to the English theatre, and native dramatists, aware of the barriers, do not waste their time trying to write great plays which they know cannot publicly be performed', wrote Gray soon after he took up his post in Cambridge. He aimed to open doors by introducing to an insular British theatre contemporary plays and practices from elsewhere in Europe and America. Inevitably, this provoked repeated disputes with the censor. 'The greater the play, the bigger the mind of the author, the less is the likelihood of the performance of the play being permitted before an English audience', Gray protested; amongst the many proposed productions over which he clashed with the Lord Chamberlain's Office were Wilde's *Salomé*, Strindberg's *Miss Julie*, Toller's *Hoppla!*, Tretiakov's *Roar China*, and several plays by Eugene O'Neill. Just as significant is Gray's claim that 'play after play passes through our hands which it would be futile even to submit to the Lord Chamberlain's department'. [83]

In 1929 Cromer demanded a series of cuts in *Hoppla!* Gray replied that it was 'not possible to suggest substitute passages in a serious foreign work of this nature' and proposed an alternative:

> May I have permission in each case to substitute the following formula:
> Scene, sentence, passage, exclamation, question, reply (as the case may require) deleted by order of the Lord Chamberlain's department?[84]

If the Office was embarrassed by practices such as this (or Gray's substitution elsewhere of the phrase 'Lord Chamberlain' when the original 'God' was banned) then it was careful not to let on. In 1931 a licence was refused for *Man and His Phantoms*, a French play which revisited the Don Juan story, and which was unanimously condemned by the members of the Advisory

Board; as Professor Allardyce Nicoll, a recent recruit who had taken the place of Sir Douglas Dawson, wrote: 'It is an play [*sic*] which leaves an impression of something evil and might, in my opinion, have a bad influence'.[85] Less than two weeks later Gray was informed that another play he had submitted—*The Eater of Dreams*, which was built partly on the Oedipus Complex—was receiving 'careful consideration', and that it would be 'some considerable time' before a decision could be reached. Gray wrote a detailed and an impassioned plea to the Lord Chamberlain:

> I am anxious to put the case of a theatre such as this, a theatre whose whole circumstances differ so considerably from those of the established professional theatre that I feel an injustice exists in connection with the administration of the censorship.

Gray pointed out that, unlike most London theatres, the aim of the Festival Theatre was not to generate financial profits, but rather 'to assist the survival and re-establishment of that aspect of the Theatre which corresponds to the best literature, to the purest form of pictorial and sculptural art, to the best music'. In order to achieve this, he explained, it was necessary to draw on 'the best intellects, the most penetrating psychologists, the most gifted dramatic artists', people whose minds were not 'bound by the narrow outlook as regards morality that circumscribes the censorship', and who were engaged with 'subjects that are of vital importance to human beings'. It was these subjects, he complained, which the theatre was being prevented from treating properly.

> The entertainment trade is allowed to treat these subjects in jest, a degree of pornography is deliberately employed to attract the public and that degree is allowed by the censorship, whereas such a theatre as this, which neither needs such pornography nor finds it in the works it seeks to perform, is denied the use of its legitimate material in consequence.

Gray received a formal and completely unhelpful reply from the Office, indicating that the aims of a theatre were irrelevant. The letter concluded with an insulting dig at Gray and his repertoire:

> That this procedure is apt to cause dislocation in your plans and the possibility of financial loss, such as you indicate, is much to be regretted. At the same time it should be pointed out that the nature of the literature you submit, which you are anxious not to have mistaken for pornography, is open to other opinions as to its character.

To add insult to injury, Cromer eventually ruled in this case that—subject to

some specific alterations—the play could be licensed; but by accident or design, he informed the Festival Theatre of his decision too late for the production to go ahead. Gray replied:

> I am obliged for your letter of November 6th. The date of performance of *The Eater of Dreams* was November 9th, and unfortunately even this theatre cannot produce a play over the weekend, so there can be no advantage in my giving you the undertakings you ask for.[86]

In 1932, when Terence Gray submitted a play called *The London Docks*, the Office described its language as 'an impertinence'. Gray reluctantly supplied a list of proposed alternatives to all the words cut, but could not resist adding: 'You will realise it is a little difficult when you insist that dock labourers shall use the language of the middle class, without the normal expletives of the latter'. He objected, too, to the assumption that a manager had the right to change the words crafted by a playwright:

> I take the strongest possible exception to the Lord Chamberlain's message. May I be informed by what ordinance I am required to step in between author and censor and make arbitrary alterations to authors' texts? . . . I do not think I should be required to understand the particular system of taboos which the Lord Chamberlain's Department endeavours to protect. I neither comprehend the system nor sympathise with it . . . I only submit plays to the Lord Chamberlain because the law obliges me to do so and I cannot see that I should be under any further obligation in the matter.[87]

Gray was well aware that the roots of the repression went beyond Lord Cromer or the Lord Chamberlain's Office. He described Baldwin's Conservative administration as 'a government of barbarians', and the Home Secretary rightly took much of the blame:

> Under the unforgettable Sir William Joynson Hicks the people of England were deprived of their liberties to an extent to which pre-war Germany was a land of freedom. Art was subjected to moral censorship only paralleled in the darkest ages of puritanism and barbarity.[88]

Shortly before abandoning theatre in 1932, Gray ended an article about censorship by quoting a poem from D.H. Lawrence, who had already suffered his own problems of repression:

> Censors are dead men
> set up to judge between life and death.
> For no live, sunny man should be a censor,

he'd just laugh,
But censors, being dead men,
have a stern eye on life.
—That thing's alive! It's dangerous. Make away with it!—
And when the execution is performed
you hear the stertorous, self-righteous, heavy breathing of the dead men,
the censors, breathing with relief.[89]

Yet the Lord Chamberlain was not the only—or perhaps even the primary—force of repression during this period. There is nothing to suggest that the abolition of the Office would, in itself, have liberated the theatre, and the opposite might have been the case. For all the damaging and unwelcome effects on theatre which were channelled through the Lord Chamberlain, he also protected the stage from some who may have been metaphorically dead, but who would have been quick enough to execute with even greater severity. It is now time to explore the practice of censorship in relation to some of the recurring themes and issues which provoked it.

CHAPTER SEVEN

No Screams from Rabbit

Horror and Religion

> It has always been the mission of the theatre to reduce, in so far as it lay
> within its power, the manners and morals of the community . . . for the
> accomplishment, if perhaps not always the intention, of all art is the
> lowering of human virtue . . . It has been kept alive by man's unregenerate
> sinfulness alone . . . And its greatest lovers and stoutest champions have
> ever been the men who most truly appreciated that beneath its pretence
> of divine origin there curled a red and forked tail.[1]

The majority of theatre censorship in the period between 1918 and 1932 was
directly connected to sexual or political anxieties, and these areas will be
explored in the three succeeding chapters. Although the boundaries are far
from absolute, the present chapter will focus on two other areas of recurring
sensitivity and suppression: horror, and religion—good and evil.

Horror

> We do not want to have audiences screaming.[2]

Theatre in the years immediately before 1918 is generally ascribed two
primary and related functions: first, to vilify the Germans and thus confirm
the continuing necessity of the war; second, to distract those at home
(including soldiers on leave from the front) from the horrors of that war
through light and escapist entertainment. In an essay called 'The War and the
Theatre', the Lord Chamberlain's Reader, George Street, spoke of the 'service
done by the theatres' in helping to maintain national morale by offering a
semblance of normality. Theatre, he says, continued to offer a crucial diver-
sion from fear and tragedy, even on nights when the threat of air-raids resulted
in smaller audiences. Street saw its actors as war heroes in their own right:

> Surely there is not an Englishman who has not felt a glowing pride in the
> nerve and pluck his countrymen and countrywomen showed on the stage
> when guns and bombs interrupted their playing . . . I think the explosions
> would have driven my 'lines' out of my head.

With the war inevitably dominating every aspect of people's lives, it is less the
explicit anti-German propaganda which Street emphasises as having been
important for audiences, and rather the need for something which 'took their
minds away from it'. Indeed, he describes watching a scene in one play which
showed Belgian women being brutally treated by German soldiers 'and
finding the people about me distressed by its inclusion'.[3] But if the staging of
'real' atrocities—in however melodramatic and patriotic a spirit—was hard
for audiences to take, then perhaps it is no coincidence that horror began to
seek expression in less direct ways. London began to import from Paris its
own version of the Grand Guignol theatre movement, with its nightmarish
atmosphere, its disturbing violence, its relishing of torture and its experiments
with death. The Lord Chamberlain's Office was unsure whether audiences
were ready for this. In June 1915 what Street called 'a characteristic Grand
Guignol' was submitted; *Baiser dans la nuit* included a scene in which vitriol
is thrown over a woman, and it required toning down for British audiences:

> Such a brutal and shocking horror would not be allowed in an English
> play. On the other hand it might be contended that Grand Guignol audi-
> ences should be allowed their thrill of exotic horror. My view is a
> compromise: that the curtain should fall before the actual throwing of the
> vitriol and the woman's shrieks eliminated.[4]

In the same year, Street found *L'horrible éxperience*—in which a man
conducting an electrical experiment to try and resuscitate his dead daughter
is strangled by her corpse—altogether 'too dreadful and horrible for public
presentation in England'. His co-reader, Bendall, may have had more realistic horrors in mind when he insisted, 'the stage seems to me no place for
surgical operations'.[5]

It was some time after the war before playwrights sought to reflect its
gruesome horrors directly. On the other hand, real horrors were all around—
in people's minds and in front of their eyes in the physical devastation of
survivors. Increasing numbers of people were understandably drawn to spir-
itualism and a desperate belief in the possibility of communicating with the
dead. Others suffered mental breakdowns or hallucinations as a result of the
nightmares they had witnessed during the last five years, and to suppress and
control unburied memories was often impossible. But blood will have blood,
they say, and a surprising relish for horrors of other kinds began to be reflected
on the stage, not least in the Grand Guignol of Lewis Casson and Sybil

Thorndike at London's Little Theatre. The taste for the macabre was one which the censorship felt the need to keep in check, though Sir Douglas Dawson was rather less protective and concerned about this issue than he was about political and sexual transgressions. He suggested in relation to *The Hand of Death* in 1920, for example, that although 'the plot is too horrible for words and we may be blamed for passing the play', he was not convinced that these were sufficient grounds for refusal: 'I doubt whether it is for us to spare the public in the matter of "horrors"', he wrote. In this instance, and following extensive internal discussions, the Comptroller attended a rehearsal and reported that the text 'read very much worse than it played'; the licence was issued with the proviso that the more disturbing incidents must be 'in no way accentuated'.[6]

As this case shows, this genre of plays frequently required the censors to deal as much or more with stage action as with the spoken word. In March 1920 they insisted on removing as 'an unnecessary horror' the visual evidence of a character having been flogged, and demanded 'a written undertaking that the towel and shoulders marked with red will be omitted'.[7] In the same year they banned 'an inferior piece of nastiness' from the Little Theatre because 'the plot hinges on a bite given the woman by the man in the act of committing adultery', and the following year allowed *Life* only after removing a scene in which a character dances with a corpse.[8] In 1921 Street described *The Hooded Death* as 'three acts of horror and gloom' and 'a farrago of rubbish', but it was his concern about the potential effect of the play on particular kinds of audience which is particularly striking: 'the horror is too silly to frighten educated people but it is a question if an average audience should be exposed to it', he wrote, and he suggested that 'the growing taste for horrors needs discouragement'.[9] *The Hooded Death* was passed, but earlier that year a licence had been refused for *Blind Man's Buff*, in which a deaf mute is hunted and tortured by a group of blind men. 'There should be a limit to the extent to which Managers should be allowed to sicken normal minds or to pander to the depraved', Street had protested, arguing that the play was 'calculated to horrify an audience beyond a permissible limit'.[10] In *Euthanasia*, 'the father of an incurable and troublesome lunatic' persuades a doctor 'to tempt him to touch certain electric fuses and so destroy himself'; the play was again submitted for performance at the Little Theatre, and though Street was prepared to argue that the theatre was 'entitled to discuss such questions as Euthanasia', he opposed a licence because of the 'bestial degeneracy' displayed by the central character. 'The continued efforts of this management to pander to morbid tastes are deplorable', he wrote. Sensitivities may possibly have been increased by the fact that the brother of the incumbent Lord Chamberlain actually held an official royal appointment as 'Chancery Visitor of Lunatics', but the main issue was whether or not a play should be refused 'on the ground, merely, that it will grossly shock and horrify an audience'. Dawson doubted this:

Morbid and horrible as the story is, are we justified in banning its production on those grounds alone? Granted that the public would be better for <u>not</u> seeing it, does that reason alone justify our preventing them doing so if they wish to?

After negotiations, a revised version was submitted, in which 'the exhibition of the lunatic's degenerate characteristics' was 'no longer dwelt upon'.[11]

Another play for the Little was licensed in January 1922 'on the clear understanding that the elements of horror it contains will be kept within bounds and toned down as much as possible'. Again, the Lord Chamberlain had delegated one of his staff to watch it in rehearsal, and he received a detailed report on *The Regiment* prior to final negotiations with the management. We may assume today that Grand Guignol productions were probably non-realistic in their style of presentation, and therefore unconvincing, but it is clear that one of the elements of the genre which most worried the censors was the realistic portrayal of extreme physical suffering, and the distress this might induce in members of the audience:

> The performance of the man suffering from hydrophobia . . . appeared to me exaggerated and horrible, and should certainly be toned down . . . The man's struggles for breath, which seemed to me too realistic to be witnessed by a public audience, should be at least intermittent, and his acute suffering need only be displayed at the moments when the light is held to his face and he is shown a glass of water.[12]

In March 1922 the Office refused as 'an exhibition of disgusting savagery and quite unfit for public presentation' a play about adultery in which a woman's head is forced into a fire, and in April they rejected another play which Street saw as 'violent and brutal for the mere sake of violence and brutality'; this second play included a hanging, and Street said the management at the Little Theatre were 'sure to make it as offensive as possible'.[13] In May, a play described by the Reader as 'a crude business of piling horror on horror' was submitted by the same theatre. 'A blind mute making inarticulate noises is a picture audiences might be well spared', wrote Street. Signals were transmitted that the new Lord Chamberlain, the Duke of Atholl, intended to institute a tougher policy over horror. 'I feel sure that on the old standard you applied to us the play would be passed', wrote Lewis Casson, 'but in the new <u>tighter</u> standard I have some qualms'. After private discussions with the manager, Atholl agreed that if 'certain modifications' were made, he would license *The Sister's Tragedy* 'in order not to disjoint the programme of the Little Theatre', and 'in view of an implied undertaking that the general policy of this theatre in regard to "shockers" is being altered'. Atholl proposed a deal which implied the introduction of greater restrictions in some areas—even on

plays already licensed—in return for freedoms elsewhere. Predictably, he was keen to counter in advance any suggestion that he was acting on his own initiative, insisting, rather, that he was reflecting the dominant public attitude.

> The Lord Chamberlain has no <u>new</u> or <u>old</u> standard but he considers that certain plays that were undesirable before, though passed, are impossible now and that if they are performed there will be a public revolt.
>
> The stage advances the view that people are more modern and broader-minded nowadays and that certain things that were held to be 'naughty' in the old days are admissible now and rightly—equally so it should admit that things that were tolerated in years gone by may also be considered too 'gross' for this enlightened age.

An example of the sort of thing which was too gross for the modern world was indicated in the conditions imposed on *The Sister's Tragedy*, where the Lord Chamberlain insisted there must be 'no screams from rabbit'.[14]

In the same month, two other horror plays were refused licences by Atholl. In *Doctor Goudron's System*, the inmates of an asylum rise up against the staff and doctors in a way which Street felt went 'beyond any legitimate limit of the horrible'. He warned the Lord Chamberlain that if they were to license this play 'no doubt the shrieks and howls and struggles and general behaviour of the lunatics would be made as loathsome as possible'. Lord Buckmaster agreed that it was time to clamp down on what he called 'the growing tendency to depict sheer naked horror', and on the 'cruelty and brutality' which he maintained were being staged 'for no obvious purpose but to gratify the depraved tastes that delight in such abominations'.[15] Also banned, on the express instruction of the Lord Chamberlain, was a play in which a medical student kisses a corpse he is supposed to be dissecting and which comes back to life and dances with him. Remarkably, far from seeing such an image as the bizarre invention of an author's imagination, Atholl read it as a dramatic metaphor for something which was evidently only too real a public concern: 'This goes very near to a specific crime, which is thought so horrible and luring to weak minds that it is dealt with In Camera in Courts', he wrote; without quite naming it, he expressed clear concern about necrophilia as a serious and dangerous obsession, which 'for some reason or another does act very definitely on certain types of weak minds'. He noted: 'I can quote two cases within my own knowledge'.[16] Presumably, the stage image of someone dancing with a corpse was in danger of attracting further imitations.

In contrast to these refusals, Shelley's *The Cenci* was licensed in the autumn of 1922; this decision was made against the advice of Buckmaster, who argued that it 'can teach no lesson it can give no warning or instruction . . . it can only sicken and terrify and distress'. The Public Morality Council protested the play would 'have an injurious effect upon the moral life and standards of

the present day', and warned that it would 'leave a modern audience exhausted and demoralised' from being exposed to the 'diabolical passion and cruel lust' of the Cenci. The Council took its cue partly from Atholl's insistence on the arrival of an enlightened age:

> However strong the nerves of the Middle Ages, modern city dwellers cannot listen to screams from torture on the rack, or watch the partial throttling of a wife without an expenditure of nervous force wholly out of proportion to any artistic gain ... the play has no message, no purpose, reason or outcome; sin and crime result in tragedy and anguish, but there is behind this no scheme bound up with religious ideals or moral purpose. The play suggests simply the ravings of a genius obsessed by a grievance.

Why, then, was Shelley's play allowed to pass while other horrors were being banned? The reason is clear—because of its status. Street pointed out that *The Cenci* was 'a famous play by a great Poet; it is universally read', and Atholl agreed that its style 'helps to put it amongst the classics', and that its appeal would inevitably be limited to 'special audiences'.[17] Similarly, horrors in the context of established opera were a slightly different matter. When Halifax Theatre Royal sought a licence for *Turandot*, Street commented: 'If this were a new Opera some caution at least about its horrors, severed heads, and torture, might be given. But as it has been played several times at Covent Garden it is rather too late for that'.[18]

Decisions about whether a 'horror' play could be allowed were based on more than the nature of the horror itself. In 1923 the Office licensed a play in which a man suffocates his rival in love by means of a clay mask which has been modelled on the face of the woman for whom they are competing. Lord Cromer, recently installed as Lord Chamberlain, disliked the horror, but the play's saving grace was its form: 'the fact of its being in verse and with music may lend so much unreality to the whole as to mitigate the shock a more serious treatment might cause to the audience', he decided.[19] In 1924 a licence was granted for *Dracula*, even though Street had advised against it on the grounds that '"horrors", for the mere sake of horror, might fitly be banned by the censorship'. Cromer agreed with the principle, but he took the advice of his Board that the story was so well known as a novel that it could not be banned. Even so, some modifications were secured: 'We no longer have the disgusting conclusion of the vampire beginning to suck the blood of his victim: he merely stands by her side'.[20]

At a time when it was not unusual to see people in public whose features had been disfigured during the war, there was also a mini-cult of plays depicting characters suffering from leprosy. Realistic or unpleasant pictures of the results of such illnesses worried the censors; in 1923 they acknowledged

that Housman's *The Little Plays of St Francis* was entirely well intentioned, but this did not absolve one scene: 'The Lepers', said Street, were 'too dreadful for representation', and even though he was basing his response on the written text alone, he confidently suggested that 'the picture of the miserable creatures . . . would be too shocking'. The play was licensed on the condition that the lepers 'should not be made horrible and repellent'.[21] In the same year, the Office attempted to prevent the more unpleasant features of *The Leper of Cairo*: 'I should like to advise the Lord Chamberlain to ban this worthless play as a whole', wrote Street, 'but I think there is no sufficient reason for that if the leper business is cut out'. He recommended that they cut the 'ghastly make up', insist on the character being veiled, and remove the incident in which the villain becomes infected by the leper. 'Perhaps it would be simpler to say that the business of leprosy . . . must be cut out all together. It is unnecessary to have such a horror introduced into a melodrama with no reason except to horrify', wrote Street. Cromer agreed:

> I see no justifiable reasons why the horrors of a dire disease should be made the theme of a play . . . and should be glad to render such a play impossible of production though I can hardly ban it. The suggestions made by Mr Street should be insisted upon and if they destroy the play, so much the better for the British public.[22]

The following year, another play was licensed subject to the leper not being made-up 'too realistically'.[23]

In 1924 the Public Morality Council complained to the Lord Chamberlain about another proposed revival of Grand Guignol plays, which it said was 'calculated to do harm'. Cromer assured the Council that the situation was under control and that standards had changed for the better: 'it is impossible to restrain theatrical managers from naming their plays "Grand Guignol"', he wrote, 'as the title is in itself one that attracts a certain section of the British public'; however, he assured the Council that 'great care has been taken to avoid the presentation of excessive horrors and Plays of too sensational nature, such as were attempted for production in London some years ago'.[24] The wish to keep as much horror off the stage as possible continued through the 1920s. In 1927 Cromer reluctantly licensed a touring melodrama on condition that 'the lion-faced man must not be made too monstrous or like an animal', that his fight with a blind mute 'must not be too realistic', and that 'the appearance of the "terror" as described on page 11 must be modified'. Typically, he also attempted to absolve himself from possible criticism by making the manager responsible for ensuring that it must not be staged 'in such a way as to cause offence to *any* member of the audience' (my emphasis).[25] In the same month the Office licensed *The Portrait of a Man with Red Hair* 'as long as torture is not portrayed on the stage', and *Frankenstein*, provided the scene in

which the monster crushes a dove was removed: 'Of course it is a dummy, but it is so contrived that the audience might easily suppose it is a live dove previously shown and be shocked', wrote Street. Often, the Office sought a compromise, endeavouring to avoid the publicity created by outright bans on plays, but demanding the removal of anything it considered too excessive. In *Jack Sheppard* it insisted that the beatings of inmates in Bedlam 'be reduced to threats', and from *Sweeney Todd* it cut the moment in which a character finds human hair and a button in a pie he is eating. [26]

In 1928 Cromer found himself embroiled in a public controversy over a play to be performed in Scotland, in which a young woman is threatened with torture by a red hot iron on her skin. 'It is high time to put a stop to this craving for horrors depicted on the stage', he wrote, perhaps thinking that such an apparently remote venue as the Theatre Royal in Inverness would provide a good opportunity to set down a new marker. Unfortunately for him, the writer and manager contrived to stir up a controversy which made headlines in the national press, and Cromer was forced to issue a statement insisting that the scene had not been banned; his concern, he implausibly claimed, had arisen only because the management had failed to tell him that the red hot iron specified in the script would be a stage property rather than a real one, which would have constituted a fire hazard. [27]

Plays known as 'Mad Scientist' dramas were also popular. One (credited to Tod Slaughter), involving an on-stage blood transfusion, was licensed only on condition that there would be no blood or simulation of blood. [28] In 1928 a play was licensed in which a surgeon transplants glands from his pet ape into his secretary, and turns the latter into a robot; a stage direction specified that the screams during the operation 'must really raise the audience', but an endorsement on the licence demanded that it 'be reduced to a minimum of horror' and that 'nothing in the business either with the ape or with other mechanical instruments of torture shall be made so revolting as to cause offence to any member of the audience'. [29] Another play which was initially refused was *After Death*—'an authentic Grand Guignol "horror"', according to the Lord Chamberlain's Reader—which centred on a professor's belief that a head can be kept alive after it has been removed from the body in an execution; in one scene the audience was to see an apparently disembodied head (the actor would be hidden in a box) opening and closing its eyes and mouth, and continuing to assert that the execution had been a miscarriage of justice. Street suggested that 'the assault on the audience's nerves is excessive', and yet again he recommended that the time had come to clamp down more strictly on horrors:

In the English Guignol season some years ago considerable licence was allowed in the way of horrors and I think worse things than this one were produced. That does not necessarily bind the Lord Chamberlain and I

think public opinion would support him in severity towards these unwholesome excitements.

Cromer was inclined to agree with Street, but his Assistant Comptroller attended a rehearsal and was persuaded that the talking head was 'not offensively done' because it was part of a medical experiment. He also found a surprisingly patriotic reason to justify licensing:

> In one way the play has a moral. That the English method of execution by hanging causes instantaneous death, while, by the guillotine method, if the medical theory advanced in the play is correct, it is not so.

Cromer would only agree to license the play if no actual head was displayed (the actor was banned from hiding in the box) and a dummy head was substituted. [30]

Worst of all, in the eyes of the censors, was the play that mixed horror with sex. Street described as 'the most repulsive "horror" I've had to read' a play centring on a creature which is half man and half bird, and which is the resulting offspring of a woman who has been raped by vultures. The monster, Veldt, has been kept in a cage in his house by Sir Gordon, whose daughter rescued the woman who gave birth to it; however, after declaring its love for a young woman in the house, the creature commits a series of violent attacks on the males whom it identifies as its rivals. The deeply unpleasant racist implications of the play are not hard to detect today, but this particular aspect was either not recognised or unmentioned; Cromer initially refused the licence because a 'half-human monster being in love with a girl and attempting murder is too disgusting', but he allowed a revised version the following month 'now that the sex element has been removed and the play reduced to a horror'. [31]

Reporting on an American melodrama in 1928, Street wrote:

> I should have said that the thrills are not out of the way and that the play, though of an undesirable class, might be safely passed. But I am given pause by a note on page 38 of Act 2, stating (after the appearance of the black-robed figure etc.) that 'the audience by this time are always screaming' and on page 40 the scream from the audience is again noted. We do not want to have audiences screaming. [32]

In this instance, he decided it was safe to recommend the play for licence in spite of the author's statement—'On the whole I think this is exaggerated boastfulness and that we need not anticipate hysterics'—but the interesting question is why the censors were so worried about horror and felt the need to be so protective of audiences. Even in the case of a serious play such as Marie

Stopes's *Our Ostriches*, the licence stipulated 'that the pains of childbirth will not be made too painful for the audience'.[33]

Horror as a genre always has the potential to be viewed as exploitative and pornographic, and the number of plays which showed women suffering as victims of torture is striking. Other horror plays relied heavily on the crudest of racial stereotypes—such as evil Chinese men torturing beautiful young English women—and the Lord Chamberlain was occasionally sensitive to the dangers and potentially iniquitous effects of this. A fairly typical example was *The Silent House* in 1923, and it is hard to be entirely opposed to the interventions as evident in the endorsement attached to the licence:

> The passages relating to torture, detailed below, will be entirely omitted at each performance of the play.
> (a) Where the girl is put into a cabinet which tortures her, and she 'turns round like a rat in a trap'. (b) When he sees the agony on the girl's face etc. If necessary, the girl may be supposed to be tortured off the stage. But the visible sign of it, and the groans heard at intervals, must be completely omitted. (c) . . . The doctor, Chan-Fu again tortures the girl—'a terrible scream' etc. This passage must be entirely omitted.[34]

Perhaps Cromer deserves some sympathy for declaring on another occasion: 'If I only knew how I could check the morbid craving of the public for this sort of exhibition, I should be only too pleased'.[35] As always, the Public Morality Council would have gone much further in its restrictions, and regularly complained about the nature of the audiences being attracted to Grand Guignol drama, and the likely effect on them of what they witnessed. In 1928 it raised again the question of whether the Lord Chamberlain could restrict admission to adults, as in the cinema; the Assistant Comptroller replied that the existing regulations did not give him the power to do this, and that anyway they had 'no reason to suppose that such plays necessarily attract persons of sadistic tendencies'.[36] In the end, it seems as if the wish to censor horror plays—especially where the action was realistic—was once again based primarily on the perceived danger of unsettling and disturbing an audience.

A very different view about the effect of horror plays was argued by Patrick Hamilton, whose play *Rope* was reluctantly licensed in 1929. Hamilton himself eschewed what he saw as the typical components of 'Grand Guignolism', which he itemised as 'the incessant round of throat-slicings, eye-gougings, thumb-screwings, floggings, burnings, brain-twistings, charred bodies and the like'; yet he described his own play as 'disgusting' and an 'essay in the macabre', calling on writers such as Poe, Shakespeare and Dickens to defend the validity of creating fear through horror:

> Personally I believe that the stimulant of horror . . . is a perfectly healthy

and legitimate stimulant. Laughter and tears and horror, after all, are the three essential features which keep the theatre alive . . . I have gone all out to write a horror play and make your flesh creep. And there is no reason to believe that this action is medically or chemically any worse for you than the other two. If I have succeeded you will leave the theatre braced and recreated, which is what you go to the theatre for.[37]

Street disliked *Rope*, but was ambivalent about whether refusing a licence would be consistent with previous decisions:

It is a revolting play, but I am inclined to think that equally revolting 'horrors' have been licensed, and that there is not sufficient reason, therefore, for banning this one. Sadistic perversity is not suggested as to the motive, though critics . . . will probably think it is and blame the Lord Chamberlain for licensing the play, if he does.

Lord Buckmaster campaigned strongly against granting a licence, describing the play as 'unrelieved horror the contemplation of which can do no good' and insisting 'I cannot imagine this play having any but the most baleful influence on those who witness it'. He challenged Hamilton's argument that horror for its own sake was acceptable:

I have always held the opinion that it is as much the duty of the Censor to protect the public against the performance of plays which consist solely of brutally horrible details as to protect them against naked immorality.

In each case the question seems to me the same. Is the horror or the immorality an incident in the development of the drama or is it the sole purpose of the work? *Othello* does not lack horror nor *Anthony and Cleopatra* immorality but each of these qualities is the essential of stupendous tragedy.

This play is nothing but sheer brutality . . . it possesses none of the element of tragedy.

But, though agreeing that *Rope* was 'detestable', Cromer reluctantly licensed it on the grounds that 'on the whole it cannot be held to be subversive of public morals'.[38]

Hamilton had denied suggestions that his play had been based on an actual American murder case, but the use of real-life crime as source material was not unknown. One example was *The Eternal Triangle*, reluctantly recommended for licence by Street in 1923:

It will be seen that the Ilford case is pretty closely reproduced. The case being over and the offenders having been hanged there is no question of the play being unfair to them—a reason why plays on cases actually going

on are not allowed. It is deplorable, however, that such cases should be vulgarly exploited the moment they are over and I wish there were sufficient reason for banning this play.

Though he did insist on removing the vision of a hangman which is witnessed by both prisoner and audience in the court room, Cromer felt there was 'no remedy except through the taste of the public' and allowed this play to pass.[39] However, he did refuse plays based on real crimes wherever he could find grounds to do so: in 1927 he rejected *Surmise* (which dealt with a recent murder case) on the specific advice of the Home Office, in 1928 he refused *Arsenic* (also based on a recent court case), and in 1929 he refused to license a melodrama based on the case of a man who had drowned several wives. 'Unless this rule is maintained', wrote Cromer, 'every "cause celebre" [*sic*] can be used as the theme of a play which is certainly undesirable', and the Home Office suggested a general policy that 'no play should be allowed which is based on a capital case if anyone who was concerned with the original incident is likely to be still alive'.[40]

Perhaps the most bizarre example of the intrusion of actuality into fiction occurred over a play which was based on the real life shooting of a British policeman, and which ended in the execution of one of the perpetrators. It was licensed by the Lord Chamberlain in 1927 as an old-fashioned melodrama, but the production created a real frisson of horror through its casting; an official letter of complaint drew Cromer's attention to this, though perhaps there may be some reason to feel slightly cynical or suspicious about the motives of the sender:

> The Actors' Association wishes to call your attention to the fact that, in a play produced last night at the Gravesend Theatre, entitled *Charles Peace*, Ellis, the ex-executioner appeared. It is obvious that his inclusion in the cast is due, not so much to his powers as an actor as the sensation attached to his late position as executioner.
>
> It is the considered opinion of the Association that the whole episode is one which is certain to have a degrading effect on the public as well being detrimental to the theatre.

Though he pointed out that he had no powers to 'prohibit or terminate the engagement of any particular person or persons in a stage play', the Lord Chamberlain was unhappy about the incident, and felt he had been tricked:

> I entirely agree that the engagement of John Ellis, the ex-hangman, to appear on the stage is the most deplorable lack of good taste, and is a thing to be deprecated most strongly . . . No one could have foreseen that a real hangman would be used in the part.

The matter was debated in Parliament, where it was proposed that it should be 'a condition in the future for the appointment of an executioner that he should give an undertaking not to engage in a public performance in such a role'.[41]

Religion

> The Lord Chamberlain is very much concerned with the Almighty. He has taken the Deity very much under his wing and protects him from calumny with the devotion of a she-bear for her cubs.[42]

Commenting on Somerset Maugham's *The Unknown* in 1920, the Reverend W.A. Kingsbury from the Actors' Church observed that 'the war has undoubtedly left as an aftermath an increase of disbelief in God'. The *Daily Express* was one of several newspapers to report at length on the controversy surrounding the production of Maugham's play 'with its atheist soldier hero and its electrifying question "Who is going to forgive God?"'. The newspaper quoted a range of opinions expressed by a number of clergymen, most of whom accepted that the play should be publicly performed, even while opposing the views expressed by those of its characters whose faiths had been destroyed. Most claimed to approve of the fact that the theatre was being used for serious purposes: 'I welcome any play which forces us to face important problems', said one clergyman.[43] So despite outrage in some quarters that Sandhurst had licensed Maugham's play, his decision received wide support from within the Church.

Successive Lords Chamberlain generally took steps to ensure that they had the backing of Church leaders for their decisions about religious plays. One might have imagined that pious dramas clearly intended to be sympathetic to the Christian faith would have been welcomed, but this was not necessarily so. Certainly, the Lord Chamberlain saw it as his duty to protect the Church, but silence was preferred to anything more active: 'I dislike Religious subjects being presented on the stage at all', wrote Cromer in 1924, and so did the Archbishop of Canterbury.[44] Partly this was because the stage was seen to keep such bad company. In 1923 a licence was withheld from a play called *The Lord's Prayer*, because the Archbishop of Canterbury disapproved of the title: 'If one thinks of what it would mean to see that title advertised alongside of an announcement about, say, "The Midnight Follies" or a score of other things, it is surely impossible to doubt that it would cause the gravest offence to very many people'. The playwright, Arthur Shirley, understandably took umbrage at the idea of changing the play's name: 'The title is calculated to elevate not to degrade the thoughts of those who witness it', he complained, and the confrontation seems never to

have been resolved.[45] However, it was not possible to exclude religion from the stage completely. In 1924, reluctantly agreeing with Cromer that there were no grounds to refuse a licence for *Judas Iscariot*, the Archbishop pointedly commented:

> I wish they did not write these plays, for the men who write them are not men qualified to handle these great subjects greatly. This good man has handled it feebly, but quite harmlessly . . . I am rather glad that Bernard Shaw does not take a play of that sort in hand for he might raise for us much more perilous issues.[46]

The problem, as perceived by the Archbishop, lay not just with a particular play he was invited to inspect but with the implications and precedents; in 1925, when asked for advice on Masefield's *Good Friday*, he replied:

> I think the Lord Chamberlain would not be well advised in forbidding the production of a work by such a man as John Masefield, handling the sacred subject with a reticence and reverence . . . The danger, I imagine, lies in the fact that to some extent you are creating precedents which may be followed by writers less competent and less reverent.[47]

Other principles remained unchanged. A licence for Masefield's *Trial of Jesus* was rejected in 1926 on the advice of the Archbishop of Canterbury; while acknowledging that the play contained 'nothing that is irreverent' or 'inconsistent with the Gospel narrative', it made the mistake of placing Christ as a character in the action:

> Once sanction it and I do not see where you could stop. Suppose, for example, some great drama were written on Miltonic lines introducing not our Lord only but even God the Father. Most people I think would be shocked.

Cromer informed Masefield that, having taken 'the highest possible Clerical opinion', he had no choice other than to disallow the appearance of Christ on stage. The Archbishop had suggested that Masefield was 'a very reasonable person and I believe would understand such a prohibition as I have suggested', but in fact the playwright had some difficulty in accepting the incongruity of what could and could not be seen on the public stage:

> Mr Masefield although urging that in the old Coventry Plays Our Lord's appearance and even words on the Stage had been admitted seemed to accept the fact that modern writers are precluded from this privilege, and I further explained that these early Plays, having been written and

produced before the days of Stage Play Licences could not be considered
in the same light. Mr Masefield left with evident disappointment.

Indeed, Masefield had already presented a private version of his play to an
audience of bishops and religious people without meeting any objection.[48]

This familiar discrepancy between what was allowed in older plays and
in contemporary plays was particularly manifest in the religious field. Between
1922 and 1928 there were regular London productions of the medieval
morality play *Everyman*, and these, of course, did not require licences. But
any attempt to stage a modern adaptation or equivalent was resisted. 'An old
morality play is one thing and a modern one another from the point of view
of religious feeling', wrote Street in 1923, in connection with a play entitled
Death. 'It differs from the medieval plays in lacking the dignity and reserve
which medieval authors managed to maintain', claimed Cromer to the
Archbishop of Canterbury in eliciting his support for banning the script.[49]
One wonders whether either of them had seen or read such plays as *Mankind*.
However, the issue here was not simply that the Voice of God was heard, but
the fact that this Voice first fails to condemn the poverty-stricken woman who
sells herself for money, and then sends Man to hell. In 1924 a licence was
refused for another modern version of a miracle play which put Christ as a
boy on the stage. Cromer had intended to license it, but was quick to change
his mind and agree with the suggestions of the Archbishop of Canterbury,
who was unhappy about putting words into the mouth of Jesus. Confirming
to the Archbishop that the play would not be allowed and that writers would
not be permitted 'to manufacture phraseology for Him', Cromer assured him
that

> The ground on which I take my stand is that modern authors endeav-
> ouring to write Religious, or would-be Religious plays, must achieve a
> standard of phraseology and spirit acceptable to the majority of devout
> minded people.

Yet perhaps part of the real problem was that a modern morality play could
hardly avoid having a political dimension, by explicitly or implicitly locating
God within contemporary situations and disputes:

> Once the door is open to this sort of play there would probably be no lack
> of endeavours to travesty medieval plays by attempting to point a moral
> in modern life under the guise of the religious.
> The difficulties and complexities of censorship in plays are quite
> numerous enough without adding to their number, and so it will be a satis-
> faction to me to feel I am right in still carefully guarding this particular
> avenue of modern imagination.

Laurence Housman continued to find his work censored, and resented the fact that 'old plays are allowed to be performed which go much further in their representation of Divinity than my own'.[50] However, he struck lucky in December 1922—almost immediately after Cromer had taken over as Lord Chamberlain—when the Office got itself into a tangle by confusing two plays, both called *Bethlehem*; one was by Housman and the other, by Rutland Boughton, was based on the Coventry Nativity Play. In order to cover their own confusion and mistake, licences were issued to both of them, even though Housman's play placed the Virgin Mary on the stage for the first time in a modern play.[51] Ironically, at the end of 1926, Boughton staged an extremely politicised version of the Coventry Nativity Play, transforming it into 'an episode in the class struggle' in which Joseph is seen as a striking miner, with Herod as the Home Secretary backed up by the army and police, and Mary as a working mother trying to nurse the infant who brings hope for a better world. The performance seems to have escaped censorship because the politics were expressed through the visual aspects of the production rather than the words.

In February 1927 a line was cut in which God was compared to 'a sort of vacuum cleaner whose one job is to suck dirty bits of clay like you up into heaven'. The simile, said Street, 'might grate too much on some people'.[52] A licence was also temporarily withheld from Terence Gray's Cambridge production of C.K. Munro's *Progress*, because the Lord Chamberlain suspected that a hymn was going to be sung in a disrespectful way which 'might create laughter among the audience'. The director was informed that 'the Lord Chamberlain will be prepared to reconsider the matter on receiving a definite undertaking from you that the hymn will be rendered in a reverent manner'.[53] After the opening performances of *Hit the Deck Again* in November 1927, the Public Morality Council wrote to Cromer to say that, while its members had approved of much of the show, it had 'felt very much hurt by the introduction of the Halleluia song in the jazzy style of a Negro Spiritual'. After an inspection by the Assistant Comptroller, a reference to 'Gabriel tooting on his horn' was duly cut.[54] In the same month the translation of an Italian play by F.V. Ratti, called *Judas*, was submitted; Cromer warned the Archbishop that 'the tendency to produce Religious plays is evidently on the increase', but he could find no reason to disallow this play. Though the Archbishop expressed his dislike of the growing tendency to 'vulgarise things which ought to stand upon a totally different level', he accepted the advice that this play could not be banned.[55] In the same year, Lord Cromer attracted the unfortunate headline 'Censor Bans Genesis', when he refused to allow lines from the Bible to be spoken on the stage in *Potiphar's Wife*, a play in which a servant spurns the sexual advances of his master's immoral wife and is then falsely accused of trying to seduce her. The lines in question, taken from *Genesis*, were: 'It came to pass after these things, that his master's wife

cast her eyes upon Joseph'. Street was in two minds, pointing out that biblical quotations had previously been 'confined, I believe, to serious plays', but adding that 'the author would, of course, say that the vindication of an innocent man is a serious matter'; moreover, in his view, the source of the quotation was 'not a sacred part of the Bible'. Cromer, however, refused to allow 'the misuse of the Bible in an objectionable play of this sort', though he reluctantly agreed to allow the lines to be included in the programme.[56]

The following year, the Archbishop was again consulted over Karel Čapek's *Adam the Creator*, which was to be produced by Terence Gray. Street was perhaps surprisingly unguarded in his original report:

> The obvious objection will be a charge of irreverence. I am convinced that no-one would be really shocked in that respect except those who sincerely believe in the historical truth of the Book of Genesis and they must be few.

The Archbishop described the play as 'a remarkable document', but queried whether it was 'justifiable to present what is really an Aristophanic Comedy in a Christian State'? He doubted whether it was, 'for it does practically make God a party to farce'. In fact Čapek's play was passed, though with a series of amendments.[57] The following year, however, a licence was refused for *East of Eden*, a 'comic fantasia on Genesis' which even Street felt went too far:

> No one now takes Genesis as literal history and Adam and Eve have often been the subject of casual jokes in plays. But a whole play making fun of Genesis and treating its God as a joke would surely shock the associations of most people intolerably.[58]

Saint Mary Ellen, a comedy described by Street as 'a strange jumble of jocosity and mysticism about the future life', was refused a licence for similar reasons; Street had been in favour of allowing it, arguing, again, that 'since it is directed against a literal view of the scriptural Heaven and Hell, which is not now widely held, it will not give offence to the intelligent'. But the censorship was not only concerned with the intelligent, and Street's recommedation was over-ruled on the grounds that many would be offended by the play's 'flippant jokes at the expense of God'.[59]

One of the cuts imposed on *Adam the Creator* had been the refusal to allow 'the Voice of God' to be heard speaking. In *The Eternal Flame*, in 1928, a surprising decision was made to allow a brief appearance by Christ, provided that a voice speaking his lines from the Bible did not do so while the figure was in view; 'As the religious intention of this is good,' wrote the Lord Chamberlain, 'I can only trust that this scene in Westminster Abbey with the impersonation of the Unknown Warrior will not give offence'.[60] A couple of

months later, the Office allowed a character to appear in another sincere Christian play even though he implicitly represented Christ—'provided there is no make up to resemble the traditional pictures of our Lord'.[61] In 1929 Street noted in connection with John Masefield's *Easter* that there was a danger of complaints about a very brief appearance by Christ, since 'one can hardly distinguish the Anima Christi from Him'. Cromer slightly inaccurately commented:

> A guiding principle, from which there has hitherto been no departure, is that no impersonation of our Lord is sanctioned on the stage. I hope this will somehow be recognised in the production of this play.[62]

He imposed no formal endorsement on this script, but inconsistencies of approach remained. In 1930 a new adaptation of the Chester miracle plays was submitted. 'These are genuine mediaeval Miracle Plays', wrote Street, 'modernized only (I think) so far as intelligibility required'. However, Cromer ruled that since they had been modernised 'they must be considered as modern plays'. Street had concerns about 'the question of realism' and worried that 'the insults heaped on Jesus . . . the scourgings and beatings and the final crucifixion . . . would be, surely, intolerably painful to a modern audience'. Yet the main problem was again the appearance of God and Christ. 'In the former case', suggested Street, 'a bright light might indicate the presence of God and the words might be spoken off the stage'. In the case of the latter, Street passed on a proposal for 'a "masking" of Jesus by the other actors'. He acknowledged that it was a strange requirement: 'I suppose this can be effectively done', he mused, 'though it must be difficult in the Passion play'. It was also, he pointed out, 'anomalous', that 'if the plays had been given in their original form this requirement would not have been necessary'.

Despite the distress and vociferous protests of those involved with the production, and even though his claim was not completely accurate, Cromer remained adamant:

> There is an accepted rule that God and Jesus Christ are not to be impersonated on the stage or to take speaking parts.
> This rule must be upheld and if these plays are produced they must be adapted accordingly.[63]

Yet in 1932, after consultation with the Bishop of London, the Office allowed Tyrone Guthrie's play *Follow Me*—despite Street's unequivocal report:

> The theme is the effect on an ordinary middle-class family of the advent of Christ and a succession of events closely parallel to those of the New Testament . . . I do not recall a play in which it has been used with so close

a parallel to the original. There is no possible ambiguity about the application.[64]

It was not only God but also clergymen who needed protection. In 1920, a comedian was banned from appearing in a sketch dressed as a clergyman, while in 1924 *The Rock of Ages* included amongst its characters a hypocritical churchman. Cromer insisted that, while 'no rule can be laid down that all parsons in plays must invariably be good Parsons', it was nevertheless essential to tone down the criticism and 'odious' insincerity of this character 'in justice to the clergy, who require support against a regrettable tendency in modern plays'. Moreover, a link between religion and politics was identified by Cromer, who observed of this play that 'the story may not be meant to embitter class feeling, but it would certainly not allay it—especially in Leicester where it is proposed the play should be acted'.[65] Even in 1931, Cromer was still insisting in relation to 'an inferior provincial melodrama, which would be extremely unpleasant, if it were not so silly', that he could 'see no reason why an odious character . . . should be a clergyman and this could with advantage be altered'.[66]

Street's attitude to the Church was slightly more cynical. Recommending a play about Mary Magdalene in 1930, he commented that it was 'always difficult' to give advice about religious plays, 'because the views of the clergy about them have changed so much in late years and are somewhat incalculable'.[67] In 1932, while proposing amendments for a musical comedy revue called *Wine, Women and Song*, he observed: 'I suppose we may as well go on protecting the Church in spite of public scandals'. Indeed, satire or criticism of the Church were generally not allowed.[68] In 1925 a licence was refused for a play set in the distant future in which churches and their followers become so fed up with waiting for the Last Judgement that 'after much argument and wrangling they decide to start without him'. In the same month, the censors also rejected a play set during the First World War and based on a partially autobiographical book, *Simon Called Peter*. The narrative centres on a parson who is so upset by his failure to influence events, and by how religion is being manipulated within the army to support its actions, that he resigns his position, falls in love with a woman, and makes a passionate speech on the supreme importance of love, and in celebration of his own supposed sin. In spite of its 'outspokenness', Street originally recommended the play for licence: 'It would be, I think, an excessive act of authority to prevent a dramatist's expressing the opinions on the inadequacy of the Church expressed in the play'. But with the Advisory Board split on the issue, Cromer consulted the Bishop of London, who was adamant that the play must not be performed. The original book, said the Bishop, had 'scandalised the clergy', and this play would 'revive the feeling', with its characterisation of a parson rethinking the meaning of his faith: 'He ends by preaching a fatuous sermon about Love

being the only thing, which if it means anything, means that all we have ever taught about self-control, chastity, is an old wives' fable'. The Bishop described *Simon Called Peter* as 'worse than *Mrs Warren's Profession*':

> I picture myself taking my house party as I do when I have a free evening to the Theatre, and any nice girl and woman would, I think, be sick at seeing any man and a woman emerge from the bedroom where they had spent the night in their night-dresses, but when one was a parson they would be positively shocked.

Again, a political dimension was identified within the play, as the Bishop suggested that the putative producer was relying 'on the fun of seeing a parson being made a fool of and his teaching laughed at, drawing an audience, and I have no doubt it will among a certain class, but I should have thought myself that the Censorship existed to <u>prevent</u> such a play being acted'.[69] The licence was refused.

There are two examples of plays refused licences on religious grounds which are worth scrutinising in some detail. One concerned the appearance of Christ on stage, the other that of God. In October 1930 the Lord Chamberlain wrote to the Archbishop of Canterbury saying that the press was beginning to query 'if a broad outlook should not be taken in the case of religious plays sincerely written and reverently performed with appropriate settings'. The *Evening Standard* was one of the newspapers campaigning for a change in the policy over religious plays, and had announced plans to publish the text of one particular play which had been refused a licence, in order to show its readers how absurd that decision had been. George Moore's *The Passing of the Essenes* had met with critical success earlier in the year when performed privately at the Arts Theatre; set twenty years after the crucifixion, it was based on the hypothesis that Christ had neither perished on the Cross nor ascended to Heaven, but had survived and become a shepherd. In the autumn of 1930, a licence was sought for public performance, and Street, evidently searching for a way to support the play, made an ingenious proposal which would almost have been worthy of Shaw at his most audacious; he argued that although the play 'contradicts a vital tenet of Orthodox Christianity', it could be maintained that this very inconsistency proved that the Jesus shown in the play could not possibly be the same Jesus as the one in the Bible, and that the play was therefore not depicting the figure who was central to the Christian faith. The trouble with this argument was that exactly the same get-out clause would, as the Archbishop of Canterbury realised, have become available to all playwrights, who might then have demanded the freedom to alter any Bible story in any way they wished, on the grounds that it was a different (and fictional) story.

However, there was considerable public support for licensing *The Passing*

of the Essenes, and Cromer was not prepared to try to face down the campaign without ensuring that the refusal to allow Christ to appear was still supported by senior Church figures. He wrote to Lambeth Palace, asking whether 'the time has yet arrived when more latitude is to be given to playwrights in the presentation of the Deity, or Our Lord, on the stage in special circumstances'. However, he clearly signalled to the Archbishop that he himself was not convinced that such a change should be introduced: 'once an exception is made . . . it will be almost impossible to stem the tide of production of certain plays that have already been banned, to say nothing of plays which may not yet even have been written'. The Archbishop replied that, while he was not against this play, he was concerned about the principle: 'If this play could stand alone there might be much to be urged in favour of its being permitted for public performance. But it cannot stand alone, and it is the question of precedent which troubles me.' Cromer confirmed that there could be no turning back, and he accordingly proposed that the licence should be refused. After discussion with other senior ecclesiastical figures, the Archbishop accepted Cromer's advice that *The Passing of the Essenes* must be sacrificed:

> If this play were permitted it would be impossible to refuse permission to other plays which might treat Our Lord as a purely human figure and weave round that figure some ingenious romance. For example, what would hinder some writer from indulging in a moving romance in which Jesus of Nazareth was presented as being in love with Mary or Mary Magdalena? The field would be opened out for all sorts of imaginative stories some of which would certainly create grave difficulty.[70]

The licence was refused.

The conflict over the American play *Green Pastures* became as much an issue of political as of religious doctrine, and though Marc Connelly's play was first submitted in June 1930, the dispute smouldered on until well into the 1960s, when a licence for public performance was again rejected. The most immediately contentious aspect of the play was the on-stage presentation of God 'as an idealized Negro preacher in dress and habits', and the scene actually opens in Heaven prior to creation, with the angels enjoying 'fish fry'. Street assured the Lord Chamberlain that there was 'no irreverence intended', and his report was as broad-minded as one might reasonably expect: 'there is no more essential irreverence in a Negro preacher's imagining God as smoking a cigar than there is in the author of Genesis making him walk in the garden', he suggested. But the Reader knew that not everyone in Britain would accept this view, and he concluded that he would recommend a licence 'only if I could be sure of audiences taking the play with understanding'. Cromer was much less sympathetic to the basic premise of the play, and either less

confident that audiences would accept it, or prepared to use this as an easy excuse for refusing to license it:

> Personally I have no hesitation in condemning it as unfit for licence in this country, not only because I consider it unsuitable to British taste and atmosphere, but also because it transgresses the basic rules of censorship in admitting the presence of God to be impersonated on the stage . . .
>
> I cannot help thinking that no matter what American religious opinion may be, all religious minded people in this country would certainly consider it blasphemous, and be highly offended with its presentation on the stage. Indeed it might lead to a breach of the peace in any theatre where it was played.

The Archbishop of Canterbury reached similar conclusions in his letter to Cromer, and, though he was not without respect for the play, his well-meant but inevitably patronising assumptions about how it might be received offer an insight into the racial attitudes of the time:

> I have read the play with great interest and with very real appreciation of it as a study of the mentality of the North American Negro and the child-like naivety of his imagination, of his blending . . . of a crude literalism with a rather pathetic mysticism. But a London or English audience would not be composed of United States Negroes or for the most part of persons capable of understanding their character and outlook on religion and life. I am certain that a large majority would find in the presentation of the Deity and in the characters of the Bible story material merely for mirth.
>
> If, as you say, it has hitherto been the accepted rule of Censorship that the Deity is not to be represented on the Stage, I cannot but think that it would be very strange and indeed indefensible to make a new beginning by allowing a representation of the Deity as an old gentleman in a white shirt with a white bow tie, a long Prince Albert coat of black alpaca, black trousers and congress gaiters, and smoking a cigar.
>
> I am quite sure that it would only be a small minority of any audience in the theatre who would have the imaginative insight to see the play from the point of view of a naïve and child like Negro, and that it would move the great majority either to ridicule or to indignation.

Subsequently, Cromer also sent the script to the King, and received a reply from his secretary: 'The King wishes me to thank you for *Green Pastures* into which his Majesty has peeped. I need hardly say that the King thinks you were quite correct in refusing the licence for this play.'

Twenty years later, another Lord Chamberlain would suggest that perhaps the play might be licensed to 'help in a small way to a better understanding

of the simple mentality of some coloured people', but the then Archbishop of Canterbury impressed upon Lord Clarendon the political implications of allowing such a play to be staged in the early 1950s:

> One of the open sores of the world at present is the position of the negros in the United States. Will they appreciate it if while in the United States their treatment presents a grave moral problem they are being represented on the London stage as a primitive race somewhere between the pitiful and the ridiculous. If the parts were taken by negros then at least one could assume that negros were content to give this representation of themselves. I confess that I feel very uneasy at the thought of Englishmen play-acting to represent the soul of the religion of the negro in this way.
>
> I think it may go further than that. There are many Africans in London and presumably they or some of them would see the play. Knowing the temper of African nationalism at the present time I wonder if this play would strike Africans as helpful or would not rather inflame their feelings. When all around negros and Africans are claiming the rights of mature people is not it rather a grave thing to have a play which represents them as a child race?

Six years after that, in 1957, the Assistant Comptroller wrote to Bernard Miles, who was hoping to stage the play at the Mermaid Theatre:

> It is merely the black man's conception of God, and being a simple sort of chap he has to project his God into a body and clothes which he can understand. That really basically is the objection, because we would not allow our own God as we know Him, or think we know Him, to appear on the stage and, therefore, we can't allow a 'nigger' to let his God appear . . . there is also the question of the feelings of 'Afrikaans'. One doesn't want to give the impression that we think them elderly babies.

The new Lord Chamberlain continued to take very seriously the points made by the Archbishop in 1951 about 'the doubtful wisdom of portraying negros as sentimental and ignorant children'; indeed, he suggested such an argument had

> acquired much more point during the last few years on account of rising African nationalism and the efforts that are being made to impress on Africans that we regard them as equals. I would expect much criticism of this play over here and of the special step of allowing it to be played after it has been banned for so long, and that criticism would be supported by all the friends of African emancipation in this country . . . I feel that the licensing of this play now would bring down on our heads a double thunderbolt.[71]

Yet these were very different from the problems and fears that caused the play to be refused a licence in 1930. As Terence Gray remarked in respect of God's relationship with the Lord Chamberlain:

> One is tempted to wonder . . . why the aforesaid Almighty, being almighty, should not be able to conduct His Own defence to His Own satisfaction, and to wonder whether He altogether appreciates the activities on His behalf of the Lord Chamberlain's department.[72]

Public Figures

> If anyone produced a play depicting your grandfather or mine in such a light that a competent critic described him as a 'sadic ogre', I have no doubt we should go and beat the author and producer with the thickest stick we could find, and keep on doing it, whatever the magistrates said, until the play was stopped.[73]

As well as sheltering religious figures, politicians and royalty from exposure on the stage, the Lord Chamberlain extended his protection to certain public figures and their relations and descendants. However, one play which he licensed in 1930 and which caused very considerable controversy was Rudolf Besier's *The Barretts of Wimpole Street*. 'This is the dreadful story of Elizabeth Barrett's elopement with Robert Browning from the dreadful possessive tyranny of her father', wrote Street; 'Everyone knows that Barrett was a monster of selfishness, but I do not know how far the evidence supports the absolute insanity and perversity attributed to him in the play'. Street was referring to passages implying the existence of what he termed 'a Cenci element', and he wondered whether there were relatives who should be consulted before deciding whether the play could be licensed. Cromer agreed with this suggestion, but details of the forthcoming production had already been announced to the press, and, according to Besier's subsequent account, the playwright immediately received 'a veritable avalanche of letters from various members of the family', demanding that they be sent the script to inspect. Besier ignored these demands, believing that 'nothing but the whitewashing of their ancestor from head to toe would satisfy the family', and subsequently received further letters from solicitors and friends of the family, including two former cabinet ministers. Besier's account of his visit to St James's Palace offers an interesting insight into how Lord Cromer may have performed his role, and how he set about achieving his aims:

> Lord Cromer received me more in sorrow than in anger. He frankly regretted the play; it was much resented by the Moulton-Barretts, a most

distinguished family; a thousand pities (and here he smiled—and his smile cheered me wonderfully) that I hadn't had the patience to wait another fifty years or so before writing it; and he felt he really must point out certain passages to me which might well be altered or altogether omitted without doing the play any serious injury as a work of art. He pointed out the passages—they were heavily scored with a blue pencil. Evidently his lordship had read the play with care. They all illustrated some of the darker aspects of Edward Moulton-Barrett's strange character, and their toning-down or omission certainly would rob the play of some of its strength. However there was no help for it. I cheerfully agreed to alterations and cuts, and left St James's Palace rejoicing to have got off so lightly. I fully believe that if the Moulton-Barretts had approached Lord Cromer with tact and diplomacy he would have forbidden the play altogether.

Despite the amendments, several reviews of the production picked up the theme of incest in describing the vicious cruelty and malevolence of the father. *The Times* then published an angry letter of protest from family descendants:

> To bring so disgusting a charge against a dead man, without any foundation, can only be deemed a monstrous abuse of the dramatic art and a gross violation of the canons of literary decency.
>
> It is a misfortune that the law provides no remedy against the gravest and most despicable libels on the dead; but surely, if it is permissible for a dramatist to endeavour to attract spectators to his plays by enduing characters in them with unspeakable vices, he should be compelled to utilize only imaginary persons for that purpose and should be restrained from defiling with his filthy imaginings the reputation of real men, whose memories are still dear to the living.

They also wrote to the Lord Chamberlain to try to persuade him to withdraw the licence:

> No playwright would be such a cad as to write a horrible inditement [*sic*] of an individual, if he knew that there were living numbers of near relatives who reverenced the said individual's memory, and, if he were such a cad, he would rightly guess that the censor would not permit its production.

Sycophantic and ingratiating letters pointed out to the Lord Chamberlain that some of the descendants were extremely important persons, whose views must be privileged and taken seriously; these included two grandsons: 'Lieut.-General Sir Edward Altham, who was a tower of strength to me in this County during the General Strike, and who is devoted to all good causes in the

County', and Colonel Edward Moulton Barrett, 'who began his service in the Northumberland Fusiliers in Egypt during your father's regime, and has often, in days gone by, told me of the kindness your father showed him as a young subaltern, when he was achieving his wonderful work in Egypt'.

Cromer arranged a conference with members of the family, Sir Barry Jackson (the play's producer), and various solicitors. The record of the meeting shows that Cromer, as so often, sought a compromise to defuse the confrontation:

> The Lord Chamberlain . . . pointed out that it was not the business of the Censorship to ensure that historical accuracy was maintained in plays of this character, but that he regarded it as part of his duty as Lord Chamberlain to ensure, as far as possible, that adequate steps should be taken by authors and producers to ascertain the views of the direct descendants of characters portrayed in plays of this nature, with a view of avoiding hurting their feelings by the presentation of incidents and the insertion of dialogue which might cause offence, and might be eliminated without spoiling the play.
>
> At the same time the Lord Chamberlain mentioned that a certain amount of licence must be allowed to authors and producers . . .
>
> A lengthy discussion ensued.

Eventually Cromer persuaded the playwright and the producer to publish a statement indicating that they had not intended to imply that incest had been involved, and to express 'regret that the play should have been erroneously interpreted'. Jackson also agreed to make further amendments to the script, but, in order to safeguard his reputation in the theatre world, Jackson's solicitors persuaded the Lord Chamberlain not to make it publicly known that he had agreed to such changes.

One further aspect of censorship over *The Barretts of Wimpole Street* is worth recounting. Following a letter of protest by the grandsons which was published in *The Times*, Bernard Shaw, always ready to lock horns with advocates of censorship, wrote a typically acerbic reply which he sent to the newspaper. The letter not only poked provocative insults at the descendants, but also firmly maintained that their grandfather was guilty:

> It is clear from the distinguished rank attained by the three that they have not suffered socially from the unfortunate circumstance that one of their parents was a detestable domestic tyrant who, having by good luck a famous poetess daughter who was beloved and married by a great English poet . . . made himself infamous by doing his utmost to separate and make them miserable in a transport of snobbery and jealousy. No dramatic poet could ignore the fact that modern psychology has made very short work

of the pretension of such jealousy to pure paternal piety; all that can be said to extenuate it now is that its victims were formerly able to disguise its real nature from themselves by a maniacal self-righteousness nourished by ecstasies of presumptuous and blasphemous prayer.

Shaw's letter remained unpublished, as did his letter of complaint to another newspaper about this non-publication.[74]

In 1926, Sir Douglas Dawson offered one definition of the role of the Lord Chamberlain's Office: 'so long as a Censor exists', he suggested, 'I would consider him the watchman that the stage is propagandist of good, and not of evil'. He reasonably added: 'To this may be answered; what is good or evil is purely a matter of opinion'.

In actual fact, getting God through St James's Palace and out the other side was probably even harder than taking the same route in the company of the red and forked tail.

CHAPTER EIGHT

Merchandisers in Muck

The Immoral Maze

That irregular sexual relations are so constant a subject of drama may be regretted.[1]

As long as the dramatist only wants to provoke the sex-laugh, he can go a long way . . . But if the dramatist has *ideas* about sex, or wants to deal with uncomfortable facts, if he wants to attack social institutions or social concealments or social prejudices in sex matters, then the Censor is liable to step in; and his motive for doing so seems to be that you must not make society feel uncomfortable by shaking the pillars of it: society is not to be informed that its sex-institutions are structurally unsound or dangerous. You must also protect the family from the suggestion that anything sexually horrific can happen within that sacred enclosure.[2]

In 1918 the Public Morality Council proposed to Lord Sandhurst that he should introduce a new regulation to be published on every licence, specifying that 'no play shall be performed which is intended or calculated to encourage or incite to immorality, or is in any other way subversive of public morality'. This would have been broadly equivalent to the injunction that a play must not 'in its general tendency, contain anything immoral or otherwise improper for the stage', which had become adopted as a standard accompaniment to licences until the 1909 Joint Select Committee pointed out that such a requirement had no basis in law. The Public Morality Council was convinced that its proposed amendment 'would give us a very much stronger hand in supporting your Lordship's department', providing a valuable weapon against plays which proved to be more disturbing in performance than might have been predicted from reading the script. Although this proposal was turned down on the grounds that no such alteration could be made without seeking changes to the law—and therefore opening up the whole issue of theatre censorship for rancorous debate—the Council continued to press similar demands in relation to specific plays.[3] At least in terms of quantity, it would be issues connected with sexual morality and

immorality which would most obviously dominate the arguments about theatre censorship for the next fourteen years.

Anyone who thought the war had been fought to restore the supposedly golden moral age of the previous century soon discovered it had not been won. In 1919 Charles Cochran staged *Afgar*, an 'extravaganza' centring on the adventures of Don Juan Junior in Morocco, which provoked outrage amongst moral campaigners, and widespread demands for Lord Sandhurst's resignation as Lord Chamberlain. A letter from the Temperance and Social Welfare Department of the Wesleyan Methodist Church complained:

> The Christian standard of morality in marriage and family life might never have existed so far as the position taken in the play is concerned. To ignore on so vital a question the existence of moral relations is to degrade the stage and to pander to the basest passions . . . The most mischievous element in the play is the successful attempt . . . to use expressions conveying a double meaning.

A series of detailed reports on the performance submitted by members of the Public Morality Council indicate the basis of many of the complaints:

> From my seat upstairs in the third row, her dress appeared to consist only of a girdle of silver coloured spangles from waist to knee, with breast shields held in position by cords . . . the upper part of her body was otherwise bare, and as she whirled her scanty 'skirt' of silver strings her tights were exhibited

Worse, 'Mr Thompson and I had glasses and we were convinced there were no tights worn by this artist'.

Cochran was the first target and enemy for the protestors; the *Sunday Express* called him 'irredeemable', and the *Daily Express* attacked him for his exploitation of the worst instincts of his audiences at a crucial moment in history: 'So long as men like Mr Cochran, who have a soul to feel art and an intelligence to understand it, pander to the baser tastes, we lose what the soul and intelligence might coin for us'. But under the headline 'Sandhurst Must Go', the *Sunday Express* was one of several newspapers to broaden the focus of its attack. In December 1919 the Lord Chamberlain reluctantly met a deputation from the Public Morality Council:

> Mr Allen prefaced his remarks by saying that any criticism he might make would be of the system, and that nothing personal was intended. He realised the difficult position the Lord Chamberlain was in, having to please all tastes, but he suggested that there were certain people who would try and get round the regulations and sail very close to the wind. With

regard to *Afgar* he submitted that it was founded on a fundamentally vicious idea, which was that of the physical inability of an elderly Oriental to satisfy his thirty wives . . . He concluded by saying that underlying the whole thing was a substratum of indecency accentuated by the acting of Delysia, and that it was offensive and unhealthy . . . One of the deputation drew attention to a phrase in the dialogue referring to a 'sparking plug' which he submitted was indecent.

As the official report on the meeting shows, Sandhurst was forced onto the back foot:

> The Lord Chamberlain in replying . . . said that when the revue was first produced he was in Scotland, and the Railway Strike prevented his taking such action as perhaps he would have done had he been in London. He agreed that the 'Daily Express' was very much against the play, but insisted that he and his officials kept a very sharp lookout in these matters . . .

He sought to reassure the deputation, by pointing out that he had now required amendments to be made, and denied that audiences were behaving improperly, as had been suggested. He even made the slightly risky admission that female members of his own family had witnessed a performance without being disturbed by it.

> The audience was in these matters a barometer, and he would point out that vulgarity was a matter of standard, that is to say the Gallery would laugh and the Stalls would merely think the joke bad taste. He was told that there were quantities of W.A.A.C.s and young men in the audience; that was not a fair statement. When he went he sat next to an elderly woman who smoked all the time and whose remarks were not at all directed to the alleged indecencies of the play.

The report of the meeting suggests that Sandhurst did not capitulate completely:

> A member of the deputation remarked that if the power in the hands of the Lord Chamberlain was not exercised it was in danger of being swept away. The Lord Chamberlain said that in his opinion if that power was exercised too severely it was still more likely to be swept away.
>
> The Lord Chamberlain further said that it was necessary to move with the times.

Cochran, meanwhile, was unwilling to make things too easy for Sandhurst, and was understandably cautious about a principle being established which

would allow the censor a second chance, by conceding the right to require changes to be made to a script after it had been licensed. He reluctantly agreed to make amendments, but he submitted a ten-page letter to the Lord Chamberlain making clear his views, and also including some of the positive comments on *Afgar* made by, amongst others, cabinet ministers.

> The position of a Manager might easily become intolerable if, after a play is licensed, and played for a long period in front of large and appreciative audiences, he is called upon at any time to make such drastic alteration as to completely alter the original play.

It is harder to judge how far Cochran's claims for the integrity of the revue should be taken seriously, and how far he was enjoying an opportunity to mock the Lord Chamberlain:

> The idea of the play is a satirical extravaganza containing an oriental analogy to certain present social and economic conditions in this country—i.e. Strikes . . . I would remind his Lordship that the whole strike of wives question was the basic idea of a farce of Aristophanes.[4]

In criticising Cochran, the *Sunday Express* had insisted that 'public taste, like all else, is now in the melting pot', and the sense of a continuing battle being fought in the years after 1918, supposedly for the moral soul of the nation, is palpable, and, at times, explicit. In the autumn of 1920, an adaptation of a French play, performed at the Little Theatre under the title *G.H.Q. Love*, provoked enormous hostility; set in a brothel attached to a fashionable French restaurant, and with prostitutes and their clients as the main characters, the play culminates in the suicide of a young man, after he witnesses the prostitute with whom he thinks he is in love in the arms of an officer. 'One can hardly stop a play because prostitutes figure in it', wrote the Lord Chamberlain; but many wanted to do exactly that.[5] One woman in the audience successfully disrupted a performance to complain about 'the importation of French filth into our theatres'. She was supported and given a voice by the *Daily Mail*: 'Although we allow that women of ill-fame exist', the newspaper reported her as saying, 'I think there is no reason for giving an entertainment about them'.[6] For Charles Palmer, an MP and assistant editor of the jingoistic *John Bull*, the real insult was the play's title, which he believed to be calculated to undermine the achievements of the last five years:

> G.H.Q. for us all stands for those Headquarters of the Army where the brains of our great generals worked out the schemes of military strategy which helped to win the war and save civilisation. And love—well, you see the pitiable idea. This underground lavatory where men and women leer

and bargain is the general headquarters of the kind of love which begins and ends in lust.

For Palmer, the project to make Britain a land fit for its war heroes was intrinsically linked to the need to establish a sexually moral and upright society. The theatre was crucial to that project:

> It never will be fit while we perpetuate wrong-doing or exalt the sordid and the vile . . . the last thing we desire as a nation is to have the vile things of the inevitable underworld turned into stage entertainment . . . What we need in our theatres and in our public policies is their very antithesis.[7]

For his supposed leniency in this and other examples, there were soon demands that the Lord Chamberlain 'ought forthwith to be removed from a well-paid post whose elementary duties he has ignored and flouted'.[8] The Westminster Catholic Federation and its Vigilance Committee fulminated against him for granting licences to 'contemptible plays which are bringing such ruin to the country', and announced a campaign against the ineffectiveness of theatre censorship. The Public Morality Council protested that plays such as *G.H.Q. Love* showed vice as commercially successful and left it unpunished: 'the ultimate triumph of virtue said to be insisted on by your officers is not apparent', they complained, protesting that the play dramatised incidents which it was 'impossible to disclose on a public stage without detriment to the morals of the younger members of the audience', and which 'could not be enacted in this country without involving a prosecution'.

Lord Sandhurst's refusal to cave in indicates that the Office realised it could not afford to endorse the reductive moral line some were urging on them:

> You will I hope understand that in the difficult and delicate duties in regard to Plays a Lord Chamberlain is called on to discharge, it is impossible to satisfy or reconcile all the different views held, not only as to the true purpose and necessary limitations of Dramatic Art, but as to the meaning and tendency of any particular play.[9]

The suggestion that nothing should be depicted on stage which would not be allowed in real life was clearly untenable, but it would recur; in 1924 the Public Morality Council complained of a play in which a boy is seduced by an older woman, partly on the grounds that 'if the incidents in *Fata Morgana* were enacted in the streets or parks, the participants would be brought before a magistrate'. But, as Street pointed out, there were 'many incidents on the stage which could not be represented in the street'. He gave an example: 'If a girl were to walk along Piccadilly dressed as a principal boy in a pantomime she would have trouble with the police'.[10]

The battle on issues of sexual morality took place on a number of fronts, and the remainder of this chapter will focus on the most important ones. Underlying all of them was the recurring complaint by some playwrights about the discrepancy between what could be alluded to for easy entertainment, and what could be discussed seriously. As Laurence Housman argued, sex remained the ultimate taboo:

> You may advocate the abolition of the House of Lords; you may even advocate the abolition of monarchy . . . You may advocate the disestablishment and disendowment of the Church of England . . . you may even advocate (what is more important still) the abolition of private property; but you may not advocate that men and women shall be allowed to live their own sex life in their own way. [11]

Another playwright, John Van Druten, agreed that in this more than in any other area, there were conventions which it was difficult to challenge:

> It is only of comparatively recent years that we have succeeded (if indeed we really have) in banishing from the stage the notion that love is the nonphysical attraction of one man to one woman, desiring no more than wedding bells and the chastest of kisses at the final curtain, a theory which still rules the musical comedy stage, and the love interest among the sympathetic characters in light comedy and in melodrama. Similarly, adultery is usually only committed by the comic or unsympathetic personages; it may excite either laughter or antagonism, but its serious consideration will be frowned at by the public.

He even mapped out the extent to which some of the codes could be stretched, and where the boundaries remained rigid:

> Supposing a dramatist wishes to present on the stage the character of a woman to be recognised by the audience either as immoral or as advanced and free-thinking, how will he do so? The answer is by indicating that she has had more than one lover. Two will be sufficient for this purpose. If two at the same time, then she is immoral; if two consecutively, then she is advanced and free-thinking. Should she allow her a third lover the censorship will probably require its excision as being unnecessary and shocking unless the woman is to be taken as definitely degraded and promiscuous.[12]

It is against that background that we will now focus on some of the specific areas of concern for the censor.

Dress

'The censoring of sex begins with clothes', wrote Laurence Housman in 1930, and as the most visible sign of provocative morality, dress was always taken seriously. Cromer declared: 'It is not the business of the Lord Chamberlain to dictate exactly as to what clothes an actress is to wear, but it is his business to be assured that she does wear sufficient clothing'.[13] In March 1926 Cromer instructed the Manchester police to inspect another Cochran revue for its possible 'audaciousness of costume'. As the country approached a general strike and the possible collapse of the social and economic order, Manchester's Chief Inspector spent his time describing an 'objectionable' dance

> by twelve girls in very short ribbon skirts, semi-ration boots, exceptionally short trunks, just covering the private parts but scarcely covering the buttocks, and leaving the leg bare from the calf to the top of the thighs . . . Their legs are thrown up and down and apart and whilst this is being done, a full view of the scanty underclothing worn is obtained.

Cochran was required to send photographs of the costumes to the Lord Chamberlain, and to make amendments to them. At the start of April, the Chief Inspector reported that they were now acceptable:

> Frills of lace have been added to their short trunks, obscuring to a great extent the objectionable feature of the trunks themselves . . . Girls execute further modified movements with their legs while still seated. [14]

Even in 1920, Lord Sandhurst was demanding full descriptions and pictures of bathing costumes to be worn in revues, and some performances were inspected specifically to check on costumes; as mentioned elsewhere the bodies wearing the costumes were themselves in danger of being censored, as when the Duke of Atholl noted that a particular dancer in Cochran's *Fun Of The Fayre*

> has got an ugly muscular back and they would certainly improve her appearance if she showed less of it above the base of her spine . . . The particular light that is used shows the imperfections of her bare legs, showing black shadows and red knees . . . she would be twice as attractive if she were in tights.

He also objected to costumes worn by the Chorus:

> There is nothing but a very tight piece of white stuff between the legs and

presumably round the waist. There must be some better covering to at least where the legs join the body and not tight flesh cover.

Inspections were sometimes carried out by Office staff, but whether this was an adequate or effective means of control is doubtful—especially when the management was aware that a performance was being scrutinised. Commenting on another dance routine in Cochran's revue, Atholl noted:

> It was difficult to see from my seat whether the dance was indecent . . . It lasted a short time and there cannot have been much wrong as I was looking for trouble . . . It is just possible, though I do not think so, that the performance was slightly watered down, as there was an individual seated not far from me who kept looking round to see if I was in my seat, when he definitely recognised me he whispered to the Commissionaire looking towards me, and went off apparently towards the stage.[15]

In 1921, anticipating problems over dancing and costumes in the spectacular musical *Cairo*, the Chief Clerk went to inspect:

> I do not think that there has ever been, in England, such an exhibition of unclad women. In the case of the Slave Market in *Chu Chin Chow*, which was so discussed, there were about twenty women dancers from the desert, stripped as much as possible to the waist. I should say that in *Cairo* there were one hundred at least, similarly clad and the exhibition of flesh is most striking.

Again, the management had evidently done its best to limit what he saw:

> I do not know whether it was done on purpose, but it was rather strange that the seat reserved for me was the last one on the left end of the front row . . . The result was, that when the dancing scene came on, my view was greatly impeded by one of the characters . . . It was only by leaning sideways that I was able to see the stage properly.[16]

The Public Morality Council complained of *Cairo* that 'the representation in England of manners and morals alien to this country as is here the case, is calculated to be subversive'; since the racial implications of this show were the source of further outrage it will be discussed in a later chapter.

It was probably not unusual for rules in this area to be bent or broken. In 1929 one of Cromer's staff inspected a musical comedy and complained to the manager, Sir Alfred Butt, about 'an unnecessary lack of clothing'. Sir Alfred apologised in writing, but it is hard to be fully convinced by his claim: 'I was horrified when Miss Ada May inadvertently, and of course quite acci-

dentally, pulled off her vest in the locker scene on the opening night'.[17] Sometimes Cromer found himself having to referee the grievances of rival managers, as when Wallace Parnell wrote a long and bitter letter of complaint:

> I can only say that I feel extremely hurt that you are permitting other shows to do things which I am not permitted to do. For instance, you have expressly stated that in my Living Pictures the girls must be covered. This in spite of the fact that at all costs I carry out faithfully the artist's conception of the original pictures . . . I go to the expense of having a complete four-way lighting system of dimmers costing over £250 to make sure that I get just the artistic lighting that the painter visualised. But you must realise how harmful it is to my business when I have to follow into a town a Show that is doing the actual pictures that I do, with the girls absolutely nude, and played in glaring white lights with no attempt whatever to copy the artist's conception, but just a desire to show as much naked flesh as they possibly can in the strongest white lights.

Parnell suggested they should send someone to see the rival performance, and that drastic action should be taken. The Lord Chamberlain did indeed have the show inspected by the Aldershot police; they reported that one performer was 'very scantily clad', and that 'her dialogue and actions are very suggestive', and expressed concern about an acrobatic dance in which a woman 'is held by the men mostly around the hips and buttocks and it seems that the slightest slip on the part of her partner might leave her in the nude'. They also described tableaux, based on classical paintings, in which a performer 'appears to be nude but owing to the lighting effects it is difficult to say whether or not she is wearing any clothing'. One of the Lord Chamberlain's staff telephoned the management to insist that the revue 'be cleaned up and the girls more adequately dressed'; he was then visited by Julie Nash, the main performer in the revue and part of its management, and discussed the situation as best he could, 'in spite of the difficulty in discussing the details of this case with a woman'. He found himself sufficiently persuaded by her arguments to advise the Lord Chamberlain that no further action was necessary:

> She stated that the revue had been on tour all over the country . . . and that the only complaint made was by the wife of Wallace Parnell, who had been following them about . . . She also stated that the girls in the tableau scene are not naked, but are made to look as such by a gauze curtain and special lighting effects . . . It appears to me that the complaint is made out of jealousy by a producer in competition. [18]

Although concern about costumes and revealing movement usually centred on 'popular' entertainment, this was not always the case. In 1926, a

performance of Andreyev's *Katerina* was interrupted by public protests from the auditorium; Cromer had already needed much persuasion to license this 'study of morbidly excessive sensuality in a woman', and he had required extensive alterations to the script. He again sent a member of staff to report on the performance, and, as always, it is the amount of detail—presented with apparent detachment and objectivity—which is striking:

> The impression intended to be conveyed is that only a single and rather scanty garment protects her from nudity . . . when, at a certain point, she sits facing the audience, the shortness of the dress makes it fairly plain (from the second row of the Stalls, at any rate) that there is nothing beneath except a narrow band of material (matching the dress) between the legs: and when she moves with her right side to the audience, part of the bare rump is occasionally exposed. (The crudity of the description is unavoidable).

The Lord Chamberlain insisted he would 'deal drastically with this case', and decreed that the manager 'should be spoken to severely' and must 'ensure no further complaints reach me about this dress question'.[19]

As mentioned previously, in the mid-1920s Cromer became caught up in an embarrassing scandal over a dress worn by the upper-class woman for her attempted seduction of a servant in *Potiphar's Wife*: 'A costume without sleeves and of net-work ceases to be a pyjama to my mind and is not a dress', ruled the King's official; 'It should either be a real feminine pyjama suit or a negligée costume'. A member of his staff who was to become the regular inspector of female attire over the next twenty years—the perhaps unfortunately named Mr Titman—was dispatched to write a report on the altered pyjamas. Titman was later to publish a book entitled *Dress and Insignia Worn at His Majesty's Court*, and the skills he would employ in describing the official dresses of His Majesty's Swan Keeper and His Majesty's Bargemaster were possibly honed through writing detailed reports on women's costumes in the theatres of London. In the case of *Potiphar's Wife*, Titman was able, with the approval of his wife, to confirm that the pyjamas were 'both adequate and decent'.[20] Nevertheless, Cromer's difficulties over *Potiphar's Wife* delighted several newspapers, and he was probably right that there had been a deliberate attempt to create a 'succès de scandale'.

Fooling an audience into believing they were seeing nudity when they were not was a widely used trick, generally achieved by the judicious use of flesh-coloured material. However, in 1932, a report for Cromer on *Beauty on Parade* expressed concern about a scene apparently featuring four naked girls with their backs to the audience. Two of the four turned out to be dummies, made out of papier-maché; remarkably, Cromer ruled that even the dummies must be clothed 'so as not to create the illusion' that the audience were witnessing

nudity. Perhaps nothing demonstrates so clearly the fact that it was the effect on an audience rather than what actually happened on stage which was the central focus for the censorship; what they <u>thought</u> they saw was what mattered.[21] If we anticipate for a moment the scandals of the 1960s over the stoning of the baby in the pram in *Saved*, or the burning of the butterfly in *US*, it is worth remembering how firmly established that principle was.

Sex Education

'I deplore the epidemic of abortion and syphilis plays, which we are suffering', wrote Dawson in 1921, but even he believed that the Rubicon had been crossed with the licensing of *Waste* and *Damaged Goods*, and that it might be too late to turn back.[22] As we know, Dawson certainly made no concession to serious plays—rather the reverse. His argument against *Matrimony*, an intelligent play about abortion and birth control which was refused a licence in 1921, advocated the exclusion of such subjects altogether:

> I have consistently opposed licenses [*sic*] for plays dealing with abortion and syphilis. I had hoped we had by now stamped out the recent epidemic of such so-called 'propaganda'. I cannot think that the stage is the place for object lessons in filthy subjects. Once admitted, one slight step further might see us faced with object lessons in unnatural crime, or even possibly the benefit to mankind of Beecham's pills.

Matrimony was resubmitted two years later under the title of *Life*, with cocaine substituted for abortion as the cause of a young woman's death. Cromer was inclined to refuse it again 'as an object lesson . . . that the Censorship is not to be hoodwinked by subterfuge'; however, on the advice of the Advisory Board he indicated that he was prepared to grant a licence.[23]

Dawson was suspicious of anything which sought to educate; writing of *Matrimony* he had commented: 'I do not believe in the bona fides of playwrights posing as propagandists on such subjects. Even granted an honest purpose, I believe that, in a mixed audience, for <u>one</u> converted <u>ten</u> are vitiated.' Overall, however, there was uncertainty about how to treat such plays—an uncertainty partly derived from a paternalistic sense of responsibility. *Was She Justified?*—a play about venereal disease—was rejected in 1921 in spite of the precedent of Brieux's play; if we accept that audiences might have been influenced by the play's arguments and claims, then it perhaps becomes harder to condemn the decision to ban it:

> I hold that this is such false and dangerous propaganda it ought never to see the light of the stage. Any good purpose which might be achieved by

emphasising the horrors consequent on venereal disease would to my mind be more than discounted by suggesting to the ignorant that its only cure lies in suicide, murder.

As Street commented—with some justification—when a revised version was submitted: 'the suggestion that syphilis is an incurable malady, is directly opposed to public interest'. [24]

Propaganda related to birth control was equally contentious, and again the Lord Chamberlain found himself attacked more for his tolerance than for his repression. In 1923 Street reported on a play which he said was 'designed to illustrate (1) the evil of a young wife refusing to have children, and (2) the evil of having too many children'. He described *Motherhood* as 'a sober statement of a tenable case', noting approvingly that 'the frank dealing is put into the mouth of a doctor', and that there was 'no sort of discussion of preventive means'. Cromer supported Street's recommendation for licensing, and justified it in terms of the play's potential for social good: 'It illustrates the evils of two extremes and thus points a moral, which may have an educational effect upon minds that need education upon so vitally important a problem in individual and national life'.[25] Street suggested that *Motherhood* 'may have been written by Dr Marie Stopes; at any rate it is in the interests of her propaganda'. Shortly afterwards, a more outspoken play on the same subject, which was indeed by Stopes, was submitted. *Our Ostriches* was a 'very direct attack on the Catholic opposition' to birth control, and Street expressed regret about the play's 'aggressive polemics', for which 'the Lord Chamberlain may not think the theatre a fitting place'. In *Motherhood*, the character advocating birth control had been a male doctor; here it was a young woman, and Dawson's typically negative response focused on this:

> I suppose I am old fashioned and out of date. But I feel Lord Simplex is well quit of a <u>girl</u> who can hold forth before a commission on birth control, syphilis, and sterilization . . . Surely the lesson it is intended to teach will be lost sight of in the feeling of horror that a young lady, just engaged to be married, should air such views in public.

A licence was eventually granted, though Cromer insisted on cutting allusions to syphilis, and demanded that the script must be revised so that 'the references to sterilization are put into the mouth of a doctor instead of the heroine'. This was not enough to prevent a conservative outcry in some circles; the Westminster Catholic Federation described *Our Ostriches* as part of 'the most deadly propaganda which has ever been agitated in this country', and unreservedly condemned all 'theatrical performances designed to forward a campaign in favour of contraceptives, the evil of which is obviously greater than that of any ordinary immoral play'. The Office's defence against these

attacks relied on arguing a general policy rather than engaging with the specific issue, but it sought to establish a very significant principle:

> With regard to the general principle of theatrical performances designed to forward propaganda on any one theme or another of public interest, your committee will doubtless recognise that, apart from propaganda of a seditious or treasonable nature, the Lord Chamberlain cannot in justice to either side of a controversial problem withhold his Licence to any Play that conforms in other respects to the Regulations governing Stage Plays.[26]

The attitude to abortion was very different; in 1924 Brieux's *Maternity* was again turned down, with the excuse that its thesis was applicable only in France, and that 'conditions are immeasurably different with us from those depicted in the play'. Specifically, the Lord Chamberlain ruled that 'the discussion of abortion which occupies the whole of Act Three renders the play unfit for public presentation in England'. In the same year, the Office also rejected *Suffer Little Children*, a play which attacked birth control by linking it with abortion. This decision could be read in different ways:

> The author will probably say it ought to be allowed as a protest against *Our Ostriches* and the censorship discriminates unfairly in favour of birth control. The answer, which I think might be conveyed to him, is of course that birth control and procuring abortion are quite different matters. His play is in fact a gross libel on the advocates of birth control.[27]

As late as 1929, a licence was refused for *Iron Flowers* because it was 'centred around an operation for procuring abortion'; of particular concern in this case was the fact that the operation was supported by 'good' characters, and Street doubted whether it was 'in the public interest to have this illegal operation practically justified'. He also feared that it might 'give grave offence to the medical profession to have a reputable doctor represented as performing it'.[28] Yet in the same year—in what it called a 'gesture of tolerance'—the Office licensed Eugene O'Neill's *Strange Interlude*, while acknowledging that until recently it would have been automatically banned 'for the suppression of one baby and the production of the other'. The knowledge that it had 'no chance whatever of being "popular" here' helped persuade the Lord Chamberlain that the play could be safely approved.[29]

Male impotence was another medical theme to which Lord Cromer took particular objection. In 1923 a licence was refused for Marie Stopes's *Married Love*; as Street's report put it:

> There can be no question about banning this play. Its theme is the impotence of a husband . . . The author would probably plead that his [*sic*] play

is meant as a warning against certain causes of impotence . . . But no excuse is sufficient for inflicting such an unnecessarily disgusting play on the public . . . the whole play is impossible, as an unnecessary and objectionable discussion of an abnormal physical condition and its consequences.[30]

In 1924 a revised version was submitted under the title of *Vectia*, and was again refused. Street suggested that it was less offensive because Stopes had now left out all references to the husband's 'secret sin' which was the cause of his impotence, but he still felt bound to oppose it. 'The author's intention is probably good, but the subject is outside of what can be discussed before a mixed audience in this country.' The Lord Chamberlain and his Advisory Board agreed unanimously:

> It is an inadequate justification to say that the description is true to life, so also would be plays dealing with unnatural vice and other instances of moral perversion. These things are not the proper subject matter for public representation in a Theatre . . .
>
> There must be some limit placed to the disclosure of all the relationships of men and women and this play is to my mind outside the pale.

Stopes was outraged. She warned Cromer that she intended to stage the play privately, and to publish the script with a preface, and she accused him of licensing plays which revelled in decadence and promiscuity, while refusing those which sought to instruct. Writing before Lady Violet Bonham Carter had joined the Advisory Board, Stopes claimed 'that all plays were considered from the man's point of view, and that anything derogatory to men was refused licence'.[31]

Reporting in 1928 on another play about an impotent husband, *Who Knows*, the liberal Street probably went as far as he dared in suggesting that 'possibly at future times such themes will be admissible'. Higgins, Buckmaster and even Dawson supported the play, but Cromer was adamant that 'however delicately handled' he was not yet prepared 'to admit impotence as a fitting theme for a play'. One adviser, Forbes-Robertson, supported him: 'We cannot have impotent husbands and neglected wives displaying their various emotions on the stage'.[32]

Sexual Perversions

'I am not prepared to consider the theme of sexual abnormality in women or men as suitable for public performance in this country', wrote Cromer in 1930. However, Nicholas de Jongh has argued that references to homosexu-

ality did sometimes make it onto the stage. He cites as 'remarkable' Street's 'ability not to see', suggesting that perhaps 'his eyes were wilfully closed' as he 'conspired in the practice of ignoring the implications' of what he read. [33] More specifically, John Deeney claims the surprising decision in October 1932 to license a German play, *Children in Uniform*, as 'an important if exceptional theatrical event in which lesbian invisibility was transgressed'. Deeney points to several reasons for the apparent leniency in this case, including the fact that its setting of a Prussian boarding school for girls could be read in nationalistic terms as 'an indictment of an "uncompromisingly German" education system'; he points out that one of the conditions of the licence was that the on-stage setting must clearly define its location as Germany. But Deeney also implies that the play escaped the censors partly because the lesbian dynamic is sufficiently muted in the text to be hidden from a reader, and is revealed only in performance; it thus 'circumvents the textually driven model of censorship as practised by the Lord Chamberlain. The censor was "reading plays", not "seeing theatre".'[34] Although it is, of course, true that censorship operated primarily in relation to the spoken word, there were—as we already know—plenty of cases where action was also imagined or anticipated, and made subject to alteration. More to the point, I think, is the issue of what the censor was *obliged* to notice. Once we recognise that Street—especially—was often much more liberal over moral issues than many critics, then choosing not to notice something can be seen as a highly plausible strategy for avoiding confrontations and arguments. The crucial issue, at least on some occasions, was whether those who wished to discredit the Lord Chamberlain and his officials would be able to argue that he had missed something which was so blatant that he had no excuse for failing to notice it. In 1921, reporting on a play called *The Trap*, Street drew attention to the line: 'there must be something pretty rotten about a girl who has such great women friends'. He noted: 'The meaning is obvious but I do not think it is conveyed in a way to call for interference', and the Lord Chamberlain neither commented nor sought further advice before licensing the play.[35] I am not suggesting any concerted plan to smuggle homosexuality onto the stage, simply that the daily practice was more a matter of compromise than of rigid laws.

Take for example the issue of cross-dressing. In *The Gay Young Bride*, a young man is entitled to his uncle's inheritance only if he marries within twelve hours; since his would-be wife is too far away, he undergoes a complete marriage service with her brother, who dresses in drag for the occasion. This was too much for the Lord Chamberlain to stomach, and he warned Herbert Clifton, the play's leading actor and manager, that 'the idea of a young man being dressed as a young woman with all the attendant business implied by the story would be too repugnant to admit a licence for performance in England'. But Clifton's indignant (and admittedly unauthenticated) response

detailed several situations where he claimed the practice was occurring without interference:

> For the last four years a Revue known as *Splinters* composed entirely of men, half of whom appear as young girls, has been toured with great success and devoid of any complaint . . .
>
> Furthermore, the Universities each year give public performances in which the students portray the part of young ladies and chorus girls. Only some two weeks ago the Life Guards gave public performances of a Revue known as *Whispers* at Windsor, which I believe was passed by your department, and only on Thursday last at the Putney Hippodrome the Metropolitan Police gave public performances at which males played the parts of young ladies, and were caressed by the other male members of the cast on the stage.[36]

Women impersonating men was usually less concerning; almost immediately after *The Gay Young Bride* had been refused, a licence was granted for *Don't Tell Timothy* in which a woman disguised as a man marries another woman: 'Of course there is nothing objectionable in a girl personating a young man (as there was in the opposite case) and it has been done in countless plays from Shakespeare downwards', wrote Street.[37]

Cross-dressing was also a tradition in pantomime and beyond. In 1924 Cromer had no real hesitation in allowing *Auntie* because 'the dressing up of Simon as a woman is in the vein of a vulgarized *Charlie's Aunt*'.[38] On another occasion, the Office received a protest about a revue act in which the comedian

> does the most indecent thing which I have ever seen in all my forty years experience. He conducts the band in semi-military uniform and with his back to the audience he undoes his trousers which he wriggles down by certain movements of the lower part of his body finally disclosing that he is wearing a pair of ladies 'undies' and his bare legs from the knees downwards. He then turns round, undoes his tunic and takes it off disclosing the top part of a lady's chemise tied with pink ribbons.[39]

The Office requested a police report, and, on being assured that the act was 'a silly joke' and that audiences were not upset, they took no further action. *Not Quite a Lady* again relied on a plot in which a man dresses as a woman in order to fake a marriage, while another man also cross-dresses in order to escape from a woman with whom he has been flirting. Street recommended licensing it:

> A man dressed up as a woman is always more or less offensive and obvi-

ously in this instance he really puts on feminine airs. But I am sure the authors had no intention of suggesting the homosexual idea and the audience will not read anything of that sort into the play.

Only one point concerned the Reader: 'I don't quite like Uncle William's kissing Paul'.[40] Of course, Street was right to imply that the plot assumes the characters are 'really' heterosexual; but then, this was presumably also true— at least ostensibly so—of The Gay Young Bride. By contrast, a gag was removed from a revue sketch in 1932 because the cross-dressing had no such excuse: 'Omit a Feminine Boy passes, stops and looks at Tom. Tom goes and takes hold of his arms: "I say that's not a girl".'[41]

De Jongh argues that 'effeminate and camp males' were more or less ignored by the censors 'as a third gender that posed no threat to men'.[42] I find no such uniformity in policy. In 1930, for example, Street noted in relation to a relatively obscure play for the Little Theatre in Leeds that 'the effeminate young man Cyril is chaffed too suggestively, though I do not think he is meant to be a practising pervert'; Cromer was then ruthless in his insistence that 'the whole of this play must be cleansed of perversity and a new script submitted before I will even consider it for Licence'. The manager was required to eliminate 'all traces of perversion in character, dialogue or insinuation' from the script: 'May this be an object lesson to those inclined to write nasty plays', wrote Cromer.[43] Again, when he read the script of Ivor Novello's Party, in which the characters are actors at a first-night party, Cromer found nothing specific to censor but was suspicious about how it might be acted: 'I will not have any young men impersonating perverts or "Nancy Boys"', he thundered; 'This is the sort of play where unpleasant business might be introduced and I do not like it'.[44] Elsewhere, de Jongh more convincingly suggests that during the 1920s 'a series of coded parallels' came into existence, allowing playwrights to use the transgressiveness of certain heterosexual relationships as metaphors to signal the forbidden subject of homosexuality in ways which the Lord Chamberlain's Office either did not see or felt unable to suppress.[45] Tempting though it is to speculate that Street, in particular, was alive to such possibilities in his sometimes generous recommendations, there is little to suggest that the censors were aware on a conscious level of any such code; indeed, it is evident that other contraventions of the moral norm were taken at face value and seen as significant in their own right. Yet their comments on Party show that the censors, whatever else they may have been, were not naïve in their assumptions about the pervasiveness of homosexuality in West End theatre circles. If we accept that Cromer saw the primary aim of censorship as being to prevent public outcry rather than to repress for its own sake, I think it is reasonable to suggest that there was a tacit acceptance that so long as a code was not penetrated by moralists, or by the majority of audience members, then there was no need to intervene or draw attention to it.

As we might expect, what could be shown also seems to have depended entirely on the context. In 1930 John Van Druten wrote:

> One of the most surprising phenomena which I have recently noticed in the theatre is the portrayal, especially in farce, revue or musical comedy, of effeminate men, mincing and wilting in what the public recognises as 'Nancy' attitudes, to the shrieking delight of an audience—and this while any attempted mention, even, of homosexuality is utterly taboo in the serious theatre.[46]

What definitely could not be allowed, of course, was anything which addressed homosexuality directly—let alone defended it. *Alone* was inevitably refused a licence in December 1930, since the play was an adaptation of Radclyffe Hall's novel *The Well of Loneliness*, which had itself been prosecuted and banned two years earlier. Street described the play as 'a study of a sexually abnormal woman and a protest against women similarly affected being regarded as pariahs and outcasts—the extent to which this happens being surely exaggerated'. In contesting the play's claims, Street confidently claimed that 'people are indifferent to the abnormality in women . . . until it becomes aggressive'; however, he described *Alone* as 'sincerely and sensitively written and quite free from offence'. Considering he must have known that to issue a licence would be quite impossible, he went as far as he could have done in supporting it, and drew a distinction which was sometimes considered highly significant: 'One would not gather from the play that Paul's abnormality resulted in definite physical action'. Unsurprisingly, Cromer ruled that since the novel had been officially banned it was 'impossible to discuss this production on the stage'.[47]

A different 'perversity' which worried the censors was incest. *The Cenci* was approved in 1922, thanks to the status of its author, but the following year Cromer rejected a modern play, *Sins of the Parents*, even though the father in this case is unaware that it is his own daughter who is the object of his lust, and even though he never gratifies that lust.[48] In 1924 a licence was refused for Benavente's *The Passion Flower*, because it focused on the secret love of a young woman for her mother's husband. 'No doubt it will be argued that it is a less horrible Play than *The Cenci*', wrote Street, but Benavente's 'realism' was seen as 'a very different matter from the poetry of *The Cenci*', and rendered it unacceptable. Dawson, meanwhile, was even more disgusted than usual, because the stepfather's love for his stepdaughter was reciprocated; 'Personally I am getting tired of these dirty stories and I am of opinion that a large number of people share my view', he wrote. Cromer agreed: 'We have more than enough of "sex complex" problems in English plays without wishing to import more of them from abroad'.[49]

In 1927 a licence was granted for *And in the Tomb Were Found*, Terence

Gray's play set in seventeenth-century Egypt, in which the royal lovers are brother and sister. Street excused it as 'historical and largely educational', and though he felt it 'conceivable that the Lord Chamberlain would be blamed for passing a play in which occurs what our civilization regards as incest', he pointed out that 'an educated audience would know of course that this is historical and inevitable'.[50] This view was accepted. In 1931 an opera based on the *Hippolytus* of Euripides, *Fedra*, was also approved: 'I do not think the motive of incest should ban the opera', wrote Street; 'Horrors in an opera are seldom as horrible as in other forms of drama'.[51]

Yet incest in a contemporary context remained unacceptable. When Cromer licensed Gray's Egyptian play in March 1927, he was simultaneously embroiled in an international argument over his refusal to license a recent French text, in which a father's sexual desire for his daughter is again unfulfilled, and in which he is again ignorant of the family connection. *The Legacy*, which had already been staged in Paris, was, said Cromer, 'too much for the English stage'. But the playwright was so angered by this decision that he elicited the support of two Presidents from the Société Universelle du Théâtre, and persuaded the British Embassy in Paris to ask the Foreign Office in London to pressurise Cromer into changing his mind. Cromer acknowledged that 'probably all foreign nations consider us peculiar as regards the stage, and perhaps we are from their point of view', but he was reluctant to concede to such a challenge to his authority: 'If once I were to give way to diplomatic pressure . . . there would be an end of all Censorship as regards foreign plays to be produced in England', he declared. He had no doubts that 'we are all better judges of what should be licensed for the British stage than any Frenchman alive', and insisted that this must be acknowledged:

> Our French friends should surely accept the fact with better grace than they have shown in this case The fact is accepted by other countries, as for instance the Italians when a play by their idol Pirandello is turned down, and by Hungarians and Americans when the plays of their most prominent young authors are refused a licence; so why not by the French . . . Paris is Paris and London is London, and the atmosphere of the twain, so far as the theatre is concerned, will never meet completely.

After protracted wrangling, the ambassador in Paris gave his official support to the British position—though not without hinting that perhaps theatre censorship in Britain was taking its role rather too seriously, and that 'very respectable French wives and mothers would admire a play of this sort'.[52]

In October of the same year another French play—*The Simoun* by Henri-René Lenormand—was also turned down by Lord Cromer. One objection was 'the talk and a certain amount of action in regard to the intercourse of

Frenchmen with Arab girls of tender age', but the main obstacle was the sexual feelings of a father towards his own child:

> This passion of a man for his daughter, though he fights against it and it is not consummated, seems to rule out the play. If the precedent of *The Cenci* is pleaded the reason, I suppose, is the difference between an historical play by a great poet and a realistic modern play.[53]

The following month, two further plays about incest were rejected. Street's report on *The Seventh Commandment* drew attention to the Office's anomalous treatment of the subject:

> A man, however unwittingly, having his own daughter as his mistress and begetting a child by her is a plot which obviously will not do in a modern play, even though it is less repulsive than that of *Oedipus Rex*.[54]

In the case of *La ville morte*, a French version of an Italian tragedy by d'Annunzio, Street agonised about its status and classification:

> The Censorship has always forbidden any approach to incest as a theme. It has however waived that rule in the case of the *Oedipus Rex* and *The Cenci*. Can the play of d'Annunzio's be taken as a classic?

Street eventually recommended licensing, because of the play's 'poetical quality'—a coded way of indicating that its potential audience was small—and because 'the incestuous passion is fought against and not given way to'. Cromer, however, turned it down without explanation.[55]

It is not difficult to understand the distaste of the censors for the recurring theme of incest, though it seems harder to credit that they really thought audiences might be encouraged or incited to commit such an act as a result of seeing a play. However, even while condemning *The Cenci*, the Public Morality Council indicated that it was not necessarily against the principle of incorporating the theme in more appropriate ways. Indeed, it conceded the possibility that the theatre could be used for positive propaganda to help warn people against incest by ensuring 'that the severity of the penalty the State inflicts for such a crime should be more generally known'.[56] Moreover, at least according to its would-be manager, *The Seventh Commandment* was based on a true and not uncommon case, and was to have been presented 'for the purpose of acting as a warning to unfortunate girls, and a deterrent to the unthinking man'. The manager even offered to give half the proceeds to charity:

> I have read the script to a prominent surgeon in one of our largest hospi-

tals, and to a Minister of the Gospel whose work lies amongst the class depicted in the play. Both of these gentlemen testify to the truth which we are endeavouring to place before the public, and give it as their opinion that, far from giving offence, the play should be a powerful instrument for the public good.[57]

Heterosexuality

There is nothing inherently indecent in a girl in bed.[58]

Despite this slightly grudging concession by one of the Lord Chamberlain's advisers, references to heterosexual sex, even between consenting adults, usually worried the censors; they were anxious both about physical details and the underlying moral lesson. An example of the former was the persistent— if unwritten—refusal to allow two people to be shown in bed together. In 1922 Atholl waived this rule for a dream sequence in which the wife of a war invalid has a vision of previous occupants of their cottage in bed together. Dawson protested that this had never been allowed previously: 'I distinctly remember telling Mr, now Sir, Alfred Butt, years ago that the Lord Chamberlain would not permit the two sexes to be shown together on the stage in bed together'.[59] But Atholl's liberal gesture remained a more or less isolated exception. In 1923 Street recommended a sentimental comedy in which an elderly couple are in bed together: 'they are elderly and there is no sort of sexual suggestion', he reported. But Cromer was adamant: 'I'm not prepared to extend the licence about bedroom scenes to a couple being in bed, no matter how elderly'.[60]

Sexual activity and even the expression of sexual desire were also fairly stringently controlled. Following complaints about *Fata Morgana* in 1924, the Lord Chamberlain sent one of his officials to witness the scene of seduction; his detailed report suggested that the physical expression generally fell within the bounds of what was acceptable:

In my opinion, the only thing which calls for action by the Lord Chamberlain is the 'business' with Mathilde, when she is seated on the sofa, on the second return of George from his bedroom.

In this 'business' she so manoeuvres her dress to show both her legs above the knees, and leans back with her arms above her head in an attitude of complete abandonment.

Last night, for a few seconds, she actually showed her leg half way up her thigh, but this was probably unintentional.

The love making between Mathilde and George is certainly passionate, but does not go beyond what is usually allowed in such scenes. He does not fondle her legs nor does he suggest in any way that he wishes to put

his hand up under her clothes ... his action throughout, though passionate when she kisses him, does not suggest sexual desire.

When complaints persisted, Cromer threatened to withdraw the licence unless his restrictions on how the scene was to be played were observed. According to a memorandum recording a meeting between the Lord Chamberlain and those responsible for the performances, 'the Producer pleaded that he had been away and that his actors were very troublesome, especially the man'; rightly or wrongly, the blame was put on the actors, who 'did not stick to what had been rehearsed'.[61]

Other plays tested the rigidity of traditional boundaries. In 1919 *Morality* was accused of expressing a 'defiant attitude' in advocating the positive advantages for a couple who live together before marriage. 'The chief characteristic is a great deal of superficial "anti-conventional" haranguing', wrote Street, though both he and Bendall thought that it remained within the limits of what was now permissible. But the Lord Chamberlain followed Dawson's advice in rejecting it:

> I cannot conceive a Censor passing a scene where a young woman offers her body (like a piece of meat) to be tossed up for by three men, the winner to seduce her that night and she to be his property for a six months leave.[62]

In *An Angel's Heart*, in the same year, an older woman who persuades a younger man to become her lover 'in order to save him from the dangers of casual intercourse' is presented sympathetically. Street thought the author intended it as 'a serious attack on what he thinks are the evils of conventional morality', but feared that, in spite of its warnings against the dangers of venereal disease, most people would simply be disgusted by the play's thesis. Ironically, Dawson saw it as well-intentioned; he worried that if the play were banned, they would be criticised by those who were 'in favour of propaganda on the stage to remedy evil, no matter how much dirt is dragged in'. Most of the Board were against licensing the play, and their view prevailed.

> If it is to be regarded as a play with a purpose, that purpose can only be to show that continence is an impossibility, and that social conventions unfairly restrain promiscuous intercourse and that a woman does a noble act in providing herself for the satisfaction of a man's desires, and incidentally of her own, so as to avoid his contracting venereal disease.[63]

In 1921 Lord Buckmaster insisted that the censorship must 'consider the teaching of a play, as well as the decency of its language and situation'; he was responding to Street's uncertainty about *Rounding the Triangle*, in which a woman offers to marry a man and share him with his mistress. 'Its conclusion

is certainly opposed to orthodox morality', Street had written, but he had found nothing in the language or the action which was itself censorable; 'The question is if an immoral thesis, decently stated, may be allowed on the stage'. The author was persuaded to rewrite the ending, and although in the revised script the same proposal was still put forward by 'the abnormally "advanced" young woman', it was now immediately and absolutely rejected by the other two.[64] A similar theme was the basis in 1923 of the same playwright's *Husbands Can't Help It*, when a wife announces that she has no intention of interfering with her husband's mistress; had the play finished there it could not have been licensed, but the ending was, as Street reported, 'happy in every sense', as the mistress walks out on the husband, telling him that his wife is too good for him.[65]

Other plays turned down in the early 1920s on moral grounds included *The Third Floor Front*, which was described as 'a sympathetic picture of immorality and licentiousness', *Anniversary*, for its 'general freedom and discussion of intimacies', and *Faisons un rêve*, because 'two adulterous people in bed (or practically so) goes beyond anything that can be allowed even to French players'.[66] Though he confessed to liking it, Cromer also rejected a French satire, *Uplift*, in which a prostitute uses her sexuality to climb the ladder of social and financial success:

> In England and in English this is impossible. The theme of demonstrating on the stage the advantages that accrue to an immoral life, openly lived by a woman who is constantly selling herself to the highest bidder would be repugnant in the extreme and would shock British public opinion.[67]

Recurring plots which were routinely rejected included a husband or wife discovering that someone with whom they are about to have a supposedly illicit relationship is actually their own partner, and a husband being tempted by either his mistress's daughter or his son's mistress.[68] Dawson found *Fledglings*, in which a nineteen-year-old boy has a relationship with his much older godmother, not only 'repulsive' because of the age difference, but 'worse to my mind where the woman is the offender'; yet rather surprisingly, the endorsement required only that she should not be his godmother.[69] In 1925 a licence was refused outright for *Rude Awakening*, which, with its discussion of a 'non-physical marriage', and its seduction of a young man by his step-mother, was according to Dawson 'the very type of play from which the rational proportion of the community look to the censor for protection'.[70] Cromer also initially rejected John Van Druten's *Young Woodley*, the story of a schoolboy's infatuation with an older woman in a public school, believing that 'its effects might be most harmful', and that 'the majority of parents would be up in arms at this sort of play being permitted'. Even the offer to remove one character completely was not enough to make Cromer reconsider, until

a private staging in January 1928 was well reviewed by the critics. The play's producer, Basil Dean, persuaded Cromer to reconsider his decision:

> I have already cut out a great deal of the undesirable element in the first act, and with your co-operation I am prepared to do so still more . . . If the Censorship were to be liberal minded in this matter after the way the play has been received, it would be a gesture of strength rather than of weakness, and go a long way towards showing that this Office is prepared to move with the times, and is indeed careful of the best efforts in English dramatic writing.

Cromer consulted Lord Eustace Percy at the Board of Education, who took the view that although he didn't like it, 'more harm is done by the vague knowledge that a play about public schools has been "suppressed"'.[71]

Once again, the censorship was not always as extreme in refusing to license plays which questioned moral conventions as some people wished it to be. In 1926 Cromer licensed *The Fanatics* by Miles Malleson, against the recommendation of his adviser, Lord Ullswater:

> I do not think that a theatre audience, composed of both sexes and persons of all ages and degrees, should be subjected to . . . having to listen to discussions on free love . . . Promiscuous sexual experiences . . . trial marriages . . . birth control . . . and so forth.[72]

Dawson agreed with Ullswater that the theatre was no place for such subjects: 'Let books, if they may, discuss free love, birth control, and other horrors of which we have object lessons in Russia today', he railed. However, Cromer not only licensed the play, but refused to intervene when Cardiff police subsequently complained to Scotland Yard that the play was 'a menace to public morality'.

In the same year, he licensed, with only minor amendments, Somerset Maugham's *The Constant Wife*. Maugham's play explored what Street called the 'cynical' philosophy that

> When a husband and wife cease to be in love with each other then his unfaithfulness matters nothing to her and she is not entitled to object, since he keeps her and (in the well-to-do class) she does nothing in return.

Street warned that this argument would 'affront the morality of most people who see it and cause considerable scandal', but Cromer—perhaps disinclined to court controversy by censoring such a well-known writer—ruled that 'I do not think I should be justified in suppressing an expression of these views on stage'.[73] Maugham's later play, *The Sacred Flame*, raised issues of euthanasia

as well as sexual morality, when the wife of a man crippled by a plane crash commits adultery with his brother; Cromer again licensed it, despite vociferous complaints from the Public Morality Council about the final Act, which appeared to excuse or even condone her behaviour:

> How such an Act received the sanction of one whose Office it is to safeguard the public morality of the Stage surpasses my comprehension. The argument of the Play is contrary to all Christian ethics and totally opposed to all Christian teaching. The danger is the greater because of the plausible way in which wrong is made to appear as right.
>
> Those who are engaged in teaching Christian morals find their work given a deliberate set-back by such plays and I think we are fully justified in making as strong a complaint as we can against such a lack of censorship.[74]

In a variety of ways, then, playwrights were seeking to use the stage to question and undermine sexual conventions and the orthodox morality which the Public Morality Council was keen to preserve from debate. Inevitably, the censors were less worried when the status quo was eventually confirmed as the natural way of living. One of the saving graces of Maugham's *Our Betters* in 1923, for instance, was that, for all 'the general viciousness, immorality and sordidness of several of the characters', it was clear that 'the effect is not sympathy with vice but intense scorn of it'.[75] Or, as Street wrote a few years later in response to a play written by Lieutenant Colonel Sir Frank Popham Young: 'I do not think there is sufficient reason for banning this play, in spite of the immoral actions of the characters. These are not presented sympathetically, as in some modern plays.'[76]

One of the most interesting examples of a play which was certainly not supportive of the status quo was *The Green Hat*, which was based on a controversial novel of the same name by Michael Arlen, and submitted in 1925. The narrative centres on a strong female character, Iris, who flouts several moral conventions, and who was played in the original production by Tallulah Bankhead. Widely blamed for her husband's suicide on their wedding night, and deserted by her friends and society, Iris pursues a promiscuous life abroad, before returning to England for the briefest of affairs with an old admirer who is about to get married. She gives birth to a stillborn child in a convent, and eventually commits suicide by driving her car into a tree. Iris's lifestyle and her outspokenness were bound to antagonise moralists, especially as the play shows sympathy for her position; 'Iris is out to destroy our sort of life. Are we going to let her?' asks someone in the play. Yet she achieves an almost tragic status—the cause of her husband's suicide at the start of the play is not Iris's behaviour but his own infection with venereal disease—and the play invites us to see her fate as emblematic: 'She's a lonely woman because she's not an idiot', says one character: 'All intelligent women are lonely'. After

Iris's death is discreetly taken to have been an accident, another female character tellingly observes that 'the only accident that ever happened to Iris was to be born into this world'.[77]

Street knew that *The Green Hat* would be seen as 'daring' and that it would 'displease some people extremely' if it were licensed. 'The play as a whole is one of those which brings blame on the Lord Chamberlain which ever course he takes', he wrote. It was apparent where the author's sympathies were located, but Street thought that Iris's death made it possible to defend the play against charges that it was condoning vice: 'It is difficult to make out if its tendency is to glorify immorality, but as there is plenty of spoken condemnation of it and it is severely punished the play is hardly immoral'. Cromer agreed that there were no longer grounds for wholesale rejection of the theme, but Dawson—who stuck to his opinions irrespective of changing fashions—took a much harder line:

> The reluctant consent to a licence for a play because, while personally disapproving the theme, we are told it panders to the public taste, does not appeal to me.
>
> Even if the public taste is vicious, . . . there is still a large proportion of decent opinion, which looks to the Censor for protection.

A forceful and determined campaign against the play was mounted by Sir Robert Cust, a Hampstead JP who declared himself to be an active member of both the Public Morality Council and the Present Day Dangers Committee. Cust's direct appeal to the Lord Chamberlain relied on patronising social prejudice:

> I do beg you, Lord Cromer, to think of the effect of such a story upon innocent or quasi-innocent folk. Read the book yourself and—may I say it as one old Etonian to another—ask yourself whether you think even as a book it ought to have been published and disseminated.

As ever, Cromer took a more pragmatic line: 'Great care is being taken to eliminate, as far as possible, everything objectionable', he replied, and the play's energy may indeed have been killed by the cuts he imposed. 'The story of the play is bound to arouse hostile criticism in certain quarters', wrote Cromer, 'so there is no reason for giving unnecessary openings for assailing the censorship over the dialogue'. Certainly, several reviewers expressed surprise at the relative tameness of the performance script by comparison with the original novel, and Cromer's willingness to license the play was in effect part of a tacit deal. 'The author has been very amenable to the requirements of Censorship', he wrote, tellingly. However, Hannen Swaffer, a frequent critic of the Lord Chamberlain, still complained about the play at length; the

racist overtones of his comments in relation to the author, Michael Arlen, somewhat outweigh the humour in his letter—though it is hard to be sure of the tone intended:

> I feel it my duty to call your attention to the fact that in *The Green Hat*, now being played at the Adelphi Theatre, the word poop is spoken twice in the first act, an act which was applauded only by the degenerates in the audience.
>
> I do not know whether Arlen, who is an Armenian of some sort, knows the meaning of this word; but I presume you do, since you are not an Armenian.
>
> Reference to the 'Century Dictionary' confirmed my opinion that it meant a breaking of the wind.
>
> I do not know whether you think this is the sort of thing which, in civilised England, should be tolerated, but in view of the fact that you are now so very much disturbed about the continuance of your Office, I must call your attention to what you and one of your underlings may have passed.
>
> There are several other gross indecencies in the play, the production of which, in this year of trouble, when we are trying to defend institutions we all hold dear, is a national scandal; but I quote only one of them since I have neither the time nor the patience to recite a catalogue of improprieties, sneers at England and dago impertinence.
>
> I am sending a copy of this letter to the Bishop of London, the Heads of all the Churches, the Premier and all the Cabinet Ministers.
>
> I have also taken steps to see that the Queen is informed of this open breach of public decency in the heart of the Empire's capital . . .
>
> In Armenia, I believe, the sewers are open in the streets. That is no reason why they should be open in the Strand, frequently though the roads are up.

Perhaps not surprisingly, an internal memorandum in the Lord Chamberlain's Office described Swaffer as 'an individual who should not be touched with the tongs'. He it was who declared that most theatre managers were 'merchandisers in muck'.[78] On this occasion, his letter was acknowledged politely, but the production was allowed to continue without further alteration.[79]

In the middle of the argument over *The Green Hat*, Noel Coward's *Fallen Angels* was submitted, with its scandalous scene of two women becoming drunk as they wait for their mutual French lover, and revealing to each other and the audience their past sexual indiscretions. Again, Cromer was keen to avoid outright rejection:

> Like most of that author's plays, it is unpleasant, but not half as much so,

to my mind, as other plays of his. This has the redeeming feature of being light and unreal and humorous. If some of the allusions to 'sex' + 'illicit' + 'illegitimate' . . . are taken out it will to some extent tone down the all too modern atmosphere.

By defining it as light rather than as a serious drama, it was easier to excuse the play—though extensive amendments were again imposed as part of the compromise with the puritan wing:

> It is not so much that I object to the actual words, as words on the stage, but their absence will help to render the atmosphere of the play less objectionable to some people who disapprove of quite unnecessary frankness of expression among women.

Cromer's stance did not satisfy members of the Public Morality Council, who campaigned to have the licence revoked on the extraordinary grounds that the play was 'utterly untrue to life' because it focused on 'only one side of human nature'; they denounced it as 'a breach of "good manners" to present so untrue a picture of human degradation'. As usual, it was primarily the potential effect on the behaviour of audiences which concerned them:

> The whole is a revolting sex-play and has not the redeeming feature of containing a moral lesson. It must have a demoralising tendency upon the minds particularly of young people who witness it and cause them to reflect that if it represents real life, then moral restraints and marital fidelity are really boring and unnatural and that to profess chastity before marriage and fidelity afterwards is sheer hypocrisy . . .
> We feel that the effect of such a production must be:-
> To gratify unhealthy sexual imaginations.
> To encourage women to be careless of their chastity.
> To lower the conception of marital relationships and consequently have a degenerate influence upon home life.

To his credit, Cromer refused to negotiate with them or to amend his decision.[80]

The Historical and the Classical

> The question is if the original comic opera's being a sort of classic and the story on which it is based being a real classic will sufficiently counter balance the objections. There will be a fuss either way.[81]

In 1922 *Peer Gynt* was finally licensed for performance in Britain. 'It would be absurd to interfere with the production of this European classic', wrote Street, and 'ridiculous to cut out anything from such a work'. Ibsen's play was thus licensed partly because the Lord Chamberlain risked becoming a laughing stock—and surrendering his authority—if he continued to reject works of art which had become widely accepted as masterpieces. Yet more important was the fact that a classic was, by definition, likely to appeal only to a 'special' audience who were better educated and therefore supposedly less susceptible to being influenced by what they saw: 'it is altogether above the heads of any but an extremely select English audience . . . There is not the faintest possibility of its appealing to popular audiences', confirmed Street, and he suggested 'treating this somewhat as one would treat Shakespeare—parts of which if written today would appear coarse. i.e. treat it as a classic'.[82] As with the licensing of *Six Characters in Search of an Author* to be performed in Italian but not in English, double standards were in operation. As we know, *The Cenci* was also afforded classic status in 1922: 'It is not as if a modern writer had invented the subject matter, which in such a case would be disgusting', explained Cromer, and Street made an explicit comparison when he gave the reason for refusing to recommend a modern play about incest:

> The authors may object that the case of *The Cenci* is much more revolting, but I do not think the Lord Chamberlain need be troubled by the inconsistency. There is a difference between a classic by a great poet and a vulgar melodrama appealing to the commonest sort of audience.

The Public Morality Council did not acknowledge this distinction and attacked the staging of any play it considered immoral. Opposing the granting of a licence to Shelley's play, members informed the Lord Chamberlain that they were 'strongly of opinion that there is no justification for the view, that has grown up, that plays that are classics should not be controlled, neither do they believe that this is the desire of the thoughtful public of this country'. However, they seem not to have understood or accepted the Lord Chamberlain's argument about the nature of the audience likely to attend a classical play; they complained that 'an average audience, varying widely in experience and age, has not the background of education which alone makes it possible to interpret wisely the different moral standards and outlook of an earlier age or of another country'.[83] The Council also contested the fact that

plays written before the passing of the censorship law were effectively exempt from the system of licensing applied to new plays. However, it should not be assumed that this apparent exemption meant that older plays were necessarily uncensored. When *The Country Wife* was staged at the Everyman Theatre in 1926, even the Public Morality Council admitted that the text was 'well expurgated' and that it had been extensively and voluntarily cut. Indeed, the management had actually submitted their version for licensing, but Cromer realised that it would be much safer to have nothing to do with the production than to give official approval to even an edited version of a Restoration play. He informed the management that no licence was required and that the script would therefore not be read, and he avoided seeing the production—perhaps so that he could plead ignorance in the event of controversy arising.

Given that the obvious and explicit immorality of plays such as Wycherley's exceeded by some way that of most of the contemporary plays which provoked moral outrage, it is easy to understand the frustration of members of the Public Morality Council when they were faced with the illogical absurdity that such plays were not susceptible to the same process of control. They sent Cromer a series of reviews and letters of complaint about *The Country Wife*, insisting that, in spite of the cuts, it remained 'vile' and lacking in 'a trace of virtue'. Trying to turn things to their advantage, they argued that the production demonstrated 'the need for further powers being given to the Lord Chamberlain . . . to deal with "Restoration Plays"', and a delegation proposed to Cromer that all plays, rather than just new ones, should henceforth require licensing. Again, the effect on certain kinds of audience was central to their argument, and one of the delegation insisted that such plays 'should only be performed to audiences of good education', since 'the effect on audiences of lower educational standard was likely to be most harmful'. They suggested that age, too, was an important factor and that, at a time when 'younger members of the community were passing through a transient stage of opinion and thought', it was the duty of the censorship to ensure 'that they should receive no hindrance from the moral atmosphere of the theatre'.[84] Their arguments had no direct effect on Cromer's decision in relation to the Everyman's production of *The Country Wife*, but it is harder to be sure whether the rarity of Restoration productions during this period had any connection with the Public Morality Council's campaigning .

Modern plays in classical or historical settings were another bone of contention. In 1925 Ashley Dukes submitted a new play called *The Man with a Load of Mischief*, which was set in the Regency period. Street commented:

> This is not of course a moral Play. The people act immorally. But there is an immense difference between immoral acts, set in an atmosphere of philosophy and poetry and the vulgarity and banality of a Play like *Fallen Angels*.

Even the Public Morality Council admitted that such a play 'presents a great difficulty to us in view of the beauty of the diction and the admirable construction'. But it reminded Cromer of an assurance he had given:

> We respectfully call Your Lordship's attention to the fact that it is not a Restoration play although apparently purporting to present the manners of that period.
>
> When our deputation brought this matter to Your Lordship some time ago, we understood that new plays dealing with the Restoration period were on the same footing as any other new play.

Cromer's reply tentatively sought to establish a principle that would allow him more leeway to relate a play not just to the period in which it was written, but also to that in which it was supposed to take place:

> The scene being laid in the Regency period, almost inevitably involves a certain degree of latitude—within limits—in both dialogue and situation, which might become more open to objection in a Play treating of a later era.[85]

In 1927 Robert Sherwood's *The Road to Rome* was submitted; Street was unsure whether its setting of the Punic Wars was sufficient to indemnify its immorality:

> Possibly the antiquity of the period may make this less objectionable, but I am afraid the production might cause considerable scandal in some quarters . . . I doubt its doing harm, but it does make a shameless woman triumph and that may be too great an objection.[86]

In the event, Cromer felt able to license it with only minor changes. In 1928 a cynical comedy about the French King Henry IV was approved for similar reasons: 'If this comedy had a modern setting it would be more doubtful', wrote Street, 'but a historical background placates moralists'. He reasoned that 'an Henri IV like our Charles II, may be allowed to be immoral', and Cromer confirmed that 'in a modern setting I agree it would not do, but in the circumstances I think it can pass'.[87] A more unusual example occurred in 1929, when a New York company announced its intention to bring to England an English translation of a German adaptation of Ben Jonson's *Volpone*. 'So far as I remember Ben Jonson', wrote Street, 'the morality of the people in this play is no more base'. However, as a modern play, the text was automatically required to 'conform more or less to our standards'. For Street, the play's saving grace was that 'the licentiousness of the play exists not for its own sake but as part of the machinery of the plot', and he recommended it for licence,

though he also proposed some fairly significant alterations. The Advisory Board, however, was divided about whether a modern as opposed to a seventeenth-century audience would accept it. Buckmaster expressed pity for 'the actors who have to learn the play and the audience who witness it', and Dawson was dismissive of what it represented:

> Having waded wearily through this most tiresome play, hoping possibly to find some redeeming feature, I have failed to do so . . . *Volpone* may have been a success in 1605, but I cannot believe in its survival of the first night today.

For Bonham Carter, on the other hand, the script, while 'undeniably coarse in the extreme', retained 'enough of the atmosphere of its period to lend the characters a certain unreality—which to modern eyes takes the edge off its indecency'. In the opinion of Lord Ullswater, however, one section went too far:

> The scene between Volpone and Colomba in Act 2 places this play beyond the pale. Elizabethan civilisation may have stomached it, but the twentieth century will not do so, and if it were presented on the modern stage there would be an indignant outcry, which would be more than justified.

Sir Johnston Forbes-Robertson, the leading actor and manager, President of the Stage Guild, and now a member of the official Advisory Board, thought Jonson's original text had been bad enough, and agreed with Ullswater: 'I look upon this modern version as being still further removed from being fit to put on the stage', he declared.

A revised version of the text was submitted, with extensive amendments, but Street still agonised about one particular scene:

> It has been modified and Volpone's most offensive gestures omitted, and might pass as an ordinary scene at the beginning of attempted rape, as it happens in harmless melodramas, except that, Volpone is in bed to begin with: this certainly enhances the 'suggestiveness'—the bed being there and his obvious intention being to return to it with Columba, though he does not as formerly try to drag her to it. It remains a scene likely to shock most people and one which would certainly not be passed in an ordinary modern play. I can only suggest, since of course the scene is essential to the play, that decency must be observed as far as possible. It might be seen in rehearsal. The offence would be considerably mitigated if for this scene Volpone were in a chair and the two never got near the bed, but it seems slightly ridiculous to insist on such an alteration before hand.[88]

Lord Cromer's decisions sometimes surprised even his advisers with their relative leniency. In 1931 he overruled reports by Street and by Titman, and licensed André Obéy's version of Shakespeare's poem *Le Viol de Lucrèce*—despite the explicit ravishing of Lucrece by Tarquin ('his whole frame can be seen jerking in a most suggestive manner', worried Titman after witnessing a private performance). The Reader had felt the script went 'too far for public representation', and Titman was convinced that—in spite of its artistic and theatrical strength, and notwithstanding the probable circumstances of any public performance—the passion and near rape were beyond what was acceptable:

> I have no hesitation in giving my opinion that it would be unwise to allow this play to be presented on the public stage in this country. In coming to this decision, I have carefully considered and allowed for the following points:- (a) that the play is a classic; (b) that the play would be presented in French; (c) that the audience would be limited to a certain extent to French linguists and to people of advanced views.
>
> I have also considered the possibility of allowing the play with the provision of an earlier curtain, but the prelude to the seduction is so long that it would be impossible to cut out part of this act—which is the object of the play—without destroying the play itself . . . The acting was marvellous—as good as ever I have seen; and it seems a pity that the public will not have an opportunity of seeing it.[89]

While still imposing some modifications on the action, Cromer decided that those circumstances—particularly the fact that it was to be performed in French—allowed him to license it.

In 1931 the Office licensed a play called *Phoenix*, in which the narrative included a young woman throwing herself downstairs in order to kill her unborn baby, and a young man marrying his father's mistress. 'I should think that few people would desire to see this play', commented Lord Buckmaster; 'the question is whether these few should be prevented'. He concluded that

> it would be an extreme measure to refuse a licence . . . a girl about to have an illegitimate child is one of the saddest spectacles of civilised life and her despair and desperation cannot be excluded from any drama that deals with realities.

Lady Bonham Carter was in agreement that it was an 'extremely unpleasant' play and had 'no doubt that it will shock and jar upon most people', but she too supported licensing it, and attempted to draw an important distinction: 'it certainly will demoralize no one, and I imagine that we exist to protect

morals rather than taste'.[90] For all the moral censorship imposed on theatres, then, the Lord Chamberlain and his advisers were by no means in the pocket of the Public Morality Council and few of them would have endorsed its goals in their entirety. As Buckmaster insisted in 1932 when recommending for licence a play he disliked: 'To edify is not . . . the chief purpose of drama. The true question is does it deprave?'[91] Yet there can be little doubt that the Public Morality Council had a significant influence on theatre—and probably on much else. Its Annual Report for 1930, for example, summed up the success of its campaign to influence the Lord Chamberlain and the theatre through the previous seventeen years, claiming that thanks to its interventions 'many alterations have been secured'. Much more striking in view of my contention that control and censorship of the theatre cannot be measured purely by looking at what happened to scripts when they reached St James's Palace, the Council claimed to have 'definite information that, but for these activities, certain plays of very doubtful character would have been submitted to the Lord Chamberlain'. If one accepts the probability of there being at least a measure of truth in this contention, then it is evident that the effect of the Public Morality Council and of unofficial censorship activities may have been much greater than is immediately apparent. It was the overall direction of theatre which was important, rather than winning individual battles over plays which had already been licensed, and the Council must have been aware that it was rare indeed for the Lord Chamberlain to revoke a licence he had granted; to do so would have been to acknowledge a mistake and to open up the probability of never-ending struggles over play after play. For the Public Morality Council, then, the importance of a battle was often less to do with the play about which it was complaining, and more to do with influencing future decisions.

In its report for 1930, the Council called for all writers and artists 'to balance the claims of liberty and social hygiene', and to act with a new sense of responsibility:

> Few could reasonably complain of the restrictions placed upon men of letters today. They are not asked to fetter their imagination, or even to be less outspoken. In their own interest and ours they are reminded that their books are accessible to people of immature and impressionable age, and are asked to avoid the obvious stupidity of besmirching what is fair, of casting ridicule on what has for countless generations been held to be honourable and of good report.

The Council had a very specific view of the proper function of art:

> To be foul-mouthed and blasphemous has ever been the hall-mark of the unintelligent, the Calibans among men . . . authors, like artists, are surely

set apart to show up the way to sweetness and light, not to degrade us, but to elevate us.[92]

One may have many reservations about the naïve assumptions, prudish narrow-mindedness, and repressive instincts of the Public Morality Council, and not least about its reductive view of art, but it is too easy to define its influence as having been entirely negative. Its report for the year 1933 included, as usual, a list of examples of 'extreme undress' in performances during the previous year. It then commented:

> Such scenes must affect the self-respect of young women, and certainly encourage undesirable men to treat them lightly, regardless of the fact that, doubtless, many young women have felt compelled to accede to this practice rather than lose employment.[93]

There is little reason to doubt that aspect of its analysis.

Our Good Humoured Community
Domestic Politics

It is not always easy to stop a play for political reasons.[1] (The Lord Chamberlain, 1926)

Lord Cromer liked to claim that censorship on political grounds was applied rarely, and only in extreme cases: 'I am always anxious, as far as possible, to cut political censorship out of the theatre', he wrote in 1931.[2] However, previous chapters have suggested that as soon as the definition of 'political' is broadened beyond the very narrow, then this hardly holds true. Perhaps it would be more accurate to say that Cromer did not wish censorship to be seen to be operating politically—which is rather different. The final two chapters of this volume will focus on five broad areas which surely cannot escape being considered under the heading 'political'. Chapter Nine concentrates on the censorship of some key aspects of what might loosely be termed internal politics—namely, the portrayal of the British monarchy, of the British army, and of class and other conflicts within British society. Chapter Ten takes an international perspective, and will concentrate on political issues which had direct implications extending beyond these islands.

Monarchy

The Lord Chamberlain frequently sent plays to the King for a ruling on whether or not they should be licensed, and he did so not only when the monarch or his relations were directly implicated in the text. Sometimes, too, George V took it upon himself to initiate debate, usually through his Private Secretary, Lord Stamfordham. Of *The Vortex*, Stamfordham wrote to Cromer: 'The King has read the papers and says evidently it is a disgusting play but, unfortunately, cannot be prohibited'.[3] In the case of Maugham's *Our Betters*, the King intervened after he had been shown newspaper reviews; Stamfordham warned the Lord Chamberlain:

Somebody has spoken to the King about a play *Our Betters*: and if the report is true His Majesty thinks it must be decidedly objectionable and he is inclined to wonder whether it was carefully considered by the Censor.[4]

Cromer hastily assured him that the play had indeed been carefully considered: 'I earnestly hope His Majesty will not be influenced by anything the *Daily Graphic* may say regarding my department'. Stamfordham reassured him that the King had not intended to find fault and that Cromer could 'rest assured that the notice in the *Daily Graphic* will not be taken too seriously'. The same letter also noted that 'the King entirely approves of your action in forbidding any Minister or Ex-Minister being personified on the stage'.

The policy of rejecting even sympathetic portrayals of the royal family or its ancestors was undoubtedly driven by the wishes of the King, or of his immediate advisers. It was unlikely that any play openly critical of the monarchy would ever have been submitted (or, perhaps, written) but even the briefest or the most positive images were forbidden, rather as God and Jesus were beyond being impersonated by actors and were therefore outside the proper scope of the stage. Sometimes, much more explicit and immediate political motives are apparent. In 1921, for example, the King intervened to prevent the granting of a licence to a play about George III and his relationship with the Quakeress Hannah Lightfoot. Street had recommended it, noting that 'the only question about its license [*sic*] is if a play about His great great grandfather would be offensive to the King'. The letter to the Lord Chamberlain from Windsor Castle suggests near paranoia:

In these days when some Thrones have disappeared, others are shaking and the wave of democracy appears to be rising, it seems to his Majesty inadvisable that the story . . . should now be given on the stage of a Glasgow or any other theatre in these Islands.

The specific worry in this instance was that George III would be 'condemned as having played a low game and merely having escaped because he was a King'; the Lord Chamberlain was categorically informed that 'His Majesty cannot agree to its production'.[5]

Queen Victoria was a magnet for some playwrights, but it had been decided that she should be kept completely free of the contamination of the stage. As always, there was a conscious strategy to avoid creating precedents which would make it harder to ban more dangerous plays, and it was easier to support an absolute ban than to allow some plays and not others; in effect, this is a more subtle form of censorship than an obviously autocratic regime which unashamedly permits sympathetic portraits and excludes criticisms. In 1922 Street yearned to recommend *The Queen's Minister*.

> The difficulty about this play is that it introduces Queen Victoria and the Prince Consort . . . the play generally, belongs to history of nearly 100 years ago, and I think it a pity the play should be debarred from dealing with it.

While agreeing there was 'nothing intentionally offensive', the Duke of Atholl was unmoveable. What he particularly objected to was the exposure of private memory to the public gaze, and the contamination of 'reality' by 'fiction':

> I personally consider it most undesirable to have Queen Victoria and the Prince Consort represented on the stage at the present moment, while so many people who knew the former are still alive. For example—my grand-mother was her lady in waiting—I should much dislike seeing the old lady (for whom I had a great affection) represented on the stage, and I can imagine how much worse annoyed His Majesty would be to find his grand-mother so represented, and doing and saying things she never said.

Writing three years after the end of the First World War, he was also worried about preserving the reputation of her husband: 'I do not think that the average public would see his constitutionalisms through his German accent and idioms. He would probably be treated at the present moment as a buffoon or with opprobrium.' Atholl said the play had been written 'twenty-five years too soon', and Dawson confirmed that it would seem 'extremely distasteful in high quarters'.[6]

The following year, Housman's *The Queen God Bless Her* was also refused a licence. Street again expressed 'regret that a great historical figure, as she has now become, should be excluded from the stage if treated with respect', and even wondered whether the story and the characters could be fiction-alised by changing their names and identities. Lord Cromer, however, ruled that this was inappropriate, and unequivocally suggested to the King that 'we have not yet reached a period when permission should be given for incidents in Queen Victoria's life to be portrayed on the stage'. Stamfordham confirmed that the King 'will not hear of this play being produced'.[7] In 1927 Street thought there could surely be no objection to a brief and silent representation of Queen Victoria and Albert at the very end of *Marigold in Arcady*, 'a pleasant, romantic comedy' and 'a blameless play', which was set in 1842; Cromer insisted on cutting the image.[8] Five years later, an equally brief and silent appearance by Queen Alexandra was written into a tableau within a large pageant, under the title *The Flaming Torch*; 'There can hardly be any objec-tion to this?', queried Street. But Cromer again insisted that 'the King would strongly object' and once again refused a licence.[9] The playwright to suffer most because of his fixation with Queen Victoria was Laurence Housman. In 1932 his series of plays about her was refused a licence without any discussion or negotiation; Street noted 'the liberty already enjoyed by literature—and I rather think the cinema', but Cromer was unmoved. He wrote to Housman, acknowledging 'all the pains you have taken towards a tactful and delicate handling of your subject', but his ruling was absolute:

> During the present reign, or at least while there are children of Queen Victoria's still living, it will not be possible without the infringement of good taste and the wounding of susceptibilities to license any play which demands the impersonation of her late Majesty on the British stage.[10]

One genre of plays which did have some freedom to dramatise monarchy as an institution was the Ruritanian fantasy set in an imaginary country. The Lord Chamberlain's Office was never quite sure whether or not such plays should be acknowledged as potentially dangerous, since to draw attention to a possible parallel might be more damaging than to ignore it. In 1932 the Lord Chamberlain licensed *Bastos the Bold*, in which a middle-class citizen is elected as King. 'No sensible person could see any satire on monarchy as it exists here', wrote Street, 'and if there were such an intention *it would be unwise* to notice it' (my italics).[11] The Office had not always been so broad-minded; in 1918 Professor Walter Raleigh had finally resigned from the Advisory Board over the refusal to license the satirical *Angelo the Ninth,* and another debate occurred in 1920 about Hamilton Fyfe's *The Kingdom, the Power and the Glory.* Street described Fyfe's play as 'a bitter satire on royalties and on the ambitions and mistakes of statesmen and generals which . . . lead deluded peoples into war'; but he was unable to decide whether it might be taken to refer to England, and whether a licence should therefore be refused: 'My own opinion is that that would be a mistaken policy', he wrote; 'The English Monarchy cannot possibly be harmed by general satire on royalties'. Dawson, however, was categorically against the play for specific political reasons: 'I think it deals with a dangerous topic, i.e. responsibility by Sovereigns for the late war'. After inspecting a private performance, Sandhurst made a pragmatic decision that it would be safer to allow the production than to acknowledge its relevance:

> There is no doubt that this play is a satire, not only on Monarchy, but also on War, Military Ambition and abuse of power . . . I must frankly say that it is not a play that one would wish Their Majesties to witness, but any satire of Royalties would be equally objectionable on this ground, and to ban all such plays would not appear to be advisable, especially in view of the British tradition of the free expression of opinion. The play is not treasonable or libellous . . . tinkering would not remove the fact that it is a satire on Royalty and would reveal an endeavour to 'make the cap fit'.[12]

It was never easy to know where to draw the line in the case of a Ruritanian play. In 1928 *The Queen's Husband*, by Robert Sherwood, was recommended by Street as 'a fantastic comedy with a dash of sentiment'; however, although set in an imaginary kingdom, its characters had English names (the King is called Eric), and Street knew that some people would detect subversive implications. He tried to pre-empt their criticisms:

> As for the play being a satire on Monarchy, I do not see that it is more so than many Ruritanian plays when Monarchs are more or less ridiculous. I do not think people would apply it to this country. And I suggest further that if any harm to the Monarchical principle could come from a play it would be more likely to do so by suppression than allowing it.

Cromer agreed that Sherwood's play was 'witty and free from impropriety', but he worried that as 'a satire on Monarchy and Royalty generally', it nevertheless went 'beyond the usual'; he sent it to his Advisory Board:

> The question really is whether in a Monarchical country it goes beyond the limits of good taste to allow such a play on the stage.
>
> In a Republican country these things do not matter and I am inclined to think it would be a great mistake to take this play too seriously, although I feel it would be regarded as bad taste by many people.
>
> It sails very near the line and I wonder if you think it sails too near to what we should tolerate in fairness to the cause of Monarchy.

Buckmaster remarked that it was 'impossible to keep the office of royalty free from satire', and Sherwood's play was eventually licensed (though not without amendments) on the quite overt principle that 'more harm would be done by suppression than by permission to perform'.[13]

The same principle was applied the following year to *The Perfect Shadow*, in which King Leopold of Otherland, having been rescued by a boy scout from an anarchist plot to kill him, falls in love with a school-teacher. Leopold is prevented from abdicating the throne and marrying her only when she herself joins with his councillors to persuade him he must fulfil his duties and accept responsibility for 'holding the State together . . . in a time of change'. Although the moral ostensibly reaffirmed the role and the importance of monarchy, Street was still anxious about how audiences might apply the message:

> Unlike other Ruritania plays this has enough intelligence to set an audience thinking of Monarchy in general and drawing applications. But this would certainly not harm the cause of Monarchy. It is true that the author exaggerates the political limitations of limited Monarchy but the upshot of the play is to insist on its importance and its power for good. An audi-

ence might see in the King the popular idea of the Prince of Wales and it is a pity he should be represented in the prologue as dissipated, but to cut that out would be to accept the application—a mistake. Apart from that, however, he is a good fellow and extremely likeable. The play is really a sincere plea for Monarchy as the author understands it.

Cromer agreed that 'interference would be a mistake'.[14]

Another related anxiety for the censorship was the danger of the British monarchy being tainted by association with other European rulers with family connections. In 1918 the Reader recommended refusing a licence for *The Russian Monk*—a very bad melodrama about Rasputin, which also touched more generally on recent events in Russia: 'at this critical moment the personal introduction upon our stage of misguided Royalties like those of Russia (closely related as they are to our own King) seems most undesirable'. There was a real fear that the Soviet Revolution might inspire something similar in Britain, and a member of the War Office who was consulted over this play commented, 'I had no idea that Sovereigns were allowed on the stage in such an unfavourable light'. Significantly, he added that 'if we pass this twaddle who will believe us if later we have to refuse something serious' and proposed that since it was 'probably only the first of many we shall get on this unsavoury subject' they should 'nip the movement in the bud'. A licence was duly refused.[15]

In the mid-1920s, *Bismarck, The Trilogy of a Fighter*—three plays about Prussia and Bismarck, by an eminent German historian—was submitted for licence. Street realised that, even though much of the action took place some sixty years previously, there would be problems over having the Crown Princess of Prussia as a significant character, since she was a member of the British royal family; 'it is, I suppose, a question of the view His Majesty takes of it', he stated. Street thought that the inclusion of the Kaiser would probably have been sufficient even on its own to make a licence impossible. 'I regret it, because this play also has educational value', he wrote, and he dared to hint at a possible shift in policy:

> I should like to suggest that the production of plays likely to enlighten and educate an ignorant public is rare and praiseworthy, and that prevention of it for personal reasons is, even when inevitable, a misfortune.

Cromer forwarded Street's comments to Buckingham Palace, and Stamfordham acknowledged their merit. However, this was outweighed by the negative aspects:

> I cannot help sympathising with Mr Street's opinion and, from an educational point of view, should like to see the play produced. But considering

> that the Emperor is still alive . . . and was, rightly or wrongly, regarded as
> a great Sovereign, it would be detrimental to the whole Monarchial prin-
> ciple, now that he is exiled, dethroned and discredited, were his action in
> the quarrel and dismissal of Bismarck emphasized on the stage of British
> Theatres with the approval of the King.

In a familiar demonstration of the preference for keeping censorship invisible, Cromer was specifically instructed by the King to speak to the intending
producer, Basil Dean, 'and endeavour to stave off any question of producing
the plays without resorting to the official procedure of banning them, and
thereby involving press publicity'. According to what Cromer subsequently
told the King's son, the Duke of Connaught, he then met Dean 'and without
using the King's name pointed out to him the undesirability of staging such
plays'. Cromer also sent the scripts and Street's report to the Duke, to ascertain whether his view was more liberal than that of his father. At the same
time, he referred to some of the difficulties he was experiencing with censorship:

> The difficult of banning plays on purely political grounds is of course too
> well known to Your Royal Highness for me to digress on this subject, and
> before any definite steps were taken in this connection I should of course
> seek the advice and support of the Secretary of State for Foreign Affairs.
> However, my object in the first place is to obtain the expression of Your
> Royal Highness's personal wishes.

Connaught replied that he could 'see no fault, or in fact anything to take
offence at' in the script, and that, in his opinion, such plays 'may do more
good than harm'. Cromer then confided that modern historical plays were a
significant and increasing problem for him:

> There is certainly a tendency abroad in literary circles to try and produce
> plays based on historical facts, and representing persons who have played
> a part in history, and the difficult point for censorship to determine is that
> of deciding how near to the present day such plays should be permitted
> to encroach, maintaining always the principle that no living personages
> should be represented on the stage.

He added that he had now discussed this play and the Prince's opinions
directly with the King, and that although 'His Majesty was deeply apprecia-
tive, as well as impressed by the views expressed by Your Royal Highness',
he was still not prepared to allow the appearance of the Kaiser. Cromer
explained that he was now involved in negotiations with the producers, and
revealed that his very deliberate intention was 'to postpone, as long as possible,

the necessity of having to condone the production'. In other words, neither Cromer nor the King wanted the publicity which would accrue from banning the plays, and a strategy of discreet procrastination was therefore employed to delay the production indefinitely. Since all the material relating to this proposed production still sits in one of the Lord Chamberlain's Waiting Boxes it seems that the strategy was successful; the trilogy was quietly forgotten about, without ever having being the subject of overt censorship or publicity.[16]

War and the Military

The monarchy was not the only British institution which had to be protected against criticism or mockery, and the army was almost equally important. In 1921 the Admiralty forwarded to the Lord Chamberlain a letter from a retired lieutenant complaining about a play in London, *My Nieces*, in which 'an individual purporting to represent a Sub-Lieutenant of His Majesty's Royal Navy appears in a disgracefully alcoholic state'; the letter demanded that steps be taken 'to abate an exhibition which represents a Naval Officer in an uncharacteristic condition'. The theatre manager was quickly instructed that henceforth the character must be dressed in plain clothes rather than in uniform, but the Lord Chamberlain also tactfully warned the Admiralty against taking the issue too seriously since 'further action would possibly lead to greater publicity'.[17] In 1924 the War Office enquired about 'a very undesirable production', and again forwarded a letter of complaint from someone whom they described as 'a very patriotic man and a staunch Monarchist'. *Rent Free* was a comic revue and a trivial entertainment, but the protests were made—and treated—with great seriousness.

> During the acting in the first scene two players dressed as soldiers were seated at a table talking generally about their officers. One tried on the colonel's hat and the other put on a Subaltern's hat. One said how do I look? and the other replied alright where's the colonel? The answer was he's in the canteen, he's never happy unless he's drunk. The two soldiers then engage in a clap trap about the colonel who they said was a low-bred fellow, and a dirty dog.

The main objections centred on a slapstick gag, in which an ordinary soldier 'accidentally' blows shaving foam over a colonel's uniform and face. Again, it was the possible effect on its Shoreditch audience that was seen as dangerous, and the complainant noted with a real sense of outrage that 'the process of wiping off the soap by the officer, who was complete with monocle, appeared to amuse the East-End audience greatly'. In his view 'the belittling of the officers and non-commissioned officers by the rank and file in this

Revue is degrading to the officer's uniform and certainly not conducive to the maintenance of necessary discipline'. He described the revue as 'Communistic Propaganda', in which 'every insult was offered to His Majesty's uniform', and soldiers in the audience were encouraged 'to insult and degrade their non-commissioned and commissioned Officers'. To insult the King's uniform, of course, was to insult the King, and therefore unforgivable:

> When I tell you that in one scene a very untidy private spits froth all over his colonel's uniform you will realise how far this matter goes towards the creation of disobedience and disloyalty. Plainly speaking nearly every scene in this wretched piece was abhorrent to a Loyalist. Personally I have seen nothing approaching it for sheer incentive to sedition.

Was the author of such a letter an absurd fanatic making a fool of himself by taking seriously something which was slight and unimportant? Not according to the War Office, which endorsed his concerns and agreed that there were very serious implications for the dignity of the army: 'Should the Revue be played in a garrison town or a naval station, the effect on the young soldiers would, I think, be most dangerous from a disciplinary point of view'. Officials were worried not just about the specific scene, but at what it might be expressing in broader terms: 'underlying the whole show there seems to be a continuous slighting of persons in authority in the Army and a lot of Communistic ideas were expounded during the performance'. The basic script of *Rent Free* had actually been licensed some time previously; Street had noted at the time that it contained 'a certain amount of military chaff', but he had pointed out that similar material had already been permitted 'in countless Revues', and that even during the war it had not proved possible 'to exclude such chaff entirely'. He was now adamant that 'nothing intended to bring discipline or the King's uniform into contempt was allowed and everything so intended in the present Revue must have been introduced since it was licensed'. Cromer obtained police reports documenting performances, and then warned the manager that his licence would be withdrawn unless cuts were made. The management admitted that unlicensed material had indeed been added, but rather than prosecute, the Lord Chamberlain chose to avoid drawing public attention to the issue. A revised script was submitted, and Cromer reaffirmed the principle which he intended to follow in relation to such themes:

> I cannot make any new rule for forbidding chaff on military matters, but I consider it my duty to see that nothing is introduced into Revues or plays that tends to be subversive of Discipline or that brings ridicule on the King's uniform in a disrespectful manner likely to be harmful.

The main assurances that I welcome is that no 'Communist Propaganda' appears in this Revue which can now be licensed.[18]

On the same day that Cromer approved *Rent Free*, Street was reporting on a farcical wartime melodrama, the plot of which centred on a wicked colonel who sends his junior on a risky mission in the expectation that he will be killed, so that he himself can marry the dead soldier's widow. Street described *Khaki* (originally entitled *Blighty*) as 'a farrago of idiocy, vulgarity and sham sentiment', but recommended that it was probably not worth censoring since 'the whole thing is so preposterously silly that the most ignorant audience could not think it represented reality'. Cromer was less sanguine, declaring it 'the sort of play I abominate', and Dawson maintained that, however harmless the intention, it was absolutely vital that in the present political climate nothing should be staged which appeared to insult the military or undermine discipline. His private memorandum also came close to accusing the Labour government of treason:

> I should ask consideration of the importance at this <u>moment</u> of upholding the good name of the Army. Revolutions only become serious when the soldier refuses to obey his officers.
>
> *A l'heure qu'il est* the agitator is at work with propaganda . . . winked at, if not supported, by the government in office. Is this the moment for a play to appear the moral of which is to cast ridicule on what may 'ere long be the only buffer left between us and revolution.

Cromer agreed with Dawson that the play was 'capable of doing much harm at the present time' and could not be licensed. The author re-wrote the text, and it was again sent in for reading:

> He makes it clear that the villain and his accomplice are in the Army by accident and they are not to be considered as representing regular soldiers in any way . . . He has reduced the temporary rank of the villain from colonel to captain, and has put over him a real and dignified colonel . . . He has toned down the chaff.

Dawson remained resolutely opposed to granting a licence, and sent another message to the Lord Chamberlain re-emphasising his view of how important it was that 'particularly at the present <u>time</u> . . . nothing even remotely ridiculing the Army in any shape or form should be allowed'.[19]

Cromer eventually licensed *Khaki* after imposing further amendments, but he continued to take very seriously anything which made fun of army officers. Later in 1924, a comic sketch under the title *A Brighter Army*—which gained its laughs from showing a scene in which 'ordinary discipline is reversed and the private is waited on by the sergeant'—was cut in its entirety from a revue. It was, said Cromer, 'the sort of scene that in my opinion <u>is</u> harmful for discipline in the minds of young soldiers and therefore to be discouraged'.[20] In 1928 *The Gay Lieutenant*—'a mixture of sentimentality and low-comedy'—was seen to trivialise military personnel. 'I do not know if there is any special objection to the Guards being mentioned', queried Street innocently, as though unaware of their long-standing connections with senior members of the Lord Chamberlain's Office. As the letter sent by the Office to the manager shows, there certainly were objections:

> All reference to the Welsh Guards to be taken out . . . the Regimental Sergeant Major smacking a Private must be omitted . . . The Lord Chamberlain will require a general undertaking that the uniforms will not be made to resemble any particular Regiment in the Brigade of Guards, and that no Regiment is mentioned by name.[21]

A much more serious play refused a licence for Cambridge in 1931 was the experimental *Roar China*, by the Soviet playwright Tretiakov. This play attacked British imperialism in China and was based on an actual incident in which the British navy had reputedly threatened to destroy a whole Chinese village in revenge for an attack on one individual. Both the Home and Foreign Offices were prepared to allow it, though they seem to have been working on the uncertain assumption that to license it for the Cambridge Festival Theatre would not preclude them from intervening and preventing it from being played elsewhere if another theatre should seek to stage it. The Admiralty took a much stronger line against such 'anti-Western civilisation propaganda', and informed the Lord Chamberlain that it was 'especially undesirable that young and inexperienced undergraduates should be subjected at their age to this kind of malicious anti-British propaganda'. Cromer refused the licence.[22]

Sensitivity about how the First World War was portrayed continued for some considerable time. Even in 1927, the Lord Chamberlain cut an incident from a play set in 1919, in which an English officer, suffering from shellshock, imagines he is killing a German prisoner; Cromer described *War and Peace* as

> a play that can do no good and could do harm in some minds. I agree that the killing of a German prisoner by an English Officer out of revenge is a highly objectionable idea and should be cut although the shell-shocked son only stabs a cushion![23]

Perhaps surprisingly, plays critical of the war and Britain's part in it were not automatically banned; in 1924 a licence was granted to Allan Monkhouse's *The Conquering Hero*, despite its dedication 'to those who hated war and went to the war'. According to Street, its sentiments were no longer a danger:

> I have read the author did not wish this play acted during the War. Rightly,
> I think, and at that time it might not have been licensed, because the
> 'Pacifist' arguments in the first part, and in the latter part the collapse of
> courage due to starvation and exhaustion and the final nervous state of the
> 'hero' might have had a bad effect. But I see no reason now for withholding
> a licence. The arguments in the play are familiar and the realities of war
> and the fact that every Englishman is not always a hero are now known.[24]

By 1928, the Office was confident that it was not necessary to ban Channing
Pollock's *The Enemy* for suggesting that there had been little difference
between British and German wartime behaviour—not that the claim could be
officially accepted, of course:

> The object of this play is to show (1) that the reactions of people to the
> War were the same in all countries and (2) that war is a horrible and futile
> affair . . . I see no reason for interfering with it. The author in a preface
> makes rather a fuss about his courage and seems to think the play will be
> thought 'pro-German' propaganda in England. I think that is nonsense.
> The assumption that there was nothing to choose between our motives
> and conduct and the enemy's is not true, but we can afford to let it be
> said.[25]

In 1929 Cromer licensed Sherriff's *Journey's End* with no alterations other
than some minor amendments to the language used by the soldiers; if such a
play could even have been written ten years earlier it would have been a
different story, but now the time was ripe for regrets.[26] This did not necessarily mean that writers had complete freedom, and commenting in 1930 on
Suspense—a play which Street noted was 'far grimmer than *Journey's End*'—
Cromer complained that 'the tendency of every war play is to try and outdo
the last'. This 'trench play' was licensed reluctantly, and 'subject to drastic
amendments'; as Street said: 'I do not know if the mention of an unpopular
corporal being shot . . . or stealing rings from a corpse . . . ought to stand'.[27]
In *The Home Front* the following month, the Reader was again worried about
a suggestion that unpopular commanding officers were shot by their own
men; however, he recommended that since 'the alleged fact has often been
stated it would probably do more harm than good to censor it'. Cromer agreed
that 'it would be impolitic to censor it, especially as some reference is made
to such episodes in a war book recently written by General Crozier'.[28] The
Office also reluctantly approved *Every Mother's Son*, in which a mother who
has lost one son in a war poisons the second when he is persuaded to volunteer to join the army; 'Hysterical though this is', wrote Street, 'I do not think

it can be prohibited. It would not be fair to assume that the authors advocate the poisoning of sons by their mothers to prevent their fighting.'[29]

Yet perhaps the most striking, theatrically imaginative, and potentially powerful anti-war play of the period did suffer heavy censorship. *The Searcher*, by Velona Pilcher, was a remarkable piece which largely eschewed naturalistic language or characterisation, drawing instead on expressionist practices to show the war through the eyes of a nurse searching for bodies at the front; it incorporated a powerful poetic language which it mixed with sections lifted from official wartime documents, and employed cinematic images, rhythm, choreography, choral speaking and a constant soundtrack of the noises of war. It is tempting to say that it was as much the aesthetics as the politics of the play which shocked the censors, but in many ways the two are indivisible; to the Lord Chamberlain's Office, the script represented 'the ravings of a lunatic'; Lord Buckmaster, openly amazed, was prepared to recommend a licence:

> if from among the people liberated on leave from asylums or not yet certified there are enough to make an audience I would not defraud them of a pleasure in which I could no more join them than in that of putting straws in one's hair.

However, others disagreed. 'In view, alone, of the ridicule it pours upon the military and medical services, it merits objection', wrote Dawson. Even Street thought the writing was spoiled by the 'hysteria' and 'mental confusion' of the playwright, and was worried by the resulting 'bitter bias against military authorities and doctors and nurses'. Part of the problem was that the censors had no way of recognising or allowing for the distinctive form and approach of *The Searcher*. In her introduction, Pilcher specifies that everything depicted—doctors and nurses dancing flirtatiously in gas masks around the bodies of the maimed, for example—is an expression of the necessarily distorted perspective of the protagonist, a woman searching for the wounded or dead body of a man she loves:

> From the opening curtain to the closing curtain all things seen, spoken and staged shall appear to us as they appear to the Searcher, whose vision we accept for this hour and through whose particular perception all action shall appear to pass. What strikes her as grotesque, what her tortured vision exaggerates and distorts, is presented to us also exaggeratedly.

Of the Advisory Board, only Lady Violet Bonham Carter seemed to have any recognition that certain actions and images were 'to be taken figuratively rather than literally'. Yet she too was adamant that much of the play was not only 'ugly and unjust' but 'too painful to produce'. Nurses could not be shown refusing to give a drink to a dying enemy; a woman could not be allowed to urge other women to refuse to give birth; and certainly, God could not be cursed in a parody of the Lord's Prayer. *The Searcher* was licensed and performed in 1930, but with extensive cuts which helped to cripple it—and perhaps to ensure that it would not survive as one of the great plays of the inter-war period.[30]

National Conflict

In the context of the revolutionary conflicts threatening society during the 1920s, the stage was constructed by the political authorities, not just as a neutral element to be kept free of politics, but as a medium which could play an active role in controlling society. In the year of the General Strike, the main theatrical newspaper, *The Era*, characterised theatre as a 'soothing influence' and 'a necessity' in helping to preserve a peaceful society; it was not for nothing that supporters of the Strike made hoax phone calls to London theatres, posing as government officials, and instructing them to close down.[31] A 240-page government report on theatre in Britain published in the same year described it as 'an unrivalled instrument for breaking down social barriers and establishing friendly relations', and even ascribed to it the potential to 'bring some element of healing and of reconciliation into the warring elements in our national life'.[32]

The paranoid responses to plays such as *Miss Julie* and *The Vortex* reflect a real fear of the imminent danger of left-wing revolution, and a belief that to expose a decadent and immoral upper middle class on the stage might help to provoke this. Even before the 1918 Armistice with Germany, opposition to the economic structures of society was creating unease about possible class conflict and civil disobedience. After the war, there was certainly disquiet in the Office about plays liable to encourage criticism of the wealthy and powerful, and a wish to protect the reputations of those in positions of power. Yet among those who advised the Lord Chamberlain there was, as we have seen, an understanding of the need to be seen to be equitable in their approach. In 1924, with a newly elected Labour government, Shaw's *Augustus Does His Bit* was described by Street as 'a very bitter and exaggerated satire on "the governing classes"', which was 'rather venomous and overshoots its mark'; however, he saw no reason to refuse a licence:

> I can imagine that such a play might have been forbidden during the War, if submitted, as tending to discouragement by representing the people running the country as half-witted. It can hardly do any harm now, especially in the change of governors, and from the point of view of the 'governing classes' indicated it would be a mistake to take it seriously.[33]

Similarly, he could see no reason to turn down Toller's *Mass-Man*: 'The revolutionary raving about conditions not existing in this country can do no harm
. . . One can take the speeches and singing of the "Internationale" as merely
dramatic.'[34] Cromer was reassured by the fact that the play was very unlikely
to reach beyond specialised audiences. Similarly, a licence was granted for
From Miner to M.P., although it was 'more bitter than the run of such things'
in attacking the British upper classes: 'There is some foolish talk about war
being "a money-making game to the privileged few"', wrote Street; but once
again he added, 'it would of course give it undue importance to interfere with
it'.[35]

Clearly reflecting contemporary paranoia, there were several more or less
comic warning plays about Britain undergoing a Soviet-style revolution. One
such in 1925 was *Reconstruction*, which showed (through the already rather
hackneyed device of a dream) a Bolshevik takeover, in which Westminster
Abbey is turned into a jazz palace, and women are sent to breeding centres.
The wealthy hero wakes from his dream 'a chastened man', and instantly
becomes more generous to his workforce. Street argued that it 'should do
good in its way, though of course no wise person really thinks that things could
happen just in that way in England'. At all events, he saw no need to interfere: 'The only people likely to be annoyed by the picture of successful
Bolshevism are the professed admirers of its working in Russia and they need
hardly be considered'. Cromer agreed the play should not be censored: 'most
of the Bolshevik methods are unpleasant and possibly the more people realise
this the less likely they are to have any sympathy for Bolshevism'.[36] It is safe
to say that a play advocating revolution would not have been treated quite so
lightly.

Most of the cuts imposed on Terence Gray's production of *Hoppla!* in 1929
were related to sexual morality rather than Toller's revolutionary politics,
though Street noted the play's 'bias against authority'. Gray's intention,
however, was to punctuate the production with short film passages, and these
caused nervousness among the censors. 'They may easily contain matter objectionable on political grounds', wrote Street. Cromer required all film material
to be submitted to the British Board of Film Censors, which reported that

> Many of the scenes in this film show soldiers firing on the unarmed popu-
> lace, including women and girls, who are seen falling, and afterwards lying
> dead.
> We regard such scenes as unsuitable for exhibition in this country.

Cromer immediately demanded an undertaking from Gray that these scenes
would be cut, though even the Board of Film Censors pointed out that 'there
would be little footage of film left' after doing this. The performance went
ahead without the film.[37]

In 1924 Cromer had dutifully forwarded to the Labour Prime Minister a script which dramatised the Fascists coming to power in Britain. *Noblesse Oblige* began by showing a group of supposedly bankrupt aristocrats either emigrating to escape taxation or awaiting the dreaded communist revolution. All the working classes lack to help bring about such a revolution is an effective leader, and this they find in Julian, a disillusioned ex-public schoolboy and soldier who feels let down by his lack of opportunities since the war. However, when Julian leads the revolution and subsequently becomes Prime Minister, he promptly betrays the workers who have supported him; he is then secretly installed as the Grand Master of the Knights of St George (the English Fascists), and allies himself with the upper classes in order to save the country. One awkward problem for the censorship was whether to acknowledge the connections between characters and actual public figures:

> In Act One the character of Lord Launceston, who is Lord Chancellor, clearly suggests Lord Birkenhead, from a hostile angle . . . but if the author denies this it would be very awkward for the Lord Chamberlain to insist that the character <u>was</u> like Lord B. I should think the best plan would be merely to insist on no make up like an actual politician, but it is a difficult point.

On balance, Street thought it would be safer to license the play with amendments, especially given the 'successful' resolution to the narrative.

> There might possibly be a political reason for banning the presentation of a Revolution 'shortly'. In my opinion that would be a great mistake, giving political importance to what need not be taken as more than a fantasy . . . I think, too, that capital and labour being reconciled by the Revolutionary hero really removes any objection from the point of view of law and order.

The Lord Chamberlain consulted the Prime Minister, Ramsay Macdonald, about 'the principle of allowing a play which imagines a Revolution in England "shortly"'; although the play was 'nonsense', said Cromer, it should be remembered that 'there are foolish people in theatre audiences, and among the press who sometimes take nonsense seriously'. Macdonald noted the slant of the play, but was apparently not disposed to worry about the potential political impact of something so removed from everyday life as commercial theatre:

> I should be very chary in interfering with these things though it looks uncommonly like Fascist propaganda. If I might offer an opinion of a general character, make no objection unless it specifically prompts to acts of disorder.

He then dryly pointed out that there was only one disorderly act in the play: 'A lady allowed a gentleman to fall asleep in her presence. That is very mild. If she had bombed him it would have been serious.' Nevertheless, Cromer met the playwright privately to guide his alterations, as a result of which Windsor was changed to Reading, and references to actual people were removed.[38]

Street's report on *Noblesse Oblige* had suggested that the revolution depicted was 'much like Mussolini's—a favourable view of the latter being taken'. Performances in the mid-1920s which incited communist revolution, on the other hand, were likely to be staged in venues other than theatres, often by the Workers' Theatre Movement; such work was of direct concern to the police but usually fell outside the jurisdiction of the Lord Chamberlain. However, there were exceptions. In 1927 Street noted that an Irish play called *The Big Drum* showed 'pronounced' sympathies for the strikers and against both the owner and the scabs; he advised that 'it would be unwise to inter-fere'.[39] In 1928 Tom Thomas's stage adaptation of *The Ragged Trousered Philanthropists* caused much greater concern. Street found the politics of the play 'of course unfair if meant to represent average conditions' in its depiction of successful capitalists; 'though no doubt there are scoundrelly employers', he conceded. But he recommended the play overall as being safe for licensing, despite its clear support for socialist views: 'In my opinion it would be unwise to forbid their expression in a play. The audience can see or hear them in papers or meetings at any time.' Street was slightly apprehensive, however, about the final climax, in which the politically conscious Owen is invited to give a final lecture, expressing his views:

> This he does at some length with the usual Socialist arguments, put crudely but with some force. With a few exceptions he wins over his audience and ends by asking the real audience in the theatre to say that Socialism is the only remedy for unemployment and poverty.

It was particularly the breaking of the boundary between stage and auditorium which caused anxiety, as the audience are invited to join with the exploited working-class characters on stage as they find their voice and call for a strike. On the whole, Street thought the provocation would not be dangerous:

> The only point about which I have any doubt is the appeal to the audience at the end, as possibly causing a row in the theatre, but I do not think it at all probable that it would be serious in our good-humoured community.

However, Cromer consulted the Home Office, before licensing the play with its specific approval, and after negotiating a series of amendments with Thomas; these included cutting the last page of the text, so as to end the play before the fourth wall is broken and the audience directly involved in the action. [40]

Class conflict was not the only threat to domestic peace. In 1924 the Lord Chamberlain refused to license a play set in Ireland in 1920, called *In the Red Shadow*. 'This play purports to be a "dramatic picture" of the state of Ireland during the reign of the "Black and Tans" and is written in a spirit of extreme bitterness', noted Street; he referred in particular to the 'passionate outburst' by one of the characters 'against a country which can employ the Black and Tan methods', and the parallel drawn between their methods and those employed by the Germans in Belgium during the war. The narrative shows an Irishman being shot by a British soldier for breaking the curfew imposed by the occupying army; his lover is then shot dead after stabbing the soldier with her hatpin, and her brother, who had previously fought with the British against Germany, takes revenge by shooting a number of British soldiers. Street pointed out that 'the event supposed is not impossible', and that the Black and Tan policy had already been condemned by many people in Britain. Moreover, no objection had been raised the previous year to 'a vehement Irish Nationalist play' called *The Jackets Green*. But there were elements of *In The Red Shadow* which made it different:

> We can afford to disregard the hatred of England. But I do not think a licence can be given to a play which ends with the shooting of English soldiers by a character with whom the audience is supposed to sympathise. It would certainly provoke an uproar in the Theatre.

Cromer agreed that 'a play of this sort, in these days and in Liverpool is quite likely to provoke an uproar', but he deliberately attempted to limit the discussion which would inevitably arise from the rejection of the play: 'The licence should be refused without any reason being given', he instructed his staff. [41]

The play resurfaced in another version for the same theatre five years later, under the title *The Whirlwind Passeth*. By that time, the events were sufficiently historical for the Reader to make a different recommendation:

> Something like this play, at least with a similar ending, has been sent in before. If that is the case I presume it was not licensed, as it is sent in again. A reason for that would be the probability of disturbance in the theatre. But at this distance of time from the events and the changed condition of Ireland I do not think there is any likelihood of that. I suppose most of us regret the Black and Tan policy and admit that outrages were committed on both sides. We can afford to be magnanimous. Therefore, though I

regret that a play should stir up this old bitterness again, and with the suggestion that if the end (of Sean shooting our soldiers) is thought too provocative it should be altered the play is recommended for licence.

It had been intended that this production would be entered for the British Drama League Festival, and Cromer was prepared to license it; however, the Chief Constable of Liverpool took a different view:

> As there is in Liverpool a large Irish population divided into different political camps and also strong sectarian views of an opposing nature, I feel it is yet too soon to permit a play of the character submitted to be performed here. Disorder might arise at the theatre and elsewhere.

Cromer did not want the responsibility of refusing to license the play. He promptly contacted the Home Office to seek confirmation that the authorities in Liverpool would have the power to ban the production even if it had been licensed by his Office. Amazingly, the Home Office was unable to give an unequivocal answer:

> I should be inclined to think that if there were clear evidence of the danger of public disturbance the Chief Constable would be in a position to take action in the special circumstances, notwithstanding that the play had been licensed, but this is a matter which would need further inquiry.

However, it saw the necessity of presenting a unified front, and came down on the side of the police:

> It would obviously be desirable on all grounds to prevent any conflict between the Lord Chamberlain's decision and the action of the local Authority.
> Liverpool with its large and vocal Irish population is of course the worst possible atmosphere for a play of this character . . . the Chief Constable appears to have good grounds for his apprehensions.

The manager of the David Lewis Theatre, who had submitted the script, argued that the events of the play 'have gone into history and are therefore legitimate material for dramatic treatment'. He also maintained that the play was not written in such a way that it could be identified as having ' propagandist intent or effect', since it offered contrasting perspectives within its narrative: 'Even if it be admitted that there is criticism (on the part of some of the characters) of the political situation obtaining at the time, this criticism is balanced by opposing points of view.' But the censorship controlled both past and future. 'It would be best to maintain the ban on this play for some time to come', advised the Lord Chamberlain. That was not the end of the story, and the manager immediately proposed a way around the problem:

> May I then beg the Lord Chamberlain to reconsider the possibility of the play being sanctioned in some other than its present form? I suggest that we might remove all our difficulties if I changed the scene from Ireland to Russian Poland, say, about 1906 . . . I could work out the dramatic thesis I desire, without the risk of hurting any English or Irish susceptibilities.

Forcibly removed from the political and historical context in which it had been rooted, the revised script was licensed almost immediately.[42]

Political Sex

In 1932 the Lord Chamberlain received a letter of complaint from an Admiral Kerr about a private production at the Gate Theatre of a play called *Adolescence*:

> The play was so filthy and disgusting and decadent that it nearly made us sick . . . there must be some way of stopping such an exhibition? Every description of unnatural sex crime is indulged in. The language is perfectly open; they say what they are doing, what they wish to do, and what they have done. You see a girl tempted physically and made to become a Lesbian, and then she retires into the bedroom with the other girl, and later comes out and says what they have done. The men are drunkards and they make filthy love to women . . . describe with whom they have been and so forth, and the women are equally frank, Drugs come into it also . . . The play is being performed again, I believe, next Saturday. It is so degrading that if there is no law to stop it one should be made.

It was not just the play itself which appalled the writer, but also the social backgrounds he encountered: 'One of the actresses was a girl who, I am told, is a Boscawen, a near relation of Lord Falmouth', he fulminated. As for his fellow-spectators:

> The audience were mostly rather peculiar. Some, I think, by the look of them, were the same class as the people being represented, but I saw a few people I knew in one group, a Peer, two Peeresses and others (but I suspect they would rather I did not mention their names), and I am sure they were equally surprised and disgusted as we were, but I did not see them at the end.[43]

Sexual morality, as considered in the previous chapter, is of itself a political matter; however, it acquires another dimension when censorship is used differentially in relation to the moral 'weaknesses' of different classes. The Public Morality Council, for example, described Coward's *Private Lives* as 'a good argument for the promoters of disorder in this country who declaim against the "idle rich"', and insisted it was far too dangerous to have been licensed: 'On what grounds it is allowed at all would puzzle anyone', complained its secretary: 'I think we should consider how best to secure a boycott of this sort of play as far as our own friends are concerned'.[44]

In the 1926 House of Lords debate on theatre censorship, Lord Buckmaster turned the tables on those who were criticising the Lord Chamberlain for the spate of recent plays which had exposed the decadence and immorality of the wealthy. Buckmaster attacked them for their hypocrisy:

> If you let the plays go through which attack the vices of the poorer people, how can you possibly justify a refusal to license a play that depicts what is alleged to be the vices of the people who are well-to-do?[45]

Buckmaster was highlighting a link between morality and politics which, he suggested, was motivating recent criticism of the Lord Chamberlain for licensing certain plays. He probably had in mind the protests against Coward's *Fallen Angels* when he pointedly observed that it was not unusual to find 'drunkenness on the part of a workman' being depicted on stage. Buckmaster also reminded them that 'cruelty to a wife, the general roughness and coarseness of the poor have been caricatured on the stage again and again and nobody complains'. But with a possible class war looming, Buckmaster's argument could not always be heard; a few months later Cromer took Dawson's side in refusing to allow Coward's *This Was a Man*:

> Every character in this play, presumably ladies and gentlemen, leads an adulterous life and glories in doing so. The only exceptions are two servants who are kept busy mixing cocktails.
>
> I find no serious purpose in the play, unless it be misrepresentation.
>
> At a time like this what better propaganda could the Soviet instigate and finance?[46]

There were those who thought that to show the upper echelons of society behaving badly might encourage some very undesirable and dangerous political outcomes, and it was therefore much more problematic than to depict the failings of the working classes.

Cromer had attracted some criticism in 1923 for licensing Somerset Maugham's *Our Betters*, a play described by Street as 'a fierce indictment of the vices of a section of English society'. Street had recommended it on the grounds that, though 'not a play for la jeune fille', its standpoint was 'not sympathy with vice but intense scorn of it'. While the censors felt no need at this point to protect a whole class, they were gallantly concerned to protect an individual who might have been identified with one of the characters; 'others will know better than I', remarked Street, in wondering whether there was any connection between the character and a well-known aristocrat:

> Pearl will suggest to many people Lady Cunard. That is pointed by her country house being called 'Feathers Nevill', as Lady Cunard used to live at Nevill Holt . . . I am not of course implying that it would be fair to her at all. But Pearl is represented as a callously vicious and mercenary person, and if any real person were obviously meant and so painted it is another thing altogether.

Even though Cromer's advisers thought there was no explicit link—'I see no more likeness to Lady C in the character of "Pearl" than to some half dozen other ladies of the same types'—he required the name of the country house to be changed 'so as to give no hint of similarity'.[47]

The following year, Cromer described Noel Coward's *The Vortex* as 'the inevitable sequence to a play like *Our Betters* by which it is evidently inspired'; this time he saw good reason to refuse a licence:

> This picture of a frivolous and degenerate set of people gives a wholly false impression of Society life and to my mind the time has come to put a stop to the harmful influence of such pictures on the stage.

Dawson agreed that such depictions of Society were dangerous:

> Especially in these days the importance of this is intensified when class hatred is preached, not only to the adult at the street corner, but to the children in the Sunday Schools.
>
> For this reason I welcome the Lord Chamberlain's remark that the time has come to put a stop to such plays, and I hope he will ban *Vortex* for, in my opinion, it is a piece calculated to convey the worst possible impression of the social conditions under which we live today.

But, to their credit, some of the Advisory Board took a very different and unexpected view. Buckmaster, while critical of the play itself, was clear about the political implications of censoring it:

> The reason suggested against it is that it holds up to unfair opprobrium the vices of the idle and the rich. Now it is quite plain that wealthy people and those who constitute what is vaguely known as Society cannot claim

immunity against publication even of extreme views of their conduct unless the same immunity is granted to all classes. No one has ever protested against plays disclosing brutalised behaviour on the part of the poor . . . The imbecilities of a ballroom and the follies and vices of prosperous and irresponsible people are just as fit a subject for the stage as the coarser vices of poorer folk.

Henry Higgins, another adviser, agreed:

I cannot help feeling that if its surroundings were those of squalid poverty and it were an 'East End' there would be no question of refusing a licence. The same observation would apply if it were dated in the Middle Ages— The real objection is that it presents the prosperous of today in an odious light and to that extent partakes of the nature of socialist propaganda . . . But that is hardly I take it a sufficient reason for banning it altogether.

Dawson took umbrage at the implications of such claims, though it was partly his own comments which had provoked them. Contradicting the implications of his previous remarks, he now insisted that 'whether a scene is laid in Mayfair or Whitechapel' it was always treated by the same principles:

I have been longer on the Board than anyone. It was created on my suggestion. I have never known the 'wealthy' or 'society' classes to be given preferential consideration. I regard the insinuation of favour to one class as a misleading opinion of the impartial way in which the Board has hitherto exercised its duties.

However, Buckmaster was so persuasive that Dawson found himself isolated, and Cromer had little choice other than to issue the licence. While he may have been influenced by Buckmaster's assurance that the effect of the play would not be 'mischievous'—and by the standard warning that a suppressed play might be more dangerous than a licensed one—we should, I think, acknowledge that, in this instance at least, a positively liberal and politically informed decision was taken.[48]

A slightly different problem presented itself in 1926 when the Countess of Cathcart wrote *Ashes*, a revealing and embittered play—apparently based on personal experiences—about sexual intrigues and betrayals among the aristocracy. The play again exposed the promiscuous decadence and cruelty of the ruling class, and the 'cynical treatment of marriage and the atmosphere of immorality' worried Cromer.

But there is another aspect.
Here is a play written by a woman notorious by self-advertisement and

her own misconduct of life, who veils her own life story so transparently that it would be obvious to everyone she wishes for revenge upon the man and woman who have been the cause of her misfortune . . . it seems to me a dangerous precedent that people with personal grievances should be able to attack the objects of their personal hatred by writing plays based on their intimate detail . . .

It may not be the business of censorship to protect people who merit 'showing-up', still I am doubtful as to the general principle.

Cromer sought legal advice from Buckmaster, who doubted 'if the Censor's powers cover the restraining of personal libels except of course in the case of well known public men'. He suggested that the names of people and places should be disguised, and, after private discussions with the King, Cromer reluctantly licensed the play on that basis.[49]

If the risk in showing the upper classes behaving immorally amongst themselves was that it might promote revolutionary sentiment, then the risk of showing aristocrats betraying their class for sexual lust was seen to carry the additional risk of encouraging such behaviour and thus destroying the pure blood of the aristocracy. This was anathema for the Lord Chamberlain's Office, and Strindberg's *Miss Julie* was rejected by Cromer in 1925 largely because it showed the daughter of a count being sexually attracted to her servant:

> In the first place there is the sordid and disgusting atmosphere, which makes the immorality of the Play glaring and crude.
> Then there is the very questionable theme in these days of the relations between masters and servants, which this play tends to undermine.

It was this second issue which Cromer thought crucial and beyond alteration, and the bias of the censorship is evident in Dawson's confirmation that 'this beastly play is the very type which *all public opinion that is worth consideration* looks to the censor to protect them from' (my emphasis). *Miss Julie* was resubmitted on several occasions over the next few years, and with careful alterations by different managements; on each occasion it was rejected. Not until December 1938—under a new Lord Chamberlain—was the play passed, with the Reader of the time observing that 'Lord Cromer always felt particularly antipathetic to this theme'.[50]

In 1928 a trivial comedy sketch was refused a licence 'on account of its ending, which clearly showed that the missing Lord Bertie spent the night with a pretty housemaid'.[51] In 1930 Cromer wrote of one scene in the revue *Mind Your Step*: 'The whole of this business of a married man making love to his maid servant and the accompanying business is I think offensively vulgar enough to ban'.[52] In the same year, a French comedy by the always troublesome Sacha Guitry was submitted, in which the central character, Desiré, is a butler sacked from his previous position 'for going to extreme lengths with his mistress, a Polish Countess'. Cromer had a meeting with the prospective producer:

> The Lord Chamberlain said that his opinion was that the theme of the play would hardly do in this country, mostly on the ground that a great many people took exception to the idea of love scenes between mistresses and servants.

The producer proposed 'that it might be possible to change the position in life of the butler by making him a gentleman', and he subsequently submitted a revised version, rewritten on those lines. Street was as outspoken as he could be about this rather crude political intervention:

> I gather that the Lord Chamberlain's chief objection was to Desiré's being a servant. I confess I do not share this objection. The man is quite as much a gentleman as his mistress is a lady—more so in fact.[53]

Concern that the nation's stock was in danger of being fatally watered down, as a result of a decadent generation of aristocrats betraying their lineage, had also been the subject of Marie Stopes's play *Cleansing Circles*, which she submitted first in 1926. The plot began, she declared, 'where *The Vortex* leaves off', and her play later went under the revised title of *The Vortex Damned*. Stopes passionately advocated the importance of her message, and the need to counter Coward's nihilistic conclusion which, she implied, envisioned the British race (or perhaps the European or even the white race) to be in terminal decline and on the point of collapse. She wrote to the Lord Chamberlain:

> I remember you told me you thought Coward's *Vortex* written with a high motive—but I felt that his curtain was weak and anti-racial and I have placed a group of people in a position such as his would have been a week after and given a curtain which will, I hope have a higher and truer moral for the public . . . There is no preaching or 'propaganda' in the play only a desire to lift the fallen to a higher and impersonal plane.

Cleansing Circles focused on a young man who is impotent as the result of his father's promiscuity, and who then offers to marry his father's mistress and preserve the family name by bringing up the illegitimate offspring of his father's adultery. However well-intentioned, such a suggestion was too morally dubious to allow. In 1930 Stopes tried once again to have the play licensed, claiming that 'things have moved rapidly in public opinion towards my way of thinking that it is the race which matters'. It was again turned down because of its explicit sexual discussions. 'These intimate revelations are surely more suitable for treatment in a book', noted the Reader, and he concluded that 'the play might be suitable for a special audience but for general production a licence is not recommended'.[54]

In *Potiphar's Wife*, a young aristocratic woman who is married to an earl forty years her senior sets out to seduce her chauffeur; when he rejects her advances, she accuses him of having molested her, and her husband presses charges. *Miss Julie* was rejected in the very month that *Potiphar's Wife* was licensed, despite the obvious similarity of theme. The difference was that in this case the woman is unequivocally shamed and condemned for her behaviour:

> There is a vicious sort of atmosphere about this play, but it cannot be called immoral since innocence is vindicated and vice trounced . . . The upshot of the play is anything but immoral. The vicious and vile slut of a woman is exposed and punished—not triumphant as in *Our Betters*.

Cromer certainly did not approve of the text, describing it as 'sickening', and 'a vicious sort of play in which the Globe Theatre Management appears to specialise'; he eventually agreed to license it with considerable reluctance, only for the Office to attract embarrassing publicity over aspects of its staging.[55]

It is perhaps understandable that in the mid-1920s the fear of a possible class revolution should have made the censorship sensitive towards some of the plays discussed above. Yet the arguments and negotiations which took place in relation to a stage adaptation of Evelyn Waugh's *Vile Bodies* demonstrate that concerns about exposing the upper classes on the public stage were still rife in the early 1930s. The script was first submitted in December 1930, when Street dismissed it as 'mostly harmless'. However, because of the adultery, the general immorality, and especially the homosexual references, he recommended that a licence should be refused. Most of the Advisory Board agreed, though Bonham Carter suggested that with judicious cutting she could see no objection; she made an interesting comparison:

> I cannot take this play at all seriously. It appears to me to be comparable to a restoration comedy—a rather fantastic satire on the moeurs and manners of the day . . . treated with cynicism rather than with sympathy.

Cromer wrote an extremely discouraging letter to the manager which was designed to kill the play once and for all, and which was less than completely honest in its summary of the responses it had received:

> The play would undoubtedly be considered a nasty play about nasty people, and this is the sort of thing which many people look to the

Censorship for keeping off the stage. Let me, therefore, beg you to dissuade either Mr Ivor Novello or Mr Basil Dean from putting them-selves to the trouble of making any revised version ... My Advisory Committee have unanimously condemned its production for public performance.

Nevertheless, Nigel Playfair, the manager, sent in a revised version which, amongst other changes, removed the lesbian references. In an effort to persuade the Lord Chamberlain to license the text for performance, he also tried to bring a very different kind of political pressure to bear on him: 'It will provide a good deal of very necessary employment', he argued; 'It contains some 42 speaking parts waiting to be filled by actors now out of work and many in great difficulty'. True to the spirit of Restoration debates, Playfair also insisted that the play took a critical rather than an indulgent gaze at the immorality it exposed, describing it as 'a very clever and stinging attack, on loose manners and morals, which is likely to do much more good than harm'; he pointed out that Waugh himself was 'a man of unblemished character and an ardent Catholic', and tried to reassure the Lord Chamberlain that the play's appeal 'will be exclusively to the more serious minded section of the public, and that queer public who seek out plays because they are "salacious" will find nothing to satisfy their craving'. In reply, Cromer told Playfair:

> It is no doubt a plausible argument that a play of this nature is merely intended as an attack on loose manners and morals, and this I understand was Congreve's defence of his own play; but it was not generally accepted.

Nevertheless, the Lord Chamberlain agreed that one of his staff should watch the private performance at the Arts Theatre. His Assistant Comptroller, who carried out this duty, described the performance as 'scandalous', and focused on the political dimension:

> The play as a whole, portraying as it does, admittedly in an exaggerated form, a class of society regarded with contempt by all decent minded people, would be to my mind admirable propaganda for the Socialist Party, and it is surely most undesirable that such a phase of life should be publicly portrayed at the present time.
> The constant imbibing of cocktails and champagne by all the characters, and light-hearted talk of open immorality would convey an impression to the more ignorant portion of an audience that such goings on were the normal habits of the more wealthy classes in the country.

The licence was refused, but in February 1932 another version was sent in. Playfair had by now withdrawn from the enterprise, but not only had scenes been completely rewritten or cut, a new character had been added—a narrator—who appeared within every scene to spell out its didactic moral. Despite his reservations about this device, Street now recommended a licence:

> I am partly influenced by the assurance of people who saw it at the Arts that it came off as a satire on the irresponsible and dissolute young people it portrays. I did not much believe in that at first—it reminded me of Congreve's answer to Jeremey Collier—but as it stands now—without so much salaciousness for its own sake introduced—I can imagine this satirical intention getting through.

After further changes, *Vile Bodies* was finally approved.[56]

In 1924 Street stated: 'It is not in the province of the Censor to exclude the expression of political opinion from plays if kept within decent limits'.[57] How those limits are defined—and who does the defining—are obviously key questions. In 1928 Street indicated the grounds on which he considered it legitimate to intervene. He did so purely in terms of the effect on an audience: 'The reason for banning a political play', he stated, 'is the probable excitation of passion and uproar'. This observation was made within his report on a 'political parable' by John Drinkwater, in which John Bull lies ill in bed, attended by Nurse Britannia and by several doctors offering alternative remedies to cure him; Sir Victor Torian, for example, 'is for going on with his own treatment of sedatives'. In order 'to avoid Press sensation and other troubles', the Lord Chamberlain followed Street's recommendation 'that the doctors should not be made-up as Baldwin, Lloyd George and Ramsay MacDonald'. However, the Office was confident that the play was 'too temperate and generally impartial to rouse any feeling', and that what Cromer described as a 'very amusing skit on national politics' was therefore safe to license. As Street observed, 'people are not as excited by politicians as they used to be'.[58]

It is not chance that one of the words which most frequently recurs in reports of licensed plays is 'harmless'. But can a political play ever be harmless? And if it is harmless, can it be political?

CHAPTER TEN

Foreign Bodies
International Politics

Villains must belong to some country . . .[1]

The final chapter of this volume focuses on the censorship of plays which involved other nations, races and cultures. It is divided into two sections: the first deals with plays where the subject matter was acknowledged by the censors as having an explicit international political dimension; the second considers racial and cultural stereotyping, and the reluctance of the censorship to acknowledge the broader implications of plays which they refused to see as possessing an international dimension.

International Relations

When the script for a spectacular musical was submitted in 1921under the title *Mecca*—'The successor to *Chu Chin Chow*'—Street knew that the basis of its appeal was intended to be its 'gorgeous Eastern scenes and dresses and unlimited local colour'. He agonised briefly about whether the performance was likely to cause offence: 'Possibly Mohammadans might object to the Mecca pilgrimage being taken lightly, but there is obviously no offence meant and no ridicule of sacred Mohammadan things'. Street did realise that the title itself might cause some offence, and he conceded that it was a reflection of regrettable ignorance on the part of the writer to show the pilgrims drinking wine; but he saw no grounds for serious complaint about the narrative: 'I never heard of Catholics objecting to Chaucer', he remarked. However, at a meeting with Mustapha Khan (a religious leader) and the Right Hon. Ameer Ali (an MP), Lord Sandhurst was told that 'the fact of the title being advertised for a production of the theatre would be regarded as derision of the Mahommedan holiest place'; Sandhurst was specifically warned that this fact 'would at any time arouse suspicion and at this moment especially be very dangerous'. The theatre manager was persuaded, with some reluctance, to change the title to *Cairo*, under which name it ran for over 250 performances at His Majesty's Theatre in the West End, and the *Islamic Review of Muslim India* wrote to thank the Lord Chamberlain 'for the sympathy which you showed to the interest of Moslems in connection with the safeguard of their religious feelings'.

Of course, Sandhurst's decision had little to do with altruism—even of a paternalistic kind—and much more to do with safeguarding control of the British Empire by not insulting and perhaps provoking its subjects.[2] Much more confrontational was the argument over *Auction of Souls*, a play submitted in 1922 which centred on the Turkish/Armenian conflict. In view of the almost exclusive concentration which is usually afforded to major London theatres in any discussions of theatre censorship, it is worth pointing out that in the case of this script—which generated so much argument and passion—the licence was being sought for a production at the Ambassadors Theatre in Southend. The apparent insignificance of the venue (when compared, for example, with the one for which *Cairo* had been licensed) was barely even registered by the Lord Chamberlain.

'It is a realistic play of Turkish atrocities and some of the examples are certainly unfit for public presentation', wrote Street in his report on *Auction of Souls*. He noted that the play was written from a very specific perspective, and that 'the audience is encouraged to "help the Armenian refugees"'. Although Street was disturbed by the physical brutality and torture depicted, it was the political context that made the production potentially dangerous; not only was the play explicitly anti-Turkish (and therefore, perhaps, anti-Muslim) but the British government and its policy were implicated as well. Yet to reject the play was not a straightforward matter:

> The Turks are of course abused all through. It is regretted . . . that England and France no longer protects the Armenians . . . I do not know if Mohammadans would be offended. The opposition of Christians and Mohammadans is insisted on throughout. I think it probable if the Lord Chamberlain refused to license there would be an outcry: the Turkish atrocities may be exaggerated but are based on facts real enough.

Dawson agreed that 'the risk of international complications' was the main objection to licensing the play, and recommended that the Foreign Office should be consulted. Historical accuracy was irrelevant; what mattered was the possibility of the unfortunate consequences which might result if the Lord Chamberlain (and the King) were seen to have approved such criticism of the Turks:

> Though the whole world is aware of Turkish atrocities on Armenians it would be inadvisable for the Lord Chamberlain to countenance the adver-

tising of them, having regard to India and Moslem problems within the
Empire.

The Lord Chamberlain announced that a licence would not be granted, and
when the manager queried the play's political relevance (and even offered to
cut out the Turks) he was informed:

> The Lord Chamberlain fails to see how the play can be regarded as other
> than political at the present moment, at a time when the subjects dealt with
> are matters requiring very delicate adjustment by those responsible for the
> conduct of foreign affairs not only in our own country but elsewhere.

A few months later, a revised version was submitted, in which all references
to Turks, Allah and Mohammed were removed, and brigands were substituted as the villains. Street, however, suspected that, despite such changes,
'an audience might infer that Turks and not brigands are really meant'; yet
he thought it 'doubtful that the play would have vogue enough to attract any
political attention'. But the Lord Chamberlain received a polite yet insistent
letter of warning from the *Islamic Review*, written by an Imam from Surrey:

> Your Lordship's predecessor, the late Lord Sandhurst, insisted on the
> name of a forthcoming theatrical production being changed from *Mecca*
> to *Cairo* in order to avoid the wounding of the Moslem's susceptibilities.
> Though the matter was trifling in itself, his action was welcomed by the
> Moslems throughout the world with a real gratitude and appreciation.
>   Today it becomes my duty to appeal to Your Lordship once again to
> exercise your powers . . . Leaving aside the present delicate situation in
> international politics, which renders highly doubtful the expediency of
> permitting the portrayal of what is, to those who pretend to any knowl-
> edge of the matter, a particularly shameless libel on the Turkish troops
> and their commander . . . I would point out that the whole production
> constitutes an even more shameless and libellous attack on the principles
> and the faith of Islam—and the knowledge that such a performance is
> being permitted here in England, with the sanction—or at any rate without
> the disapproval of—the authorities is likely to create a very painful—I may
> say disastrous impression among Moslems in every land.

The Imam asked Atholl to ensure that the play was suppressed 'before the
knowledge that such performances are taking place, reaches Moslems over-
seas', and he left him in no doubt about the potential seriousness of allowing
performances to go ahead:

> The British Moslem Society had unanimously resolved to some form of

public action—but in deference to my suggestion, they are now agreed that it would be far better . . . for the matter to be dealt with by Your Lordship . . . My position enables me to judge more accurately than another of the state of public feeling among Moslems generally and Indian Moslems in particular—but the thoughtless exploitation of reckless and unprincipled propaganda which English audiences may or not take seriously, may well, in the hands of anti-British agitators, become a very serious obstacle to that peaceful adjustment to the situation to which all men of goodwill—Moslems or Christians—are today looking anxiously forward.

Further alarmed by the threatening implications of such a letter, Dawson demanded that the play must be stopped because 'its production risks unnecessarily giving provocation, where it is of vital importance to avoid doing so'. Atholl agreed that even the revised version remained beyond acceptable limits: 'I am of opinion that neither in fact nor in spirit has the play been materially altered', he ruled, and his concern focused on the fact that the settings and the names still signalled that the events were located in a real place. However, since he was also under what he described as 'very strong pressure' to allow the play, he continued to seek an alternative to the imposition of a total ban: 'Are the brigands dressed as Turkish soldiers', he asked, 'and are they obviously Turks?'. The Office invited the manager to resubmit yet another version: 'If the Turks are represented as brigands of no particular nationality, the Lord Chamberlain is of opinion that the religious question is obviated unless the tortures are carried on in the name of Allah'. Eventually, a licence was promised, with the following stipulations:

> That there is no mention of Turkey or Turks throughout the play.
> That no character is made up to represent a Turk.
> That no character is called Kiamil Basta or Kiamil Pasha or any other Turkish sounding name.[3]

The seductive power of the exotic inspired a number of more or less exploitative and inaccurate plays set in different parts of the British Empire, and a political dimension was frequently unavoidable. In 1921 the Lord Chamberlain licensed *Kishna,* an extravagant drama which relied for its appeal on 'effects of Indian music and dresses, live snakes . . . fire-breathing . . . and so forth'. The narrative also involved a villainous priest and a representation of the God Shiva, but the Office had few anxieties about cultural appropriation or distortion, or even about a human actor representing a non-Christian God: 'It seems to me that there might be some offence to possible Indian spectators in the priest and the Shiva business', acknowledged Street, 'but that sort of thing has often been done before and this show is merely spectacular'.[4] The following year the Office also licensed William Archer's *The Green Goddess*, a melodrama set in a part of the Himalayas beyond British control and occupied by savage inhabitants under the rule of an anti-British Rajah:

> I do not think there need be any objection to the play from the point of view of Indian susceptibilities: . . . the place is outside India and the savage religion has nothing to do with Buddhism or Mohammadanism. The Rajah hates us but he is outside our system.[5]

However, one drama which was banned because of its possible effect on the political situation in relation to India was *The Call of Kali*. The play's heroine was a beautiful young Indian woman who has been brought up in Britain and America, but who returns to India as a famous singer:

> She is at first bitterly hostile to the British Raj but comes to see that it is necessary for India, and uses her influence against the degraded ritual of Kali worship presided over by the high Priest Ramapai, an evil and sinister figure.

Other characters included a German spy disguised as a Brahmin priest, a Jewish banker and a Russian Bolshevist, and the plot involved a conspiracy to bring down the British government and provoke a war. The religious rituals which we see taking place in temples (and which involve human sacrifice) are really a front for political intrigues, and Street agonised over his recommendation:

> I should think it unlikely that the play would reach India, and of course it could be censored there if advisable. Here it is to be done at matinees and I should not think it likely to go into an evening bill. How far it may be unwise to represent a High Priest as a ruffian and his ritual as including human sacrifice (if possible) and vaguely mentioned obscenity I do not know . . . Personally, as we have had many plays with sinister native priests and so on without any untoward result I should think there would be no harm in passing it.

Cromer was more cautious, and sent the script to the India Office for advice. He said that there was 'nothing in it which would in the ordinary course come under the ban of the Censorship as regards morality', but explained that he was concerned about the references to Indian religious ritual, and, by implication, the political dimension of the script:

> Personally I am of opinion that this sort of melodramatic business has

nothing likely to affect the British Public one way or another, but it might give offence to Indian susceptibilities and do harm among Indian students in London, and reports might reach India that their religion is being libelled on the London stage. Further it is not a play which should be produced in India.

India Office officials took the matter extremely seriously, and professed themselves appalled by the 'gross ignorance' and 'absurdities' of the play and the damage which it might do. They had no doubt that such a play would be

> gravely offensive not only to anyone on the lookout for a stumbling block of offence, but to decent Hindu sentiment. So also would the representation of the High Priest as a man of abandoned morals engaged in a treasonable conspiracy. The *mise en scène*, showing an Indian state as a hotbed of sedition, is also calculated to offend in another direction . . . references to . . . national volunteers conspiring with Bolshevik and German spies are also politically objectionable. The main objection, however, is that the whole play is calculated to give justifiable offence to average Hindu religious susceptibilities.

The India Office told Lord Cromer he would be unwise to issue a licence, and he accepted its opinion.[6]

Again on the specific recommendation of the India Office, Cromer also refused a licence in 1927 for *The Pool*, a romantic melodrama involving Hindu temples, princesses, torture and English soldiers:

> At the present time, for one reason and another, Indian and particularly Hindu sentiment is unusually sensitive of any imagined attack upon Hindu institutions. This play, the plot of which turns upon the disloyalty of a Hindu Prince and his tribesmen, and the vengeful nature of the form of Hindu religion which they are supposed to observe, might well give offence.

The manager was informed that in the light of the 'forthcoming visit of the Indian commission to India, and the delicate nature of their investigation, it is felt that it is particularly desirable to avoid starting up any controversy'.[7]

Three years later, Sir Alfred Butt, who in addition to being the managing director of Drury Lane Theatre was also a serving Conservative and Unionist MP, ran into similar problems of political sensitivity when he submitted a musical comedy, *Song of the Drum*, for Drury Lane. Street equivocated:

> The important matter, I think, is if a play about India, with a disaffected Rajah, should be allowed while the Round Table Conference is sitting and

many Indian Princes are in London. Perhaps on the whole, since so many plays of the sort have been produced, and no one ought to take a Musical Comedy seriously, it can be allowed.

Cromer told Butt that he was obliged to consult with the India Office to ascertain whether it was acceptable that such a piece should be performed at a time when 'so many questions of high policy affecting India are at present in the balance'. He advised Butt that 'in some quarters certainly, it would be considered highly impolitic to produce a play of this description, which is so liable to misinterpretation by Indians and in India'. Once again, the India Office argued forcefully that a play with such a theme would have 'a deplorable effect', and strongly objected to its being produced:

> The leit-motif underlying it is a plot of an Indian Prince who is in touch with a Bolshevik spy to upset British rule, and he tries to seize an English girl for immoral purposes . . . Such a play would be regarded by Indian Princes as positively insulting, though the wicked Raja has a virtuous nephew who sides with the British.

Cromer informed Butt of the situation, and the familiar solution of transferring the action into a different location was proposed:

> Sir Alfred quite understood this objection and is going to arrange to change the setting of the piece to a more vague and mythical part of Turkestan, or somewhere possibly on the Borders of Persia. He expressed his desire to introduce a Persian element if possible, in order to make use of Persian dresses and colourings. He also spoke of introducing into the plot some foreign menace from Russia.

However, there was always the risk that such a switch might do no more than transfer the same problem elsewhere, as one of the Lord Chamberlain's staff warned Butt:

> I told him that in avoiding the objections of the India Office I did not wish him to run into a further set of objections from the Foreign Office, so I begged him to be careful as regards anything that was likely to be offensive to foreign countries—even the Russians, although Bolsheviks deserve no sympathy.

As always, the best solution from the political point of view was to avoid any references to real places: 'My indications to him were to make this play as fantastic and impersonal as possible as regards localities and nationalities, and this he will endeavour to do'. A revised and fantastic version—which Butt promised would be 'more reminiscent of the *Arabian Nights* than anything else'—was duly submitted and allowed.[8]

In 1929, the Office did cautiously license another potentially controversial play set in India, *The Flight Lieutenant*. This drama opened in the air force mess at Delhi, and was permeated, said Street, by 'talk of the black Rajah . . . of a native rising and the necessity of warning the Prince of Wales on his tour'. Though the Reader felt such talk 'will not do', he judged that it was probably rendered 'innocuous' by the fact that the dangerous predictions voiced in the play proved to be 'all nonsense, the raving of a dying native mad, at the time'. Lord Cromer was reassured—just—by the context of the performance: 'I trust this play will not get beyond Greenock', he commented.[9]

It was not only concerns about the British Empire that motivated censorship in relation to international contexts, and plays involving other European countries were also carefully watched. In 1928, for example, a comedy about cuckoldry and adultery in diplomatic circles, entitled *The Command to Love*, was refused a licence; the problem was its plot, which centred on a French military attaché, whose post requires him to manipulate Spanish politics by making love to the wives of leading statesmen. Ironically, the fact that he proves to be physically not up to this task was a further cause of anxiety for Lord Cromer, who was always touchy about any references to male impotence. However, the manager—Sir Alfred Butt again—correctly assumed that the major reason for the refusal was fear that the play 'might offend the susceptibilities of foreign countries with whom we are upon the most friendly terms'. A revised version which removed the names of the countries was also turned down, because of fears that the identities might still be 'self-evident to the audience', and that 'the characters may be regarded as real representatives of a friendly power'. A third version of the text was submitted:

> It is now in the form of a 'jeu d'esprit'. It takes place in no particular epoch of time. The characters have no more reality than those of a Punch and Judy Show . . .
>
> Quite possibly this entirely new treatment of the play will be found at the same time to have removed all the entertainment value. But that is not a matter with which your department will concern itself.

After viewing a private performance, the Assistant Comptroller recommended that the script could now be safely licensed since 'the characters now belong to no particular country and the place where the action takes place is left vague'. More than a year after it had first been submitted, and after five different playwrights had worked on the script, Cromer was satisfied that few people were likely to be shocked by the performance. A licence was granted for *Command to Love* in March 1930, but the Public Morality Council was still outraged by the play's immorality—and especially by the responses of certain sections of the audience. It complained at length to the Lord Chamberlain, in an unsuccessful attempt to persuade him to withdraw his approval. Part of its complaint was on purely moral grounds:

> This is a very objectionable play from every point of view. Marriage and other of the best things in life are ridiculed . . . Such remarks as, that the unfaithful wife is only doing what every fashionable woman does, won screams of laughter from the young women in the gallery and one wonders what sort of wives and mothers are going to be the result of such plays . . . most of the laughter came from the gallery. One wonders why such plays need be allowed to be on the English stage, there is no genuine demand for them and they are quite alien to English feeling.

However, this hostility was also crucially informed by the political and class context of the drama:

> It deals with life in diplomatic circles . . . it is to be hoped that it libels rather than portrays the conditions of things existing in these exalted spheres . . . Adultery is deliberately advocated as the most effective instrument for the achievement of political aims . . . it parodies every virtue, it flaunts lying, seduction and adultery, it appeals by suggestion to the basest instincts of human nature and it elevates a liar and a libertine to the level of a hero.

But the relative priorities of the Lord Chamberlain's Office were clear; such objections were minor and could be safely ignored, provided only that international diplomatic codes and conventions were not breached.[10]

The opinion of the Foreign Office was frequently sought over plays involving other countries, and actual representatives of the countries concerned might also be approached. In 1923, for example, Lord Cromer contacted the Foreign Office about 'an extremely lurid melodrama of the recent Hungarian Revolution' which contained some fairly explicit scenes of torture:

> The point on which I should much value the expression of your opinion is whether the present Hungarian Minister, and other Hungarians in London, are likely to resent a play depicting certain episodes, imaginary or not, in the somewhat recent history of Hungary? Personally I do not think that patriotic and right-minded Hungarians could be offended by such a play, as they must deplore atrocities committed in the course of revolution as much as right-minded people would do in any other country.

Cromer stressed that the play was unlikely to reach the West End or a significant commercial audience, and indicated that he was reluctant to refuse the licence, unless there were strong reasons for doing so: 'Plays about revolutions are constantly being acted so that it is not advisable to withhold a licence to any play unless it is really offensive to a foreign nation with whom we have amicable relations'. On this occasion the Foreign Office had no objections, and Cromer issued a licence.[11]

There were no family links between the British and Hungarian rulers; it was a different story the following year with *The Grand Duchess*, an adaptation of Alfred Savoir's French comedy about the survivors of the former Russian royal family and their lifestyle in exile. Street was certain it would have been banned in the past, and thought the policy should remain unchanged:

> I suppose that the rule about reigning houses does not apply now, but this presentment of contemporary Grand Dukes and a Grand Duchess, even if imaginary, must give so much offence in some quarters that I imagine the Lord Chamberlain would be right in not permitting it. I hope so, for considering what they have gone through and how most of them have died I think the taste of this ridicule of imaginary survivors thoroughly vile.

Cromer agreed that such a play was in 'very dubious taste' and 'impossible on the English stage', since it contained 'satire and ridicule of the Russian Imperial Family *and thus of Royalty*' (my emphasis). But even though he suspected audiences would see through the disguise, he was prepared to consider allowing it if the country and the characters were fictionalised:

> This would probably be the best solution, as it is a play that may suit Republican France, but is out of place in England, where endeavours are still being made to keep aglow the embers of good taste, and also to respect the misfortunes of those in high places who misused or abused pre-Revolutionary days in foreign countries to their present discomfiture.

He employed the deliberate strategy of procrastination in order to postpone the performance:

> I am inclined not to ban the play as a play or for any specific reason, but to raise objections to a number of points of principle and detail which may result in the producer re-considering the advisability of producing the play at all.

Cromer sent the script of *The Grand Duchess* to his Advisory Board, advising them that he would also be referring it to the King. Most of the Board were quite conscientious in trying to decide whether there were legitimate grounds for refusing it, even though they instinctively objected to its theme; perhaps they feared exposure and mockery in the press if they were seen to be taking too hard a line. Lord Buckmaster, for instance, was clearly shocked by the comic class reversal which showed the son of a president working as a waiter; such an insult, he said, was 'beyond excuse', and he proposed that the 'suggestion I formally made so that plays prejudicially affecting members of the Royal Family ought not to be permitted applies in principle to all people occupying eminent public positions'. Yet he maintained that 'to scoff and jeer at the misfortunes of people fallen and in exile is a matter of bad taste with which by itself the Censorship has no concern'. Another member of the Board, the Chairman of the Grand Opera Syndicate and Director of the Carlton and Ritz, Henry Higgins, agreed that 'any class of the community may be criticised or satirised in a play'; however, he, too, denounced the attempt 'to hold up the Russian Royal Family to ridicule and contempt which quite apart from their near connection with our own Royal Family is quite inadmissible'. A revised version of the play, which removed the direct references and fictionalised the story, was duly licensed the following year. Street was convinced that 'everyone will still think of Russia', but, as so often, Cromer judged that less controversy would be generated by allowing the play to be performed than by banning it. 'Further restrictions may only end in every point being discussed in the Press, according to the modern method of some managers', he shrewdly observed.[12]

As the previous example suggests, censorship involving Russia and the Soviet Union was often focused on the depiction of the royal family—reflecting a concern which derived principally from the links between that family and the British monarchy. In 1927 extensive negotiations and revisions occurred over *Red Nights of the Tcheka*, a Grand Guignol melodrama staged by Terence Gray at Cambridge. The main objection was to the suggestion that the Grand Duchess Olga, daughter of the late Tzar, was now acting as a spy for the Bolsheviks. Gray changed her name and also cut lines, after being instructed by the Lord Chamberlain that it was 'undesirable that anyone connected with the Russian Royal Family should abuse the Tsarist regime'. These changes did not go far enough, and Gray was informed that no licence could be issued 'until the Script has been so revised as to eliminate all references to the Imperial Family'.[13]

In 1929 Hubert Griffith's *Red Sunday*—which chronicled the history of the Russian Revolution from 1905 to 1917, and included amongst its characters Lenin, Trotsky, Rasputin and the Tzar and Tzarina—was refused a licence, following a direct intervention by the King on behalf of Russians exiled in London.[14] A licence was also refused two years later for *A Woman of Destiny*, a play about the last days of the Tzar and Tzarina, even though it was intended to be entirely sympathetic to them, and was to have been performed for charity under the auspices of the Bishop of Chichester. 'Normally the play would be recommended', wrote the Lord Chamberlain's new Reader, Henry Game, 'but I understand that the historical incidents treated here are of too recent nature to allow their presentation on the stage'. The author complained bitterly 'that in these days only foul libels of the late Tzar and Tzarina are permitted in public places of entertainment and that such that give the truth are officially withheld'; but typically, it was less the play itself to which the censors objected than the fact that it could have been seen in the future as a precedent. To allow a subject to be dramatised and therefore fictionalised is to acknowledge the possibility of alternative versions of reality; or, as Game put it, although this particular play was 'a sincere attempt at presenting the truth, the difficulty arises that if one play on this subject is allowed and another disallowed it leads one to debatable questions of historical fact'. Cromer's revealing response explained the policy very clearly:

> There is little in this to which exception need be taken except that it involves the impersonation of the late Emperor and Empress of Russia which has hitherto been disallowed on the stage (mainly owing to the close relationship between the British Royal Family and the Imperial Family of Russia).
>
> Licensing of this play would open the door to any number of plays with a similar theme.

The same points were reiterated in a letter sent by Cromer to his royal master: 'Subject, therefore, to the King's approval I propose to say that the play involving the impersonation of the late Emperor and Empress of Russia deals with such recent history that I do not see my way to granting a license [*sic*]'. However, Cromer also warned him: 'Of course the time will come when such plays will have to be permitted, but this can no doubt be left to the fullness of time and need not be yet awhile'.[15]

The protection of other nations by the British censors extended also to the United States of America—and some plays were refused licences in England even when they had already been performed in the United States. In 1927 Cromer initially refused a licence for the musical *Chicago*, which had caused a degree of controversy in America for its attack on corruption in the legal and political professions and in the media, in relation to a murder trial. 'If Chicago deserves a tenth of it it must be a deplorable place', wrote Street; however, he advised that 'since the play has been allowed in America I do not think it our business to protect Chicago'. Cromer, however, sent the script to his Advisory Board, giving an unmistakeable indication of what he expected from them: 'Although this play has been published and has been produced in America, I would gladly seek every opportunity of preventing its production in this country', he informed them. Most of the Board took the hint. 'I know Chicago well', wrote Sir Johnston Forbes-Robertson; 'It is the most corrupt city in America, but I know many honourable folk there who would be greatly relieved did they hear that the Lord Chamberlain had declined this play a licence'. Lord Ullswater reasoned that its having been staged in America itself was no excuse for allowing such a play to be performed in England: 'The public in the USA will stand criticism from their own people which they will resent coming from a foreigner', he declared, and Higgins agreed that 'the fact that such a performance has been permitted in the USA only convinces me that the introduction of some more effective system of Censorship than exists at present should be introduced in that country'. Dawson was even more strongly opposed to it: 'I have waded through this garbage with difficulty and disgust . . . Only a diseased mind could sit through it without blaming the Censor for passing it'. Not for the first time, it is Dawson's argument which is perhaps most revealing, with its assumption that the theatre has more to do with propaganda than with honesty or integrity:

> It is only an ordinary international courtesy to prevent such a criticism of American methods (however true) being shown in London. The more justified the criticism, the more this argument applies.[16]

Race

In January 1931 the Committee of the Girls' League of the Wesleyan Methodist Missionary Society in Liverpool wrote to the Lord Chamberlain asking 'if there is any legislation governing references in modern drama which are of such a nature as to be derogatory to members of the coloured races'. The letter was apparently provoked by a recent performance containing material which the committee considered 'could have been construed as expressing an outlook strongly prejudiced against the coloured races', and they maintained that in a city in which theatre audiences were likely to be ethnically diverse, there was a real danger that 'such remarks tend to cause misunderstanding between the races'. The Society acknowledged that it might be accused of exaggerating the importance of something which was quite minor, but astutely observed that 'it is often by seemingly trivial and casual remarks that public opinion is confused or educated'. A politely dismissive reply from the Lord Chamberlain's Assistant Comptroller assured the Society that 'every care and consideration' was given to such matters. The evidence hardly supports such a contention.[17]

There were plenty of comic foreigners to be found on the stage in the 1920s, and in most cases the censorship saw no reason to intervene; a sketch consisting of 'an American negro waiter . . . saying pointless rude things to the customers, getting into a rage about nothing and making an idiotic speech' was described as 'imbecile but harmless'.[18] A comic opera about cannibals, performed at a Boy Scout charity in Moretonhampstead, featured a German trader who saves himself from being eaten by 'frightening the savage with a wireless set'; the script was described as 'harmless nonsense'.[19] A Chinaman scaring old ladies in a flat by hunting for rats to use in his curries was 'mild and harmless fun'.[20] There was no need for hesitation over a play set in Central Africa in which 'a fat black schoolteacher provides comic relief'.[21] On the other hand, a sketch called *Mussolini's Lunch*—which was included in the script for a revue at the Hampstead Everyman in 1929—was 'absolutely impossible', since it contained 'insults to a leading statesman of a friendly country'.[22]

Melodramas with evil Chinese characters were everywhere. Of *The Yellow Snare* in 1921—a typical story in which the Chinese villain dopes an English woman in his opium den—Street commented: 'I do not like these plays which tend to make bad blood, but this is no worse than fifty others'.[23] In 1922 he reluctantly recommended a melodrama about cocaine and wicked Chinamen set in 'the House of a Hundred Horrors and Ling Foo's Den', and involving much screaming and violence: 'This sort of rubbish may tend to provoke animus against Chinamen—with talk of their abducting white women—which may be unjustified, but this does not do so any more than many previous plays', he wrote.[24] In 1923 he felt inclined to recommend turning down *The Vengeance of Li Fang Foo*, but was unable to do so:

> This is one of those repulsive plays of Chinese opium dens of which the supply seems to be inexhaustible. The idea of Chinese 'fiends' decoying or drugging English girls and proposing to violate them, of which so far as I know there is no evidence, is undesirable in itself and the details are always vulgarly sensational. However, these plays have not so far been banned and this is no worse than many of them.[25]

This was the other side of refusing to license a theme which might be taken as a precedent; once something had appeared on the stage, it was hard to prevent its reappearance or to draw a line.

Reluctantly recommending *His Chinese Bride* in 1921, Street had commented that

> the real objection to such plays is that they stir up hatred, for no reason, against the Chinese. I do not suppose it goes far and this is only one of many, but I sometimes wonder the Chinese Authorities do not object.[26]

In 1925 those authorities did object, focusing on what Street had described as 'a good melodrama', with the title *The Man from Hong Kong*. The villain of this piece, Li Tong, is the mixed-race offspring of an English man and a Chinese woman, and is able as a result to exert strange powers through his mysterious ability to 'look at will either a Chinese or an Englishman'. After the script had been licensed and performed without official objections, the Chinese Consulate General wrote to the Lord Chamberlain on behalf of Chinese people living in London, expressing disquiet about the genre of which this play was one example:

> The Chinese community felt that this drama not only misrepresented, in a very objectionable form, aspects of Chinese life and customs, but also was of a nature tending to produce international ill-feeling, since in these days of a cheap press and facile communications, what happens in this country is at once made known without difficulty in the Far East.
>
> This piece has now fortunately been withdrawn, but in view of the regrettable tendency to portray aspects of Chinese life and characteristics of the Chinese people which belong now-a-days to fiction and not to fact, it is hoped that you will be good enough to bear in mind the considerations which I thus respectfully urge, should any future plays of a similar type be brought to your notice for approval . . .
>
> This is no casual expression of opinion, but the considered representations of the Chinese community who have, for a long time, noticed with regret the tendency of authors to overlook the consequence of dramatic misrepresentations in their efforts to secure a popular financial success.

Cromer replied courteously that he would 'be pleased to bear in mind the considerations you have mentioned', but he rejected the accusation: 'in melodramas of this nature', he informed the Consulate, 'there is no intention on the part of the author or producer to show hostility towards the peoples in any particular country they may select for the characters and settings of their plays'.

The Chinese Consulate officials were wrong in assuming the production had closed altogether, and when it was revived in Edinburgh shortly afterwards, they sent a letter, similar to their previous one, to the city's Chief Constable; he forwarded it to Scotland Yard, who sent it to St James's Palace, but Cromer still refused to intervene: 'I regret that the Chinese community should take this play so much to heart', he wrote; 'If it misrepresents Chinese life and customs in an exaggerated manner it must be too fantastic to be taken seriously and objection is hardly reasonable'. Where Cromer had been prepared to take action to avoid upsetting Hindu and Mohammedan communities for the sake of the British Empire, he had no intention of taking any notice of these complaints; indeed, he now counter-attacked on grounds of etiquette and procedure:

> In my opinion the Chinese Consul General in London has no right to go writing letters of this sort to officials in this country about 'international

ill-feeling' etc. as that is the business of the diplomatic representative and
is not a consular business.

The Foreign Office spoke with an official representative of the Chinese
Consul and—at least in its own version of events—put him firmly in his place:

> Mr Chu, the Chargé d'affaires, when interviewed, tendered his apologies.
> He said he was himself to blame . . . The Chargé d'affaires now under-
> stands his mistake and will, no doubt, see that the ardour of the
> Consul-General is curbed.[27]

Three years later, in 1928, the Chinese Legation took up the issue again
over a number of plays, writing directly to Sir Austen Chamberlain at the
Foreign Office to ask for his support in seeking to end 'the increasing tendency
in Dramas and Plays which are now being produced in London to represent
Chinese people in consistently vicious and objectionable form'. This, they
protested, was an issue which was 'greatly occupying the attention of Chinese
residents in this country, and which is, in addition, being adversely noticed in
the Far East'. The letter cited as examples five unpleasant and offensive plays
currently being performed in London, and insisted that 'no other oriental
nation is thus singled out for objectionable dramatic treatment'. It also warned
the Foreign Office of the dangers of allowing the trend to continue:

> It is hardly necessary to lay stress on the educational value of the Drama
> so far as public opinion is concerned, and for this reason, it is most inad-
> visable to permit any theatrical productions, which may have the
> regrettable effect of causing ill-feeling between the two nations, and of
> creating misconceptions which may operate to mutual disadvantage.

The Foreign Office sought advice from Cromer on how best to respond. He
replied that, while it was perhaps 'rather regrettable that playwrights have used
the Chinese in this way', there was nothing he could do about it. He refused
to accept that it would result in any 'serious misconception' on the part of
audiences; 'No doubt', he added, 'English men and women are portrayed
badly on stage elsewhere'.[28]
    There was no need, then, to censor racial stereotyping, and Chinese villains
and their drug and torture businesses continued to be a staple ingredient of
melodrama after melodrama. In April 1928 Street commented of *The Green
Beetle*: 'I can understand the Chinese being annoyed by so many Chinese
villains on the stage, but this is nothing out of the way and villains must belong
to some country'. Cromer agreed: 'The play cannot be banned because the
villain is a Chinaman!'.[29] In September, Cromer himself noted of *The
Twister*—which was set in Chang's Torture Chamber and featured cocaine

gangs—that 'this is the sort of play to which exception has been taken by the Chinese Legation, but it can hardly be banned on that account'.[30] In November, he licensed *Yellow Vengeance*, in which Wong Koo, a doctor, threatens to inject the son of an Englishman, Gerard Pearson, with tetanus, unless Pearson sacrifices his second wife to Koo's lust, as revenge for Pearson having violated Koo's betrothed twenty years earlier. It is hard to argue with Street's description of *Yellow Vengeance* as 'the Chinese rubbish play reduced to a very simple form', and Cromer noted that it was just the sort of play to which the Chinese consulate was 'constantly taking exception'. However, Koo actually turns out to have been bluffing, and is 'much less a villain than the usual Chinese play type', so Cromer was more easily able to justify his decision: 'as the Chinaman comes out of it all with credit, I can hardly object to the play on either political or moral grounds'.[31] Of *The Yellow Hand* in 1929—'A very feeble example of the Chinese-dope melodrama . . . innocuous by reason of its extreme puerility'—Cromer again admitted that it was just the sort of play which was offensive to many Chinese people, but insisted that it could 'hardly be banned on that score'.[32]

In refusing to accept the validity of Chinese complaints about *The Man from Hong Kong*, Cromer had explicitly stated: 'We make no bones about discountenancing Anglo-Chinese matrimonial alliances'; he had also suggested that the play might be useful as 'a warning to white women who are foolish enough to be beguiled by Chinamen'.[33] In other words, the fact that someone of mixed-race descent was characterised as evil could be viewed as positive propaganda against the perceived dangers of mixed-race relationships. The sexual allure of non-white races, and the possibility of such relationships developing, was a recurring theme, and one on which the censorship took a very definite position. Commenting on a scene in a 1925 revue, *Overtime*, Street suggested that 'a black man being kissed by girls is not pleasant. I think it might be required that either he should not be black or should not flirt with the girls.' Cromer agreed: 'This <u>must</u> be insisted upon before licence'.[34] Although changing the title of *Mecca* to *Cairo* four years earlier may have served to appease some Muslims, the 'exhibition of unclad women' and of dancers 'exercising all sorts of evolutions' caused a predictable outcry among moralists. Moreover, there was a particular element to the performance which, as Street's comments on one dance make clear, raised the temperature of the complaints: 'The intention is sensual and the effect is extremely unseemly. Girls dance frantically with dark skinned men, all more or less naked to the waist, the men fight for them and so on.' Following Street's report, the manager was immediately informed by the Lord Chamberlain that in future none of the male performers must be 'got up to give the appearance of coloured men'.[35]

The images which were compulsorily removed from *Cairo* and *Overtime* nevertheless signalled and admitted the possibility of inter-racial sexual attraction. Though the censorship disliked the stage being used to advertise the fact that such relationships even existed, it was generally accepted as a theme, so long as the relationship was shown to be doomed to inevitable failure and tragedy. In 1922 Street saw Maugham's *East of Suez* as a powerful play about 'the union of an Englishman and a half-caste', and recommended it for licence as 'a painful story with a practical moral against such connections'. He noted approvingly that 'the character of the half-caste, Daisy, is vile and evil and the presentment of her is a sort of wholesome warning', in which she is ultimately shown to have 'relapsed to her mother's race'.[36] *Her Egyptian Husband*, in 1923, was inspired, said Street, 'by a recent revolting case'. The Lord Chamberlain commented: 'This sort of thing is detestable, but is difficult to eliminate from the stage. The only hope is that these sort of plays deter some white women from marriage with men of black blood.'[37] In 1926 the Japanese Embassy complained to the Lord Chamberlain about *Kimono*, an anti-Japanese play based on a novel. Cromer recorded his subsequent meeting with a senior member of the Embassy staff:

> Mr Shuh Tomii, First Secretary of the Japanese Embassy called to see me yesterday morning with reference to an announcement he had read in the newspapers that this play was shortly to be produced . . . If the dialogue was identical with that of the novel published some years ago, he felt bound to point out that several passages would certainly offend Japanese suscep-tibilities . . . he hoped all cause for offence might be eliminated. I . . . told him that I well remembered reading the novel, and that I could well under-stand that the general theme of the play might arouse Japanese susceptibilities. At the same time, I felt bound to tell him that, although the story might seem inimicable [*sic*] to Japan, its object was primarily to deprecate the question of mixed marriages as between different races. This I explained was quite a legitimate theme. Plays were constantly written and produced bearing on this particular question.

In deference to Japanese sensitivities, the censorship did remove all references to slit eyes, the suggestion that all Japanese were liars, and the line 'they're as dull as dolls and they turn a white man's brain yellow'. The sexual aspect was another matter, however, and in an internal memorandum Cromer noted: 'The story is of course intended to prove the undesirability of mixed marriages as between East and Western races. This theme is of course quite justifiable on the stage.'[38] In the same year, Street described *Bongola*, a play set in South Africa, as 'a well-written object lesson of the harm of mixing white and black'. Cromer agreed that 'this sort of play may have its uses', and unhesitatingly confirmed that 'anything that helps towards discouraging marriage between black and white races is to the good of the human race generally'.[39] It was for the same reason that he licensed O'Neill's *All God's Children Got Wings*, described by Street in 1929 as 'a dreadful warning against a mixture of black and white in marriage'; Cromer explained that 'much as I detest the "black and white" theme, I agree there is no justifiable ground for interference in this play'.[40]

There are plenty of similar examples of plays in which messages we now recognise to have been deeply unpleasant and racist remained uncensored; however, though it is perhaps disappointing to find George Street's relative liberalism barely extending into such areas, it would be knocking at an open door to accuse Lord Cromer and his advisers of prejudice. They were largely reflecting the dominant ideological beliefs and fear about the 'contamination' of their own race, and could hardly be expected to escape the assumptions of their time. On the other hand, while the past may be another country where they do things differently, it borders and shapes our own; much that is still shocking about the attitudes of a previous generation is exposed by looking at these plays and the censors' responses to them. Even the boundaries between past and present cannot be clearly drawn; if theatre not only reflected contemporary attitudes and behaviour but helped to shape them—and the presumption that it did so was the whole basis for the continued existence of censorship—then there may be significant lessons to learn from examining such material and its reception. Probably there is more than one story to be read from the plays, for the extent to which the taboo of mixed-race relationships fascinated both playwrights and audiences is certainly striking; moreover, although some of the comments of the Lord Chamberlain's Office clearly reflect a tangible fear and a desperate need to discourage something which threatened the very spirit of the Empire and its colonial relationships, many of them also seem to embody a realisation that they were fighting a losing battle.

Popular plays dealing with mixed-race relationships were usually variations on a few stock narratives with generally offensive stereotypes; most obviously, these included the violent sexual assault on a white woman by a black man who is unable to control his animal instincts, and the white man working in a remote part of the Empire, who succumbs to heat, drink and the wiles of attractive native women. There is also a fairy-tale version with a happy ending, in which the object of white desire unexpectedly turns out to be European (or part-European), thus saving the play from suggesting the unacceptable. In *East is West*, for example, an American man is apparently in love with a Chinese woman, but it eventually transpires that she had been stolen from an American mission as a child, in an act of revenge against the Americans for converting Chinese children to Christianity. Street felt secure in recommending the play on those grounds:

It is found that she is the daughter of an eminent American and all is well. One is prepared for this throughout by her hating Chinese and taking to

American ways, praying secretly to a crucifix and so on, and this fact of course takes away any unpleasantness of racial intermixture.[41]

The so-called 'Arab sheik' was a particularly popular stage figure in the 1920s (as he was in film), generally seen trying to lure an innocent white woman into both a literal and a metaphorical desert. In versions where the woman is unable to prevent herself from finding her sheik attractive, he too will inevitably turn out to have a convenient secret. In *Love and the Sheik* in 1924, for example, Ahmed ben Hassan is finally revealed as the son of a British officer.[42] In the case of *Sheik of the Desert*, Street's report, which recommended the play for licence, identified a similar revelation:

> The story of a sheik carrying off an English woman to the desert and then eventually marrying her has formed the plot of more than one play, I think, already . . . This one . . . is much more agreeable than the others, being free from excessive 'passion' and violence and the heroine's virtue remaining intact. The sheik, Ahmed, is the son of an Englishman who deserted his mother.[43]

So sensitive was Cromer to any suggestion of sexual attraction across the races that he sometimes stipulated that the 'real' racial identity of a character should be made apparent to an audience throughout the play, rather than only emerging at the denouement when the characters discover it. Thus in the case of *The Sheik of Araby*, he insisted to the manager that he would issue a licence 'only on receiving a written undertaking from you that Sheik Ahmed, although dressed as an Arab, is to all appearances an Englishman and not of swarthy complexion'.[44] Similarly, in approving 'a sham-Eastern play' called *Sands of the Desert*, Street commented approvingly: 'I do not think this is any more objectionable than the Sheik Plays . . . the audience knows all the time that he is a white man'.[45] By contrast, an Arab without European parentage was generally either evil or pathetic. In 1929 the Lord Chamberlain agreed to license 'a lurid melodrama', *Sinister House*, only after 'an intrigue' between an Arab called Hassan and a white woman had been reduced to a kiss. In the revised version, Street reported that 'he now wants to marry Faith, not to make her his mistress, which makes it a little better'. Hassan was allowed to retain the hopeless desire and the helpless gaze, but these are the limits of his achievements, and he is duly shot dead by another Arab. 'The play is now merely a lurid melodrama and not worse than others which have been licensed', said Street.[46]

White men usually fell for the charms of black women in either the relatively idyllic world of the South Seas, or a nightmare vision of Africa derived from Conrad's *Heart of Darkness*. In *Man's Desire* in 1924, Sir Kenneth, a British spice merchant, 'sniffs at a "native" powder' and then dreams he is living with a half-Polynesian mistress on a remote island: 'Perhaps it is a pity he dreamed he was living with a Polynesian', commented Street, 'but it was only a dream'.[47] In 1929 in *Amoya*,

> Frank Granger arrives at Talao with correct ideas and denounces the concubinage of white and native . . . But Frank falls a victim to the charm of Amoya, a (supposed) native girl, beautiful and of light colour, and devoted to him.

Fortunately, Amoya turns out to be the daughter of the brother of the president of the company by a native princess, and, crucially, an audience could be expected to realise this: 'Amoya's birth, which the audience will probably guess early, removes something of the white-and-native unpleasantness'.[48] In 1925 a licence was refused for *Human Wreckage*, in which white men marooned on a remote island become sexually involved with local women; the following year, *Kongo*, a desperate melodrama full of intrigue, disease and violence, was rejected partly because of its excessive brutality, but also because there was 'far too much amorous business' between white and black characters.[49] In *Out East* in 1927, a white man in Burma 'succumbs to . . . a beautiful girl child of fourteen', but pays the price after his wife comes out from England to reclaim him; he discovers that the feelings of his mistress 'go deeper than the ordinary Burmese girls' when she shoots his wife and drowns herself. This was clearly a warning play and good propaganda, and Street thought it would be 'squeamish' to object; however, he did recommend that 'it should be impressed on the management that the girl must not be made too much a child'.[50] *The Leopard Men* in 1924 had a similar starting point and message; a white planter, who has been living in Nigeria, makes the mistake of bringing out his wife from home, and is himself viciously murdered (on-stage) by the native woman with whom he has been living. Such women are shown as uncontrollably dangerous and voracious in their passions, resembling wild animals; for the planter's body is found 'face deathly white, with four livid claw marks across one side of his face and the blood-stained handkerchief round his throat'. Somewhat optimistically, Cromer merely asked for 'a written undertaking that these scenes are played with discretion'.[51]

The successful and up-market theatrical model for many such dramas was *White Cargo*, a play by Leon Gordon which ran for two years in London's West End between 1924 and 1926 and which was subsequently made into a film. It was a controversial play which attracted so many protests that Cromer came to doubt the wisdom of having allowed it; but the protests were not about the offensively racist assumptions and language—so obvious to us—which pervade almost every line of the play, and which are never questioned. *White Cargo* was set amongst Europeans who, while managing a rubber plantation in tropical Africa, are trying to resist the evils with which prolonged absence from civilisation gradually tempts and seduces them:

WITZEL: Black bread is better than no bread at all. We all come to Mammy-palaver sooner or later.
MISSIONARY: Not all!
WITZEL: Pretty damn nearly . . . A man must have something.
MISSIONARY: Do you call taking one of these native women, something? Is there any fellowship of thought, any companionship of mind in such a union? These women have practically no mentality and they have no more reaction than automatons.
WITZEL: Well, beggars can't be choosers . . . Tondeleyo is the only really good looking nigger I've ever seen. She may be more than half white, but her skin and her instincts are all nigger.
MISSIONARY: The only concession she made to her French father are her features and her brain. She's a bad example to the natives and a menace to the whites. Tondeleyo is the worst kind of . . . harlot . . . What the others do through ignorance she does from sheer wantonness.[52]

Described by Street as a 'powerful study of the deterioration of a white man on the West coast of Africa', the narrative demonstrates how the upright values and morals of the white men are gradually sapped by the tropical climate and the sexual power of an irresistible, half-native prostitute; a new and upright arrival from Britain is shown degenerating to a point where he not only allows himself to be seduced by Tondeleyo, but—worse still—insists on marrying her. Inevitably, Tondeleyo proves to be interested in nothing but the material possessions he can provide, and has no intention of remaining faithful to him; she is not only sexually insatiable, but also expects and requires men to physically beat her. Incapable of understanding concepts such as marriage or loyalty, Tondeleyo attempts to poison her husband in order to be free of him, but is forced by another European to drink the poison herself, before disappearing, 'jabbering', into the bush.

Several local authorities refused to allow *White Cargo* to be performed in their theatres, and the visual images used to advertise performances were the subject of much complaint, and led to at least one police prosecution. However, it was not the racism itself which caused the protests, and the play's bigoted and xenophobic assumptions seem not to have been visible to the censors or to those who objected. The only significant concern of the Lord Chamberlain's Office was that the evil Tondeleyo, played of course by a white actress browned up, must not reveal too much flesh or behave so seductively that she tempted the audience. The management was required 'to increase the lady Tondeleyo's clothing, both at the waist and the hip', and to ensure that 'in the love making scene the lady be less demonstrative and does not paw her victim to the extent that she does at present'. All the subsequent protests (and the campaign against the play) centred on the dangers of her sexual attractiveness as an apparently non-white woman, and on the depiction of immorality and degeneration in a European.[53]

In 1924 a licence was refused for *Coloured Love*. As Street's report insisted:

> This is a disgusting play and I have no hesitation in advising the Lord Chamberlain to refuse a licence . . . The whole thing is clearly impossible, with its rape of a white woman by a black man and its general atmosphere of sexual business between white and black. It is altogether an affront to decent taste.

Cromer confirmed that 'under no consideration would I grant a licence for so revolting a theme'.[54] Again, it was not the construction of the black man as rapist that worried the censors. Five years later, Street described *The White Assegai* as 'an impressive play'; its central narrative showed how civil war is fostered between the good (loyal) and the bad (rebellious) natives in a British colony, largely because the selfish wife of the English governor forces him to betray his 'children' by threatening to divorce him unless he abandons his post and returns to England. The main themes, reported Street, were 'the devotion of a fine type of Englishman to his work among "natives" together with their devotion to him . . . and the harm done to this work by the wrong sort of English woman'. Only one element worried the censors—the sexual attack by a black servant on a white woman. Mrs Giles, the wife of the station-master, has just arrived in the country, and does not realise that her 'native boy' will be so 'inflamed' by seeing her in a dressing gown that he will be completely unable to control his animal instincts. The Reader commented:

> The only part of the play open to objection is the rape by a native of Mrs Giles . . . We only see the terrified woman running away and the man following and hear a scream and a moan. The author does not make it clear if we are to suppose the rape carried out or only attempted.

As usual, it was not the characterisation of the African that was considered offensive, but the very idea of mixed-race sex. Street thought it should be made clear that no intercourse actually takes place, and Cromer agreed:

> I attach much importance to this, as every Englishman would do who has lived among coloured races.
> There must be no 'low moaning' business and it must be made clear that no rape takes place.

Yet what is even more shocking to discover today is that rape of a white woman by a black man was potentially less disturbing and more acceptable than consensual sex: 'Personally I do not think the passage need be banned', wrote Street; 'it is not disgusting as it would be if the woman were willing'.[55]

Only desperation and the tropics could persuade a white man that a black woman was attractive, and no white woman could be shown willingly entering a sexual relationship with a non-white man—or even being attracted by him—unless he turned out to be half-European after all. There were, too, degrees of blackness. 'The pursuit of a white woman by an Arab is unpleasant', wrote Street in connection with one play, 'but . . . an Arab is not a nigger'.[56] Not for the first time, the boundary between sex and politics dissolves. In the struggle to hold the Empire together, the British political establishment was fearful about the possible effect of presenting images which suggested the sexual immorality and degeneracy of white society—especially since the new electronic performance media could broadcast images across the Empire itself. In 1926 *The Times* reported a speech made by the Prime Minister, Stanley Baldwin, to John Reith and the retiring directors of the BBC, in which he voiced his concern about the 'influence on civilization of the moving picture'; Baldwin declared that there was 'one aspect of it upon which I look with the gravest apprehension', namely, 'the effect of the commoner type of film, as representing the white races'. He explained what he meant:

> In my view the whole progress of civilization in this world is bound up with the capacity that the white races have, to help the races of the world to advance, and if their power to do that be impeded by false ideas of what the white races stand for, it may well be that their efforts will not only fail, but that the conception of the white races generated in the hearts of the coloured races throughout the world may be the initial step in the downfall of those white races.[57]

In the same year, the Bishop of London announced during a parliamentary debate on theatre censorship: 'I want to be able, in my tour of the Empire, to point to our stage as an example to the whole British Empire'.[58] If there were fears during the 1920s that an inherently superior blood-line was in danger of being diluted and destroyed by sexual promiscuity across the class divide, then concerns about the survival of the white race as a distinct and unsullied entity were equally prominent. It was vital, then, that ideas about race and sexuality were policed. Once again, in understanding the role of censorship, what is allowed—and by definition encouraged—is as important as what is banned. The weight of responsibility being placed on the theatre as an agent to help preserve the status quo was considerable.

A Gentler Process of Prevention

> We do not in this country deprive a class of citizens of their ordinary rights, we do not place their produce under the irresponsible control of one not amenable to Law, *by any sort of political accident!* That would indeed be to laugh at Justice in this Kingdom!.. We do, we *must* believe that a just and well-considered principle underlies this arbitrary Institution; for else it would not be suffered to survive for a single moment.[1]

This apparent apologia for theatre censorship was actually part of a satire by John Galsworthy, published in pamphlet form in 1909, with the intention of embarrassing and, perhaps, influencing the enquiry of the Joint Select Committee. In what pretended to be an anonymously authored text which had fallen into his hands by chance, Galsworthy's fictitious author confidently defines stage censorship as 'a bulwark for the preservation of average thought and sensibility', which is designed to keep 'the average citizen, happy in the groove within which his birth and associations have embedded him'. By comparing specific pairs of plays where one had been approved and the other refused a licence, Galsworthy sought to demonstrate the underlying ideological assumption about the role theatre was assigned and permitted to fulfil in contemporary society:

> the drama must entertain, and not instruct, must follow and not lead, and, conforming to the conventions and taste of the majority at the moment, in no sense attempt to be a moral renovator . . . the endeavour of the Censorship is to promote the pleasure, protect the feelings, and maintain unaltered the aesthetic and moral standards of our greater Public.

Galsworthy's imaginary advocate confidently concludes that the existing system, which has the advantage of not being 'hampered by the Law', is opposed only by those 'wedded pedantically to the liberty of the subject, or resentful of summary powers vested in a single person responsible only to his own conscience'.

The full title of Galsworthy's satire was *A Justification of the Censorship of*

Plays (Together with a Demand for the Extension of the Principle of that Office to Other Branches of the Public Service). It is particularly through the pamphlet's evangelical—yet essentially logical—demands that the same principles of censorship should be extended into other arts and beyond, that Galsworthy intends to shock his readers, and draw attention to the implications:

> If Censorship of the Drama be, as we have shown, in the real interests of the people . . . then Censorships of Art, Literature, Religion, Science, and Politics are in the interests of the people . . . it is time to urge the Legislature to provide these branches of the public service with those protecting Censorships which have too long been lacking.

In each case, he spells out the supposed advantages for humanity and society of imposing a similar system of censorship to that already applied to theatre; as, for example, with science:

> Had a judicious Censorship existed over our scientific matters, such as for the last two hundred years has existed over Drama, scientific works would have been no more disturbing and momentous than those which we are accustomed to see produced by our nicely pruned and tutored stage. For not only would the more dangerous and penetrating scientific truths have been carefully destroyed at birth, but scientists, aware that the results of investigations offensive to accepted notions would be suppressed, would long have ceased to waste their time in search of a knowledge repugnant to average intelligence, and have occupied themselves with services more agreeable to the public taste, such as the re-discovery of truths already known and published.[2]

Twenty years later, William Joynson Hicks, who as Home Secretary for much of the 1920s had been accused, he admitted, of trying 'to establish a dictatorship in the realm and literature of morals', published a real 'justification' of censorship, under the rhetorical title *Do We Need a Censor?*. Hicks described stage censorship as 'one of those curious factors in the English constitution, which are not founded on any logical position, but which work, as so many of our laws do, quite satisfactorily'. He based his justification on the argument that the government had both 'a general responsibility for the moral welfare of the community' and the duty 'of combating such dangers as threaten the safety or well-being of the State'. It would be, he warned, 'a bad day for the country when we cease in our legislation and administration to found ourselves on morality and to allow any and every form of filth to pollute the minds of the young unchecked'.[3] Hicks denied that there was any reason for taking into account the views of those on the receiving end of censorship; one hopes that his breathtaking assumption that to be accused of an offence apparently debarred the artist from arguing a defence did not extend into all his dealings as Home Secretary: 'I am not prepared to assent to any criminal or body of criminals deciding whether their own acts are, or are not, criminal', was his confident declaration in response to a statement made by the World League for Sexual Reform which had proposed that 'obscenity and impropriety are matters too subjective and indefinite to serve as a basis for laws'.[4]

Stage censorship, as Galsworthy understood, was a crucial strand within a system of ideological control, intended to preserve as far as possible the status quo. The individuals who carried out the requirements of the Office were not the issue; some may have been pleasanter, more lenient and more flexible than others, but they inevitably acted their roles within a system, the limitations of which they may have been barely able to conceive. Writing in the same year as Galsworthy, and with a similar purpose, the playwright Henry Arthur Jones mused on his personal knowledge of George Redford's predecessor as Examiner of Plays—an essentially 'liberal-minded, advanced man'—and asked how 'the easy, genial, broad, amiable, cultured Mr Pigott of private life' could turn into 'the narrow, suspicious, illiberal Mr Pigott the Censor'. Jones answered his own question: Pigott, he said, became 'the creature of his office'.[5] Similarly, it is evident that the Reader during the latter half of the period covered in this volume, George Street, was in many ways very broad-minded for his time; some of the Advisory Board—and even Lord Cromer—were far from the reactionary caricatures one might associate with censorship. Yet while they might have been more generous—at times significantly more generous—than many (including the government) would have had them, and while it is no doubt true that they liked to see themselves as licensers of plays rather than censors, they were inevitably powerful agents of repression. Indeed, the position of relative liberalism also became a way of preserving and prolonging their control, avoiding the head-on challenge which might have brought down the censorship. In a letter to the King in 1924, Cromer predicted that 'censorship will every year require more and more delicate handling'; he explained that 'the more articulate portion of the community' was generally 'hostile to censorship', and to ensure its survival, he concluded, it was necessary to tread with considerable care:

> All sensible minded people realise that a censorship in some form must continue to exist, but the fact remains that censorship, like most forms of restriction, is unpopular in the community and for that very reason can look for no support in the public Press which, for reasons of its own, has to remain on the popular side ... though its advocates may be numerous, they persistently remain inarticulate as far as open support is concerned ... If ever censorship were administered in too high-handed a manner, it might easily result in a popular clamour and a Press campaign for its complete abolition, which some governments might not feel willing to withstand.

Buckingham Palace described Cromer's memorandum as 'excellent',[6] and the way in which Cromer set out his plans to manipulate the owners of theatres and the licensees so that they, rather than he, would be seen as the censors of private play-producing societies typifies the deviousness with which the system maintained itself:

> Rather than imperil their licences, most of the licensees would be prepared to deal drastically with the private societies . . . but if on the other hand the Lord Chamberlain were to deal directly with the private Dramatic Societies, and to place an absolute veto on the production of any play that has not been licensed, I do not think it would be long before the whole question would be raised of revising the Censorship system in this country.[7]

Writing in 1913, Fowell and Palmer spelled out the specific ideological origins of stage censorship. The theatre censor, they said, had always served as 'a sort of bodyguard to Authority', and his primary 'duty was to see that the people were not indiscreetly encouraged from the stage to make faces at their rulers'. As if responding to Galsworthy's satirical call for the extension of a similar practice into other fields, they suggested that he had in the past been part of a much more elaborate system:

> The Censor was only one of a number of court policemen whose duty was to prevent the throwing of intellectual bombs . . . Anything tending to destroy or challenge the supremacy and authority of Church and State was ruthlessly eliminated. These were poisons the social body could not tolerate, and it promptly purged itself of them. [8]

It is beyond the scope of this book to consider how far it had become an isolated practice of control, and how far, and in what ways, censorship in those other fields remained significant. However, Fowell and Palmer also argued that the sphere of operation within which theatre censorship was exercised had become much wider in the first decade of the twentieth century than in previous eras. Certainly, as we have seen, it had become more devious, often attempting to hide itself. As Fowell and Palmer pointed out—and the evidence of the correspondence files certainly supports them—'it has been a frequent practice in the Lord Chamberlain's office to anticipate the presentation of a play by suggesting to the manager who is about to produce it that he had better not ask for a licence'.[9] For the same reason, it was the constant strategy of the Office to negotiate changes in scripts, so that a play appeared to be licensed and uncensored when it had in fact gone through a sometimes considerable degree of censorship and a long process. As Pigott had put it in the 1890s, 'it is in substituting for abrupt repression a gentler process of prevention that scandals are avoided'. This advice and strategy were quite consciously adopted and imitated by Pigott's successors—indeed, Pigott's long memorandum of policy was used as a Bible by those in the Office who were required to give evidence to the 1909 Committee. That being the case, it is also worth drawing attention to Pigott's almost Machiavellian suggestion that it might sometimes be a necessary and an effective tactic to license material which would normally be rejected, as a way of manipulating public attitudes :

> The public, no doubt, have sometimes thought that the Examiner's indulgence was carried too far; but I confess it has sometimes occurred to me that but for such occasional relaxations the public might be disposed to imagine that any restraint was uncalled for, and, indeed, that there was nothing to restrain.[10]

From that perspective, the criticisms of the Lord Chamberlain for sometimes allowing 'dubious' material to be performed take on a different dimension.

When a Noel Coward play was refused in 1926, Dawson declared that 'it was apropos of just this sort of play that, during my time in Paris, nice French people remarked to me—"Would that we had a Censor"'.[11] Whatever the truth and the implications surrounding this claim, the records do show that there was a number of diplomatic legations from other countries—as varied as, for example, Czechoslovakia and Peru—which sought specific advice from the Lord Chamberlain's Office during the 1920s on the principles and practice of stage censorship, and how to apply it. Conversely, one of the arguments frequently thrown against the censorship by the more advanced managers and producers—usually with little effect—was that Britain risked making itself a laughing stock by refusing plays which had been widely performed in other countries. Yet it was a more or less fundamental tenet of the censorship that the stage in Britain should have 'higher' standards than elsewhere, precisely as a manifestation of national superiority. As Cromer noted in 1930 in relation to one French play: 'In Berlin, Paris and possibly in New York such a play would be applauded and passed, but not in London I hope'.[12] In the same year, refusing to license a play which had proved popular and successful in the United States, he commented 'our views of what makes a suitable entertainment for the people differs from that held in America'.[13] More explicitly, when he refused to license Chicago, he insisted with complete confidence that 'British standards are higher than American in all things and it will be a sorry day for this country when these standards are not maintained'.[14]

Censorship is only necessary when it is believed that what is being censored has power—potential or actual. Throughout the period covered in this present volume, the British establishment—from the King downwards through Parliament and beyond—considered control of the stage to be crucial to the preservation of the moral and social values which they wished to maintain.

Pigott's warning and apprehension at the end of the nineteenth century retained its credit for a long time—longer, probably, than it deserved to. Plays, Pigott had insisted, were much more dangerous than the press, and therefore in much more need of tight control if the world was to stay largely unchanged:

> A theatrical representation enhanced by all the accessories of the stage, upon a mixed audience of a thousand or two thousand men and women of all classes, to be repeated for two or three hundred nights in succession, and at all the large towns throughout the kingdom. Here you have eyes and ears at once assailed . . . by living flesh and blood . . .[15]

Underlying the belief in censorship, then, was the assumption that people's behaviour and actions could be significantly changed by what they saw in the theatre. Writing in 1926, the theatre critic S.P.B. Mais had little doubt that decadent theatre was at least partly to blame for 'making slack our moral fibre' as a nation:

> The revolt against conventional morality has led many thoughtless and unstable people into a parlous morass, and there are a great number of weak wives and husbands who now have reason to curse the day when they allowed themselves to be influenced by what they saw on the stage or read in books. The subtle poison has worked its way into the very vitals of a great number of people who would never have been made restless or discontented had they avoided theatres and novels.

Criticising 'books and plays which definitely aim at ridiculing or undermining the moral code', Mais said it was crucial to know that there was 'a power waiting to pounce on those who go beyond the limits of decency'; with a strange mixture of nostalgia and naivety, he called on playwrights and novelists to 'paint life as it really is and show us that honour and chivalry are in reality no more dead than they ever were'.[16] In the House of Lords debate on theatre censorship in the same year, the Bishop of Southwark spoke of the need for effective control, 'because a large number of people drift into the theatre where they find the great broad issues of life hopelessly confused and evil presented in an attractive shape'. In the same debate, Lord Braye had no doubt about the importance of the theatre in shaping behaviour and society:

> The politics of a nation are the outcome of the ethics or morals of a nation, and if you bring up a nation inured to the sight of immoral things and to the hearing of immoral dialogues you cannot be surprised, when young people grow up, that they should have a very different idea of what their duty is to the State and to their own families from that which is sanctioned by Christian principles.

Developing the Bishop of London's protest that 'nobody wants these filthy plays to be given on the stage to do harm to boys and girls', Braye—in a claim which we may well find familiar from more recent debates on the control of other media—declared that plays led directly to crimes of imitation in real life: 'Boys have before now been brought up before the Courts for committing violence and they have said that they first learned the excitement of these doings by seeing plays', he declared. More specifically—and perhaps somewhat implausibly, given that he admitted that he never went to the theatre himself—Lord Braye suggested that boys were becoming so 'carried away with excitement' by plays which featured 'the heroic goings-on of highwaymen of the eighteenth century', that they were seeking to 'emulate these adventurous gentlemen' by turning 'to larceny and even to worse misdemeanours'.[17] Today, we probably resist the neatness of the equation; yet arguments about the extent to which susceptible members of an audience are liable to imitate behaviour they see enacted still continue. Van Druten, a playwright who was frustrated by the fact that important subjects could be treated lightly but not in serious drama, also acknowledged the problem:

> Actually, the reason which would probably be given for such a policy is that a serious or intellectual presentation of such subjects demands a corresponding degree of intelligence in the audience, and that what is all very well as nourishment for, let us say, the brain of University standard may well be too strong meat for Standard VIII. In other words, that it is protecting the mentally inefficient against subjects too advanced for them, as one might protect a child of ten against entering a class on the Criminal Law Amendments Acts.

Van Druten was driven to muse on the possible merits of introducing a two-tier system:

> One theatre, subject to censorship, where the audience could be thereby insured against having either their sensibilities shocked or their intellects assailed, and another where, free from censorship, they entered at their peril?

Interestingly, he acknowledged that, in effect, exactly such a system had 'indeed been partially attempted by the Sunday Societies and by such institutions in London as the Arts Theatre Club and the Gate Theatre Salon'.[18]

It is clear that one of the pressures on the censors to intervene and actively guard against controversial and disturbing material was the fact that the system within which they worked was presided over by a member of the King's household. The result of this structure was that any play which was licensed carried 'the *imprimatur* of the Lord Chamberlain', and therefore might be presumed to enjoy the support and even the endorsement of the monarch, and in effect of the British political establishment.[19] In 1909 the novelist and playwright Hall Caine told the government's Joint Select Committee that this system ensured that every play became in effect 'a national act, carrying a sort of national responsibility', as opposed to simply an 'individual act' expressing the views of an individual playwright.[20] In the 1926 House of Lords debate, Lord Morris's opening speech proposed that if 'objectionable' material was going to be presented on stage, then 'it would be far better to have no censor at all than the approval of a great officer of State'.[21] This fact was, indeed, fundamental to complaints by foreign embassies, governments and nationals about how their countries were shown on the stage. The choice of 1932 as the ending date for this volume excludes some of the most significant censorship of political theatre in an international context which emerged from 1933 onwards in relation to Hitler's accession to power and the rise of Nazism; that will form one of the key starting points for the second volume. But it is worth noting here that the banning of explicit or even implicit criticism of the Nazis was rooted in the fact that the German Embassy protested vociferously about such material, largely on the basis that anything expressed on the public stage was—*ipso facto*—a statement of official belief and policy.

Yet to have abolished the role of the Lord Chamberlain in relation to censorship would have been to detract from the power of the monarch. In 1909, when there seemed a real possibility of a Bill being passed which might have done this, the Lord Chamberlain—Lord Althorp—met the King's Private Secretary and then wrote to the Home Office: 'if the censor of plays were abolished', he warned them, 'a part, admittedly a small part, but still a part, of the Royal Prerogative would go too'.[22] It was for the same reason that the King carefully let it be known later that year that it would not be acceptable for the newly convened Advisory Board to have authority over the Lord Chamberlain. Power must stay at the top. So stage censorship was trapped in a circular double bind, where every script licensed, however dreadful, had the full endorsement of the King, but the system could not be changed because to do so would have undermined his authority.

From a modern perspective, it is not difficult to be alternately amused by the pettiness and appalled by the serious effects of the Lord Chamberlain's decisions. However, the assumption that the Lord Chamberlain's Office exerted rigid and godlike authority, or that its actions represented an absolute will to repress, is patently not supported by the evidence. The truth is much more complicated than that, and I have argued that the Office was itself under constant and not always resistible pressures from powerful and committed organisations and individuals. Its principles were conflicting rather than uniform, and sometimes surprisingly flexible in reflecting changing political, cultural and social climates. Arguably, the most fundamental and constant principle, which dictated policy and practice, was the institution's instinct for its own survival and perpetuation.

Meanwhile, I am painfully aware that at times—in the last chapter in particular—I found myself being drawn close not only to accepting that there may have been a need to control what was allowed on the stage, but even that in areas such as racial stereotyping the Lord Chamberlain should have listened more to those who complained. Again, if we consider the use of the female body in revues and living statuaries, the Public Morality Council may often seem absurd in its puritanism, but some of its concerns can be seen to imply a relatively radical critique of prevailing capitalist structures, in which the drive for profit and the rule of the market have transformed human beings into disposable fodder. The critic Hannen Swaffer argued that 'we should not need a Censor if all our managers were decent-minded men, which they are not. There has to be a Censor to keep them straight.'[23] In 1934 he wrote an open letter to the Bishop of London offering his support in the drive to clean up the stage. It is hard to argue with some of his perceptions about the exploitative relationships which too often prevailed:

> I see you are once again attacking what you call indecency on the stage. And once again, I see, managers pretend they do not know what you are talking about. Never mind what they say. They know very well.

Swaffer was not, he insisted, arguing against nudity *per se*, but against the way it was being used:

> What I object to is the cynical, leering way in which, for years, certain London managements have staged nudity not as Art but as Business. They have sometimes boasted to me that they have 'got it by' the Lord Chamberlain.

He went on to attack the 'smug hypocrisy' of those who conveniently argued that the victims were always in control of the situation and making their own choices:

> One newspaper I read seemed desirous of proving that the girls liked it! That is just bunk. Stage nudity persists because certain managers know that it causes talk. It is cheap advertisement. It saves money, not only in clothes, but in publicity . . . it is introduced into theatrical productions merely to cause a sensation and for no other reason.

Swaffer concluded:

> Censorship is wrong in theory. But, in practice, it stops those managers who, in a few years, would, without it, become mere merchandisers in muck . . . It is our job to put them out of business.[24]

We are back to Wilfred Coleby's 1913 satire, *The Censor*, where the disillusioned playwright complains bitterly to the entrepreneurial agents, whose goal is profit, about the state of contemporary theatre:

> The muck rake, that's what the public are after just now. Something that stirs up just what's got to be controlled and suppressed in chaps of my age, unless they want to go to the devil.[25]

Swaffer wrote: 'Although I object to censorship on principle, I find that, in practice, it works out very well'.[26] Was this a legitimate perspective? One obvious counter was the argument that it didn't work out very well at all, because the material which suffered censorship included some of the most serious and advanced work of important contemporary artists, while perhaps some of the more obviously exploitative productions found their place on the stage with relatively little difficulty. But to free the artist to experiment while restricting the businessman would have been impossible (and possibly invidious) even if there had been a political will to undertake this. Obviously, 'decent-minded' and 'exploitative' are not hard and fast categories, and their boundaries will depend almost entirely on who has the power to define them. The other argument against Swaffer's acceptance of the need for censorship was that there were other laws which could have helped limit or prevent exploitation in the theatre, and which would have remained fully available even if the specific law on stage censorship had been repealed. After all, all laws are, in effect, a form of censorship—as Joynson Hicks explicitly argued, when attempting to explain the incontrovertible justification for censorship:

> It is as much a crime against the community to commit an act of public indecency as to commit a theft, and exactly in the same way as the Government of the day is a censor of burglars, so it is a censor of those who offend against the Acts of Parliament . . . It is according to common law, that is, law without any statute, that the conscience of mankind deems it a felony to commit a murder, and that it is a misdemeanour to publish any indecent matter tending to the destruction of the morals of society and to deprave and corrupt those whose minds are open to immoral influence. No man has any more right to publish in this country matter which tends to the destruction of morals than he has to commit any other crime.[27]

This book has focused primarily (and, I think, justifiably) on powers exerted by and through the Lord Chamberlain's Office. But I have also argued that the practice of theatre censorship also had a very active life beyond St James's Palace. In 1927 the Home Office carried out a survey designed to allow it to consider how different parts of the country exerted control over what went on in their theatres; while the licence of the Lord Chamberlain was an important element, it was by no means the be-all and end-all of that control, as the resulting report showed:

> In certain towns particular care is taken to ensure that there is no impropriety in the performances. In Birmingham a Superintendent of Police visits on Monday in each week and three women inspectors report as to the nature of the performance, the conduct of the house and the provision for the comfort and convenience of the audience and the artists . . . At Leeds Superintendent or Inspectors of Police visit one day a week usually the first day of the performance . . . the theatres are supervised at Manchester by experienced Police Officers in plain clothes who specialise in this class of work. They visit twice a week or oftener if necessary. A licensed script is demanded when objectionable passages are noticed . . .
>
> At Huddersfield, the Chief Inspector of Police, three or four members of the Force and a woman police assistant or one or more of them visit once a week; at Northampton the Police visit generally . . . the Chief Inspector of Police is responsible at Walsall but the patrol inspectors and police women visit almost nightly.
>
> Members of the Watch Committee visit at Leicester in order to satisfy themselves that the performance is unobjectionable and at Bury the Watch Committee all have passes. Magistrates visit at Halifax if there is any suspicion that the performance is of a doubtful character . . . The police visit daily at Wigan and once a week at Blackburn, Darlington, Dudley, Great Yarmouth, Norwich, Portsmouth, Preston and Sunderland. Senior Officers of the Police visit weekly at Dewsbury and Sheffield . . . The Authorities of 25 towns merely say that regular inspections are carried out by the police . . . at Birkenhead, Gateshead, Liverpool, Middlesbrough, Wallasey and Wigan children under fourteen are prohibited from entering a theatre at any time unless accompanied by parents or guardians . . . at Blackburn they are prohibited from entering after six thirty p.m. and at Carlisle after 9.00 p.m . . . . Carlisle prohibits children under six from entering a theatre and Sunderland prohibits children under seven unless in charge of a person over fourteen . . .[28]

Such diversity of practice in a cross-section of towns and cities not only indicates some of the control which existed separately from the Lord Chamberlain, but also hints at the pressures which must have been faced by touring companies—pressures which would clearly have been exacerbated if their relative authority and status had been increased. Moreover, it suggests that if the Lord Chamberlain's powers had been abolished, it is possible that the immediate effect would have been to usher in more extreme repression, and probable that the practice of censorship would have become even more inconsistent. Partly this would have depended on the nature of any system superseding the Lord Chamberlain, but the evidence suggests that in some areas (by which I mean both geographical and ideological) the censorship would have become more severe. Perhaps this would have provoked more conflicts and revolutions against an unsustainable system—it is pointless to speculate too far—but one must at least acknowledge that if the role of censor had passed to the Home Office, or if the principle and apparatus of centralised licensing had been dismantled, the outcome would not have been a panacea for progressive writers or directors.

Yet it is undeniable that the restrictive and repressive practices employed in this country against imaginative and intelligent writers and artists severely damaged the development of British theatre. Even now, we may be living with some of the consequences. Had the centralised requirement for licensing for public performances been dismantled, then at least the more adventurous and determined managers—Granville Barker, Terence Gray, Peter Godfrey and Gertrude Kingston, for example—would have been free to take risks and invite the authorities to prosecute them under other laws.

Finally, we might wonder how far the Lord Chamberlain's Office—or even those who exerted pressure on that Office—should actually be seen as little more than extreme manifestations of a deeper and more pervasive cultural instinct, inhabiting and inhibiting the British psyche. During the period covered in this volume, there is a recurring argument—voiced by those who felt crushed by its weight—that Britain lived in a culture of repression, revelling in its peculiar national mindset. Terence Gray complained about 'the tinpot censors and moralists' who were exerting 'a moral stranglehold on the healthy instincts of the English people'; but he believed that the fundamental problem lay not with those who created or sought to impose and maintain the taboos—the 'block-heads, puritans, boot-faces and boll-weevils'—but rather with the willingness of the majority to honour and respect them. There was, he avowed, 'no law or regulation so fatuous or so ludicrous, so flagrantly stupid, unjust, idiotic, degrading or contemptible that every Englishman will not bow down to it and obey it without a murmur'. Thomas Beecham said something similar, when he described the system of theatre censorship as 'one of our most characteristic institutions', and again suggested that it was the willingness to endure—and even embrace—the imposition of control which was remarkable: 'to the average Englishman there clings a vestige of the old Adamic taint that stands in need of constant repression', he suggested. Gray called for 'a revival of the spirit of rebellion in the English people', but Beecham identified an innate resistance in the national character to challenging tradition:

> In most countries when a custom outwears its use it is abolished; with us hardly ever, even though it be quite obsolete or has long been crying out for reform. But no one can do anything about it, for a mysterious force,

almost an occult influence, creeps insidiously through the body politic and social to head us away from the folly and danger of change . . . nor does it matter in the least that our conservatism is not only an inconvenience to ourselves but the object of ridicule to others . . . abuses or absurdities that would make some nations blush for shame and others rush to the barricades we endure cheerfully for the sole reason that they are our own, just as indulgent parents delight to protect the weakly among their offspring.[29]

Equally telling, perhaps, was the argument that it was actually the attitude to theatre which lay at the heart of the problem. 'The ease with which an audience can be collectively shocked in the theatre by things which would in no way shock each individual member in real life is quite extraordinary', wrote John Van Druten; while bemoaning the crippling effect on playwrights of 'an audience's distaste for serious drama', he made a crucial distinction:

> I would suggest that the censorship itself is hardly to blame. It makes an honest attempt to keep the theatre in line with general public opinion— not public opinion on the matters which are discussed or portrayed, but public opinion on the amount of licence which the theatre-going public is prepared to tolerate in the *stage* discussion or portrayal of those matters.

What was needed, he said, was 'some means of altering the attitude of the public towards the theatre', for censorship was as much the function as the cause—'the mouthpiece of that attitude'.[30]

'Nothing does so much good as a good play', affirmed the Bishop of London in 1926.[31] That statement, positive in itself, is the other side of the same coin which makes censorship logical; for the Bishop doubtless intended his audience to understand, also, that nothing does so much harm as a bad play. One obvious way of reading the story of the changing role of the Lord Chamberlain as censor of the stage in the twentieth century is as a reflection of the declining importance of the medium of theatre, in terms of its perceived relevance to, or capacity to influence, society. I began by drawing attention to the claim by an MP at the start of the century that 'multitudes of young men and young women form their ideas of what is right and wrong in no small degree from what they witness on the stage'.[32] Such an assumption informs many of the debates and decisions on censorship which have been referred to in this book. It is harder, however, to think that such a claim would find much of an echo in the 1968 debate, which would culminate in the abolition of the Lord Chamberlain's responsibility to decide what could and could not be performed in public. It could therefore be argued that the dismantling of this particular apparatus of control was allowed to take place once the stage itself was no longer seen to matter. That is a thesis to which the second volume of this history will return.

Notes

Note on Archive Referencing

There are two separate archives in the British Library Manuscript Collections on which I have drawn substantially and which are referenced; both come under the general heading: 'The Play Collection'.

The texts of plays submitted for licensing between 1900 and 1968 are referenced here as LCP (Lord Chamberlain's Plays) followed by the year and box number. This is the referencing system used within the archive and its index.

The material in the Lord Chamberlain's Correspondence Files 1900–1968 is also referenced here as in the archive, using the abbreviation LCP CORR to indicate the archive.

Material relating to plays which were licenced is filed separately from that related to plays which were refused licences. In the case of a *licensed play*, LCP CORR is followed by the year under which it is filed, the file number and the title of the play. For an *unlicensed play*, LCP CORR is followed by the title of the play, LR (indicating 'Licence Refused') and a year. There is also correspondence relating to plays which were neither licensed nor refused. These are known as 'Waiting Box Plays'. To reference these, LCP CORR is followed by the title of the play, WB (indicating 'Waiting Box') and a year.

In addition to the above, in June 2001 a further extensive collection of theatre files from the Lord Chamberlain's Office was deposited with the British Library. As yet, these have not been catalogued, but the collection is identified under the title 'Lord Chamberlain's Office Files, transferred from the Royal Archives at Windsor to the British Library, June 2001, not catalogued'. Within these Notes, extracts from these files are referenced as LCO Theatre Files, not catalogued.

Occasionally, I also cite the Lord Chamberlain's Daybooks. These are the Register which were kept in the Lord Chamberlain's Office to record basic details of plays submitted, but they sometimes contain notes or comments as well. The Daybooks are also part of the archive in the British Library Manuscript Collections.

Introduction

1   Terence Gray writing in *The Festival Theatre Review*, 55, February 1929, p. 9, after the refusal to grant a licence for Toller's *Hoppla!*
2   Terence Gray writing in *The Festival Theatre Review*, 83, October 1931, p. 8, after the refusal to license either *Man and His Phantoms* or *The Eater of Dreams*, both by the French playwright Lenormand.
3   Reported in *The Times*, 17 October 1910, p. 6.
4   Board of Education, Adult Education Committee, *The Drama in Adult Education* (London: HMSO, 1926), p. 199.
5   Lord Cromer made this observation in September 1930 in relation to *Warren Hastings*, written by Feuchtwanger and licensed for the Festival Theatre, Cambridge. See LCP CORR: 1930/9919 *Warren Hastings*.
6   *Report from the Joint Select Committee of the House of Lords and the House of Commons on the Stage Plays (Censorship) Together with the Proceedings of the Committee, Minutes and Appendices* (London: Government Publication, 1909), p. 50.

7   Dan Rebellato, *1956 And All That* (London: Routledge, 1999), p. 188, discussing the report of Ronald (Rebellato calls him Rudolf) Hill, a member of the Lord Chamberlain's Office, who had been sent to view *We're No Ladies*. Hill commented on both the reactions and the perceived sexual inclination of the audience, and Rebellato argues that 'Neither the Lord Chamberlain's jurisdiction nor Hill's brief covered audience behaviour'.

8   *Report from the Joint Select Committee*, p. 190.

9   On 18 August 1909, the Lord Chamberlain wrote to the Prime Minister: 'My dear Asquith, Ponsonby writes to me from Marienbad by the King's desire on the subject of the Joint Committee on the Censorship. I copy the passages which I think you should know.' Dawson's evidence to the Joint Select Committee of Enquiry in August drew on this advice—see memoranda in the LCO Theatre Files, not catalogued.

10 From a memorandum by Pigott dated 15 March 1883, sent by Redford to the Comptroller in November 1907 and described by the Lord Chamberlain on that occasion as 'excellent and most interesting'. A number of Dawson's statements to the 1909 Committee of Enquiry draw very closely on Pigott's statements. See LCO Theatre Files, not catalogued.

11 From the report of a meeting which took place on 7 March 1903. LCO Theatre Files, not catalogued. Cunynghame was Under Secretary of State at the Home Office.

12 See correspondence between the Public Morality Council and the Lord Chamberlain, December 1926 in LCO Theatre Files, not catalogued.

13 Debate on Stage Plays in the House of Commons, 16 April 1913. *See Parliamentary Debates (Official Report), Volume LI, House of Commons, 31 March 1913–18 April 1913* (London: HMSO, 1913), column 2062.

14 The Chief Constable's letter to the Lord Chamberlain on 2 April 1931 was written in connection with a performance by Max Miller. See LCP CORRS: 1931/10,243: *Merrie Tales*.

15 Henry Arthur Jones, *The Censorship Muddle and a Way Out of It* (London: Samuel French, 1909), p. 43.

16 See LCP CORR: *Dingo* WB (1964). The play, written by Charles Wood, was submitted by Tynan and Olivier for the National Theatre at the Old Vic in December 1964.

17 *Enslaved by the Mormons* was written by Frederick H.U. Bowman, a playwright whose supposed excesses and penchant for melodramatic violence caused frequent problems and disgust in the Lord Chamberlain's Office. This play was licensed in May 1913 for performance at Kelly's Theatre, Liverpool, and on tour. See LCP CORR: 1913/1720: *Enslaved by the Mormons*.

18 G. Bernard Shaw, 'The Censorship of the Stage in England', *North American Review*, 169, 1899, pp. 251–262.

19 See LCO Theatre Files, not catalogued.

20 John Russell Stephens, *The Censorship of English Drama 1824–1901* (Cambridge: Cambridge University Press, 1980), p. 1.

21 John Allan Florance, 'Theatrical Censorship in Britain: 1901–1968', unpublished Ph.D. thesis, University of Wales, 1980.

22 Anne Etienne, 'Les Coulisses du Lord Chamberlain: La Censure Théâtrale de 1900 à 1968', unpublished Ph.D. thesis, L'Université d'Orleans, 1999.

23 Richard Findlater, *Banned!: A Review of Theatrical Censorship in Britain* (London: MacGibbon & Kee, 1967).

24 John Johnston, *The Lord Chamberlain's Blue Pencil* (London: Hodder & Stoughton, 1990).

25 Nicholas de Jongh, *Not in Front of the Audience: Homosexuality on Stage* (London: Routledge, 1992) and *Politics, Prudery and Perversions: The Censoring of the English Stage 1901–1968* (London: Methuen, 2000).

26 L.W. Conolly, *The Censorship of English Drama 1737–1824* (San Marino, California: Huntington Library, 1976).

27 Letter from Lord Cromer to Laurence Housman, 23 September 1922. See LCP CORR: *The Queen's Progress* LR (1932).

28 Internal note by Lord Cromer, 4 January 1926. See LCP CORR: *Cradle Snatchers* LR (1926). It seems the script was subsequently licensed in a revised form as *Sauce for the Gander*.

29 Stephens, *Censorship*, p. 155.

30 *The Censor* by Wilfred T. Coleby was performed at the Haymarket theatre in 1913. Extracts taken from unpublished manuscript in LCP 1913/2140.

Chapter 1

1 G.B. Shaw, 'Impressions of the Theatre', *Review of Reviews*, 32: 190, October 1905.
2 See *The Times*, 16 May 1900, p. 9. The speech was also published as a pamphlet: Samuel Smith, *Plays and Their Supervision: A Speech made by Samuel Smith Esq., MP in the House of Commons May 15th 1900, and the Reply of the Home Secretary* (London: Chas. J. Thynne, 1900).
3 From the report in *The Times*, 16 May 1900, p. 9.
4 'A Plea to Keep our Theatres Clean' was the headline of a leader column in the *Daily Express*, 14 October 1904, p. 4, which attacked the licensing of Pinero's *A Wife Without A Smile*.
5 See Smith, *Plays and Their Supervision*.
6 This was Sir Douglas Dawson's claim when the discrepancy between the wording of the official Statute and the endorsement habitually included on the licence was pointed out to him. See *Report from the Joint Select Committee of the House of Lords and the House of Commons on the Stage Plays (Censorship) Together with the Proceedings of the Committee, Minutes and Appendices* (London: Government Publication, 1909), p. 47.
7 G.B. Shaw, 'The Censorship of the Stage in England', *North American Review*, 169, 1899, pp. 251–262.
8 *The Times*, 29 October 1907, p. 15.
9 Anuual Report of the Public Morality Council for 1907, dated 31 December 1907.
10 E.F.S. [Edward Fordham Spence], *Our Stage and its Critics* (London: Methuen & Co., 1910), p. 160.
11 First performed at Wyndham's Theatre in October 1904. The script was published as Arthur Wing Pinero, *A Wife Without a Smile* (London: Chiswick Press, 1904).
12 'The Dirty Drama' in *The Free Lance*, 22 October 1904, pp. 9–10.
13 LCP CORR: 1904/388: *A Wife Without A Smile*.
14 Redford's letter is dated 19 October 1904. See LCP CORR: 1904/388: *A Wife Without A Smile*.
15 An internal memorandum written by Sir Douglas Dawson on 6 February 1912 noted that the Lord Chamberlain 'remembers having a conversation with King Edward' in which this view was expressed. See LCP CORR: 1914/2840: *Monna Vanna*.
16 Reader's Report on *Monna Vanna* by Ernest Bendall, 12 July 1913. See LCO Theatre Files, not catalogued.
17 *The Era*, 21 June 1902, page 17.
18 Shaw, 'Impressions of the Theatre'.
19 E.F.S., *Our Stage and its Critics*, p. 157.
20 E.F.S., *Our Stage and its Critics*, pp. 161–162.
21 *Report from the Joint Select Committee*, p. 73.
22 See LCP CORR: 1909/494: *L'Assommoir*.
23 Internal memorandum from Dawson to the Lord Chamberlain, 17 June 1909. See LCP CORR: 1909/494: *L'Assommoir*.
24 Shaw, 'Impressions of the Theatre'.
25 'The Incorrigible Censor', *The Nation*, 29 May 1909, pp. 310–311.
26 See Edward Garnett, *A Censured Play. 'The Breaking Point'. With Preface and a Letter to the Censor* (London: Duckworth & Co., 1907).
27 See 'Granville Barker on the Censor', *The Sketch*, 23 October 1907, p. 36.
28 Barker was detailing his experience of the censorship of *Waste* to the Joint Select Committee's enquiry of 1909. See *Report from the Joint Select Committee*, p. 37.
29 The comment that '*Waste* has wasted me' was made in a letter to Gilbert Murray; cited in Dennis Kennedy, *Granville Barker and the Dream of Theatre* (Cambridge: Cambridge University Press, 1985), p. 92. For the use of the phrase 'Dry Nurse' to describe the Lord Chamberlain see 'The Theatre: The Next Phase': a lecture given by Granville Barker on 9 June 1910', published in H.G. Barker, *Offprints of Contributions by Granville-Barker to Various Publications* (London: publisher unknown, 1910). For the other remarks quoted here, see *Report from the Joint Select Committee*, pp. 36–37.
30 From the report of a meeting which took place between Cunynghame, who was Under Secretary of State at the Home Office, and senior staff in the Lord Chamberlain's Office on 7 March 1903. See LCO Theatre Files, not catalogued.
31 See LCO Theatre Files, not catalogued. The letter was not made public or published in the proceedings of the Joint Select Committee.
32 The disparaging reference is in a letter from Redford to the Lord Chamberlain in June 1909,

responding to criticisms of the lack of a written or transparent code in the practice of censorship expressed in a letter to *The Times* by Granville Barker. See LCO Theatre Files, not catalogued.

33 *Report from the Joint Select Committee*, p. 26.

34 *Report from the Joint Select Committee*, p. 13.

35 See *The Lord Chamberlain's Daybook* for 1907.

36 Licensed for performance at Drury Lane Theatre, September 1903.

37 Cecil Raleigh, 'The Rag and the Gag', *Daily Mail*, 30 September 1903. See also LCP CORR: 1903/350: *Flood Tide*.

38 Extracts taken from unpublished manuscript of *Flood Tide* in LCP 1903/22.

39 See Frank Fowell and Frank Palmer, *Censorship in England* (London: Frank Palmer, 1913), pp. 229–230.

40 LCP CORR: 1903/350: *Flood Tide*.

41 Raleigh, 'The Rag and the Gag'.

42 *Daily Mail*, 1 October 1903, p. 4.

43 He had another confrontation over a music-hall sketch dealing with the secret marriage between the future George III and a commoner, Hannah Lightfoot. Again, it was the King who insisted absolutely that such a theme should not be licensed, and the Office stonewalled a series of increasingly outraged and provocative letters from Raleigh in which he reasonably demanded to know why this one sketch should be singled out for special attention when a blind eye was being turned to everything else performed in music-halls. See LCO Theatre Files, not catalogued.

44 LCP CORR: 1908/190: *The Woman of Kronstadt*. Based on a novel by Max Pemberton published in 1898, the stage adaptation was credited to Pemberton and 'George Fleming' (Constance Fletcher), and licensed for the Garrick Theatre in January 1908.

45 When asked in a letter from the secretary to the Joint Select Committee of 1909 to comment on the suppression of this play, Dawson originally replied on 11 October 1909 that it had been licensed in 1896 and remained free for performance since then. He subsequently corrected this in a second letter, adding that it was now licensed under the title *Secrets*. See LCO Theatre Files, not catalogued.

46 Extract from unpublished manuscript of *An Englishman's Home* by Guy du Maurier, in LCP 1908/28.

47 LCP CORR: 1908/184: *An Englishman's Home*. The play opened at Wyndham's Theatre in January 1909.

48 From unpublished manuscript of *Mr Turnbull's Nightmare* in LCP 1909/5. Written by the MP Mark Sykes, it was licensed for performance in March 1909.

49 See LCP CORR: 1909/333: *Mr Turnbull's Nightmare*.

50 In 1909 Dawson apparently submitted this letter, dated 13 March 1895, as evidence to the Joint Select Committee enquiry that the Reader had been issued with clear procedural instructions. He also submitted at the same time a letter from himself to Redford dated 28 June 1909—just a month before the Enquiry began hearing evidence—instructing the Reader that:

> The Lord Chamberlain wishes you, whenever matter of any nature contravening his Regulations, appears in a Play submitted for your examination, to interview the Manager of the Theatre concerned and thus, if possible, ensure that the objectionable matter is eliminated without friction or further discussion.
>
> In submitting a Play which has been thus dealt with, the Lord Chamberlain would like <u>always</u> to be told of what has passed on the subject, previous to the alterations, which, in your opinion, have rendered the Play eligible for Licence.
>
> Should your personal interview with the Manager prove abortive, in other words should the objection you see to the Play be likely to produce a deadlock in the negotiations the Lord Chamberlain wishes you at once to inform him.

See LCO Theatre Files, not catalogued.

51 LCP CORR: 1909/385: *The Devil*. The play was adapted by Henry Hamilton from Molnár's *Az Ördög*, and opened at the Adelphi in April 1909.

52 From unpublished manuscript of *The Devil* in LCP 1909/8.

53 The exchange of letters took place in April 1909. See LCP CORR: 1909/385: *The Devil*.

54 *The Proud Prince* by Justin Huntly McCarty had been licensed for the Vaudeville Theatre in 1903. The correspondence between Dawson and Althorp occurred in September 1909—see LCP CORR: 1903/340: *The Proud Prince*.

55 In her detailed analysis of the censorship of this play, Anne Etienne suggests the possibility of a conscious identification by Shaw of himself with the character of Blanco, and explores the effect of substituting the words 'Lord Chamberlain' for 'God' in certain passages. See Etienne, 'Les Coulisses du Lord Chamberlain: La Censure Théâtrale de 1900 à 1968', unpublished Ph.D. thesis, L'Université d'Orleans, 1999, pp. 121–129. See also LCP CORR: 1909/22, and 1916/91: *The Shewing Up of Blanco Posnet*.

56 *Report from the Joint Select Committee*, p. 73.

57 Stanley Weintraub (ed.), *Shaw: An Autobiography,1898–1950: The Playwright Years, Selected from his Writings by Stanley Weintraub* (London: Reinhardt, 1971) , p. 61.

58 *The Times*, 24 May 1909, p. 12.

59 Letter from Shaw to *The Times*, 26 June 1909, p. 10, published under the headline: 'The Censor's Revenge'.

60 Letter from Redford to Althorp, 27 June 1909. See LCP CORR: 1909/80: *Press Cuttings*.

61 Redford's memorandum of 10 August 1909 explained that the revised script now submitted for licensing was accompanied by 'a note in the handwriting of the author' to this effect. See LCP CORR: 1909/80: *Press Cuttings*.

62 Memo from Dawson to Althorp, 17 June 1909, LCP CORR: 1909/494: *l'Assommoir*.

63 *The Times*, 29 October 1907, p. 15.

Chapter 2

1   From Max Beerbohm's assessment of the report on theatre censorship by the 1909 Joint Select Committee of Enquiry. See the *Saturday Review* 20 November 1909, pp. 625–626.

2   See the official terms of reference as they appear on the title page of the *Report from the Joint Select Committee of the House of Lords and the House of Commons on the Stage Plays (Censorship) together with the Proceedings of the Committee, Minutes and Appendices* (London: Government Publication, 1909).

3   Dawson's letter of 25 September 1909. See LCO Theatre Files, not catalogued.

4   Althorp's letter of 20 June 1909, describing the situation as 'pretty hopeless'. See LCO Theatre Files, not catalogued.

5   *Report from the Joint Select Committee*, p. 188.

6   *Report from the Joint Select Committee*, p. 96.

7   Evidence of W.F. Fladgate, solicitor to the Society of West End Theatre Managers. See *Report from the Joint Select Committee*, p. 28.

8   *Report from the Joint Select Committee*, p. 174.

9   Correspondence between Dawson and Fladgate of July 1909. See LCO Theatre Files, not catalogued.

10 Mr W.P. Byrne. See *Report from the Joint Select Committee*, p. 11.

11 Mr Oswald Stoll. See *Report from the Joint Select Committee*, p. 146.

12 See LCO Theatre Files, not catalogued.

13 *Report from the Joint Select Committee*, p. 195.

14 *Report from the Joint Select Committee*, pp. 44–47.

15 Letter from Redford to the Lord Chamberlain, June 1909. See LCO Theatre Files, not catalogued.

16 This view was expressed by W.L. Courtney, a writer who had been responsible for a recent adaptation of *Oedipus Rex* which had been refused a licence. See *Report from the Joint Select Committee*, p. 88.

17 See *Report from the Joint Select Committee*, p. 21.

18 See *Report from the Joint Select Committee*, p. 64.

19 *Report from the Joint Select Committee*, p. 176.

20 See *Report from the Joint Select Committee*, pp. 129–133. Carr argued that licences should be issued to playwrights rather than to managers.

21 *Report from the Joint Select Committee*, pp. 101–102.

22 See *Report from the Joint Select Committee*, pp. 122–123. George Edwardes was an experienced theatre manager specialising in musicals.

23 *Report from the Joint Select Committee*, p. 51.

24 Letter from Dawson to Byrne, 17 November 1913. See LCO Theatre Files, not catalogued. Dawson claimed in his letter that 'The truth is the whole system of theatre and music-hall management and censorship of plays is working admirably and no redress of grievance is required, because there is only an imaginary grievance on the part of the authors and no-one else'.

25 See *Report from the Joint Select Committee*, p. 203.
26 *Report from the Joint Select Committee*, p. 25.
27 *Report from the Joint Select Committee*, pp. 21–22.
28 *Report from the Joint Select Committee*, p. 67.
29 *Report from the Joint Select Committee*, p. 72.
30 From an article in the *Daily Express*, 14 October 1904, p. 4.
31 *Report from the Joint Select Committee*, p. 174.
32 *Report from the Joint Select Committee*, p. 111.
33 *Report from the Joint Select Committee*, p. 158.
34 *Report from the Joint Select Committee*, p. 97.
35 *Report from the Joint Select Committee*, pp. 138–139.
36 *Report from the Joint Select Committee*, p. 146.
37 *Report from the Joint Select Committee*, p. 106.
38 Grein was writing in relation to Granville Barker's *Waste* in the *Sunday Times* 1 December 1907.
39 *Report from the Joint Select Committee*, p. 78.
40 *Report from the Joint Select Committee*, p. 138.
41 *Report from the Joint Select Committee*, p. 97.
42 *Report from the Joint Select Committee*, pp. 75 and 139.
43 *Report from the Joint Select Committee*, pp. 100–104.
44 The playwright Henry Arthur Jones declined an invitation to give evidence to the Committee, but submitted a pamphlet. See *Report from the Joint Select Committee*, p. 199.
45 *Report from the Joint Select Committee*, p. 188.
46 *Report from the Joint Select Committee*, p. 12.
47 *The Stage* reporting on proceedings, 12 August 1909.
48 Unsigned memorandum from the Home Office of 9 August 1909. The writer also pointed out that 'it would be open to the Lord Chamberlain to take proceedings if he thought necessary under section 14 of the Act of 1843'. See LCO Theatre Files, not catalogued.
49 'The Theatre: The Next Phase': a lecture given by Granville Barker on 9 June 1910, published in H.G. Barker, *Offprints of Contributions by Granville-Barker to Various Publications* (London: publisher unknown, 1910).
50 *Report from the Joint Select Committee*, p. 23.
51 Hall Caine; see *Report from the Joint Select Committee*, p. 160.
52 *Report from the Joint Select Committee*, p. 75.
53 *Report from the Joint Select Committee*, p. 18.
54 See Laurence Housman, *The Unexpected Years* (London: Jonathan Cape, 1937), p. 191.
55 *Report from the Joint Select Committee*, p. 18.
56 *Report from the Joint Select Committee*, pp. 188–192.
57 All quotations taken from the conclusions of the *Report from the Joint Select Committee*, pp. 185–195.
58 Undated and unsigned internal memorandum in the Office of the Lord Chamberlain, which recommended 'no drastic change'. See LCO Theatre Files, not catalogued.
59 Private letter from Dawson to Althorp, 14 June 1909. See LCO Theatre Files, not catalogued.
60 Private letter from Althorp to Asquith, 20 June 1909. See LCO Theatre Files, not catalogued.
61 From Carr's undated reply to Dawson's letter of 30 July 1909. See LCO Theatre Files, not catalogued.
62 *Report from the Joint Select Committee*, p. 138.
63 Private letter from Althorp to Asquith, 18 August 1909. See LCO Theatre Files, not catalogued.
64 Private letter from the King's Private Secretary, Stamfordham, to the Lord Chamberlain, 10 January 1910. See LCO Theatre Files, not catalogued.
65 Undated private letter from Redford to Althorp, June 1909. See LCO Theatre Files, not catalogued.
66 *The Stage*, 12 August 1909.
67 *Report from the Joint Select Committee*, p. 137.
68 *Report from the Joint Select Committee*. Redford's evidence is pp. 11–21; Dawson's is pp. 41–50.
69 Correspondence July 1909. See LCO Theatre Files, not catalogued.

70   *Report from the Joint Select Committee*, pp. 11–12.
71   Private letter from Althorp to Higgins, 31 October 1908. See LCP CORR: 1908/119: *Samson et Delilah*. The opera by Saint-Saens and Ferdinand Lemaire was licensed for performances at Covent Garden in April 1909.
72   *Report from the Joint Select Committee*, p. 17.
73   *Report from the Joint Select Committee*, p. 46.
74   Telegram from Althorp to Redford, 24 February 1909. Redford actually completed the licence form for the sketch, a burlesque on *The Englishman's Home*, but Dawson informed him that this was being cancelled. It was then apparently scheduled for performance as part of an evening of entertainment at the Apollo Theatre by the Follies Company. However, an MP wrote from the House of Commons to the Home Office on 1 March 1909 to ask why this was being permitted. After a discreet phone call from the Lord Chamberlain's Office, on 26 February 1909, London County Council contacted all music-halls under their control to say they would 'view with displeasure the production of such a stage play in any music-hall licensed by the council'. See LCP CORR: *Chips* LR (1909).
75   Correspondence September 1909. See LCO Theatre Files, not catalogued
76   Letter from Redford to Althorp, 17 September 1909. See LCP CORR: 1903/340: *The Proud Prince*.
77   See correspondence between Dawson, Fladgate and Althorp in September 1909. LCO Theatre Files, not catalogued.
78   Private correspondence between Dawson and Byrne, 18 and 19 October 1909. See LCO Theatre Files, not catalogued.
79   Private letter from Byrne to Dawson, 12 November 1909. See LCO Theatre Files, not catalogued.
80   From the minutes of a meeting held 7 January 1910, attended by Sir Douglas Dawson, Sir Almeric Fitzroy (of the Privy Council), Sir Charles Mathews (Director of Public Prosecutions) and Mr C.P. Byrne (Assistant Under-Secretary to the Home Office). See LCO Theatre Files, not catalogued.
81   Private correspondence between Dawson and Mathews, both letters dated 21 January 1910. See LCO Theatre Files, not catalogued.
82   Max Beerbohm, *Saturday Review*, 20 November 1909, pp. 625–626.
83   *The Observer*, 25 February 1912, p. 7.
84   John Palmer, writing on the recent appointment of Brookfield under the title 'The Dear Old Charlie', in the *Saturday Review*, 2 December 1911, pp. 697–699.

Chapter 3

1   *The Times*, 14 November 1910, p. 12.
2   Mr Ellis Griffith, Under-Secretary of State for the Home Department, was speaking in the House of Commons debate of 16 April 1913 in response to Robert Harcourt's motion proposing 'that the system of licensing stage plays before production in Great Britain . . . by means principally of the perusal of a manuscript should be abolished'. See *Parliamentary Debates (Official Report), Volume LI, House of Commons, 31 March 1913–18 April 1913* (London: HMSO, 1913), columns 2036–2081.
3   From a private letter from Dawson to Byrne sent on 31 January 1910, reporting on a meeting he had held with three leading theatre managers (Tree, Irving and Bourchier) who all sought the introduction of a 'dual licence' for theatres and music-halls which would give them comparable freedom. See LCO Theatre Files, not catalogued.
4   Private letter from Althorp to Dawson of 8 November 1910, written during acrimonious correspondence with Laurence Housman over the refusal to issue a licence for *Pains and Penalties*, which included the character of Queen Caroline. 'The real question is the broad principle of presenting on the stage a play dealing with a painful episode in the life of an ancestress of The King', wrote Dawson to Althorp privately on 11 July 1910. See LCP CORR: *Pains and Penalties* LR (1910).
5   Private letters from Redford to Dawson 23 September 1910 and from Althorp to Dawson, 26 September 1910. See LCP CORR: 1910/790 *The Sins of London*. The play was written by W. Melville and licensed for the Lyceum.
6   Letter from the Editor of *London Opinion* to the Lord Chamberlain, 30 November 1910. See LCP CORR: 1909/264: *How Girls Are Brought to Ruin*. Written by M. Powell, the script had been licensed for the Queen's Theatre, Farnworth, Bolton, in January 1909. It appears that additional material had been illegally introduced during performances at the Britannia

Theatre, Hoxton, in November 1910.

7   See Frank Fowell and Frank Palmer, *Censorship in England* (London: Frank Palmer, 1913), p. 342.

8   Letter from Beecham's Opera Company to the Lord Chamberlain, 24 October 1910. See LCP CORR: 1910/815: *Salomé*.

9   Thomas Beecham, *A Mingled Chime: Leaves from an Autobiography* (London: Hutchinson, 1952), p. 103.

10   See LCP CORR: 1910/815: *Salomé*.

11   Beecham, *A Mingled Chime*, p. 105.

12   See Dawson's letter of 2 July 1914 in LCO Theatre Files, not catalogued.

13   See LCP CORR: *Pains and Penalties* LR (1910).

14   See *The Times* obituary of William Mansfield, First Viscount and Second Baron Sandhurst, 3 November 1921, p. 13.

15   *The Times*, 14 November 1910, p. 12.

16   Dawson's letter to members of the Advisory Board dated 25 January 1911, accompanying the script of *Waste*, which had been resubmitted. See LCO Theatre Files, not catalogued.

17   The play was *The Dawn of Eternity*, eventually refused a licence because it dealt with the life of Christ. Dawson's letter of 27 October 1911 to the Advisory Board warned them that 'If this play were passed we should have the whole church from the Archbishop downwards, not to speak of the "Non-Conformist Conscience" down on us at once', and that 'The Lord Chamberlain is very anxious I should impress on you the importance of the matter'. See LCO Theatre Files, not catalogued. Also LCP CORR: *The Dawn of Eternity* LR (1911).

18   All extracts from correspondence on *Miss Julie* of December 1912. The play was submitted for licence for performance at the Court Theatre in January 1913, but was turned down. LCO Theatre Files, not catalogued.

19   From Dawson's letter of resignation of 21 January 1931, written during a debate on the licensing of a stage adaptation of Waugh's *Vile Bodies*. LCO Theatre Files, not catalogued.

20   From a letter by Housman published in *The Times*, 15 November 1910, p. 12.

21   See LCP CORR: 1910/814: *Oedipus Rex*. The play was licensed for the Haymarket Theatre in November 1910.

22   Letter from Dawson to Althorp, 15 September 1911. LCO Theatre Files, not catalogued.

23   Dawson's letter to Redford was dated 11 October 1911, and Redford's appeal to Althorp 14 October 1911. The Lord Chamberlain's reply is undated. LCO Theatre Files, not catalogued.

24   Letters and memoranda from Dawson, October 1911. LCO Theatre Files, not catalogued.

25   Correspondence December 1911. LCO Theatre Files, not catalogued.

26   The *Star*, 2 January 1912, p. 2. *The Pity of It* and *Tricked*, described as Grand Guignol plays, were submitted for performances at the Royal Court in November 1911, and the latter was turned down on the recommendation of Redford. Cowan then claimed it was extracted from *The World, The Flesh and the Devil*, which had been licensed three years earlier. For correspondence and memoranda relating to this and written between November 1911 and January 1912 see LCO Theatre Files, not catalogued.

27   All correspondence December 1911 to March 1912. LCO Theatre Files, not catalogued.

28   John Palmer writing in *the Saturday Review*, 2 December 1911, pp. 697–699.

29   From 'The Incorrigible Censor', *The Nation*, 29 May 1909, pp. 310–311.

30   Letter from Dawson to the Bishop dated 17 February 1912. LCO Theatre Files, not catalogued.

31   Charles Brookfield, 'On Plays and Playwriting', *National Review*, November 1911, pp. 420–421.

32   Undated petition. LCO Theatre Files, not catalogued.

33   On 26 November 1911. The audience passed the resolution. LCO Theatre Files, not catalogued.

34   See the *Saturday Review*, 2 December 1911, pp. 697–699.

35   In a letter to the Prime Minister, 28 November 1911. LCO Theatre Files, not catalogued.

36   Letter from Dawson to the Prime Minister, February 1912, informing him that the King had approved the appointment and asking 'if Mr Asquith would like to make any remarks on the subject'. LCO Theatre Files, not catalogued.

37   The Lord Chamberlain's Office was advised that this question would be asked in Parliament by Mr Lynch on 30 November 1911. LCO Theatre Files, not catalogued.

38   Letter from Dawson to Sir Edward Carson, 29 November 1911. LCO Theatre Files, not catalogued.

39 The Duke of Atholl writing on 30 August 1922. See LCP CORR: 1922/4401: *The Secret Woman.*
40 Letter from Dawson to Professor Raleigh, 12 February 1912. See correspondence on *The Secret Woman* in LCO Theatre Files, not catalogued.
41 Cited by Fowell and Palmer, *Censorship in England*, pp. 266–267.
42 Letter from Dawson to Raleigh,12 February 1912. LCO Theatre Files, not catalogued.
43 Letter from Dawson to Bourchier, 28 March 1912, in relation to the resubmitted version of *A Man in the Case*. LCO Theatre Files, not catalogued.
44 Petition to the King, 11 June 1912. Published in appendix of Fowell and Palmer, *Censorship in England*, pp. 374–378.
45 Petition to the King, 29 February 1912. Published in appendix of Fowell and Palmer, *Censorship in England*, pp. 378–379.
46 According to the account by Fowell and Palmer, *Censorship in England*, pp. 310–312, a deputation was received in January 1912 by the Home Secretary, who assured them 'that they would find the Home Office only too anxious to carry out the wishes that had been expressed'.
47 See *The Times*, 17 October 1910, p. 6, reporting Zangwill's speech in a public debate on censorship.
48 Fowell and Palmer, *Censorship in England*, p. 335.
49 Fowell and Palmer, *Censorship in England*, p. 236.
50 H.W. Massingham, 'Two Plays and the Censor', *The Nation*, 9 March 1912, pp. 944–945.
51 Fowell and Palmer, *Censorship in England*, p. 350.
52 Correspondence April 1912. LCO Theatre Files, not catalogued.
53 See *Parliamentary Debates (Official Report), Volume LI, House of Commons, 31 March 1913 –18 April 1913.*
54 Undated internal memorandum in the Lord Chamberlain's Office following the viewing of the private matinée of Philpotts's play at the Kingsway Theatre on 22 February 1912. LCO Theatre Files, not catalogued.
55 *Parliamentary Debates (Official Report), Volume LI, House of Commons, 31 March 1913–18 April 1913.* Ellis Griffith's speech is pp. 2052–2059.
56 *Parliamentary Debates (Official Report), Volume LI, House of Commons, 31 March 1913–18 April 1913.* p. 2065. The speaker was Mr Francis Neilson.
57 *Parliamentary Debates (Official Report), Volume LI, House of Commons, 31 March 1913–18 April 1913.* p. 2051.
58 *Daily Mail*, 12 November 1913, pp. 9–10.
59 'The Mistakes of Puritanism', *Daily Mail*, 15 November 1913, p. 4.

Chapter 4

1 Mr Walter Rea speaking in the House of Commons debate on theatre censorship, 16 April 1913. See *Parliamentary Debates (Official Report), Volume LI, House of Commons, 31 March 1913 – 18 April 1913* (London: HMSO, 1913), columns 2036–2081.
2 *Ghosts* was finally licensed for public performance at the Haymarket Theatre in July 1914. For the debate in the Lord Chamberlain's Office cited here, see LCP CORR: 1914/2853: *Ghosts.*
3 From the Reader's Report by Ernest Bendall, 17 April 1914. The play was eventually licensed for St Martin's Theatre in March 1917. For Bendall's report and discussion of this play extending from 1914 to 1963, see LCP CORR: 1917/837: *Damaged Goods.*
4 See LCP CORR: 1914/2853: *Ghosts*
5 See the Reader's Report of 11 March 1915. Written by B.T. Selbit, the revue was licensed for the Palace Theatre, Bath, in March 1915; however, it appears that it had previously been performed without a licence in Dover, and that when it reached the Eastbourne Hippodrome the manager there received a warning to this effect from the Lord Chamberlain. The Eastbourne performances were then watched by the police. See LCP CORR: 1915/3343: *Very Mixed Bathing.*
6 See LCP CORR: 1916/416: *Zulu.* The script was licensed for the Palace Theatre, Manchester, in September 1916.
7 Letter from Dawson to Cochran, 21 August 1915. *More* was scripted by Harry Grattan and licensed for the Ambassadors Theatre in June 1915. See LCP CORR: 1915/3534: *More.*
8 Internal memorandum, 21 April 1915, written after an inspection of the performance. See LCP CORR: 1914/3011: *Odds and Ends.* The script was by H. Grattan and was licensed

for the Ambassadors Theatre in October 1914.

9   'The Music-halls Must Be Criticised', *Daily Mail*, 15 November 1913, p. 4.

10   The comments were included in a letter sent to the management on 8 August 1918. The Office had been concerned about the potentially revealing nature of medieval costumes, and insisted on drawings being submitted. The part of Mephistophilis was to be played by Delys, a well known actress and dancer who frequently provoked controversy. See LCP CORR: 1918/1690: *As You Were*. The script was written by A. Wimperis, and licensed for the London Pavilion in July 1918.

11   Letter from the Archbishop of Canterbury to the Office, 19 June 1911. See correspondence related to *The Birth of Christ—a Nativity Play*, in LCO Theatre Files, not catalogued.

12   E.F.S. [Edward Fordham Spence], *Our Stage and its Critics* (London: Methuen & Co., 1910), p. 88.

13   See *The Great Unknown* and *The Carpenter* in The Lord Chamberlain's Day Book, 8 February 1913 and 26 March 1914. Both cited in John Florance, 'Theatrical Censorship in Britain: 1901–1968', unpublished Ph.D. thesis, University of Wales, 1980, pp. 148–149.

14   *A Life Of Man* by Leonidas Andreiev was licensed for Edinburgh Lyceum Theatre in June 1915. See LCP CORR: 1915/3452: *A Life of Man*.

15   *The Upper Room*, by Robert Hugh Benson, was submitted in January 1915, but not licensed until 1921 for performance at Philbeach Hall, Earls Court; even then, the licence carried an official endorsement: 'This play shall not be produced anywhere in Great Britain, except under conditions that shall be approved by the Lord Chamberlain'. See LCP CORR: 1921/3433: *The Upper Room*.

16   See LCP CORR: 1913/1446: *Joseph and his Brethren*; 1913/1447: *Job*; 1913/1955: *Joseph in Canaan*.

17   See LCP CORR: 1913/1810: *Parsifal*. The script was licensed for the Royal Opera House, Covent Garden, in July 1913.

18   See LCP CORR: 1913/1446: *Joseph and his Brethren*.

19   See correspondence in May 1912 in LCO Theatre Files, not catalogued. Also LCP CORR: *La Dame de Chez Maxim's* LR (1912).

20   For the Office's discussions of *The Coronation* see LCO Theatre Files, not catalogued. The play was co-written by Christopher St John and K. Charles Thursby, and was refused a licence.

21   Written by Leonard T. Durell, the script was licensed with amendments for the King's Theatre, Southsea, and the Grand, Derby, in July 1913. See LCP CORR: 1913/1843: *The Ambassadors*.

22   *At the Point of a Pistol* (author unknown) was licensed for Glasgow Athenaeum in November 1912, despite Dawson's reservations, but only after amendments. See LCO Theatre Files, not catalogued. Also LCP CORR: 1912/1154: *At the Point of a Pistol*.

23   *The Sunshine Girl* was a musical play licensed for the Gaiety Theatre in February 1912. See discussion of February 1912 in LCO Theatre Files, not catalogued. Also LCP CORR: 1912/212: *The Sunshine Girl*.

24   For full and extensive correspondence and other material, including the undated newspaper extract from the *Pall Mall Gazette* cited here, see LCP CORR: 1913/2233: *Romance of India*. The 'Spectacle' was to have opened at Earl's Court in December 1913.

25   *Mr Wu* had been licensed and first performed at the Strand Theatre in October 1912, but the confrontation over the play took place in November 1913. See LCP CORR: 1912/1088: *Mr Wu*.

26   *The Tsaritza* had been adapted from Lengyel and Biro by Herbert Thexton for the Garrick Theatre and for Arthur Bourchier, and was to have been performed in July 1913. Discussions about possible amendments to secure a licence continued until January 1914, but the play never received one. See LCP CORR: *The Tsaritza* LR (1913).

27   See LCP CORR: 1913/214: *The Great Catherine*. Shaw's play was licensed for the Vaudeville Theatre in November 1913.

28   See LCP CORR: *A Thumbnail Sketch of Catherine the Great of Russia* WB 1915.

29   Brookfield's comment in his Reader's Report was written on 11 March 1913. The report is with the script of the play in the LCP: *The White Slave Traffic*: 1913/10. Written by A. Middleton Myles, it was licensed for the Foresters Theatre in March 1913, though the title was apparently changed later to: *Should The Preacher Tell?* See also LCP CORR: 1913/1515: *The White Slave Traffic*.

30   The play (author unknown) was submitted in June 1910. See LCP CORR: *Champions of*

Morality LR (1910).

31 *Abode of Love* by Walter Satoun was eventually licensed in a revised version in July 1915 for performance at the Elephant and Castle Theatre. For comments and discussion see LCP CORR: 1915/3955, *Abode of Love.*

32 The play was intended for performance at the Coronet Theatre, Notting Hill Gate, in August 1914, by a group called 'Woman's Theatre' under the direction of the Actresses' Franchise League. See LCP CORR: *Where Are You Going To?* LR (1914).

33 For all correspondence and discussion see LCP CORR: 1924/5632: *Mrs Warren's Profession.* The play was eventually licensed in September 1924 for the Edinburgh Lyceum Theatre.

34 Ernest Bendall's Reader's Report, September 1917. LCP CORR: 1924/5632: *Mrs Warren's Profession.*

35 Comment made on behalf of the Archbishop of Canterbury in December 1918 and sent to the Lord Chamberlain in opposition to licensing another play by Brieux, *Maternity.* The Archbishop was drawing a distinction between the supposed usefulness of *Damaged Goods* and the unhelpfulness of *Maternity.* See LCP CORR: *Maternity* LR (1924).

36 From the Reader's Report by Ernest Bendall, August 1917. See LCP CORR: 1917/1115: *Tainted Woman.* The play, by R. Graham, was licensed for the Cinema Theatre, Evesham, in the same month.

37 *Her Escape,* by J.H. Wharncliffe, was licensed for the Palace Theatre, Maidstone, in June 1917. See LCP CORR: 1917/995: *Her Escape.*

38 All extracts taken from 1917 correspondence; see LCP CORR: *Is Vice Worthwhile?* LR (1917). Frederick H.-U. Bowman's play was eventually licensed for the David Lewis Theatre in Liverpool forty years later in February 1958.

39 *His Childless Wife* by Clifford Rean had been submitted for performance at the Hippodrome Theatre, Huddersfield, in July 1918, but was never licensed. For discussion and correspondence see LCP CORR: *His Childless Wife* LR (1918)

40 See LCP CORR: *Maternity* LR (1924). This play was eventually licensed for the Regent Theatre in October 1932, in a different translation by John Pollock. For further correspondence see LCP CORR: 1932/11470: *Maternity.* In 1933 the play's title was changed to *Broken Lives.*

41 The original intention was for this play, written by R. de Flers and G. de Caillavet, to be performed in its French original in London in October 1917 as *Le Roi.* The rights were then sold to an American company which applied for a licence to present it in an English version at the Prince's Theatre in the summer of 1918 as *Angelo the Ninth.* It was eventually licensed—after Raleigh's resignation—in a new and revised version for the Shaftesbury Theatre in November 1918, under the title *Change for a Sovereign.* For all correspondence relating to the play and to Raleigh's resignation from the Advisory Board see LCP CORR: *Le Roi/ Angelo the Ninth* LR (1917).

Chapter 5

1 *National News,* 7 July 1918, p. 7.

2 Paul Fussell, *The Great War and Modern Memory* (London: Oxford University Press, 1975). See especially Chapter VI, 'Theater of War', pp. 191–230.

3 Samuel Hynes, *A War Imagined: The First World War and English Culture* (London: Bodley Head, 1990), pp. 122–126.

4 Hynes, *A War Imagined,* pp. 79–80.

5 Shaw, Introduction to *Heartbreak House* (London: Constable, 1919), p. 39.

6 L.J. Collins, *Theatre at War, 1914–1918* (Basingstoke: Macmillan, 1998), pp. 179–182.

7 Extracts taken from unpublished manuscript in LCP: 1913/2941: *England Expects.* The script was licensed for the London Opera House in September 1914.

8 The play was written by J. Lateiner (?) and originally licensed in March 1909 for the theatre at Mile End. See LCP CORR: 1909/343: *Man and Wife.* The title of the play was subsequently changed to *The Soldier's Bride.*

9 This play by Gavault and Morton had been licensed for the Playhouse in February 1910. See LCP CORR: 1910/256: *Tantalising Tommy.*

10 This melodrama by A.J. Shelley-Thompson (a barrister-at-law of the Middle Temple) was licensed for the Empire Theatre, Liverpool, in January 1915. See LCP CORR: 1915/3181: *Honour Gains the Day.*

11 The play (author unknown) was licensed for Devonport Hippodrome in January 1915. For discussion see LCP CORR: 1915/3163: *The Master Hun*.

12 *The Glorious Day*, by Leonard Mortimer, was licensed for the Elephant & Castle Theatre in February 1915. See LCP CORR:1915/3187: *The Glorious Day. Somewhere in France*, by Herbert Sidney, was licensed for the Scala Theatre, Seacombe, in April 1915. See LCP CORR: 1915/3284: *Somewhere in France*.

13 The play was licensed for the New Theatre in May 1915. Written by a relatively well known author of mostly religious plays, it was also published: Stephen Phillips, *Armageddon* (London: John Lane, 1915). For correspondence see LCP CORR: 1915/3411: *Armageddon*.

14 This play, written and performed by Edmund Frobisher, was licensed for the Pavilion Theatre, Hawick, in August 1915. It was also published as a five-page leaflet which described it as 'AN ORIGINAL, TOPICAL, PROTEAN PLAYLET'. See LCP CORR: 1915/3685: *Gott Strafe England*.

15 Credited to Millane and Shirley, the play was licensed for Salford Hippodrome in January 1915. See LCP CORR: 1915/3160: *War and a Woman*.

16 The play, by Andrew Emm, had an alternative title: *Comrades in Arms*. It was licensed for the New Princes Theatre in May 1915. See LCP CORR: 1915/3392: *For England, Home and Beauty*.

17 The play was *What Happened to Jane*, by Chris Hamilton, licensed for the Colchester Hippodrome in January 1915. See LCP CORR: 1915/3331: *What Happened to Jane*.

18 A revue in five scenes, this script was licensed for the Hippodrome, Southend, in March 1915. See LCP CORR: 1915/3229: *Cheer Up*.

19 Written by Lauri Wylie, Alfred Parker and Clifford Harris, the script was licensed for the Palace Theatre, Leicester, in July 1915. See LCP CORR: 1915/3580: *Kiss Me Sergeant*.

20 This script by Geo de Gray was licensed for the Osborne Theatre, Manchester, in April 1915. See LCP CORR: 1915/3297: *The Gates of Mercy*.

21 Licensed for the Alexandra in Hull in December 1915, the script was by J. Cassidy. For discussion and details of negotiations over licensing, see LCP CORR: 1915/3930: *His Mother's Son, V.C.*

22 Hynes, *A War Imagined*, pp. 53–54.

23 In fact, the play's title was subsequently changed again to *The Princess and the Soldier*. Written by Dorothy Mullord, it was licensed for the Willesden Hippodrome in April 1915. For discussion see LCP CORR: 1915/3342: *The Nun and the Hun*.

24 Written by John G. Brandon, the play was licensed for the Balham Hippodrome in April 1915. In 1918, the title was changed to *The Red Cross*. For discussion of details of licensing and the endorsement see LCP CORR: 1915/3384: *There Was a King in Flanders*.

25 Licensed for His Majesty's Theatre in May 1915, this script was by the well-known playwright Edward Knoblock and was subsequently published: Edward Knoblock, *Marie Odile* (Ottawa: G.H. Popham, 1915). For details of the complaints and other responses see LCP CORR: 1915/3493: *Marie Odile*.

26 The title was also changed, first to *Delores* and then to *The Victim*. Written by E. Hill-Michelson, the play was licensed for the Theatre Royal, Middlesbrough, in November 1915. See LCP CORR: 1915/3840: *Delores*.

27 See 'God's Lovely Lust', *The Antidote*, 4, 12 June 1915. Cited in Hynes, *A War Imagined*, p. 223.

28 Arnold White, 'Efficiency and Vice', *The Vigilante*, 20 April 1918, p. 4. Cited in Philip Hoare, *Wilde's Last Stand: Decadence, Conspiracy and the First World War* (London: Duckworth, 1997), p. 89.

29 W.R. Colton, 'The Effects of War on Art' *The Architect*, 45 17 March 1916, pp. 199–201.

30 Edmund Gosse 'War and Literature', *Edinburgh Review*, 220, October 1914, p. 313. Cited in Hynes, *A War Imagined*, p. 12.

31 James Barrie, *Der Tag* (London: Hodder & Stoughton, 1914). The play was licensed for performance at the Coliseum in London in October 1914. See also LCP CORR: 1914/3077. *Der Tag*.

32 Hynes, *A War Imagined*, p. 231.

33 *The Glorious Day* by Leonard Mortimer, see n. 12.

34 Written by Horace Hunter, the play was to have been performed at the Nottingham Hippodrome in June 1915, but was refused a licence. See LCP CORR: *Outraged Women* LR (1915).

35 The play, written by C.V. Proctor, was licensed for the Elephant & Castle Theatre in June 1915, though not in its original version. For subsequent complaints and discussion as well

as details of modifications made before the licence was issued see LCP CORR: 1915/3549: *The Unmarried Mother.*

36   See LCP CORR: 1917/837: *Damaged Goods.*

37   Details and figures cited in Hynes, *A War Imagined*, pp. 370–371.

38   The play was licensed for the St Martin's Theatre, London, in March 1917. For full details of the discussion about whether or not to license it, see LCP CORR: 1917/837: *Damaged Goods.*

39   Collins, *Theatre at War*, p. 201.

40   The play was eventually licensed for the Little Theatre, Leeds in October 1926. See LCP CORR: 1926/7132: *Black 'Ell.* It had been published as follows: Miles Malleson, *'D' Company and Black 'Ell*, (London: Hendersons, 1916).

41   Hynes, *A War Imagined*, p. 152.

42   Hynes, *A War Imagined*, pp. 216–217.

43   Jones's play was licensed for the Kingsway Theatre in June 1917. For details see LCP CORR: 1917/989: *The Pacifists.* It was also published under its full title: Henry Arthur Jones, *The Pacifists: A Parable in a Farce in Three Acts, Showing How Certain Citizens of Market Pewbury Acted Upon the Exalted Principle of Peace at Any Price, and How the Town Fared in Consequence* (London: Chiswick Press, 1917).

44   It was written by John Brandon and licensed for the Empress Theatre, Brixton, in October 1918. See LCP CORR: 1918/1824: *The Pacifist.*

45   Written by A. Middleton-Myles, the play was licensed for the Palace Theatre, Battersea, in October 1918. See LCP CORR: 1918/1828: *Beware Germans.*

46   Hoare, *Wilde's Last Stand* and Michael Kettle, *Salomé's Last Veil: The Libel Case of the Century*, (London: Hart-Davis MacGibbon, 1979).

47   Michael Kettle makes this judgement on Billing, p. 311. Cited in Hoare, *Wilde's Last Stand*, p. 210. For Billing's comment cited here, see *The Vigilante*, 9 February 1918, p. 1.

48   'Michael Orme', *J.T. Grein: The Story of a Pioneer 1862–1935* (London: John Murray, 1936), p. 167.

49   Grein's application for a licence was to allow the play to be performed at the Prince of Wales's Theatre in April 1918. Wilde's script was eventually licensed for the Lyceum Theatre in Edinburgh in 1931, and correspondence relating to earlier submissions of the play for licensing are filed in relation to that application. See LCP CORR: 1931/10553: *Salomé.*

50   The Deed of Constitution was published in *The Vigilante*, 9 February 1918, p. 3.

51   *The Imperialist*, 26 January 1918, p. 3.

52   'The Music-halls Must Be Criticised', *Daily Mail*, 15 November 1913, p. 4.

53   *The Vigilante*, 16 February 1918, p. 1.

54   LCP CORR: 1931/10553: *Salomé.*

55   A (supposedly) verbatim report of the original proceedings at Bow Street Police Court in April 1918, and condensed but extensive extracts from the subsequent trial of Rex against Pemberton-Billing at the Old Bailey in late May and early June, were published in successive issues of *The Vigilante* between 6 April and 15 June. All quotations here are taken from these edited transcripts.

56   Hynes, *A War Imagined*, p. 229.

57   See 'Vanoc' [Arnold White], 'Our Handbook: The Wider Issues', *The Referee*, 9 June 1918, p. 2. Also, Arnold White, 'Efficiency and Vice', *The Vigilante*, 20 April 1918, p. 4.

58   *The Hidden Hand* was written by Laurence Cowan—presumably the same person who had brought a legal action against the Lord Chamberlain in 1911 (as discussed in the previous chapter). It was licensed for performance at the Royal Court Theatre, Liverpool, in May 1918. For all discussion about licensing, see LCP CORR: 1918/1588: *The Hidden Hand.*

59   *National News*, 7 July 1918, p. 2.

60   The play in question was *The Man with the Club Foot*, by A. Crawford and V. Williams, licensed for the Apollo in April 1918. The cast included the Kaiser. See LCP CORR:1918/1530: *The Man with the Club Foot.*

61   *A Spy in the Ranks* was a melodrama by Mrs F. Kimberley, and was originally licensed for the Theatre Royal, Wolverhampton, in May 1918. For details of subsequent alterations responding to complaints, see LCP CORR: 1918/1563: *A Spy in the Ranks.*

62   Written by Samuel Shipman and Aaron Hoffman, the play was duly licensed for the Haymarket in January 1919. For the extensive internal arguments and debate see LCP

CORR: 1919/1975: *Uncle Sam* (*Friendly Enemies*).

63   This play, by Margaret Mayo and H.J. Foreman, was to have been performed at the Kingsway Theatre in February 1919. For details of why the licence was refused, see LCP CORR: *The World's Enemy* LR (1919).

Chapter 6

1   'On Censors and Censorship', *The Times*, 12 April 1922, p. 13.

2   The Lord Chamberlain having demanded that the word 'God' be omitted from *Absorbing Perdita* before he would license it for the Festival Theatre, Cambridge, Terence Gray wrote to him on 8 October 1927 to ask for permission to substitute 'the Lord Chamberlain'. The reply from the Assistant Comptroller of 10 October, quoted here, granted this permission on behalf of Lord Cromer. See LCP CORR: 1927/7835: *Progress*.

3   'On Censors and Censorship', *The Times*, 12 April 1922, p. 13.

4   George Street, 'The Censorship of Plays', *Fortnightly Review*, DCCV, 1 September 1925, pp. 348–362.

5   His essay on Wilde was published in: G.S. Street, *People and Questions* (London: Martin Secker, 1905), pp. 137–142.

6   See Street's 'Introduction' to *The Comedies of William Congreve: Volume One* (London: Methuen, 1895), pp. vii–xxxiii.

7   Reader's Report by Street on Maugham's play, written 6 December 1928. See LCP CORR: 1928/8717: *Sacred Flame*.

8   Street was writing on 13 August 1924 as part of a discussion on a revue containing 'military chaff' and said by some to be 'Communistic Propaganda'. See LCP CORR: 1924/5482: *Rent Free*.

9   Cromer's prediction came in a letter to a member of his Advisory Board, written on 30 November 1924. See LCP CORR: 1926/6767: *The Passion Flower*.

10   See House of Lords Debate, 'Censorship of Plays', *Parliamentary Debates (Official Report), Volume LXIV, House of Lords, 4 May – 15 July* (London: HMSO, 1926), columns 365–392.

11   Buckmaster's original statements of principle in a letter of 19 November 1924 were part of his contribution to the debate on whether or not to issue a licence for Noel Coward's controversial play *The Vortex*. Buckmaster's argument helped persuade other members of the Board and the Lord Chamberlain that they should license the play for the Everyman Theatre in November 1924 in spite of their considerable dislike of the text. See LCP CORR: 1924/5762: *The Vortex*. His additional amendment was made the following month, on 13 December 1924, in relation to *The Grand Duchess*, a play about former Russian aristocrats living in exile, adapted by Harry Graham from the French of Alfred Savoir. Buckmaster again concluded that there were no proper grounds for interference in what he defined as 'a matter of bad taste with which by itself the Censorship has no concern'. The play was duly licensed (after alterations) for performance at the Globe Theatre in January 1925. See LCP CORR: 1925/5900: *The Grand Duchess*.

12   Dawson writing on 29 May 1921, recommending a play for licensing which Street had actually opposed. See LCP CORR: 1921/3591: *The Queen of Hearts*. Written by Philip Rodway, the script was licensed in December 1921 for the Theatre Royal Birmingham, though it also appears to have been previously licensed for the London Pavilion in May 1921.

13   Dawson was writing in July 1924, and opposing the licence for this play by 'Joshua Jordan' (really, Lord Kilmarnock). An amended version was licensed for the Wimbledon Theatre in that month, and the title changed to *The Dream Kiss*. See LCP CORR: 1924/5600: *The Dream Kiss*.

14   The phrase was used in the obituary for Sandhurst published in *The Times*, 3 November 1921, p. 13.

15   See LCP CORR: 1927/7864: *Robespierre*. Written by Andrew Emm, the play was licensed for the Grand in Brighton, in October 1927.

16   This revue, credited to Albert de Courville, Wal Pink, Frederick Chappelle, Archibald de Bear and Leslie Haslam, was licensed for the Royalty Theatre in May 1921 with this proviso. See LCP CORR: 1921/3540: *Pins and Needles*. The attack came in the *Daily Graphic*, 16 May 1921, p. 4, under the headline 'Censored—by the Papers'.

17   See correspondence of June 1926 in LCO Theatre Files, not catalogued.

18   House of Lords Debate, 1926, 'Censorship of Plays'.

19   See correspondence of June 1926 in LCO Theatre Files, not catalogued.

20   For 'Bulgaria' see LCP CORR: 1929/9027: *Bang*. The script was by Geo. R. Gordon, and
     it was licensed for the Southport Coliseum in May 1929. For 'blurry' see *The Mendip
     Mystery*, written by Lynn Brock and licensed for the Bristol Little Theatre in December
     1930. See LCP CORR: 1930/10,044. For *Shadow of a Gunman*, licensed for the Court
     Theatre in May 1927, see LCP CORR: 1927/7638. See also, for example, the Lord
     Chamberlain's 1922 ruling: 'the joke about smelling feet is to be omitted' in relation to
     Auction of Souls by Betty Fairfax, licensed for the Ambassadors Theatre, Southend, in
     August 1922; LCP CORR: 1922/4357.

21   See LCP CORR: 1928/8337: *The Decline and Fall of the Water Hens*. The playwright was
     Hanworth Browning, and the play was licensed for the Garrick Theatre in May 1928. The
     title was changed to *Call Me Georges*.

22   See LCP CORR: 1927/7606: *Asleep*. The script was by Cyril Campion, and it was licensed
     for the Q Theatre, Kew, in April 1928.

23   See LCP CORR: 1927/7947: *Eve's Flesh*. Written by David Gill, the script was licensed for
     the West Pier Theatre, Brighton, in November 1927. The title was later changed to *Eve's
     Price*.

24   See LCP CORR: 1927/7647: *The Return*. The play was written by Charles Bennett and
     licensed for the Everyman Theatre in May 1927.

25   For *Journey's End* by R.C. Sherriff, licensed for the Savoy Theatre in January 1929, see
     LCP CORR: 1929/8757: *Journey's End*. For *The Life and Misdoings of Charley Peace* by
     Edward Percy, licensed for the Ambassadors Theatre in September 1929, see LCP CORR:
     1929/9153: *The Life and Misdoings of Charley Peace*.

26   The play was *Every Mother's Son*, written by Winifred and John L. Carter, and licensed for
     the Strand Theatre in May 1930. See LCP CORR: 1930/9671: *Every Mother's Son*.

27   *Children of Darkness* by Edwin Justus Mayer was licensed for the Apollo in June 1930. See
     LCP CORR: 1930/9809: *Children of Darkness*.

28   *Cape Forlorn* by Frank Harvey was licensed for the Fortune Theatre in March 1930. See
     LCP CORR: 1930/9628: *Cape Forlorn*.

29   *Down Our Street*, by Ernest George, was licensed for the Vaudeville Theatre in April 1930.
     See LCP CORR: 1930/9662: *Down Our Street*.

30   *The Zoo*, by Michael Arlen and Winchell Smith, was licensed for the King's Theatre,
     Southsea, in May 1927. See LCP CORR: 1927/7608: *The Zoo*.

31   *The Reappearance* by H.A. Bland was licensed for St Catharine's Hall, Liverpool, in February
     1930. See LCP CORR: 1930/9502: *The Reappearance*.

32   Buckmaster was writing in January 1930. See LCP CORR: 1903/9539: *Wealthy and Wise*.
     Written by Eleanor Carol Chilton (?) and Herbert Agar (?), this play was licensed for the
     New Theatre in February 1930.

33   He was writing in 1929. See LCP CORR: LR (1929) *The Last Lover*.

34   Henry Vincent Higgins, the Chairman of the Grand Opera Syndicate and Director of the
     Carlton and Ritz, was writing in November 1924 as an active member of the Advisory Board.
     See LCP CORR: *The Passion Flower*: 1926/6767.

35   Adapted from Waugh's novel by Dennis Bradley, the script was refused a licence in
     December 1930 and again—in a revised version—in October 1931. It was eventually
     licensed for the Vaudeville Theatre, at the end of March 1932. See LCP CORR:
     1932/11133: *Vile Bodies*. The censorship of this play is also discussed in Chapter Nine.

36   Buckmaster's observation was made in December 1927 while discussing whether or not to
     recommend for licence Sacha Guitry's play *L'Amour Masque*. In this instance the licence
     was refused. See LCP CORR: *L'Amour Masque* LR (1928).

37   The Italian original was licensed for the New Oxford Theatre in June 1925. See LCP CORR:
     1925/6179: *Sei personaggi in cerca d'autore*. The English translation was licensed for the
     Globe Theatre in May 1928 (having been performed privately and unlicensed at the Arts
     Theatre). See LCP CORR: 1928/8393: *Six Characters in Search of an Author*.

38   See LCP CORR: 1928/8569: *Knock*. The play was licensed for the Prince's Theatre,
     Manchester, in October 1928.

39   Simon Gantillon's play had been performed privately in English at the Gate Theatre in
     November 1927 and the Arts Theatre in January 1928, and in French at the Arts in June
     1929. The licence was applied for by Terence Gray in May 1929, who intended to perform
     it publicly at the Festival Theatre, Cambridge, but was refused. Gray applied again in July
     1931, following the announcement of further private performances in London, but was
     again turned down. See LCP CORR: *Maya* WB (1929).

40   Cromer's statement of policy came fairly soon after he took office, in August 1923. See LCP CORR: *Monte Carlo Scandal* WB (1923). Adapted by Robert Fenemore from *Le Scandale de Monte Carlo* by Sacha Guitry, and previously titled *The Morning After*, the script was first submitted in June 1922 on behalf of the Devonshire Park Theatre, Eastbourne. It was resubmitted in August 1923 with a new second act, and again, with further revisions, in April 1924.

41   The correspondence between the Lord Chamberlain and the British Embassy in Washington took place between January and March 1926. See LCP CORR: *The Cradle Snatchers* LR (1926).

42   House of Lords Debate, 1926, 'Censorship of Plays'.

43   Cromer received a large deputation from the Public Morality Council to discuss 'The Atmosphere of Stage Plays' in the Armoury at St James's Palace on 31 January 1923. For the report on the meeting see LCO Theatre Files, not catalogued.

44   Cromer was writing in January 1924. See LCO Theatre Files, not catalogued.

45   See LCO Theatre Files, not catalogued, June 1925.

46   Letter to the Home Office from the Assistant Comptroller in the Lord Chamberlain's Office, 21 May 1925. See LCO Theatre Files, not catalogued.

47   House of Lords Debate, 1926, 'Censorship of Plays'.

48   See LCP CORR: 1927/7715: *Love and Money*. Written by Lester and Lee, the script had been licensed for the Brighton Hippodrome in July 1927.

49   House of Lords Debate, 1926, 'Censorship of Plays'.

50   Correspondence between Cromer and the Home Office, March–July 1926. See LCO Theatre Files, not catalogued.

51   The comment was made by George Crichton in March 1928, following complaints received from Cardiff, Eastbourne and Westminster about *Fanatics* by Miles Malleson, which had been licensed for the Ambassadors Theatre in May 1926. See LCP CORR: 1926/6917: *Fanatics*.

52   Writing to the Clerk to the Borough Justices of Halifax in February 1923, following complaints about alleged indecencies in a touring revue which had been licensed a year earlier, Dawson informed them of the letter from the Home Secretary which had been circulated. He commented: 'If the provincial police will so co-operate . . . the prevention of such incidents as are reported in your letter will be ensured'. See LCP CORR: 1922/4000: *Rockets*. The revue, by Charles Henry, had been licensed for the Empire, Newcastle, in January 1922.

53   Office memorandum of 26 April 1932 by George Titman, who had carried out an inspection of a performance on behalf of the Lord Chamberlain, following a complaint by the East Ham and Barking Free Church Council. See LCP CORR: 1932/11166: *The Gas Inspector*. The script, by Con West and Herbert Sargent, was licensed for the Holborn Empire in April 1932.

54   Letter from the Assistant Comptroller to the Chief Constable of Newcastle on 25 March 1931, declining the request to consider a prosecution on grounds of indecency in respect of *Merrie Tales*. See LCP CORR: 1931/10,243: *Merrie Tales*.

55   He was commenting in August 1928 in relation to a melodrama for which he was issuing a licence. See LCP CORR: 1928/8485: *John Ord's Mistress*. The script was by A.B. Bell, and it was licensed for the Town Hall, Musselburgh, in August 1928.

56   The Chief Constable was writing in April 1931, following performances in Newcastle of *Merrie Tales*—the cast of which included Max Miller. See LCP CORR: 1931/10,243: *Merrie Tales*. The script had been licensed for the Boscombe Hippodrome in February 1931.

57   See LCP CORR: 1930/9909: *Une Nuit Excitante*. The script had been licensed for the Empire, Bristol, in September 1930. William Henshall, the producer, was quoted in the *Newcastle on Tyne Evening Chronicle* on 3 December 1930.

58   *Report from the Joint Select Committee of the House of Lords and the House of Commons on the Stage Plays (Censorship) Together with the Proceedings of the Committee, Minutes and Appendices* (London: Government Publication, 1909), p. 189.

59   See correspondence between the Lord Chamberlain's Office and the Home Office between January 1925 and February 1926 in LCO Theatre Files, not catalogued.

60   See report of meeting and correspondence between Cromer and Joynson Hicks, April 1926, in LCO Theatre Files, not catalogued.

61   See correspondence and memoranda, March and April 1926, in LCO Theatre Files, not catalogued.

62   *The Star*, 13 May 1929, quoting Cathleen Nesbitt, the leading actress in *The Shanghai*

Gesture, a play performed privately because the licence had been refused.

63 Sir Alfred Butt in March 1929. See LCO Theatre Files, not catalogued.

64 Memorandum of 27 May 1926. See LCO Theatre Files, not catalogued.

65 Letter from Major Colin Lindsay Gordon, Assistant Comptroller of the Lord Chamberlain's Office, on 11 June 1929, replying to a letter from the Home Office of 8 June expressing concern that the controversial *The Shanghai Gesture* by John Colton had recently been performed. The play was eventually licensed thirty years later in 1957. See LCP CORR: *The Shanghai Gesture* LR (1926) and 1957/9617: *The Shanghai Gesture*.

66 Peter Godfrey and Velona Pilcher were fined a total of 20 guineas at Bow Street Police Station on 21 May 1928 'for allowing the public admission to the Gate Theatre Studio during the performance of stage plays'. According to the evidence presented by the Director of Public Prosecutions on 28 March 1928, 'two officers, each accompanied by a lady, visited the theatre on the 23rd and 24th of March and purchased tickets at the pay-box . . . and witnessed a performance'. See LCO Theatre Files, not catalogued.

67 See *The Stage*, 15 September 1932, p. 12. The censorship of *Green Pastures* is discussed in Chapter Eight.

68 See correspondence and memoranda, September to December 1932, in LCO Theatre Files, not catalogued.

69 Street had noted in his Reader's Report on *Children on the Dole* of 26 April 1927: 'It is inconvenient that the Lord Chamberlain's licence should cover such things . . . but I suppose it cannot be helped'. Cromer was having none of this, and issued his response on 27 April. See LCP CORR: 1927/7618: *Children on the Dole*. The script, by Tom G. Hanlon, was licensed for the Regent's Theatre, Longton, Staffordshire, in April 1927.

70 Cromer, writing on 7 February 1929. See LCP CORR: 1928/8829: *What a Night*. The script, originally entitled *Variety Round-Up*, was licensed for the Southend Hippodrome in February 1929.

71 A letter from Gordon, the Assistant Comptroller, to the Home Office on 20 May 1932, contrasting revues with the newly introduced 'revudeville'. See LCO Theatre Files, not catalogued.

72 The sketch was entitled 'Scholasticism', and was subsequently licensed under this title for the London Music Hall, Shoreditch, in September 1925. Apparently written by George Wilma and Hector Littlefield, it seems to have been plagiarised from Will Hay's *The Schoolmaster and Scholar* (or *The Schoolmaster and the Boy*)—certainly Wilma pleaded that it had already been performed in that context and therefore did not need licensing. See LCP CORR: 1925/6316: *Scholasticism*.

73 The Lord Chamberlain had actually been asked for clarification on 8 March 1929 by the Provincial Entertainments Proprietors and Managers Association Ltd; he passed the query on to the Home Office, whose reply was dated 15 April 1929. See LCO Theatre Files, not catalogued.

74 In March 1932, the Assistant Comptroller wrote to the illusionist Signor Arvi: 'I am to inform you that the illusionist display of Living Statuary described by you as "The Grand Arvi Mystery" not being a Stage Play, can not be covered by the Lord Chamberlain's Licence . . . kindly return the licence issued to you in January 1930 for *A Sunburst in Vaudeville*, when a fresh licence will be issued for such items as come under the heading of Stage Plays'. However, partly as a result of pressures from, on the one hand, the Public Morality Council, and on the other, the theatre managers who wanted the security of licensing, he was not able to hold this line for long. See LCP CORR: 1930/9477: *A Sunburst in Vaudeville*. The script had been licensed in January 1930 for the Olympia, Bulwell.

75 See correspondence between Gordon and the Home Office, May and June 1932, in LCO Theatre Files, not catalogued.

76 See Obituary in *The Times*, 14 May 1953, p. 10. Hannen Swaffer, 'If I Were the Censor', *Behind the Scenes* (London: George Newnes, 1929), p. 34.

77 Joynson Hicks sent Bourchier's speech to the Lord Chamberlain on 1 April 1926, reporting that it had been recently given at a mass meeting at a theatre in Sheffield. See correspondence, April 1926, in LCO Theatre Files, not catalogued.

78 From a memorandum written by Cromer, 9 March 1926, detailing a recent meeting with Dean, who had come to complain about the refusal to license two recent plays—one of them *Young Woodley*. See LCP CORR: *Why Not?* LR (1926). The authorship of this play was credited to Scott and Garth.

79 The play was *The Lady-in-Law*, translated and adapted by Bertha Murrey from the French

of Georges Berr and Louis Verneuil. See LCP CORR: *The Lady-in-Law* LR (1927) and 1927/7807: *The Lady-in-Law*. This revised version was licensed for Wyndham's Theatre in September 1927.

80   Censorship of this play, which was written by Edgar Middleton and licensed for the Globe Theatre in August 1927, is discussed more fully in Chapter Seven. See LCP CORR: 1927/7743: *Potiphar's Wife*.

81   LCP CORR: 1927/7807: *The Lady-in-Law*.

82   Swaffer, 'If I Were the Censor'.

83   Gray regularly used the pages of *The Festival Theatre Review* to record his clashes with the Lord Chamberlain, and to attack the principles and practice of theatre censorship. The quotations here are from issues 21, 1927; 66, 1931; and 18, 1927.

84   Toller's play was licensed for the Festival Theatre, after very significant cuts, in February 1929. See LCP CORR: 1929/8795: *Hoppla!* Gray himself claimed, in *The Festival Theatre Review*, issue 55, 1929, that the play had been presented in 'mutilated' form.

85   See LCP CORR: *Man and His Phantoms* LR (1931). The play was by the French playwright H.R. Lenormand.

86   *Eater of Dreams*, also by Lenormand, was licensed for the Festival Theatre in September 1932, a year after it had been first submitted. See LCP CORR: 1932/11443: *Eater of Dreams*.

87   *London Docks* by Willm Rupke was licensed for the Festival Theatre after extensive changes in November 1932. See LCP CORR: 1932/11509: *London Docks*.

88   *The Festival Theatre Review*, issue 80, 1931.

89   Terence Gray, 'Was That Life? Swat It!', *The Gownsman*, 6 June 1931, pp. 14–15.

Chapter 7

1   George Nathan, *The House of Satan* (London: Knopf, 1926), pp. 3–5.

2   George Street's Reader's Report, 18 August 1928. See LCP CORR: 1928/8496: *The Mystery Of The Red Tavern*. Written by John Floyd, and licensed for the Lyceum, Edinburgh, in August 1928.

3   From his essay 'The War and the Theatre', published in George Street, *At Home in the War* (London: Heinemann, 1918), pp. 106–112.

4   From Street's report, 8 June 1915, on *Baiser dans la nuit* by Maurice Level. The play was licensed with some changes for the Coronet Theatre in June 1915. See LCP CORR: 1915/3494: *Baiser dans la nuit*.

5   The licence for this Grand Guignol piece by André de Lorde and Alfred Binet was refused in June 1915. See LCP CORR: *L'horrible expérience* LR (1915).

6   See LCP CORR: 1920/3074: *The Hand of Death*. The play, again by André de Lorde and Alfred Binet, was licensed for the Little Theatre in August 1920.

7   See LCP CORR: 1920/2769: *The Secret Mother*. The play (author unknown) was licensed for the Theatre Royal, Jarrow-on-Tyne, in March 1920.

8   See LCP CORR: *Save the Mark* LR (1920); the script is credited to Nancey and Manoussey. LCP CORR: 1921/3898: *Life*. This play, by M.D.W. and Alex Fisher, and subtitled 'a play of human life', was licensed for the Holborn Empire in November 1921.

9   This play by Dennis Clyde and Annette Howard was licensed for the Queen's Theatre in September 1921. See LCP CORR: 1921/3743: *The Hooded Death*.

10   See LCP CORR: *Blind Man's Buff* LR (1921). Adapted from the French of Charles Hellem and Poll d'Estor, the play was to have been performed at the Little Theatre in 1921 but was refused a licence. It was refused again in 1928, though it had been performed privately at the Arts Theatre in 1927.

11   The play, by Winifred Graham and H.L. de Caux, was intended for the Little Theatre in October 1921, but was licensed only in its revised version in December. See LCP CORR: 1921/3983: *Euthanasia*. It is not quite clear if the licence was actually issued.

12   *The Regiment* by Robert Francheville, adapted by Lewis Casson, was licensed for the Little Theatre in January 1922. See LCP CORR: 1922/403: *The Regiment*.

13   See LCP CORR: *Coals of Fire* LR (1922), and LCP CORR: *The Gentlemen of Havre* LR (1922). Authors unknown.

14   See LCP CORR: 1929/4229: *Sister's Tragedy*. Credited to R. Hughes, the play was licensed for the Little Theatre in May 1922.

15   André de Lorde's play was refused a licence for the Little Theatre in May 1922 . See LCP CORR: *Doctor Goudron's System*: LR (1922).

16 See LCP CORR: *The Death Day Party* LR (1922). The play (author unknown) was never licensed.

17 Shelley's play was licensed for the New Theatre in October 1922, after several previous refusals. See LCP CORR: 1922/4437: *The Cenci*.

18 See LCP CORR: 1929/9229: *Turandot*. The licence was issued for performance in September.

19 The play was *The Mask*, by Robert Mason, and it was licensed for the Palladium in November 1923. See LCP CORR: 1923/5148: *The Mask*.

20 The adaptation was by Hamilton Deane for Derby's Grand Theatre in May 1924. See LCP CORR: 1924/5485: *Dracula*.

21 Housman's *The Little Plays of St Francis* was licensed for St Peter's Small Hall, Bournemouth, in March 1923. See LCP CORR: 1923/4796: *The Little Plays of St Francis*.

22 The title of this play by E. Hill-Mitchelson was changed to *Forbidden Fruit* before it was licensed for the Theatre Royal, Leicester, in August 1923. See LCP CORR: 1923/4992: *The Leper of Cairo*.

23 *The Phantom*, by the Reverend H.J. Boyd, was licensed for the Gaiety Theatre in Hastings in January 1924. See LCP CORR: 1924/5267: *The Phantom*.

24 For correspondence see LCP CORR: 1920/3135: *Private Room no. 6 (The Glove)*. Written by André de Lorde and Pierre Chaine, the play was licensed for the Little Theatre in October 1920. (*The Glove* was the original title.)

25 See LCP CORR: 1927/7877: *The Black Triangle*. The play (author unknown) was licensed for the Hippodrome, Mexborough, in October 1927.

26 *The Portrait of a Man with Red Hair*, adapted from Hugh Walpole's novel by Benn Levy for the Strand Theatre, was licensed in November 1927. See LCP CORR: 1927/7925. *Frankenstein*, in an adaptation by Peggy Webling, was licensed for the Empire, Preston, in November 1927. See LCP CORR: 1927/7975. *Jack Sheppard* was adapted from Henry Ainsworth's novel and licensed for the Elephant and Castle Theatre in April 1928. See LCP CORR: 1928/8322. *Sweeney Todd* was licensed for the Palace Theatre in Hammersmith in March 1928. See LCP CORR: 1928/8259.

27 See LCP CORR: 1928/8311: *Danger*. Written by Norman Lee, the play was licensed for the Theatre Royal, Inverness, in April 1928.

28 See LCP CORR: 1928/8432: *Spring Heeled Jack*. Written by Geoffrey Carlisle and Tod Slaughter, the play was licensed for the Grand Palace, Clapham, in July 1928.

29 *A Surgical Adventure*, by H. Hodgson Bentley, was licensed for the Ambassadors Theatre, Southend in December 1928. See LCP CORR: 1928/8700: *A Surgical Adventure*.

30 Written by Réné Berton and translated by Virginia and Frank Vernon for performance at the Little Theatre, a licence was refused in April 1928 and then granted for a revised version in May. See LCP CORR: 1928/8366: *After Death*.

31 Simply called *The Horror*, this play (author unknown) was licensed for the County Theatre, St Albans, in August 1928. See LCP CORR: 1928/8479: *The Horror*.

32 See LCP CORR: 1928/8496: *The Mystery of the Red Tavern*.

33 Originally licensed in 1923 for the Court Theatre, a revised version by Stopes was submitted for licensing in April 1930 for the Royalty Theatre. See LCP CORR: 1923/5104: *Our Ostriches*.

34 *The Silent House* by J.G. Brandon was licensed in August 1923 for the Croydon Empire. See LCP CORR: 1923/5005: *The Silent House*.

35 Letter from Cromer to Buckmaster in December 1927, discussing the appearance of an executioner on stage in *Charles Peace*. See LCP CORR: 1927/8030: *Charles Peace*.

36 Letter from the Comptroller to the Public Morality Council, April 1928. See LCP CORR: 1927/7925: *The Portrait of a Man with Red Hair*.

37 Patrick Hamilton, 'Preface on Thrillers', published as introduction to *Rope* (London: Constable & Co., 1929), pp. vii–viii.

38 Hamilton's play was licensed for the Ambassadors Theatre in April 1929. See LCP CORR: 1929/8958: *Rope*.

39 It was written by Charles Clifford and licensed for Stanley Hall, South Norwood, in January 1923. See LCP CORR: 1923/4692: *The Eternal Triangle*.

40 *Surmise* by Frank Vosper was turned down in August 1927. See LCP CORR: *Surmise* LR (1927). *Arsenic* by Talbot Ponsrow was refused in July 1928. However, a revised version by B.M. Fox was licensed for the Palace Theatre, Pengam (Monmouthshire), in August. See LCP CORR: 1928/8472: *Arsenic*. *The Bride in the Bath* (author unknown). See LCP CORR:

The Bride in the Bath LR (1929).

41 This play—one of several about this case—was written by William Hargreave and licensed for the Grand Theatre, Gravesend, in December 1927. See LCP CORR: 1927/8030: *Charles Peace*.

42 Terence Gray writing in *The Festival Theatre Review*, 21, 1927, after the Lord Chamberlain refused to license Oscar Wilde's *Salomé* for production in Cambridge.

43 *Daily Express*, 11 August 1920, p. 5.

44 Cromer was writing in November 1924, as part of the discussion on how to respond to *Judas Iscariot*, a play written by TempleThurston. No licence was issued (though the play was never officially refused) but there was a single private performance at the Scala Theatre in November 1924. See LCP CORR: *Judas Iscariot* WB (1924).

45 Again, *The Lord's Prayer* was never officially turned down. See LCP CORR: *The Lord's Prayer* WB (1923).

46 See LCP CORR: *Judas Isacriot* : WB (1924).

47 Masefield's play was licensed for the Century Theatre in April 1925. See LCP CORR: 1925/607: *Good Friday*.

48 See LCP CORR: *Trial of Jesus* LR (1926).

49 The play was written by Leonard Carlisle for performance at the Victorian Theatre, Stanley, in September 1923, but was refused a licence. See LCP CORR: *Death* LR (1923).

50 Housman was writing to Sir Douglas Dawson in January 1923. See LCP CORR: 1923/4688: *Bethlehem*. Also 1914/2867: *Bethlehem*.

51 Housman's play was licensed for the Little Theatre in January; Boughton's was licensed for the Town Hall, Streatham, in the same month. See LCP CORR: 1923/4654: *Bethlehem*.

52 *Jazz Patterns*, by Cecil Lewis was licensed for the Everyman Theatre in February 1927. See LCP CORR: 1927/7451: *Jazz Patterns*.

53 The play was licensed for the Festival Theatre, Cambridge, in October 1927. See LCP CORR: 1927/7835: *Progress*.

54 This musical comedy was licensed for the Alhambra in Glasgow in October 1927. See LCP CORR: 1927/7850: *Hit the Deck Again*.

55 Translated from the Italian by F. O'Dempsey, the play was licensed for the Arts Theatre, Leeds, in November 1927. See LCP CORR: 1927/7983: *Judas*.

56 See LCP CORR: 1927/7743: *Potiphar's Wife*. Edgar Middleton's play was licensed for the Globe Theatre in August 1927. See also the *Evening Standard*, 6 August 1927, p. 7.

57 *Adam the Creator*, by Karl and Josef Čapek, was licensed for the Festival Theatre, Cambridge in May 1928. See LCP CORR: 1928/8304: *Adam the Creator*.

58 Written by Christopher Morley to be performed at the Lyceum, Edinburgh, in June 1929, the play was turned down by the Lord Chamberlain. See LCP CORR: *East of Eden* LR (1929).

59 The play was written by J.R. Gregson. See LCP CORR: *Saint Mary Ellen* LR (1930).

60 The playwright was C. Mill, and the play was licensed in September 1928 for performance at the Theatre Royal, Leamington Spa. See LCP CORR: 1928/8552: *The Eternal Flame*.

61 *The Bidden Guest*, by Frank Anthony, was licensed for the Winter Gardens, Margate, in December 1928. See LCP CORR: 1928/8683: *The Bidden Guest*.

62 See LCP CORR: 1929/9021 *Easter*. Masefield's play was licensed in May 1929 for the Music Room, Boars Hill, Oxford.

63 See LCP CORR: 1930/9837: *Chester Miracle Plays*. 'Done into modern English by J.S.O. Breton King', the script was licensed for West Wycombe Park in July 1930.

64 Guthrie's play was licensed for the Alhambra, Glasgow, in October 1932. See LCP CORR: 1932/11497: *Follow Me*.

65 See LCP CORR: 1920/2759: *The Elixir*. Written by Sidney Lester, the musical was licensed for the Grand Theatre, Walsall, in May 1920; however, an official wrote to the manager: 'I am desired to inform you that the Lord Chamberlain assumes that the comedian will not be dressed as a Clergyman in the last scene, and so make such a character ridiculous'. He was changed to a registrar instead. *Rock of Ages* by R.Y. Drew and F. Lindon was licensed for the Royalty Theatre, Chester, in November 1924. See LCP CORR: 1924/5741: *Rock of Ages*.

66 See LCP CORR: 1931/10289: *Moths of the Night*. Written by E. Hill-Mitchelson, the play was licensed after amendments for the Grand Theatre, Walsall, in February 1931.

67 See LCP CORR: 1930/9710: *The Rose Of Magdala*.

68 Licensed for the Brighton Hippodrome in April 1932. See LCP CORR: 1932/11154: *Wine, Women and Song*.

69 Written by Jules Eckert Goodman, the play was intended for the New Oxford Theatre in May 1925, but was never licensed. See LCP CORR: *Simon Called Peter* LR (1925).

70 See LCP CORR: *The Passing of the Essenes* LR (1930).

71 See LCP CORR: *Green Pastures* LR (1930). The last failed applications for performances were in 1961 (a Cambridgeshire village society and—separately—Watford Technical College), 1962 (Rose Bruford College) and 1963 (Nottingham Technical College). The script was never approved.

72 Terence Gray, *The Festival Theatre Review*, 21, 1927.

73 Letter from John Bernard Seeley to Lord Cromer, October 1930, complaining about the depiction of his grandfather (as reviewed in *Punch*). See LCP CORR: 1930/9770: *The Barretts of Wimpole Street*.

74 Rudolf Besier's play was licensed for Birmingham Repertory Theatre in July 1930. For all discussion of censorship see LCP CORR: 1930/9770: *The Barretts of Wimpole Street*. Also, Rudolf Besier, 'The Besier-Barrett Controversy', *Time and Tide*, 13:8, 20 February 1932, pp. 194–197.

Chapter 8

1   From a report by Lord Buckmaster for the Advisory Board in February 1920. See LCP CORR: 1920/2729: *Tom Trouble*. Written by John Burley, this script was licensed for the Holborn Empire in February 1920.

2   Laurence Housman, 'Sex and the Censorship', *World League for Sexual Reform: Proceedings of the Third Congress*, edited by Norman Haine (London: Kegan Paul, Trench, Trubener & Co. Ltd, 1930), pp. 311–316.

3   Letter from the Public Morality Council to the Lord Chamberlain, 7 June 1918. See LCP Theatre Files, not catalogued.

4   Cochran's revue was licensed for the London Pavilion in September 1919. See LCO CORR: 1919/2464: *Afgar*. See also the *Daily Express* and the *Sunday Express* generally in the autumn of 1919.

5   *G.H.Q. Love* was adapted by Sewell Collins from the French of Pierre Rehm, and opened at the Little Theatre in September 1920. See LCO CORR: 1920/3059: *G.H.Q. Love*.

6   See *Daily Mail*, 9 October 1920, p. 5.

7   See *National News*, 10 October 1920, p. 8.

8   A letter of protest to the Lord Chamberlain in October 1920 claimed to be citing a recent article published in *Plain English*. See LCO CORR: 1920/3059: *G.H.Q. Love*.

9   *Ibid.*

10 The play, adapted from the Hungarian of Ernest Rajda by J.L.A. Burrell and Philip Moeller, opened at the Ambassadors Theatre in September 1924, and created considerable scandal. See LCO CORR: 1924/5640: *Fata Morgana*.

11 Housman, 'Sex and the Censorship'.

12 John Van Druten, 'Sex and Censorship in the Theatre', *World League for Sexual Reform: Proceedings of the Third Congress*, pp. 317–322.

13 Lord Cromer was writing in April 1926, following protests by audience members and a subsequent visit by one of his staff to see the production of *Katerina* at the Barnes Theatre. See LCO CORR: 1926/6701: *Katerina*. The play, in a translation by Herman Bernstein, had opened there in February of that year. For Housman's comment, see his essay 'Sex and the Censorship'.

14 See LCO CORR: 1926/6773: *Charles B. Cochran's Revue*. The revue was licensed for the Palace Theatre, Manchester, in March 1926, and reached the London Pavilion in April 1926.

15 See LCO CORR: 1921/3807: *Fun of the Fayre*. The revue opened at the London Pavilion in October 1921.

16 See LCO CORR: 1921/3627: *Ali Shar*, and 1921/3672: *Cairo*. Written by Oscar Asche and Percy Fletcher, the show was licensed for His Majesty's Theatre, Haymarket, in June 1921, but appears not to have opened until October.

17 See LCO CORR: 1929/9813: *Follow Through*. Written by Laurence Schwab and B.G. De Sylva, this musical comedy was licensed for the Empire in Southampton, before opening London's Dominion Theatre in October 1929.

18 See LCO CORR: 1932/11247: *Beautés de Paris*. This revue was licensed for the Opera House, Leicester, in June 1932.

19 See LCO CORR: 1926/6701: *Katerina*.
20 See LCO CORR: 1927/7743: *Potiphar's Wife*. Written by Edgar Middleton, the play was licensed for the Globe Theatre in August 1927 and became a prolonged embarrassment for the Lord Chamberlain as a result of extensive newspaper reporting of his confrontations with the management.
21 See LCO CORR: 1932/11592: *Beauty on Parade*. The revue was licensed for the Piccadilly Theatre in November 1932.
22 Despite his comment, Dawson said he could 'see no special reason for refusing in the case of this play', since a precedent had been established. See LCO CORR: 1921/3387: *The Trail of Shame*. The script (author unknown) was licensed for Paisley Theatre, Glasgow, in February 1921.
23 See LCO CORR: *Matrimony* LR (1921). Written by Harris Deans and F.R. Littler, the altered version was submitted as *Life* in October 1923, when Cromer indicated he was prepared to license it for the Kingsway Theatre. See LCO CORR: 1923/5328: *Life*.
24 *Was She Justified*, by Collin F. Heather, was submitted for production at the King's Theatre, Gainsborough, in February 1921 by the Gordon-Heather Repertory Company, and resubmitted in a slightly altered version for the Empire Theatre, Egremont, Cumberland, in January 1922. Both applications were rejected. See LCO CORR: *Was She Justified* LR (1922).
25 See LCO CORR: 1923/4965: *Motherhood*. Written by A. Miller (?), the script was licensed for performance at the Palace Pier, Brighton, in July 1923. The title was subsequently changed to *Has a Wife the Right?*
26 Stopes's play was licensed for the Royal Court Theatre in October 1923. See LCO CORR: 1923/5104: *Our Ostriches*.
27 See LCO CORR: *Maternity* LR (1924). Also *Suffer Little Children* LR (1924); this latter play was by Howard McKent Barnes, and the licence was sought and rejected for the Theatre Royal, Aldershot.
28 See LCO CORR: *Iron Flowers* LR (1929). The playwright was Cecil Lewis.
29 See LCO CORR: 1929/8932: *Strange Interlude*. O'Neill's play was licensed for the London Pavilion in March 1929.
30 See LCO CORR: *Married Love* LR (1923). Had it been approved, the play was to have been staged at the Royal Court.
31 See LCO CORR: *Vectia* LR (1924). The application was for performance at the Little Theatre.
32 See LCO CORR: *Who Knows* LR (1928). The play was submitted under the name 'John Lord', but the quotation marks presumably indicate this was a pseudonym. The performance would have taken place at the Ambassadors Theatre if a licence had been granted.
33 See Nicholas de Jongh, *Politics, Prudery and Perversions: The Censoring of the English Stage 1901–1968* (London: Methuen, 2000), pp. 92–97.
34 John F. Deeney, 'Censoring the Uncensored: The Case of "Children in Uniform"', *New Theatre Quarterly*, 16:3, August 2000, pp. 219–226.
35 See LCO CORR: 1921/3543: *The Trap*. Credited simply to 'Jonathan', the play was licensed for the Kingsway Theatre in May 1921.
36 See LCO CORR: 1923/5182: *The Gay Young Bride*. Apparently licensed for the Theatre Royal, Kidderminster, in November 1923, the script was by Captain Leslie Peacock.
37 See LCO CORR: 1923/5169: *Don't Tell Timothy*. Written by Mark Arundel, the play was licensed for the Royal Court in December 1923.
38 See LCO CORR: 1924/5360: *Auntie*. The play was written by H.C. Sargant, and licensed for the County Hall, St Albans, in February 1924. Its title was subsequently changed to *Mix Up*.
39 See LCO CORR: 1925/6332: *Cranky*. This touring revue was licensed for the Pavilion, Southport, in September 1925.
40 See LCO CORR: 1932/11295: *Not Quite a Lady*. Written by Gerald Anderson and S. Frederick Carlton, the script was licensed for the West Pier Theatre, Brighton, in June 1932.
41 See LCO CORR: 1932/11247: *Beautés de Paris*.
42 De Jongh, *Politics, Prudery and Perversions*, p. 99.
43 The play was *Threshold* (author unknown) and was performed at Leeds Little Theatre in July 1930. See LCO CORR: 1930/9834: *Threshold*.
44 See LCO CORR: 1932/11229: *Party*. Ivor Novello's script was licensed for the Strand Theatre in May 1932.

45 Nicholas de Jongh, *Not in Front of the Audience: Homosexuality on Stage* (London: Routledge, 1992), p. 124.

46 Van Druten, 'Sex and Censorship in the Theatre'.

47 The stage version was credited to Marion Norris, and the Kingsway Theatre sought a licence for performance in December 1930. See LCO CORR: *Alone* LR (1930).

48 The author was Aimée Grattan-Clyndes, and the Theatre Royal, Stratford East, sought a licence for performance in July 1923. See LCO CORR: *Sins of the Parents* LR (1923).

49 A licence was subsequently granted for performance at the Everyman Theatre in March 1926. See LCO CORR: 1926/6767: *The Passion Flower*.

50 Gray's play was licensed for the Festival Theatre, Cambridge, in April 1927. See LCO CORR: 1927/7568: *And in the Tomb Were Found*.

51 LCO CORR: 1931/10455 : *Fedra*. The opera, by Alfredo Lenozoni and Romano Romani, was licensed for the Royal Opera House in May 1931.

52 Translated by Sidney Harris from *La Riposte*, by Francois Nozier, the play was to have been performed at Wyndham's Theatre in March 1927. See LCO CORR: *The Legacy* LR (1927).

53 Lenormand's play was translated from the French by M. Boyd and J. O'Neal for Kew's Q Theatre in October 1927. It was not licensed. See LCO CORR: *The Simoun* LR (1927).

54 Written by W.T. Ivory and Maurice Duncan, the play was turned down in November 1927. See LCO CORR: *The Seventh Commandment* LR (1927). A rewritten version, specifically excluding the incestuous relationship, was licensed for the Burston Hippodrome in January 1928; see LCO CORR: 1928/8082: *The Seventh Commandment*.

55 The French version of the play was refused a licence in November 1927. See LCO CORR: *La ville morte* LR (1927). In September 1903, a licence had been refused for performance in the original Italian, under its title *La città morta*.

56 Letter to the Lord Chamberlain from the Public Morality Council in December 1922. See LCO CORR: 1922/4437: *The Cenci*.

57 See the LCO CORR: 1928/8082: *The Seventh Commandment*.

58 Lord Buckmaster was offering his advice in July 1922 on a script entitled *Monte Carlo Scandal*. See LCO CORR: *Monte Carlo Scandal* WB (1923).

59 See LCO CORR: 1922/4056: *The Enchanted Cottage*. Written by Arthur Pinero, the play was licensed for the Duke of York's Theatre in February 1922.

60 See LCO CORR: *Emily Plays Trumps* WB (1923). The script was by Charles Thornton, and the licence was sought for the Kennington Theatre in July 1923.

61 See LCO CORR: 1924/5640: *Fata Morgana*

62 See LCO CORR: *Morality* LR (1919). The playwright is identified only as Owen.

63 See LCO CORR: *An Angel's Heart* LR (1919). This script was credited to 'M.P.'.

64 The play was written by Eliot Crawshay Williams and licensed for the Little Theatre in April 1921. See LCO CORR: 1921/3524: *Rounding The Triangle*.

65 Also written by Mr Crawshay Williams for the Little Theatre, in December 1923. See LCO CORR: 1923/5170: *Husbands Can't Help It*. The title was later changed to *This Marriage*.

66 See LCO CORR: *The Third Floor Front* LR (1922). No author is identified, but the play was to have been produced at the Trinity Rooms, Leeds. LCO CORR: *Anniversary* LR (1922). The playwright was Frederick Witney. LCO CORR: *Faisons un rêve* LR (1922). The writer was Sacha Guitry.

67 See LCO CORR: *Uplift* LR (1922). No further details are known.

68 In *A Warning to Men* by Gertrude Vickers in 1924, for example, Cromer insisted that a daughter be changed to an adopted daughter, and in 1925 he refused to license *Maica*, a French play by Louis Verneuil, in which a father attempts to seduce his son's mistress. See LCO CORR: 1924/5414: *A Warning to Men*. The play was licensed for the Burslem Hippodrome, in March 1921. Also LCO CORR: *Maica* LR (1925). The script was licensed ten years later.

69 The play was adapted by Marguerite Rea from *Les Noces d'Argent* by Paul Geraldy, and licensed for the St Martin's Theatre in November 1923. See LCO CORR: 1923/5108: *Fledglings*.

70 See LCO CORR: *Rude Awakening* LR (1924). Written by Captain Wilfred Miles, the play was intended for production at the Q Theatre, Kew, in January 1926.

71 See LCO CORR: 1928/8174: *Young Woodley*. Van Druten's play was licensed for the Playhouse in February 1928.

72 Miles Malleson's play was licensed for the Ambassadors Theatre in May 1926. See LCO CORR: 1926/6917: *The Fanatics*.

73 See LCO CORR: 1928/7322: *The Constant Wife*. Maugham's play was licensed for the Strand Theatre in December 1928.
74 Maugham's play was licensed for the Playhouse in December 1928. See LCO CORR: 1928/8717: *The Sacred Flame*.
75 See LCO CORR: 1923/4877: *Our Betters*.
76 See LCO CORR: 1926/6972: *A Dog's Chance*. The play was licensed for the Q Theatre in Kew, in June 1926.
77 From the unpublished manuscript of *The Green Hat* by Michael Arlen in LCP 1925/30.
78 In an open letter to the Bishop of London, 1934.
79 See LCO CORR: 1925/6280: *The Green Hat*. The play was licensed for the Adelphi Theatre in September 1925, having been submitted in January.
80 See LCO CORR: 1925/6100: *Fallen Angels*. Coward's play was licensed for the Globe Theatre in April 1925.
81 Street was reporting on the script of *Lovely Helen*, an adaptation by A.P. Herbert of *La belle Hélène*. See LCO CORR: 1931/10893: *Lovely Helen*. The script was licensed for the Manchester Opera House in December 1931.
82 Ibsen's play was eventually licensed for the Royal Victoria Hall, in February 1922. See LCO CORR: 1922/4067: *Peer Gynt*.
83 See LCO CORR: 1922/4437: *The Cenci*, and *Sins of the Parents* LR (1923).
84 See correspondence of December 1926 between the Lord Chamberlain's Office and the Public Morality Council concerning the production of Wycherley's play at the Everyman Theatre, in LCP Theatre Files, not catalogued.
85 See LCO CORR: 1925/6158: *The Man with a Load of Mischief*. Ashley Dukes's play was licensed for the Haymarket Theatre in June 1925.
86 Sherwood's play was licensed for the Strand Theatre in May 1928. See LCO CORR: 1928/8363: *The Road to Rome*.
87 See LCO CORR: 1928/8309: *The Good King*. Written by Raoul Auernheimer (?), the play was licensed for the Theatre Royal, Glasgow, in April 1928.
88 According to the title page of the script, Jonson's original text had been 'freely adapted by Stefan Zweig', and then translated back into English by Ruth Langner. This version was eventually licensed for the London Pavilion in May 1929. See LCO CORR: 1929/8930: *Volpone*.
89 Obéy's play was licensed for the Ambassadors Theatre in July 1931. See LCO CORR: 1931/10535: *Le Viol de Lucrèce*.
90 See LCO CORR: 1931/10323: *The Phoenix*. The play was by G.C. Vernon, and was licensed for the Everyman Theatre in February 1931.
91 Buckmaster was discussing *The Vinegar Tree* by Paul Osborne in May 1932, a play which had been rejected in an earlier version of 1929 under the title of *My Mistake*. See LCO CORR: *My Mistake* LR (1929), *The Vinegar Tree* LR (1932), and *The Vinegar Tree*. This revised version was licensed for the Theatre Royal, Brighton, in May 1932.
92 See the Public Morality Council's Annual Report No. 30, published 1929.
93 See the Public Morality Council's Annual Report No. 34, published 1933.

Chapter 9

1 Letter from Lord Cromer to the India Office, 22 November 1926. See LCP CORR: *The Call of Kali* LR (1926).
2 Letter from Lord Cromer to the Home Office, 10 April 1931. See LCP CORR: *Roar China* LR (1931).
3 Letter from Lord Stamfordham to the State Chamberlain (Sir Douglas Dawson), 22 November 1924. See LCP CORR: 1924/5762: *The Vortex*.
4 Letter from Lord Stamfordham to Lord Cromer, 18 September 1923. See LCP CORR: 1923/4877: *Our Betters*.
5 See LCP CORR: *Fair Hannah Lightfoot* LR (1921).
6 See LCP CORR: *The Queen's Minister* LR (1922). Housman's play was eventually licensed in 1937 as *The Queen's Ministers*.
7 See LCP CORR: *The Queen, God Bless Her* LR (1923).
8 See LCP CORR: 1927/7500: *Marigold*. Credited to L. Allen and F.R. Abbott, the amended script was licensed for Devonshire Park, Eastbourne, in March 1927.
9 See LCP CORR: 1932/11215: *The Flaming Torch*. The script was written by Percy Corkhill

(?), and licensed for the Royal Court, Liverpool, in May 1932.

10 See LCP CORR: *The Queen's Progress* LR (1932).

11 *Bastos the Bold* by Leon Regis and Francois de Veynes was licensed for the Festival Theatre, Cambridge, in January 1932. See LCP CORR: 1932/10912: *Bastos the Bold*.

12 Hamilton Fyfe's play was licensed for the Comedy Theatre in December 1920. See LCP CORR: 1920/3298: *The Kingdom the Power and the Glory*.

13 Sherwood's play was licensed for the Crane Hall, Liverpool, in February 1929. See LCP CORR: 1929/8840: *The Queen's Husband*.

14 The play was written by H.N. Gibson, and licensed for St Andrews Hall, Alexandra Park Road, in February 1929. See LCP CORR: 1929/8844: *The Perfect Shadow*.

15 See LCP CORR: *The Russian Monk* LR (1918). The censorship of this play is discussed in more detail in Steve Nicholson, *British Theatre and the Red Peril: The Portrayal of Communism 1917–1945* (Exeter: University of Exeter Press, 1999), pp. 10–18.

16 The play was by Emile Ludwig. See LCP CORR: *Bismarck, The Trilogy of a Fighter* WB (1927).

17 *My Nieces*, by Percy Greenbank and Howard Talbot was based on Pinero's *The Schoolmistress* and licensed for the Queen's Theatre in August 1921. See LCP CORR: 1921/3693: *My Nieces*.

18 This revue was licensed for Halton Camp, Wendover, Buckinghamshire, in April 1924. See LCP CORR: 1924/5482: *Rent Free*.

19 See LCP CORR: 1924/5673: *Khaki*. The script was licensed for the Lewisham Hippodrome in September 1924.

20 The revue itself was called *Pages*, and was licensed for the Penge Hippodrome in September 1924. See LCP CORR: 1924/5760: *Pages*.

21 Written by Frank E. Franks, the play was licensed for the Hippodrome, Newcastle upon Tyne in January 1928. See LCP CORR: 1928/8113: *The Gay Lieutenant*.

22 The play was a translation by Barbara Nixon from the original Russian text of Sergei Tretiakov. See LCP CORR: *Roar China* LR (1931). For further discussion of the censorship of this play, see Nicholson, *British Theatre and the Red Peril*, pp. 22–25.

23 Written by H.S. Barnes, the play was licensed for the Rudolph Steiner Hall in January 1927. See LCP CORR: 1927/7394: *War and Peace*.

24 See LCP CORR: 1924/5316: *The Conquering Hero*. Monkhouse's play was licensed for the Albert Hall, Leeds, in February 1924.

25 Pollock's play was licensed in May 1928 for the King's Theatre, Edinburgh. See LCP CORR: 1928/8373: *The Enemy*.

26 Sherriff's play was licensed for the Savoy Theatre in January 1929. See LCP CORR: 1929/8757: *Journey's End*.

27 See LCP CORR: 1930/9608: *Suspense*. The play was written by Patrick Macgill and licensed for the Duke of York's Theatre in March 1930.

28 See LCP CORR: 1930/9723: *The Home Front*. Written by Diana and Bruce Hamilton, the play was licensed for the Birmingham Repertory Theatre in April 1930.

29 The play was written by Winifred and John L. Carter, and licensed for the Strand Theatre in April 1930. See LCP CORR: 1930/9671: *Every Mother's Son*.

30 Velona Pilcher's play was licensed for the Grafton Theatre in April 1930. See LCP CORR: 1930/9450: *The Searcher*.

31 The *Era*, 6 January 1926, p. 10.

32 Board of Education, Adult Education Committee, *The Drama in Adult Education* (London: HMSO, 1926), pp. 120 and 198.

33 Shaw's play was licensed for the the Everyman Theatre, Hampstead, in June 1924. See LCP CORR: 1924/5544: *Augutus Does His Bit*.

34 See LCP CORR: 1924/5502: *Mass Man*. The script was licensed for the New Theatre in May 1924.

35 See LCP CORR: 1924/5356: *From Miner to M.P.* Submitted under what was apparently a pseudonym of 'May Dana', the script was licensed for the Hippodrome, Ellesmere Port, in February 1924.

36 See LCP CORR: 1925/6308: *Reconstruction*. The play (author unknown) was licensed for Rusholme, Manchester, in September 1925.

37 Toller's play was licensed for the Festival Theatre, Cambridge, in February 1929, in what Terence Gray described as a 'mutilated' version. See LCP CORR: 1929/8795: *Hoppla!* For a fuller discussion of Gray's confrontation with the censors over this text, see Steve

Nicholson, ' "Nobody Was Ready for That": The Gross Impertinence of Terence Gray and the Degradation of Drama', *Theatre Research International*, 11:2, Summer 1996.

38   The play was written by Frank Stayton and licensed for the Manchester Opera House in July 1924. Its title was subsequently changed to *The Home and the Man* . See LCP CORR: 1924/5525: *Noblesse Oblige.*

39   See LCP CORR: 1927/7874: *The Big Drum.* This comedy thriller was licensed for the Q Theatre, Kew, in October 1927, and transferred to the Adelphi Theatre.

40   Thomas's script was licensed for performance at Edmonton Town Hall in March 1928. See LCP CORR: 1928/8204: *The Ragged Trousered Philanthropists.*

41   See LCP CORR: *In the Red Shadow* LR (1924). The play was written by E.J. Cairns. *The Jackets Green*, by John McLaren, was licensed for the League of the Cross Hall in February 1923.

42   Credited to J. Cairns, this play was rejected in November 1929, but then licensed in a revised version for performance at the David Lewis Theatre, Liverpool, the following month. See LCP CORR: 1929/9386: *The Whirlwind Passeth.*

43   The Lord Chamberlain replied that since the performance was private, it was outside his jurisdiction. No licence for public performance appears to have been sought for this play, author unknown. See LCP Theatre Files, not catalogued.

44   See LCP CORR: 1930/9823: *Private Lives.*

45   See House of Lords Debate, 'Censorship of Plays'. *Parliamentary Debates (Official Report), Volume LXIV, House of Lords, 4 May – 15 July 1926* (London: HMSO, 1926), columns 365–392.

46   See LCP CORR: *This Was a Man* LR (1926).

47   Maugham's play was licensed for the Globe Theatre in May 1923. See LCP CORR: 1923/4877: *Our Betters.*

48   See LCP CORR: 1924/5762: *The Vortex.* Coward's play was licensed for the Everyman Theatre in November 1924. The licence was issued within a couple of weeks of the script being submitted.

49   *Ashes* was licensed for the Prince of Wales's Theatre in March 1926. See LCP CORR: 1927/6739: *Ashes.*

50   See LCP CORR: *Miss Julie* LR (1925), and 1938/2153: *Miss Julie.* In 1925 the Chelsea Palace had sought a licence for the translation by Horace B. Samuel. In 1938 it was a version by C.D. Locock published by the Anglo-Swedish Literary Foundation which was finally licensed for the Westminster theatre, after the removal of the line 'You think I love you because the fruit of my womb thirsted for your seed'. For further discussion and details of the censorship of Strinderg's play see Steve Nicholson, ' "Unnecessary Plays": European Drama and the British Censor', *Theatre Research International*, 20:1, Spring 1995.

51   See LCP CORR: *Disappearance of Lord Bertie* LR (1928).

52   *Mind Your Step*, by Roy Roberts and Reg Powell, was originally licensed for the Ipswich Hippodrome in 1929. A revised version was licensed for the Palace Theatre, Burnley, in December 1930, and the title was subsequently changed to *Cheer Up*. See LCP CORR: 1929/9261: *Mind Your Step* and 1930/10069: *Mind Your Step.*

53   See LCP CORR: 1930/9735: *Desiré.* The script was licensed for the New Theatre, in its translation by John Leslie Firth, in June 1930.

54   See LCP CORR: *Cleansing Circles* LR (1926).

55   Edgar Middleton's play was licensed for the Globe Theatre in August 1927. See LCP CORR: 1927/7743: *Potiphar's Wife.*

56   The script was eventually licensed for the Vaudeville Theatre in March 1932, though it had been performed at the Arts Theatre in October 1931. The stage adaptation was credited to Arthur Boscastle. See LCP CORR: 1932/11133: *Vile Bodies.*

57   Street was writing in August 1924 in connection with *Rent Free*. See LCP CORR: 1924/5482: *Rent Free.*

58   See LCP CORR: 1928/8558: *John Bull Calling.* The script was licensed for the London Coliseum in October 1928.

Chapter 10

1   This observation was made by George Street in a Reader's Report in April 1928, recommending for licence 'a very ingenious example of the wicked Chinaman play' even though he predicted there might be resentment among the Chinese community. See LCP CORR:

1928/8302: *The Green Beetle*. The play was written by John Willard and licensed for perform-ance at the Theatre Royal, Bristol in April 1928.

2 See LCP CORR: 1921/3672: *Cairo*. Written by Oscar Asche, the script was licensed for His Majesty's Theatre, Haymarket, in October 1921.

3 Written by Betty Fairfax, the script eventually received a licence for performance at the Ambassadors Theatre, Southend in August 1922. See LCP CORR: 1922/4357: *Auction of Souls*.

4 Written by H. Kenneth Gordon, the script was licensed for the Hippodrome, Stratford-upon-Avon, in December 1921. See LCP CORR: 1921/3932: *Kishna*.

5 Archer's script was licensed for the St James's Theatre in March 1922. See LCP CORR: 1922/4135: *The Green Goddess*.

6 See LCP CORR: *The Call of Kali* LR (1926). The play's author was G. Stuart Ogilvie, and the first performance would have taken place at the Globe Theatre.

7 The play was by Dorothy Quick. See LCP CORR: *The Pool* LR (1928).

8 This musical comedy by Guy Bolton and Fred Thompson was eventually licensed for the Theatre Royal, Drury Lane, in December 1930. See LCP CORR: 1930/9994: *Song of the Drum*.

9 LCP CORR: 1929/9815: *The Flight Lieutenant*. The play was licensed for the Argyll Theatre, Greenock, in August 1929.

10 LCP CORR: *Command to Love* LR (1928) and LR (1929). Also 1930/9600: *Command to Love*. The original script was credited to Rudolph Lothar and Fritz Gottwald, and adapted by Herman Bernstein and Brian Marlow, but the 1929 and 1930 versions were revised by Bernard Merivale. The licence was eventually issued for the New Theatre in March 1930.

11 See LCP CORR: 1923/5128: *The Blue Flame*. The script was by Earl Carroll, 'arranged for the English stage' by Randle Ayrton. It was licensed for the Willesden Hippodrome in November 1923.

12 Harry Graham's adaptation of the French play, originally written by Alfred Savoir, was licensed for the Globe Theatre in January 1925. See LCP CORR: 1925/5900: *The Grand Duchess*.

13 The play was licensed after alterations in May 1927. See LCP CORR: 1927/7645: *Red Nights of the Tcheka*. It was translated by Terence Gray from the French of André de Lorde and Henri Bauche.

14 See LCP CORR: *Red Sunday* LR (1929). Hubert Griffith's play was staged privately at the Arts Theatre under the direction of Fyodor Komisarjevsky, with a cast which included John Gielgud as Trotsky. It was not allowed to transfer for public performances. For a fuller discussion of this, see Steve Nicholson, *British Theatre and the Red Peril: The Portrayal of Communism 1917–1945* (Exeter: University of Exeter Press, 1999).

15 See LCP CORR: *A Woman of Destiny* LR (1931). The play was written by Cayley Calvert, for a charity event under the patronage of the Bishop of Chichester.

16 Maurine Watkins's script for the Ambassadors Theatre was turned down in January 1928. See LCP CORR: *Chicago* LR (1928).

17 See correspondence between the Office and the Girls' League of the Wesleyan Methodist Missionary Society in January 1931, in LCO Theatre Files, not catalogued. It is unclear which play provoked the correspondence.

18 See LCP CORR: 1922/4563: *Dark Town Follies*. The script was by J.C. Glass, and it was licensed for the Palace, Tottenham, in November 1922.

19 See LCP CORR: 1926/6816: *Umgumwanga*. The script (author unknown) was licensed for Dink (?) Hall, Moretonhampstead, in March 1926.

20 See LCP CORR: 1922/4568: *Chin Chin*. The script was by J.L. Plunkett, and it was licensed for St George's Hall in November 1922.

21 See LCP CORR: 1927/7935: *Mavana*. Written by Frank Worthington, the script was licensed for the Savoy Theatre in November 1927.

22 See LCP CORR: 1929/8999 : *Morning, Noon and Night*. This revue, by E. Middleton, was licensed for the Everyman Theatre, Hampstead, in May 1929.

23 See LCP CORR: 1921/3633: *The Yellow Snare*. Written by Henry Oscar, the script was licensed for the Kennington Theatre in June 1921.

24 See LCP CORR: 1922/4319 : *Traffic in Souls*. The script (author unknown) was licensed for the Woolwich Empire in July 1922.

25 See LCP CORR: 1923/4693: *The Vengeance of Li Fang Foo*. Written by W.P. Sheen, it was licensed for the Alhambra, Stourbridge, in January 1923.

26   See LCP CORR: 1921/3631: *His Chinese Bride*. The script was by A. Howard, and it was licensed for the Elephant and Castle Theatre in June 1921.
27   See LCP CORR: 1925/6232: *The Man from Hong Kong*. The play was written by Mrs Clifford Mills and licensed for the Queen's Theatre in July 1925.
28   See correspondence of March 1928 in LCO Theatre Files, not catalogued.
29   See LCP CORR: 1928/8302: *The Green Beetle*.
30   See LCP CORR: 1928/8547: *The Twister*. The play (author unknown) was licensed for the Grand Theatre, Brighton, in September 1928.
31   See LCP CORR: 1928/8659: *Yellow Vengeance*. The play (author unknown) was licensed for the Theatre Royal, Worthing, in November 1928.
32   See LCP CORR: 1929/9058: *The Yellow Hand*. The script was written by Frank Price and licensed for the Bilston Hippodrome in May 1929.
33   See LCP CORR: 1925/6232: *The Man from Hong Kong*.
34   See LCP CORR: 1925/6131: *Overtime*. The revue was licensed for the Grand in Woking in May 1925.
35   LCP CORR: 1921/3672: *Cairo*.
36   Maugham's play was licensed for performance at His Majesty's Theatre in May 1922. See LCP CORR: 1922/4209: *East of Suez*.
37   The script, by J. Baker Howard, was licensed for the Assembly Rooms, Andover, in December 1923. See LCP CORR: 1923/5173: *Her Egyptian Husband*.
38   Written by William Pollock, the play was licensed for the Q Theatre, Kew, in July 1926. See LCP CORR: 1926/7013: *Kimono*.
39   See LCP CORR: 1926/6857: *Bongola*. The play was written by Lilian Cornelius and C. Owen Payne, and was licensed for the Q Theatre, Kew, in April 1926.
40   See LCP CORR: 1929/8977: *All God's Children Got Wings*. O'Neill's play was licensed for the Court Theatre in April 1929.
41   See LCP CORR: 1920/2868: *East is West*. Written by Samuel Shipman and John B. Hymer, the script was licensed for the Queen's Theatre in May 1920.
42   See LCP CORR: 1924/5410: *Love and the Sheik*. The playwright was Royce Carleton, and the play was licensed for the Alexandra Theatre, Hull, in March 1924.
43   See LCP CORR: 1923/5099: *Sheik of the Desert*. The script was by A. Douglas and was licensed for the Empire, Ushaw Moor, in October 1923.
44   See LCP CORR: 1924/4926: *The Sheik of Araby*. The playwright was Val Gurney, and the script was licensed for Dover Hippodrome in June 1923.
45   Written by C. Douglas Carlile and licensed for the Ambassadors Theatre, Southend, in January 1924. See LCP CORR: 1924/5289: *Sands of the Desert*.
46   See LCP CORR: 1929/8862: *Sinister House*. The script was by Denis Mayne, and was licensed for the County Theatre, St Albans, in February 1929.
47   Written by Richard E. Goddard, the play was licensed for the Brighton Repertory Theatre, in January 1924. See LCP CORR: 1924/5261: *Man's Desire*.
48   See LCP CORR: 1929/8925: *Amoya*. The play was by Leslie Vance, and it was licensed for the People's Theatre, N17, in March 1929.
49   See LCP CORR: *Human Wreckage* LR (1925). The playwright is listed only as Langley. Also, LCP CORR: *Kongo* 1926 (LR), for which Devonde and Gordon were identified as the authors.
50   See LCP CORR: 1927/7995: *Out East*. The play was by Eliot Crawshay Williams, and it was licensed for the Little Theatre in December 1927.
51   Written by Harry J. Clifford, this play was licensed for the Crown Theatre, Eccles, in September 1924, and again in a revised version the following month. See LCP CORR: 1924/5656: *The Leopard Men*, and 1924/5728. The title was subsequently changed to *African Love*.
52   Leon Gordon, *White Cargo: A Play of the Primitive* (Boston: The Four Seas Company, 1923), pp. 28–30.
53   See LCP CORR: 1924/5494: *White Cargo*. Gordon's play was licensed for the Playhouse, in May 1924.
54   See LCP CORR: *Coloured Love* LR (1924).
55   See LCP CORR: 1929/8747: *The White Assegai*. The play was by Allan King, and it was licensed for the Birmingham Repertory Theatre in January 1929.
56   See LCP CORR: 1929/8862: *Sinister House*.
57   *The Times*, 17 December 1926, p. 7.

58   See House of Lords Debate, 'Censorship of Plays'.*Parliamentary Debates (Official Report),* *Volume LXIV, House of Lords, 4 May – 15 July 1926* (London: HMSO 1926), columns 365–392.

Conclusion

1   John Galsworthy, *A Justification of the Censorship of Plays* (London: Heinemann, 1909), p. 16.
2   Galsworthy, *A Justification*, pp. 10–14.
3   William Joynson Hicks, *Do We Need a Censor?* (London: Faber and Faber, 1929), pp. 5–20.
4   Hicks, *Do We Need a Censor?*, p. 18.
5   Henry Arthur Jones, *The Censorship Muddle and a Way Out of It* (London: Samuel French, 1909), p. 16.
6   Private correspondence between Cromer, the Home Secretary, the King, and the King's Private Secretary, Lieutenant Colonel Rt. Hon. Arthur John Bigge Stamfordham, October 1923 to February 1924. See LCO Theatre Files, not catalogued.
7   See correspondence between Cromer and the Home Office, March–July 1926 in LCO Theatre Files, not catalogued. This strategy is explored in more detail in Chapter Six.
8   Frank Fowell and Frank Palmer, *Censorship in England* (London: Frank Palmer, 1913), pp. 325–326.
9   Fowell and Palmer, *Censorship in England*, p. 191.
10   Pigott's Memorandum was dated 15 March 1883, and was sent by Redford to the Lord Chamberlain in November 1907. See LCO Theatre Files, not catalogued.
11   See LCP CORR: *This Was a Man* LR (1926).
12   See LCP CORR: *Les Criminelles* LR (1930).
13   See LCP CORR: *The Last Mile* LR (1930).
14   See LCP CORR: *Chicago* LR (1927).
15   Pigott's Memorandum, 15 March 1883. See LCO Theatre Files, not catalogued.
16   S.P.B. Mais, 'Poison Novels and Plays', *Daily Graphic*, 17 March 1926, p. 7.
17   See House of Lords Debate, 'Censorship of Plays'. See *Parliamentary Debates (Official Report), Volume LXIV, House of Lords, 4 May – 15 July1926* (London: HMSO, 1926), columns 365–392.
18   John Van Druten, 'Sex and Censorship in the Theatre', *World League for Sexual Reform: Proceedings of the Third Congress*, edited by Norman Haine (London: Kegan Paul, Trench, Trubener & Co. Ltd, 1930), pp. 317–322.
19   The point was made by Lord Morris in his opening speech in the House of Lords Debate, 'Censorship of Plays', 1926.
20   See *Report of the Joint Select Committee of the House of Lords and the House of Commons on the Stage Plays (Censorship) Together with the Proceedings of the Committee, Minutes and Appendices* (London: Government Publication, 1909), p. 163. Caine claimed to have worked on a play about Mohammed with the backing of Sir Henry Irving, before being privately warned by the then Lord Chamberlain not even to consider applying for a licence.
21   See House of Lords Debate, 'Censorship of Plays', 1926.
22   Letter from the Lord Chamberlain to the Home Office, April 1909. See LCO Theatre Files, not catalogued.
23   Hannen Swaffer, 'If I Were the Censor', *Really Behind the Scenes* (London: George Newnes, 1929), p. 34.
24   Hannen Swaffer, open letter to the Bishop of London, 1934.
25   From *The Censor* by Wilfred T. Coleby. See unpublished manuscript in LCP: 1913/2140.
26   Swaffer, If I Were the Censor', p. 34.
27   Hicks, *Do We Need a Censor?*, pp. 6–11.
28   From the report sent from the Home Office to the Lord Chamberlain's Office in December 1928. See LCO Theatre Files, not catalogued.
29   See Terence Gray, 'Was That Life? Swat It!', *The Gownsman*, 6 June 1931, pp. 14–15. Also Thomas Beecham, *A Mingled Chime: Leaves from an Autobiography* (London: Hutchinson 1952), p. 102.
30   Van Druten, 'Sex and Censorship', p. 318.
31   House of Lords Debate, 'Censorship of Plays', 1926.
32   Samuel Smith, *Plays and their Supervision: A Speech made by Samuel Smith Esq., MP in the House of Commons May 15th 1900, and the Reply of the Home Secretary* (London: Chas. J. Thynne, 1900).

Select Bibliography

Archival Material
The Lord Chamberlain's Correspondence Files (Manuscript Room, British Library).
The Lord Chamberlain's Office Files, transferred from the Royal Archives at Windsor to the British Library, June 2001, not catalogued (Manuscript Room, British Library).
The Lord Chamberlain's Collection of Licensed Plays 1900–1968 (Manuscript Room, British Library).
The Lord Chamberlain's Daybooks (Manuscript Room, British Library).
Production Files (Theatre Museum)

Government and Parliamentary Reports
Report from the Joint Select Committee of the House of Lords and the House of Commons on the Stage Plays (Censorship) Together with the Proceedings of the Committee, Minutes and Appendices (1909).
Parliamentary Debates (Official Report) Volume LI, House of Commons, 31 March 1913 – 18 April 1913 (London: HMSO, 1913), columns 2036–2081.
Parliamentary Debates (Official Report), Volume LXIV, House of Lords, 4 May 1926 – 15 July 1926 (London: HMSO, 1926), columns 365–392.
Hansard's Parliamentary Debates.
Board of Education, Adult Education Committee, *The Drama in Adult Education* (London: HMSO, 1926).

Books, Articles and Unpublished Dissertations
Barker, Harley Granville, 'The Theatre: The Next Phase', in H.G. Barker, *Offprints of Contributions by Granville-Barker to Various Publications* (London: publisher unknown, 1910).
Beecham, Thomas, *A Mingled Chime: Leaves from an Autobiography* (London: Hutchinson 1952).
Besier, Rudolf , 'The Besier-Barrett Controversy', *Time and Tide*, 13:8, 20 February 1932, pp. 194–197.
Brookfield, Charles, 'On Plays and Playwriting', *National Review*, November 1911, pp.419–435.
Chandos, John, pseud. [John Lithgow Chandos MacConnell], *To Deprave and Corrupt: Original Studies in the Nature and Definition of Obscenity* (London: Souvenir Press, 1962).
Collins, L.J., *Theatre at War, 1914–1918* (Basingstoke: Macmillan, 1998).
Colton, W.R., 'The Effects of War on Art', *The Architect*, 45, 17 March 1916.
Conolly, L.W., *The Censorship of English Drama 1737–1824* (San Marino, California: Huntington Library, 1976).
Dawson, Sir Douglas Frederick Rawdon, *A Soldier-Diplomat* (London: John Murray, 1927).
de Jongh, Nicholas, *Not in Front of the Audience: Homosexuality on Stage* (London: Routledge, 1992).

de Jongh, Nicholas, *Politics, Prudery and Perversions: The Censoring of the English Stage 1901–1968* (London: Methuen, 2000).

Deeney, John F., 'Censoring the Uncensored: The Case of "Children in Uniform"', *New Theatre Quarterly*, 16:3, August 2000, pp. 219–226.

E.F.S. [Spence, Edward Fordham], *Our Stage and its Critics* (London: Methuen & Co., 1910).

Etienne, Anne, 'Les Coulisses du Lord Chamberlain: La Censure Théâtrale de 1900 à 1968', unpublished Ph.D. dissertation, L'Université d'Orleans, 1999.

Findlater, Richard, *Banned!: A Review of Theatrical Censorship in Britain* (London: MacGibbon & Kee, 1967).

Florance, John Allan, 'Theatrical Censorship in Britain 1901–1968', unpublished Ph.D. dissertation, University of Wales, 1980.

Fowell, Frank, and Palmer, Frank, *Censorship In England* (London: Frank Palmer, 1913).

Fussell, Paul, *The Great War and Modern Memory* (London: Oxford University Press, 1975).

G.M.G., *The Stage Censor: An Historical Sketch: 1544–1907* (London: Sampson Low & Company, 1908).

Galsworthy, John, *A Justification of the Censorship of Plays* (London: Heinemann, 1909).

Garnett, Edward, *A Censured Play. 'The Breaking Point'. With Preface and a Letter to the Censor* (London: Duckworth & Co., 1907).

Gosse, Edmund, 'War and Literature', *Edinburgh Review*, October 1914.

Gray, Terence, 'Was That Life? Swat It!', *The Gownsman*, 6 June 1931, pp. 14–15.

Hamilton, Patrick, 'Introduction', *Rope* (London: Constable & Co, 1929).

Hicks, William Joynson, *Do We Need a Censor?* (London: Faber and Faber, 1929).

Hoare, Philip, *Wilde's Last Stand: Decadence, Conspiracy and the First World War* (London: Duckworth, 1997).

Housman, Laurence, 'Sex and the Censorship', *World League for Sexual Reform: Proceedings of the Third Congress*, edited by Norman Haine (London: Kegan Paul, Trench, Trubener & Co. Ltd., 1930), pp. 311–316.

Housman, Laurence, *The Unexpected Years* (London: Jonathan Cape, 1937).

Hubert Griffith, 'Preface', *Red Sunday: A Play in Three Acts with a Preface on the Censorship* (London: Cayme Press, 1929).

Hynes, Samuel, *A War Imagined: The First World War and English Culture* (London: Bodley Head, 1990).

Johnston, John, *The Lord Chamberlain's Blue Pencil* (London: Hodder & Stoughton, 1990).

Jones, Henry Arthur, *The Censorship Muddle and a Way Out of It* (London: Samuel French, 1909).

Kennedy, Dennis, *Granville Barker and the Dream of Theatre* (Cambridge: Cambridge University Press, 1985).

Kettle, Michael, *Salomé's Last Veil: The Libel Case of the Century* (London: Hart-Davis MacGibbon, 1979).

Knowles, Dorothy, *The Censor, the Drama and the Film* (London: Allen & Unwin, 1934).

Lawrence, D.H., *Sex, Literature and Censorship*, edited by Harry T. Moore (London: Heinemann, 1955).

Nicholson, Steve, ' "Nobody Was Ready for That": The Gross Impertinence of Terence Gray and the Degradation of Drama', *Theatre Research International*, 11:2, Summer 1996, pp. 121–131.

Nicholson, Steve, ' "Unnecessary Plays": European Drama and the British Censor', *Theatre Research International*, 20:1, Spring 1995, . pp. 30–36.

Nicholson, Steve, 'Censoring Revolution: The Lord Chamberlain and the Soviet

Union', *New Theatre Quarterly*, 8:32, November 1992, pp. 305–312.

Nicholson, Steve, *British Theatre and the Red Peril: The Portrayal of Communism 1917–1945* (Exeter: University of Exeter Press, 1999).

Nicholson, Watson, *The Struggle for a Free Stage in London* (London: Archibald Constable & Co., 1906).

O'Higgins, Paul, *Censorship in Britain* (London: Nelson, 1972).

'Orme, Michael', *J. T. Grein: The Story of a Pioneer 1862–1935* (London: John Murray, 1936).

Palmer, John, *The Censor and the Theatres* (London: T. Fisher Unwin, 1912).

Shaw, George Bernard, 'The Censorship of the Stage in England', *North American Review*, 169, 1899, pp. 251–262.

Shaw, George Bernard, 'Impressions of the Theatre', *Review of Reviews*, 32:190, October 1905.

Smith, Samuel, *Plays and their Supervision: A Speech made by Samuel Smith Esq., M.P. in the House of Commons May 15th 1900, and the reply of the Home Secretary* (London: Chas. J. Thynne, 1900).

Stephens, John Russell, *The Censorship of English Drama 1824–1901* (Cambridge: Cambridge University Press, 1980).

Stopes, Marie C., *A Banned Play ('Vectia') and a Preface on the Censorship* (London: J. Bale & Co., 1926).

Street, George, 'Introduction', *The Comedies of William Congreve: Volume One* (London: Methuen, 1895), pp. vii–xxxiii.

Street, George, *People and Questions* (London: Martin Secker, 1905).

Street, George, 'The Censorship of Plays', *Fortnightly Review*, September 1925, pp. 348–357.

Street, George, *At Home in the War* (London: Heinemann, 1918).

Swaffer, Hannen, 'If I Were the Censor', *Behind the Scenes* (London: George Newnes, 1929).

Swaffer, Hannen, 'Open Letter to the Bishop of London', *John Bull*, 56:1488, 22 December 1934, p. 10.

Travis, Allen, *Bound and Gagged: A Secret History of Obscenity in Britain* (London: Profile Books Ltd, 2000).

Van Druten, John, 'Sex and Censorship in the Theatre', *World League for Sexual Reform: Proceedings of the Third Congress*, edited by Norman Haine (London: Kegan Paul, Trench, Trubener & Co. Ltd, 1930), pp. 317–322.

Weintraub, Stanley (ed.), *Shaw: An Autobiography, 1898–1950: The Playwright Years, Selected from his Writings by Stanley Weintraub* (London: Reinhardt, 1971).

White, Arnold, 'Efficiency and Vice', *The Vigilante*, 20 April 1918, p. 4.

Young, Eugene J., *Looking Behind the Censorship* (London: Lovat Dickson, 1938).

Newspapers, Periodicals and Reports

The following have been particularly and frequently valuable sources:

Annual Reports of the Public Morality Council
Daily Graphic
Daily Mail;
The Era
Festival Theatre Review
Imperialist / Vigilante
The Nation
New Statesman
The Referee
The Stage
The Times

Index